PIMLICO

651

# SIX ARMIES IN NORMANDY

John Keegan is the Defence Editor of the *Daily Telegraph* and Britain's foremost military historian. The Reith Lecturer in 1998, he is the author of many bestselling books including *The Face of Battle*, *The Mask of Command*, *Battle at Sea*, *The Second World War*, *A History of Warfare* (awarded the Duff Cooper Prize), *Warpaths*, *The Battle for History*, *The First World War*, and most recently, *Intelligence in War*.

For many years John Keegan was the Senior Lecturer in Military History at the Royal Military Academy Sandhurst, and he has been a Fellow of Princeton University and Delmas Distinguished Professor of History at Vassar. He is Fellow of the Royal Society of Literature. He received the OBE in the Gulf War honours list, and was knighted in the Millennium honours list in 1999.

# SIX ARMIES IN NORMANDY

From D-Day to the Liberation of Paris
June 6th–August 25th, 1944

----

## JOHN KEEGAN

PIMLICO

*To my mother*
*in thanks for a happy*
*wartime childhood*

Published by Pimlico 2004

2 4 6 8 10 9 7 5 3 1

Copyright © John Keegan 1982

First published in Great Britain by
Jonathan Cape Ltd 1982

First Pimlico edition 1992

Second Pimlico edition 2004

Pimlico
Random House, 20 Vauxhall Bridge Road,
London SW1V 2SA

Random House Australia (Pty) Limited
20 Alfred Street, Milsons Point, Sydney,
New South Wales 2061, Australia

Random House New Zealand Limited
18 Poland Road, Glenfield,
Auckland 10, New Zealand

Random House South Africa (Pty) Limited
Endulini, 5A Jubilee Road, Parktown 2193, South Africa

Random House UK Limited Reg. No. 954009

A CIP catalogue record for this book is available from the British Library

ISBN 1-8441-3739-2

Papers used by Random House UK Limited are natural, recyclable
products made from wood grown in sustainable forests. The manufacturing
processes conform to the environmental regulations of the country of origin

Printed and bound in Great Britain by Bookmarque Ltd, Croydon, Surrey

# Contents

# 3 Canada: to the South Shore

# 4 Scottish Corridor

# 5 Yeomen of England

# 6 The Honour of the German Army

# *Illustrations*

## Plates

# Maps

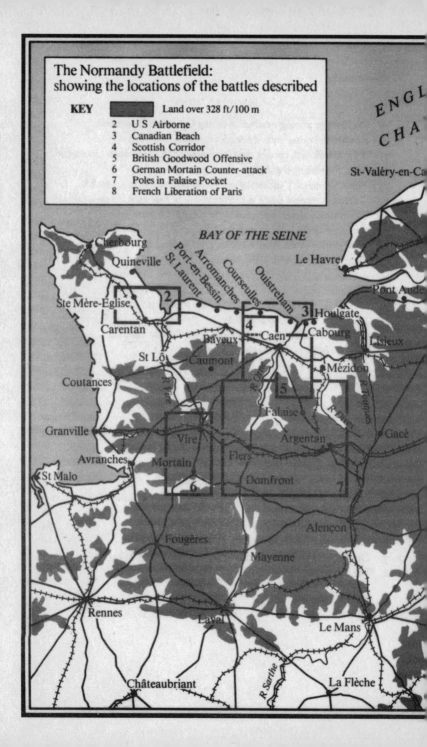

The Normandy Battlefield:
showing the locations of the battles described

**KEY**      Land over 328 ft/100 m

2   U S Airborne
3   Canadian Beach
4   Scottish Corridor
5   British Goodwood Offensive
6   German Mortain Counter-attack
7   Poles in Falaise Pocket
8   French Liberation of Paris

# *Foreword*

Five years ago, in a book I called *The Face of Battle*, I set out to explore the predicament of the individual on the battlefield. Though a practising military historian, and the colleague in my academic life of professional soldiers, I had no understanding of the risks which the warrior faced in his encounter with his enemy, or of the means he found to quell his terrors and master himself at the 'point of maximum danger'. What I discovered, however near to the truth it was, surprised me. I learnt of the universality of fear, of the operation of inducements and coercion in its conquest but, above all, of the importance of male honour, as judged by a man's immediate comrades, in sustaining the soldier's resolution.

But, despite my concentration on the individual and the small group, I was also drawn to a recognition of the peculiar nature of the larger body to which both belong, the army itself. Armies are universal institutions which, in the dimension of purpose and authority, closely resemble each other. Yet each is also a mirror of its own society and its values: in some places and at some times an agent of national pride or a bulwark against national fears, or perhaps even the last symbol of the nation itself; elsewhere and otherwise an instrument of national power deprecated, disregarded and of very last resort. It seemed to me worth finding some episode through which the varying status of national armies might be exemplified. And in the Normandy campaign of 1944 I believed that I had stumbled upon it. I knew the battlefield well. I had long been struck by the very different motives inspiring the armies which action conjoined there. And, over the years, I had become familiar with the wealth of corporate history and personal reminiscence which the campaign has thrown up. What follows is therefore another attempt to understand, from a different angle of vision, the role which warfare and its institutions play in social life.

# Acknowledgments

I have been fortunate enough to visit the battlefields of Normandy several times, first as a schoolboy in 1953 when memories of the events of 1944, still strong today, were in the forefront of Norman minds; again in 1965; and finally in 1977, while this book was in preparation. I am grateful to all those who have talked to me about D-Day and its aftermath, particularly those whom I heard speak on the ground where they had actually served. They include General Sir John Mogg, Lieutenant-General Sir Napier Crookenden, Major-General Sir James d'Avigdor-Goldsmid, Major-General G. P. B. Roberts, Brigadier D. M. Stileman, Brigadier P. Young, Brigadier R. M. Villiers, Brigadier M. E. Peppiatt, Captain P. G. C. Dickens, RN, Oberst H. von Luck, Oberst R. Freiherr von Rosen, Lieutenant-Colonel R. H. Hastings, Lieutenant-Colonel W. McElwee, Lieutenant-Colonel A. J. M. Parry, Lieutenant-Colonel E. J. Warren, Major W. H. Close, Major D. F. Cunliffe, Major J. Howard, Major G. Ramsay, Major J. A. N. Sim, Major J. N. Taylor, Captain A. R. Jefferson, Mr C. W. Adams, Dr R. Cox, Mr T. D. Miller, Mr P. Walter and Mr D. Woodcraft. I am also grateful for help with the procurement of documentary and manuscript material to Captain L. Milewski, of the Sikorski Institute, London, to Mr C. P. von Luttichau, of the Office of the Chief of Military History, Washington, to Dr R. Suddaby, Keeper of Archives at the Imperial War Museum, London, and to the staffs of the Militärgeschichtlichesforschungsamt, Freiburg and the Service historique de l'armée, Vincennes. M. Albert Grandais, a Norman historian and author of *La Bataille de Calvados* (Presses de la cité, 1974) was especially helpful with local material, and my friends Jean-Claude and Marie-Hélène Cuirot, of Bretteville-sur-Odon, were kind hosts.

Much help came as always from fellow members of the academic staff at Sandhurst, among whom it is such a pleasure to work: David

Chandler, Eric Morris, Richard Holmes, Nigel de Lee, Christopher Duffy, Ian Beckett, Paddy Griffith, Bob Godfrey, David Johnson, John Pimlott, Buck Ryan, Keith Simpson, Michael Orr, Tony Thomas, Francis Toase, Ned Wilmott, Tom Maley and Paul Thomas. John Hunt, our Librarian, put the resources of the Central Library at my disposal as generously as ever, and I am grateful to him and his staff, particularly Miss King and Mrs Stevens, and to Mr George Parker for his assistance with inter-library loans. Kenneth White, the Librarian of the Staff College and a veteran of Normandy, again allowed me to borrow freely from his shelves and also put his detailed knowledge of the campaign at my disposal. I also owe particular debts for help to John Jolliffe, Derek Anyan, Brian Mitchison, Professor Michael Howard and Professor Richard Cobb, and to Malcolm Deas, of St Antony's College Oxford. The College, which made me a Senior Member while (though not because) this book was in progress, has been a happy haven of retreat from the typewriter. What I produced on it was made legible by Miss Monica Alexander, formerly principal secretary at the Staff College and a princess among typists. I am grateful as always for the support and encouragement of Liz Calder, Tom Maschler and Graham Greene of Jonathan Cape, of David Machin, formerly of Jonathan Cape, of Alan Williams of the Viking Press, and of Anthony Sheil, Gill Coleridge and Paul Marsh of Anthony Sheil Associates; I hope I have not disappointed them after all they have done.

Finally, thanks for help and family hospitality while writing to Mary and Maurice Keen, Clare and Christopher Dow, Francis and Julia Keegan, Mollie Keegan, Martin and Susan Everett and Charles and Vanessa Everett; and, last of all, love returned to my children, Lucy, Thomas, Rose and Matthew, and my darling wife, Susanne.

JOHN KEEGAN

*Sandhurst*
*March 29th, 1980*

# Credits

The author would like to thank the following for permission to reproduce the photographs: Bundesarchiv, Koblenz, 4, 5, 26; Robert Hunt Library, 1, 6, 7, 8, 9, 10, 11, 13, 16, 17, 24, 25, 27, 34, 37, 39, 40, 42; Imperial War Museum, London, 3, 12, 18, 19, 20, 21, 22, 23, 28, 29, 30, 31, 32, 33, 36, 41, 43; Keystone Press Agency, 2, 14, 35, 38; Popperfoto, 15; and is grateful for permission to quote material to George E. Koskimaki, author of *D-Day with the Screaming Eagles*; Leo Cooper Ltd (*Lion Rampant* by Robert Woollacombe); the Souvenir Press (*Caen, Anvil of Victory* by Alexander McKee); Paul Elek Ltd (*The Battle of the Falaise Gap* by E. Florentin); Macmillan Ltd (*Night Drop* by S. L. A. Marshall); Harper Inc. (*Soldier* by Matthew B. Ridgway) and Hutchinson Ltd (*Currahee* by Donald Burgett).

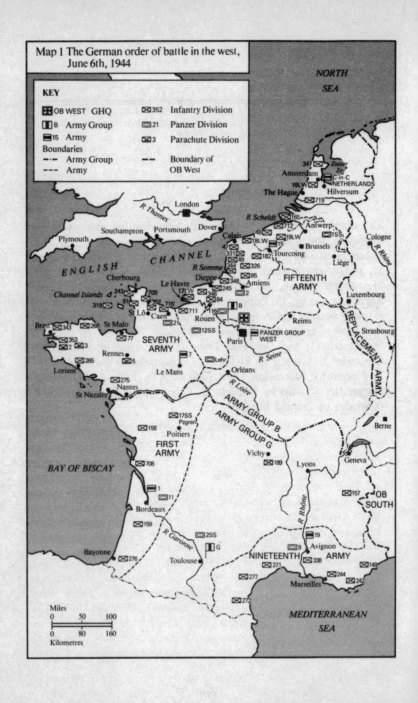

Map 1 The German order of battle in the west, June 6th, 1944

KEY

| | |
|---|---|
| OB WEST GHQ | ⊠ 352 Infantry Division |
| B Army Group | ⊠ 21 Panzer Division |
| 15 Army | ⊠ 3 Parachute Division |

Boundaries
– · – Army Group
– – – Army
– – Boundary of OB West

# PROLOGUE

## *In the Invasion Area*

I HAD A good war. It is not a phrase to be written, still less spoken, with any complacency, breathed as it has been on clouds of *bonhomie* in saloon bars from one end of the Home Counties to the other during the last thirty years. But in my case it is accurate none the less: the good war not of a near-warrior at the safe end of one of the sunnier theatres of operations, but of a small boy whisked from London at the first wail of the sirens to a green and remote corner of the west of England and kept there until the echo of the last shot fired was drowned in the sighs of the world's relief in August 1945.

I was not, unlike so many other children swept from harm's way in September 1939, an evacuee. On the contrary – and it was this which did so much to make my war good – I was transplanted in an intact family from one reassuring fireside to another, with nothing but the excitement of the journey and new surroundings to mark the change. It was the evacuation programme, none the less, which took me to the West Country, for my father's war work was to help administer it. An Inspector of Schools, he had in the years before the war supervised teaching in one of the most densely populated districts of south London, deemed by the government after the scare of Munich to be one of the likeliest targets for German air attack. Its schools had therefore been among the first directed to disperse their pupils to the countryside, and for the first week of the war he had shuffled manila-labelled children, teachers, burst suitcases and mislaid gas-masks between the platforms of Paddington station and seen them off westward to their billeting areas. At the end of it he followed the last train he had filled, too exhausted to be moved by the pathos of this extraordinary diaspora, to rejoin his wife and family, sent ahead to set up temporary home on the outskirts of the county town where

he was to have his office. For the rest of the autumn we saw little of
him. His days were taken with settling schools, half-schools, frac-
tions of schools into church halls and village institutes the length of
the Quantocks and Mendips and coaxing children and teachers back
into the routine of the time-table. Meanwhile my mother, losing
patience with the gimcrack villa to which long-distance arrangements had brought us, found a pretty white Regency cottage in the
fields beyond the town, into which she settled her three children and
their nursemaid, a kindly middle-aged soul in an advanced but
harmless stage of religious mania, for the winter. By Christmas my
father's daily round had slowed to the pace of our own, and there, for
the next five years, our share of the war stopped.

Petrol rationing had already brought silence to the high road
which ran beyond our front garden wall, broken only by the buzz of
the infrequent rural bus, the roar of a very rare tractor passing from
one field to another and the clatter of hooves of ponies seeking to
escape the whiphand of an intimidating breed of leather-faced
landed ladies, whom the war had put back into governess carts long
cobwebbed and forgotten. My father, categorized as an essential
user, retained his car and set off each morning, exactly as he had
done days without number in London before the war, to call on
headmasters and headmistresses, monitor standards of reading
among eight-year-olds, cast an eye on probationary teachers, discuss
leaving certificates with their seniors and in general uphold the
austere but uplifting ideal of standard and compulsory education for
all which inspectors of schools had represented since Matthew
Arnold's appointment to the first inspectorship a hundred years
before. I often accompanied him, my private-school holidays overlapping the terms of the state schools in his care, an anomaly to
which at the age of six or seven I gave no thought at all. Thus I
began my discovery of the secret world of the English countryside –
in 1940 literally secret, for among the flurry of anti-invasion
directives issued after the fall of France was one ordering the
uprooting of all rural signposts. Whatever twist that measure might
have given to the wanderings of vagabond German parachutists, it
had the effect of taking the two of us down every other wrong
turning which offered itself. These false starts were corrected only
by random knocking at the doors of remote cottages inevitably
occupied by crones who regarded all strangers as foreigners, and so
to be denied any but the most misleading information, or by shouted

conversations with ploughmen following their horses in the middle
distance of fields too muddy to enter. Staple Fitzpaine, Curry Rivel,
Curry Mallet, Isle Abbotts, Isle Brewers, Hatch Beauchamp,
Thornfalcon, Buckland St Mary, Combe St Nicholas: how slowly
and circuitously did my father's car learn to pick its way from one
hidden place to another through a countryside as silent and empty as
it had been before the coming of the railways.

As I grew a little and learnt to bicycle, these expeditions became
my own, no doubt of short range but in memory of immense extent,
excitement and mystery. The war having taken the young men from
the farms, and forced their employers to concentrate on essentials,
hedges and roadside trees grew unchecked from one springtime to
the next, turning every lane in summer into a green tunnel,
waist-deep at the verge with campion and cow-parsley, and trellised
overhead at harvest with the yellow of corn stalks scraped from the
tops of wagons bringing grain to the threshing machines. Near by
the tunnels led to farms from where eggs, pots of cream and
sometimes an unplucked chicken found their way, in the teeth of all
rationing regulations, on to neighbours' tables, our own included;
farms where there were ricks to be scaled, pigs poked, rats chased,
cats followed to their litters of kittens in high, hot, dusty hay-
lofts, and sheds filled with obsolete horsedrawn machinery to be
examined, with much squeaking of rusty levers and squealing of
long-frozen gears.

Farther away the tunnels led to stranger destinations, to secret
lakes in overgrown woods where swans rose screaming from their
nests with a flap of wings which we children believed, with the force
of gospel truth, could break a man's arm at a single blow; to small
waterfalls tinkling bright in the gloom of stream-cut grottoes under
bridges at the turn of an oak-hung road; to short-tufted upland sheep
runs where we improvised picnics in the wheeled, hump-backed
sheds in which shepherds lambed their ewes; to an isolated crossroad
forge, dark as midnight within even at high summer and pungent
with the smoke of hooves burning under red-hot iron – I was seeing
the last days, know it though I could not, of a thousand years of
heavy-horse farming. In summer the horses came to the fields
behind our house and we rode beside their drivers on machines
seemingly no different from the cast-offs discovered in our explora-
tion of the neighbouring out-houses, waiting for the word to lift the
blades on the turn and leave the long swathe of mown grass to lie like

a broken wave on the stubble behind; a day or two of sun took us out again with pitchforks to turn the drying crop and then, mounted behind a horse rake, to gather the drift into lines, watch it pitched on to wagons and, last of all, brought to the stacks for thatching against the storms of winter.

And yet I remember no wartime winter. The German Sixth Army froze in its filthy, iron-hard foxholes at Stalingrad; I pined for snow on a bright Christmas Eve and thought myself cheated when the morrow brought not a flake. The PQ convoys skirted the edge of the pack on the north Russia run, shrinking by every mile of sea room they could find from the basilisk eye of the Luftwaffe; I scouted the hedge-bottoms for a ditchful of bearing ice and came home with wet socks. The Hunger Winter of 1944 sent Dutch families to scratch for overlooked potatoes in the twice-dug earth of north Holland; I cracked hazelnuts in the November sun on Sunday afternoon walks with my father and returned to hot treacle flapjack by the kitchen fire. Perhaps there were other corners of war-enwrapped Europe where children lived as well-fed, warm and carefree as us. But I wonder if any retain, as I do, a memory of six years so consistently illuminated by sunlight, so deeply suffused by happiness, so utterly unmenaced by danger? Today conscience attacks memory with accusations of involuntary guilt at what I was spared. But at the time it was simply as if the war was not.

Chance decreed that I had no close relatives of an age to serve in the armed forces; nor apparently had any of the families who lived round about. Our nearest neighbour with military connections was a long-retired colonel of Indian Mountain Artillery, venerated by me for his gift of a patent field-sketching pencil presented to him on his relinquishing command of a screw-gun battery at Aden in 1903. His incomprehension of current military realities was as total as my own. Locality ensured that not a bomb fell within thirty miles of our retreat; on one thrilling night of, inevitably false, alarm, we were taken in our pyjamas to sit in the cellar of the large house across the way, and on another my parents stood in the garden for an hour after the nine o'clock news to watch the glow of Bristol burning beyond the horizon. But on neither night, nor on any other, did we hear as much as the engine-note of an errant German bomber. Parental protectiveness shielded us entirely from disturbing facts or rumours. My father, who had spent what I now realize to have been two horrible years on the Western Front in 1917–18, was nightly badgered by my sister and me for stories of what he had done in the 'First War', as he called it; but the world of active service he conjured up was all friendships, horses and rest from the trenches in billets as warm and secure as the darkened bedroom in which we prompted him down his train of entrancing, evasive memories. Habits of rural independence and self-sufficiency spared us any real want; in a countryside of mixed farming cultivated by yeoman tenants as close-fisted in their dealings with the War Agricultural Committees as they had always been with landlords, there was inevitably a tithe of produce which escaped the official collection, circulating by barter, payment in kind or down-to-earth cash from larder to larder within the parish. The only deprivations I therefore suffered were entirely psychological and largely formed by reading. I yearned in particular for the company of Roger, Susan, Nancy and the rest of Arthur Ransome's *Swallows and Amazons* children, whose Lakeland life seemed so enviably and eventfully different from ours but which, save for the absence of a dinghy and a stretch of navigable water, I now recognize mine must have closely resembled.

And yet, in this unruffled pool of peace, the war entirely possessed me. I walked to school each morning – a walk along paths I again recall permanently dappled by sunshine, against which we wore curious regulation grey flannel hats apparently inspired by E. H. Shepard's drawings of Christopher Robin – in the pleasant confidence that between arithmetic and Latin there would be half an hour of commando raids behind the football hut, or hard-driven bargains in Dinky Toy models of Blenheims and Hurricanes, or detailed technical discussions of the Lee-Enfield and its laughingly obvious superiority to the Mauser and the Mannlicher-Carcano which, as the possessor of a small brown linen-covered manual of small arms, I knew to be the contemptible equipment of the Italian army. I also possessed an out-of-date edition of Jane's *Fighting Ships*, which I had read even more often than *Swallows and Amazons*, a complete set of Ministry of Information pamphlets on the war effort (*Combined Operations, Bomber Command* and the rest, now collectors' pieces and still a model of what sensible propaganda can achieve), and a file of articles on military subjects torn from *Picture Post*, including a particularly informative one on the Red Army. This last provoked my father, who held unchangingly to the view that we had declared war in solidarity with Poland and could not forgive Stalin for partitioning it with Hitler, to contemptuous snorts.

As a result of this diet of print, I can still recite the characteristics of most models of British equipment from the earlier half of the war with as little effort as the two-times table – Supermarine Spitfire Mark II, top speed 365 miles per hour, service ceiling 35,000 feet, armament eight ·303 Browning machine-guns, HMS *Norfolk*, six 8-inch guns, 10,000 tons displacement, 33 knots – and instantaneously recreate their silhouettes without the need to shut my eyes. It is only the earlier models with which I have this trick; later and improved types, like the Typhoon fighter-bomber or the Dido-class cruisers, interested me but failed to imprint themselves in the same way. Perhaps this was because they lacked the very striking grace of the designs conceived in the interwar years, when aesthetics could stake a claim beside mere lethality, but chiefly because, I conclude on reflection, of the fixed conviction I had formed as soon as my consciousness grasped the issues – and which therefore made improvements in equipment quite irrelevant – that *Britain was going to win the war*. But that formula does not convey the strength of my conviction strongly enough. It was rather the case that I knew, with an unshakeable moral and intellectual certainty, that Britain *could not lose*. So powerful was this sensation that my feelings towards Hitler, a figure whom the newspapers rarely let one forget and who was represented by every medium of public information as a mixture of monster and leper, were those of protective indulgence. If only, I used to muse, I could get him to myself for a moment or two, talk things over, put the facts straight, open his eyes, he'd have to see that there was no point in going on, that it would be better to chuck the towel in at once and ask to be let off. The sense of silent and unconsummated communion with the Führer had the parallel effect of compromising and devaluing for me all official efforts to put heart into an anxious and uncertain people to which the British were subjected during the war years. My disapproval was particularly aroused by a National Savings Committee poster, displayed month after month over the ping-pong table in one of my prep-school day-rooms, which showed an exaggeratedly aggressive lion snarling into mid-distance over the caption *The Spirit of 1943*. I thought it tastelessly overstated as an expression of the national spirit, which I was certain the artist, had he only made the right inquiries, would have found as sublimely confident of ultimate victory as my own.

My conviction had its roots, I now diagnose, in two circumstances. The first was my sense of place at the centre of an enormous empire. Not only did our school atlas show its extent in red ('Couldn't Hitler see ...?') and not only did we know that Australians, Canadians, New Zealanders, South Africans, Indians were back here, as they had been in the First World War, to take their place at our side, but, in my class of eight-year-olds, the life of the empire was actually an immanent presence. One classmate's father was the squadron leader who held the record for long-distance flying between Britain and Australia, another's a district commissioner in West Africa, while the boy with whom I shared a desk was the son of a soldier commanding a brigade on the North-West Frontier of India, standing where Pakistan, a country not yet invented, and Afghanistan, then totally disregarded, now meet. By not one flicker of prescience was it suggested to us that within five years India, the jewel in the crown of empire, would have fallen away and within twenty all but the smallest seed pearls would have followed. The very scale of the empire was a guarantee to us of its unshakeable permanence.

That quality determined the second reason for my confidence in the war's outcome. It was clearly the reassuring stability and solidity of Britain's imperial power which had brought all those other people, unlucky enough to live outside its boundaries, to join us also. If you counted them all in, Chinese and Russians and Norwegian and Dutch and Free French and the bits of empire (not, of course, to be spoken of in the same breath as our own) which some of them owned, you found that almost everyone was against Hitler. ('Couldn't he see ...?')

Moreover, these co-belligerents were not propaganda figments, like the overdone lion in the day-room. Their representatives, wearing British uniform differentiated by cloth shoulder patches which read 'Netherlands' or 'Free French' or 'Belgium', were here in Britain among us and could occasionally be seen walking the streets of the county town. Religion assured that I should meet a disproportionate number in the flesh, for ours was a Catholic family and the local church, a very solitary beacon of the faith in the deeply Protestant west, was a natural haven for uprooted and lonely fellow-believers. There were some oddities and mistakes among the acquaintance Sundays brought us. My father formed an inexplicable affection for a community of conscientious objectors, bearded men and sandalled women otherwise largely clad in untanned sheepskins, who had one day confronted our austerely orthodox parish priest – a man I held in considerable awe for his ability to transfer himself from the ground to the seat of the monumentally upright bicycle on which he paid his parish calls by a process akin to levitation – with a request to be 'received' *en masse*. Many subsequent afternoons were consequently spent at their settlement, a handsome Georgian mansion tepidly vandalized by their occupation, where my father carried on high-minded conversation across the tea-table and I avoided as far as possible the copious offerings of unrefined peanut butter on which the community appeared principally to subsist. Less innocuous was another of his church-door adoptees, an Italian prisoner-of-war paroled to a local farmer. Swarthy and almost dwarfish, he was, I suppose, a Sicilian or Calabrian peasant boy for whom the Duce's call to live dangerously can never have sounded very loud, if indeed it had meant anything at all in whatever southern dialect he spoke. He had none the less learnt a sort of English and on his first, only and never-again-to-be-mentioned visit he subjected my parents to a lengthy description of what they eventually grasped to be his single-handed massacre of a platoon of Australians in the Western Desert. This wholly incredible tale lapsed into a deepeningly distasteful pantomime of hand-to-hand combat, from which my father took refuge in a hasty armchair nap while my mother sat the fable out in frozen politeness to its loathsome end. Christian charity did not extend to a second invitation.

Other military transients were more warmly welcomed, the Slavs in particular. I can still recreate the slightly stable-like odour left in the car by a Czech soldier, given a lift on a rainy day, and though it offended me at the time it was, I now realize, simply a soldier's smell, compounded of infrequent baths and shoddy khaki. It clearly repelled my father, who must have recognized it from the trenches, not at all. He and his hitch-hiker passed an agreeable twenty miles in companionable deprecation of the small miseries of military life. But his regard for the Czechs, whom he illogically associated with Chamberlain's appeasement policy, took second place to what he felt for the Poles. They were peerless: Catholic, high-spirited, heroes of the Battle of Britain, undaunted by exile, they satisfied every one of his exacting tests of warriordom, and he sought out their company whenever he could find it. 'Always glad to help a Pole' invariably concluded the street directions he offered them, answers to questions stumbled out often so haltingly that it was clear even to me that the sentiment was quite lost on the hearers (though not perhaps the good will).

The arrival of a Polish squadron at a near-by airfield allowed ampler scope to his Slavophilia; thither his car developed a habit of calling on its roundabout journey from one refugee school to another, to wait outside the mess while within he imbibed hospitality and far-fetched dog-fighting stories with indiscriminate pleasure. My harder-headed mother was less susceptible to Polish charm. It was the chance appearance of peacetime friends, transformed by khaki and the open air into bronzed and gallant cavaliers, which brought out the girlishness in her, sent her tripping to conjure up cream teas and bottles of sherry from cupboards which should have been bare, and tempted her to listen to talk laced with the shorthand of wartime English – 'Gib' and 'Alex' and 'the Med' – without for once any of that impatience I sensed she otherwise felt for a world suddenly, self-importantly and sadistically masculinized.

I too was entranced by these incursions, for our visitors brought with them the flavour of the 'real' army, quite different from that of the few, drab, static units which populated our operational backwater. The county town, true, was the depot of an ancient regiment of the line, the lintel of whose castellated Victorian gatehouse bore the deeply incised name of a Kiplingesque North-West Frontier siege; but the guard at the gate was mounted by pensioners. Convalescents in unbecoming bright-blue flannel suits occasionally found their way from a local hospital on to the benches of the municipal park. And though a unit of the Royal Artillery was billeted in one of the larger houses in the town, it was equipped only with searchlights. I knew that elsewhere the military scene must be more glamorous, for I had a small book which depicted the badge of every regiment of the army underneath a picture of the coloured side-cap proper to each: green and yellow for the Inniskilling Dragoon Guards; cherry red for the 11th Hussars; scarlet for the 12th Lancers; purple and navy for the Essex Regiment; black and grey for the Leicesters; maroon and black for the East Yorkshires; yellow, blue and Lincoln green for the Sherwood Foresters. I searched the horizons for this brilliant millinery. In vain: the only soldiers I saw wore khaki from top to toe, khaki so ill-cut, shapeless and hairy that I could find almost nothing in its wearers to admire. 'Battledress' was the official description of the outfit; but it was not thus clad, I knew, that Wellington's infantry had stood in square to receive the charge of Napoleon's Cuirassiers at Waterloo.

The 'real' army, of course, was elsewhere, capturing, if the propaganda photographs were anything to go by, Italians by the acre in the Western Desert. Term by term the boys at the top of the senior school left to join it – less often the navy or the air force – news of their service occasionally percolating back to us, commissionings, decorations, sometimes a death in action. I had known them too little to be touched. The only death which at all punctured my cocoon of serenity was that of a stupid, jolly sixth-former, who, the masters despairing of his passing exams, had been allowed to spend his last term learning to manage a pipe and a shotgun, equipped with which he had become a familiar sight under the rookery which swayed in the tops of the gigantic elms below the cricket field. Almost as soon as he left, it seemed, he was reported killed in the Sicily landings, a private soldier, not quite eighteen years old. By then, as I can now date it, the army had left North Africa and begun the invasion of Italy. But still there was no sign of the soldiers who, failing the arrangement of my *tête-à-tête* with Hitler, were going to bring the war to an end. There were hints of their existence. Once a glittering battery of 25-pounders came to the school to give a demonstration of firepower, to such effect that the shock of their first salvo almost dislodged me from the walnut tree in which I had established a vantage point, my neck-saving clutch at a branch sending a cascade of ripe nuts to patter a muffled answer to the echo of their thunder on the soft turf below. On another afternoon a squad of Herculean young commandos, training for some amphibious derring-do, came tumbling over our garden wall in flight from the 'enemy' and took refuge among the fruit trees and vegetables. Their heavy breathing and wordlessly transmitted wish that I should stop staring so pointedly at their hiding place and play elsewhere remained to thrill and disturb me long after the crash of their departure through the strip of adjoining woodland had died behind them. But thrills and disturbances by anything resembling a genuine menace to the Germans were so few and irregular that, had I not been possessed by my unreasoning certainty in victory, I might, with a little reflection, have allowed myself to question during 1942 and 1943 how it was ever going to be won.

And then, suddenly, there were the Americans. There had been portents of their coming, in particular the appearance of a US Office of War Information booklet, snapped up by me from a town bookstall, on the Eighth US Army Air Force (USAAF), filled with photographs of the construction of the airfields from which it was to begin its bombing campaign over Europe, and containing a cut-away drawing of the Flying Fortress, for which, through counting the enormous number of machine-guns it mounted, I quickly formed almost as strong a regard as I already had for the Spitfire. There had been outriders, a scattering of officers in the unfamiliar rig of olive jacket and beige trousers – 'pinks and greens', as I subsequently learnt veterans nostalgically describe it – whom I used to see walking home on warm sunlit evenings to the lodgings which had been found for them on the outskirts of the town. On one of these, astounding myself by my forwardness and in flagrant violation of family rules, I tried the formula, which I knew to be in universal circulation, 'Got any gum, chum?' and was rewarded by an embarrassed halt – my embarrassment was altogether greater – a rummaging in pockets and the presentation of a packet of Spearmint. As it happened, I did not like chewing gum. But the superiority of the American over the British product, and particularly the sumptuousness of the wrapper and the lustrous simplicity of its design, instantly and deeply impressed me. Much of that evening, which would normally have been spent reading at a gap illicitly opened in my bedroom curtains, I devoted to a study of its elements, struggling in an increasingly trancelike state to draw from its symbolism the message which I sensed the designer sought to convey. Thus I made my first encounter with the science of semeiotics; but also with the bottomless riches of the American economy.

They were shortly to be made manifest in super-abundance. Towards the end of 1943 our backwater, which British soldiers had garrisoned so sparsely for four years, overflowed almost overnight with GIs. How different they looked from our own jumble-sale champions, beautifully clothed in smooth khaki, as fine in cut and quality as a British officer's – an American private, we confided to each other at school, was paid as much as a British captain, major, colonel – and armed with glistening, modern, automatic weapons, Thompson sub-machine-guns, Winchester carbines, Garand self-loading rifles. More striking still were the number, size and elegance of the vehicles in which they paraded about the countryside in stately convoy. The British army's transport was a sad collection of underpowered makeshifts, whose dun paint flaked from their tinpot bodywork. The Americans travelled in magnificent, gleaming, olive-green, pressed-steel, four-wheel-drive juggernauts, decked with what car salesmen would call optional extras of a sort never seen on their domestic equivalents – deep-treaded spare tyres, winches, towing cables, fire-extinguishers. There were towering GMC six-by-sixes, compact and powerful Dodge four-by-fours and, pilot fishing the rest or buzzing nimbly about the lanes on independent errands like the beach buggies of an era still thirty years ahead, tiny and entrancing jeeps, caparisoned with whiplash aerials and sketchy canvas hoods which drummed with the rhythm of a cowboy's saddlebags rising and falling to the canter of his horse across the prairie. Standing one day at the roadside, dismounted from my bicycle to let one such convoy by, I was assaulted from the back of each truck as it passed by a volley of small missiles, which fell into the ditch beside me with the same soft patter I had provoked under my grandstand at the artillery display. But when I burrowed in the dead leaves to discover the cause I unearthed not walnuts but a little treasure of Hershey bars, Chelsea candy and Jack Frost sugar-cubes, a week's, perhaps a month's ration, of sweet things casually disbursed in a few seconds. There was, I reflected as I crammed the spoil into my pockets, something going on in the west of England about which Hitler should be very worried indeed.

For a time it was only as the distributors of haphazard largesse that the Americans impinged, though the town soon began to be surrounded by encampments of neat, weathertight wooden huts, again altogether superior in quality to the straggling settlements of corrugated iron which housed British units; one formed a large modern hospital which was to survive the war and become the town's alternative medical centre. But gradually personal contacts were made, the first by our pretty, black-ringleted, Welsh nursemaid, Annie, who had appeared soon after the evening when a drunken British parachutist had made an assault on the bedroom window of her dottily pious predecessor. Annie came to us from a convent, where she had emphatically not been preparing to enter the sisterhood. The look assumed by my mother, as Annie swayed towards GI territory in the centre of the town on her afternoons off, her pink, plump and rather wobbly legs covered for the outing in a bottled brown preparation called 'liquid stockings' which did wartime duty for the real thing, implied a nagging anxiety that she was flirting with another sisterhood, from which the convent had presumably been enlisted to rescue her. But though silk stockings materialized to replace liquid ones, as did supplies of Hershey bars and Spearmint on a scale which rapidly devalued mine, Annie was apparently asked to give nothing in return or, if asked, not pressed. My mother's alarm subsided.

Quite soon my parents had collected an American circle of their own. One member, a major of engineers, became a lifelong friend and, in 1945, godfather to a new daughter, the second of two children born into the family in the war years. Others, also encountered at the church door, came to replace the earlier wave of expatriates who had called for tea on Sunday afternoons. Most, like them, seemed to want no more than an occasional glimpse into a domestic interior as a comforting leaven in their austere but enthralling military experience. A few gentler souls became more dependent and appeared more often. One, Sontag – I knew him in no other way – a thin, dark-haired, soft-eyed young man, must have been acutely afflicted by homesickness and perhaps by the fear of what lay ahead. Squirrel-like, he accumulated in a spare corner of the house a store of small, valueless personal possessions, which he called to fuss over at intervals and one day, after which he was not seen again, asked my parents to keep safe for him. Their overheard murmur of agreement at lunch months later that 'Sontag won't be coming back' awoke in me a guilty, prurient curiosity, and that afternoon I picked his little store over, and found a GI torch, a webbing belt and a Pocket Book edition, in gritty grey paper, of *A Tree Grows in Brooklyn*. It seemed a small enough stake to have put down in the country.

But by then – it must have been in the winter of 1944 – there was very little left at all of the Americans' transient presence. It had during that spring swollen to almost all-pervading proportions, so that there seemed more Americans than natives in the district (as there may well have been). American transport monopolized the roads, American uniform became as commonplace as that other uniform of the penultimate war year, the high-shouldered overcoat, wedge-heeled shoes and turbaned head so often seen on its arm. American accents, much enjoyed, much, if badly, imitated, passed as an alternative local dialect and some of the ease, nonchalance and generosity of American manners had permeated and softened local formality. The feudal west would never be quite the same again, and a good thing too thought many, particularly the young. We relentlessly patriotic little prep-school boys, imprinted with our idea of the paramountcy of the British empire, to which we knew the United States represented a principle in some way antithetical, held out longest against American charm. I particularly resisted admitting that the US Navy had demoted the Royal Navy to second place among the world's fleets, even after the facts had told me differently. But in time it got to us too. There was something in particular about jeeps, and the way they were driven with one high-booted leg thrust casually outside the cab, which softened even the most chauvinist ten-year-old heart.

And, as spring became summer in 1944, yet more exciting manifestations of American military power thrust themselves on our attention. The GIs whom we had got to know had, we now grasped, been engineers, builders and truck drivers, who had been creating settlements for the fighting troops still to come. They were now among us. And with them they brought a new wave of equipment, half-track scout cars, amphibious trucks and gigantic transporters, laden with tanks and bulldozers – a machine previously unknown in Britain – which held to the main roads and, when in convoy, were usually seen heading southward, towards the ports of Hampshire and Dorset, on the Channel coast opposite France. American aircraft, too, appeared in great numbers, Liberators, Dakotas and occasionally the dramatically twin-boomed P-38 Lightning, glimpsed rocketing across the sky like a shape of things to come. Dakotas were the most common, and the source of the most arresting experience I underwent that fresh, green spring. Some forgotten journey brought me unexpectedly upon an airfield, over which a cloud of aircraft hung, turning and swooping. But it was unlike any formation I had ever seen, in that the planes were linked together in pairs by spider-thin cables. Suddenly and successively the cables fell slack and the second in each pair of aircraft began to descend towards the runway. Strangest of all, they had neither propellers nor engines, their descent was silent and, when they touched ground, they came to a halt within a few yards. From their interiors men tumbled out and formed ranks, from which brilliant red and green flares were shot in spluttering arcs towards the departing Dakota tugs. I had had my first sight of a method of war which I had not dreamt, a glider assault on the rear of the enemy.

But not my last. One evening some weeks later the sky over our house began to fill with the sound of aircraft, which swelled until it overflowed the darkness from edge to edge. Its first tremors had taken my parents into the garden, and as the roar grew I followed and stood between them to gaze awestruck at the constellation of red, green and yellow lights which rode across the heavens and streamed southward towards the sea. It seemed as if every aircraft in the world was in flight, as wave followed wave without intermission, dimly discernible as darker corpuscles on the black plasma of the clouds, which the moon had not yet risen to illuminate. The element of noise in which they swam became solid, blocking our ears, entering our lungs and beating the ground beneath our feet with the relentless surge of an ocean swell. Long after the last had passed from view and the thunder of their passage had died into the silence of the night, restoring to our consciousness the familiar and timeless elements of our surroundings, elms, hedges, rooftops, clouds and stars, we remained transfixed and wordless on the spot where we stood, gripped by a wild surmise at what the power, majesty and menace of the great migratory flight could portend.

Next day we knew. The Americans had gone. The camps they had built had emptied overnight. The roads were deserted. No doubt, had we been keeping check, we would have noticed a gradual efflux of their numbers. But it had been disguised until the last moment and the outrush had then been sudden. The BBC news bulletin told us why. 'Early this morning units of the Allied armies began landing on the coast of France.' The message was transmitted often that morning, June 6th, 1944, drawing listeners anxiously to their sets before each advertised broadcast in the hope of hearing some heartening change in the anodyne form of words passed by the censor. I had no patience with their incertitude. The doorman at my father's office, a figure of weight and importance to me because, as a retired policeman, he was allowed to keep a pistol in the drawer of his desk the better to repel any fifth columnist bent on capturing the files of the County Education Committee, caused particular irritation by being too busy with the controls of his set – bending his head to the speaker and fussily adjusting the volume – to show me the gun as he usually did. He just, he said, wanted to hear how things were going. Irritation gave way to scorn. What was the point of wondering how things were going? A cross-Channel invasion was not, as it happened, how I had visualized the war would be won. I had formed no picture at all of the means by which the German army was going to be brought to decisive battle. If anything, I had imagined some gigantic, climacteric duel of aircraft, in which Spitfires without number would have overwhelmed the Germans first in the sky and then on the ground. But if a cross-Channel invasion it was to be, that was an end to it. The Allies had determined a means different from that I had visualized. But the outcome was no more in doubt than it had ever been. They were going to win. The Germans were going to lose. News of events would add colour and interest while we waited, and should be enjoyed in that spirit. But the outcome was not in doubt. *Allons, enfants de la patrie; le jour de gloire est arrivé*.

And thus, in a curious way, the war released me from its grasp. Another world of the imagination, that of the more distant past, had already begun to possess me and, for what remained of my enchanted exile in the countryside, it was there that I dwelt. The surrounding landscape was planted particularly thickly with medieval churches, and dotted with villages and townships on which Georgian domestic builders had laid a wide and kindly hand. I had got to know many of these buildings well in my travels, learnt to distinguish Norman from Perpendicular and both from Victorian Gothic (on which I directed a scorn untinged by Betjemanite doubt), come to admire eighteenth-century proportionality and the gentle adaptation of Doric and Corinthian severity to cosy market-place front doors. And I peopled them with the dwellers who seemed to me proper to their spirit; the churches with pre-Reformation parsons best resembling the Benedictines at our neighbouring abbey, Oxford and Cambridge men who interspersed their plain chant with rough shooting and rugger; the houses with decorous, benevolent, politely educated Jane Austen families differing only from their current retired-colonel occupants by way of buckled shoes and lace. Both sets of characters I found deeply attractive, and I surrounded them with the appropriate cast to play supporting roles – with pious, sparsely prosperous villeins, craftsmanly, wordless guildsmen, white with stone-chippings or sawdust, packhorse drovers looking for packhorse bridges, millers, merchants, carters, bargemen, village schoolmasters with a thumb in Chapman's *Homer*, town worthies with a deep pocket and an eye for a classical cornice, scarlet-coated grenadiers soberly supping ale beside their sprig-muslined maids. The two worlds ran together in the mind's eye as easily and naturally as, in the prettier townscapes, did the two architectures, producing a vision of the past at once Catholic and Anglican, Plantagenet and Hanoverian, feudal and municipal, pastoral and mercantile, and throughout friendly, easeful and utterly pacific.

Time, teaching and reading would show me that it was all the most perfect nonsense; that the world of the past was not a potpourri of its quainter elements but as getting-and-spending a one as that of the present, the getting harder, the spending stingier; that its prevailing mood was not harmony but conflict, which man's nastier qualities were more often deployed to resolve than charity or reason; that the lyrical emotions it aroused in me, dissolving all differences of class, interest, period and place in a poetic haze, were a positive obstacle to grasping its passions, hopes and needs. I struggled against the death of romance and the dissolution of my peaceable kingdom. How could an age that had built Glastonbury Abbey not be kinder than that which had built cotton mills? How could a world of hand tools not be more satisfying to work in than a world of machines? How could travel by horse not be more fun than by steam or oil? Who would not choose to live under thatch instead of slate, eat stone-milled instead of shop-bought bread, wear broadcloth instead of rayon? Disease, I accepted, was a hazard which afflicted the inhabitants of my imagined and vanished England with a frequency and severity we were spared. But that they were afflicted also in the vast majority by seasonal hunger, winter cold, constant poverty, backbreaking labour for little return, legal inequity, illiteracy, ignorance and frequent disorder was a view to which I retreated reluctantly, step by step, and with a lingering conviction that the sun-warmed stones of cloister and market-cross could not really lie.

And of course they do not altogether. But to begin to see how and why was to take as much time as unlearning the myths of beauty and peace they had spoken to me of in the first place. In the process I was taught a great deal about other places and times than the England of the late middle and early modern age and of other subjects than the social and cultural history which were my starting points. I learnt enough imperial history to accept that it had two sides, enough political history to perceive that power was important and parties had purpose, enough intellectual history to distinguish between debate and dissent, enough economic history to see that work was about business not pleasure, enough military history to grasp the cardinality of force, dubiety of valour and marginality of the just cause. A child of war, it was military history which particularly aroused me. In time I grasped that I had lived through great events and that the determinism I had imposed on them – the certainty of victory, the indulgent contempt for the enemy, the patronizing acceptance of allies – was merely an index of how limited and local had been my viewpoint. Britain, I learnt, had not been strong, but weak. The long delay in bringing the Germans to decisive battle had been a matter of necessity, not choice. The Russians, whose war I had thought entirely marginal, had, I discovered, fought the greatest of the land campaigns. The empire, whose sheer size I reckoned the principal source of Allied power, had, I learnt, been unable to arm itself. The European allies, whom I had thought important by reason of their number alone, had, I gathered, been little better than refugees. The Japanese, of whom I had not thought at all, had, I found, come close to making the Pacific their own. And the Americans . . .

It was my misunderstanding of their place in things which was hardest to correct. They had been all about me and yet I had had no curiosity about what had brought them. During the period of Britain's isolation I had counted them, when I did so at all, as benevolent spectators, clearly on our side because they spoke English but, since we had Australia, Canada and South Africa with us, not wanted or even necessary as allies, a viewpoint which I presumed was also their own. When, nevertheless, they had begun to appear in England, it was, I supposed, because of a failure of patience, similar to that I had felt, with Hitler's effort to win a war he was bound to lose. And, in their coming to England, I very definitely presumed that they were putting themselves, if not under British command, at least at Britain's disposal. We, after all, had established property rights in the war and latecomers would be obliged to respect them.

There, as childish perceptions go, I may not have been so wide of the mark. Popular sentiment, though overflowingly warm to the Americans as individuals, was not, after years of exposure to the themes of 'blood, toil, sweat and tears', 'taking it', 'the few' and 'standing alone', at all adaptable to the acceptance of parity of British and American effort, still less of any British subordination to American authority. That the invasion should have been mounted under the operational control of a British soldier, General Montgomery, and that British Commonwealth troops should have been in the majority on the invasion beaches therefore accorded with national feeling about the fitness of things. Had it been possible to take a poll of popular strategic attitudes in June 1944 it would probably have revealed an expectation that, though the Americans might in time come to supply the larger number of men in the battles for the liberation of Europe, and naturally the lion's share of the equipment, the direction of the campaign would be determined by British minds and exercised by British commanders, even if General Eisenhower might, for diplomatic reasons, have to be accorded a titular primacy over the armies in the field. And the justification for that division of responsibility would have been that the invasion was, after all, a British conception, an endeavour long promised, by Churchill to the country, by the British to themselves, an act of historical vindication, a paying back five-, ten- and twenty-fold for the nation's expulsion from the continent four years before and for all it had subsequently suffered.

It was hidden from the majority, hidden from all but a very few in the inmost circle of policy-making, that this simple, legalistic view of how strategy had been made and would thenceforth unroll was quite at variance with reality. And it would remain hidden until long after the war. Only in the early 1950s would it start to become apparent that a cross-Channel invasion, for all its obviousness as a cardinal means to defeat Hitler, had carried nothing like unanimous assent in the Allied camp. Gradually it would be revealed that, despite much lip service to the concept, the British had shown nothing like the commitment to it that the Americans had done; that they had not merely advanced practical objections when it was right to do so, during the periods of Allied inferiority, but had, even after the reversal of the balance of strength, argued so persuasively for alternative approaches to Hitler's heartland that the Americans had come to suspect a lack of resolution in their allies. The 'Second Front debate' was, it gradually became clear, the crux of the most important of all wartime Anglo-American misunderstandings.

# CHAPTER I

## *Journey to the Second Front*

THESE REVELATIONS of hidden Allied discord had for a child – in the 1950s a schoolboy – who had been reared not merely in the political atmosphere but on the substance of Anglo-American co-operation, the power to shock, strongly enough to set up walls of disbelief. With all the fervour of a convert, once brought to accept the hollowness of Britain's splendid isolation, I had replaced that faith with another which distinguished not at all between the interests of the United States and the United Kingdom, scarcely, indeed, between the identities of the two societies. Britain and the United States, it seemed to me, were one unit, the British and the Americans almost one people; and that their leaders could have disagreed, could have pursued different military ends, could in the process have formed resentments, nurtured suspicions, manoeuvred, equivocated, dissembled, treated with third parties, played for time were ideas that I simply could not credit. And I was right to doubt. For, in the history of the wartime alliance, it is the unity and good faith of the two powers which stands out, and their differences of opinion and divergence of aims which seem trivial and secondary. But it was also right to be taught to look beyond the appearance of unanimity. In the real world the Britain in which I grew up was a power already in decline, the United States poised on the brink of succession to her place and vibrant with the confidence and wealth which would carry her into it. But the United States was also a land which had eschewed military development and involvement in European politics, whose armed strength lay largely in her navy and whose foreign entanglements, where they existed, lay largely in the Pacific. Her decision, once war was thrust upon her, to make her main effort in Europe remains, therefore, even in retrospect, a remarkable one. And the paths by which she arrived at it, and held her chief ally to her chosen method of implementing it – the invasion which we have come to call D-Day – retains an equally compelling interest. How she chose those paths is best understood by following the footmarks of the professional military men who translated their political leaders' will to victory into reality.

Seven – and one civilian – personify the principles and predicaments of the strategies by which their nations strove to achieve victory or avoid defeat in the years when the Second Front was in the making: Stilwell, whose career incarnated the poverty and backwardness of the American army in the interwar years and his country's strategic involvement with Asia rather than Europe; Wedemeyer, the military technocrat, whose European training helped to commit the United States none the less to a continental invasion by a mass army; Eisenhower, whose intellectual flexibility and political touch found the means to give American strategy a coherent direction; Molotov, remembrancer of Russia's agony to Britain and the United States; Marshall, Roosevelt's strategic conscience; Brooke, book-keeper of Britain's dwindling strategic assets and editor of Churchill's wayward genius; Montgomery, his battlefield executive; and Rommel, on whom devolved responsibility for translating the folly of Hitler's ambitions into military sense.

The story of the Second Front begins with Stilwell at the moment when Japan, by her unannounced attack on the American Pacific Fleet at Pearl Harbor in Hawaii, ended a year of skirmishing and indecision and irrevocably committed herself and her ally, Germany, to war against the United States.

# Stilwell

Japan's attack on Pearl Harbor brought post-haste from Monterey to Washington one of the unlikeliest officers of the United States army. Joseph Warren Stilwell – Warren to his family, already Vinegar Joe to subordinates and superiors who knew the whiplash of his tongue – was commanding III Corps on December 7th, 1941. Until very recently a formation as large as a corps – 50,000 soldiers with artillery, transport and signals to match – had existed in the United States only on paper, and even in the late autumn of 1941, after two years of rearmament, III Corps's real and paper strength were still embarrassingly different from each other. But Stilwell had been raised in the old army of tiny and scattered units, had marched on his chin-strap in the weary pursuit of Filipino rebels, eaten the dust of summer on the Chinese plains, and camouflaged genteel poverty behind the white clapboard of officers' quarters at Leavenworth and Fort Benning. A corps, however filigree its fabric, and incomplete in its establishment, was a command of which as a turn-of-the-century West Pointer he could scarcely have dreamed and as a Great War veteran in the Depression years had abandoned hope of seeing again. To have watched III Corps come into being was to sense life pulsing again in the moribund army of the United States; to have been given command of it was to feel on his brow the crowning laurels of a soldier's career.

The call to Washington meant not only separation from his family but farewell to their beloved Carmel on the Monterey peninsula, where he and his wife had come to settle before the First World War and where the headquarters of III Corps had later been fixed. Its dark cypress groves and operatic crags, the Steinbeckian charm of the waterfront and the rag, tag and bobtail of the crowd which peopled it – Polish sardine-canners, Italian seine-boat fishermen, Chinese grocers, the hoboes from the Palace Flophouse and the dollar-a-day privates from the regiment in the Presidio – made it an unlikely setting for a military headquarters. Perhaps because of that Stilwell had reacted with uncharacteristic alarm to news of an imminent Japanese descent upon its enchanted coast during the first weeks of the war. 'Jap fleet 20 miles south, 10 miles west of Monterey', he wrote in his diary, 'I believed it like a damned fool . . . two [US] battalions along the coast . . . two battalions in reserve for 175 miles . . . six tanks coming from Fort Ord. (The others won't run) . . . Had the Japs only known, they could have landed anywhere on the coast, and after our handful of ammunition had gone, they could have shot us like pigs in a pen.' By December 22nd, when the call from Washington came, he had regained his objectivity and it was only the general unpreparedness of the nation which continued to give him 'that old sinking feeling'.[1] But to leave the Pacific, which had consumed his professional life, and the Salinas Valley, which possessed his heart, required a deliberate effort of will. Going was made easier by the speed of departure. He had an overnight stop with his family. Then on December 23rd he took the plane eastward.

Trans-continental flights in 1941, flown at 170 miles per hour in the ubiquitous DC-3 in stages of 500 miles, still lasted over a day. But for a sublimated romantic like Stilwell the long passages from San Francisco to Salt Lake City, Kansas City and Cincinnati was bearable because the route constituted a sort of pilgrimage across the heartland of the 'old Army's' past. It began north of the deserts of Arizona, where the black regiments of US Cavalry – 'buffalo soldiers' to the Indians – had endured the Saharan summers of the American interior, ran south of the hunting grounds of the Sioux, for which Custer had died in battle at the Little Big Horn, and then across the endless steppe of the Great Plains dotted by the stockaded outposts of settlement, Forts Kearney and Niobrara, Omaha and Sydney, Dodge, Ellsworth, Hawker, Hays and Wallace, a few thriving and populous, most garrisonless and forgotten, through which the army had shepherded the trek west. At Kansas City he left behind one of the most sacred places of the army's emotional geography, holier even than Battle Monument at West Point or the eternal flame at Arlington National Cemetery, where at Leavenworth, on the bluff above the Missouri still scarred by the abandoned Oregon–Santa Fé trail, stands the tiny memorial chapel of the regiments which fought for the frontier in the Indian wars of the 1860s and 1870s. It is there in the low-eaved gloom, between the cannon barrels which serve as pillars to the roof, among the slips of commemorative marble to scalped subalterns, that the American officer reminds himself of the days of 'real soldiering'; days when men sweated their necks sore, swallowed spit and chewed their boots for supper, rode all day to the musical creak of the McClellan saddle, slept to the dying fall of 'Taps' – 'Fades the light/And afar/Goeth day/Cometh night/And a star/Leadeth all/To their rest' – and celebrated return to the safety of the palisaded camp with eye-burning shots of rye and all the sweet water a soldier could swallow. It is the shrine of those Indian-fighting troopers whom Frederick Remington has immortalized in paint for the American nation and whose days on the prairie he has left as a vision of the perfect life to the freemasonry of Uncle Sam's army.

And, to the long-service soldier of Stilwell's stamp, it was a vision which cut deeper into the imagination even than the panoramas of glory and tragedy composed in blood on the great battlefields of the south – Atlanta, Chattanooga, Spotsylvania and the Wilderness – which lay beyond the horizon as he winged onwards from St Louis to Cincinnati. The Indian wars had been the private concern of 'a homogeneous class – straight, lean, square-jawed, clear-eyed, moustachioed soldiers, professionally going about their business without a flicker of fear or a moment of self-doubt', the American equivalents of Stalky and Co. and inhabitants of a world equally self-contained. The Civil War had been a war of the people, miscellaneously armed, shoddily clad, often unwillingly conscripted and corruptly officered, ragged in step, clumsy in drill, uncertain and sometimes panic-stricken in the face of the enemy – blue or grey. They had formed armies over which the West Point classes of the 1840s had wrung their hands in despair and with which their descendants from the Long Gray Line still felt less fraternity than with the disregarded apprentice regulars who had been driven from Washington by the British in 1812.

But, as Stilwell might have reflected as he touched down on the reclaimed swampland along the Potomac on December 24th, it was again a people's war which he had come to organize. The army of the white-painted officers' quarters which – as if for a stage setting of a Carson McCullers novel – line the lawns in front of the War College, where he called that afternoon, was almost as unfitted to fight a world conflict as was Winfield Scott's that which had broken out between the states in 1861. True, it no longer ranked 'nineteenth among the world's armed forces after Portugal' or 'forty-fifth in per cent of population under arms' as in September 1939. In the 27 intervening months it had multiplied its strength eight times, from 190,000 to 1·5 million, and its 93 battalions of infantry and 14 regiments of cavalry had been lost inside an army of new large formations – 30 divisions of infantry, 2 of cavalry and 5 of the new Armoured Forces, equipped with tanks (for which the American general staff in the interwar years had shown even less enthusiasm than the British). But tanks were as yet arriving from the hastily mobilized factories in dribs and drabs and, as with the aircraft for the 40 new Air Groups, much of the production was earmarked for shipment to Britain or Russia. American industry, like a knight in rusty armour, groaned to put forth its strength; meanwhile little equipment reached the divisions training in the hundreds of hutted camps hastily thrown up all over the south-eastern and western United States. Eight million Americans were docketed for drafting into the army, but the officers who would lead them still knew little more of their duty than they had been taught in afternoons at college ROTC courses.

None of this mattered as much, however, as the lack of a plan by which to employ the army when it eventually graduated from the training camps and, fully equipped, stood ready to face the enemy.

Not that there were not plans. There was indeed a plethora, an embarrassment of plans, their number reflecting the diffusion of responsibility for strategic direction which had prevailed in the War Department until almost the day before yesterday, and the still imperfect organization for co-ordinating all the ingredients of strategic decision – economic, logistic and diplomatic as well as military – which the unexpected arrival of foreign war had imposed upon a nation unprepared for it. The War Department of the United States had been reformed only twice in its history, first by Elihu Root in 1903, then by General Pershing in 1921. The first reform had ended a century of internal warfare between the military commander of the army and the heads of its internal bureaux; the second had provided the military commander – called, since 1903, the Chief of Staff – with a General Staff specifically organized to plan and wage war. But even in this new General Staff exact responsibility for the crucial issue of command – setting strategic aims and choosing where, how and by whom they should be realized – remained divided between its four original divisions, called G-1, G-2, G-3 and G-4, concerned respectively with personnel, intelligence, training and supply, and a new section, War Plans Division (WPD). In a misguided attempt to simplify the strategic planning process, Marshall, the new Chief of Staff, had actually set up in July 1940 yet a third agency, General Headquarters. It was to take on from the War Plans Division its latent responsibility for wartime command, meanwhile occupying itself with the training of the hundreds of thousands of draftees the Selective Service Act of September would bring into uniform. Training was, however, the direct responsibility of the G-3 Division, which left GHQ really no clear-cut function, except the obvious though unintended one of quarrelling with G-3 in particular and the divisions in general, an activity all the more readily stimulated by its distance in the suburban War College from their offices in central Washington.

Little wonder that almost every soldier above the rank of major in the capital in December 1941 had his own ideas about how the war should be won. The notorious 'colour' plans of the 1930s – Green for a war against Mexico, Black against Germany, Orange against Japan, Red against Britain, Orange and Red against Japan and Britain combined – were still current, even though they had been conceived in a spirit of 'pure staff thinking', without reference to real diplomatic circumstances, actual or anticipated. Since May 1939, however, they had been overlaid in importance by five so-called Rainbow plans prepared by the Joint Army and Navy Board, fore-runner of the Joint Chiefs of Staff, in which the two services were supposed to agree joint plans of action. The multiplication of plans and planning authorities did not end there. The American–British Staff Conversations, which had opened in great secrecy in Washington in January 1941, bequeathed both a plan (ABC-1) generally conforming to Rainbow 5, and two further consultative bodies, a British military mission to Washington and an American one to London. And while the former, being part of the highly centralized Whitehall machine, would indeed only consult, the latter was to have 'authority to collaborate in formulating military plans and policies'. The future Marshal of the Royal Air Force, Sir John Slessor, a member of the Washington Staff Conversations and an incredulous observer of the American governmental scene, reported on his return: 'It is fascinating to anyone who has been in close contact with our Committee of Imperial Defence and War Cabinet system to watch the way even the most capable Americans shy off any attempt to formalise or regularise the governmental system.'

Much of the failure to formalize or regularize was the deliberate omission of President Roosevelt. His temperament was hostile to bureaucratic style; he 'kept channels open, fought routine, sabotaged institutionalisation', worked through a network of unofficial friends and advisers (of whom the most important throughout the war would be the puckish and irreverent Harry L. Hopkins). He ran the White House very much on the relaxed lines of his Hudson Valley seat, Hyde Park, to which he retreated for days or even weeks on end when the need for country air and family gossip overcame his otherwise apparently inexhaustible zest for the intrigue, vote-bartering, compromise, high-minded moralizing, cynical dispensation of flattery and endless, teasing flirtation with the press which comprised the art of presidential government as displayed by its greatest practitioner. But he had another reason for declining to formalize methods of strategic decision. A single, strong, inter-service staff, with authority to agree on priorities and to co-ordinate land, sea and air action, would inevitably, however unintentionally, have driven the United States down a one-way street.

And he himself had not come to any ultimate decision before December 7th, 1941. He had committed the American taxpayer to a great programme of national rearmament. He had committed American diplomacy to a policy of 'all aid short of war' for Britain and of 'much aid' to Russia and China. But 'short of war' was his sticking point. It was not that, like Hitler the year before, or Schlieffen two generations earlier, he was seeking some antidote to the danger of fighting a war simultaneously on two fronts, east and west. He was seeking on the contrary to avoid war altogether, hoping that by the 'demonstration of his determination to mobilise and use America's enormous war potential . . . [he] might save Britain, deter Japan and make war unnecessary'. But to play that game of deterrence and dissuasion, he needed to manoeuvre day by day between enemies, friends and neutrals with a freedom, as much emotional as political, he could not hope to enjoy if admirals or generals stood at his elbow ready to warn that today's diplomatic concession vitiated yesterday's strategic decision or tomorrow's half-promise would compromise next week's binding commitment. 'This is a period of flux. I want no authorisation for what may happen beyond July 1st, 1941', he had told Knox, the Secretary of the Navy, late in 1940, but he had withheld all authorization far beyond that date, even though by December 1941 his position at home had been secured by his second re-election and Britain's acute predicament much eased by Hitler's attack on Russia.

Presented with a series of strategic proposals – Admiral Stark's Plan Dog of November 1940, which put the 'Atlantic First' and prefigured Rainbow 5, Rainbow 5 itself and its inter-Allied version, ABC-1 – he had done no more than 'familiarize' himself with their contents, meanwhile withholding both approval and disapproval. The clearest glimpse – and it was no more than a glimpse – that he had given of his strategic inclinations – and they were no more than inclinations – had come in a meeting with his 'War Council', an informal assembly of the Secretaries of State for War and of the Navy and the two chiefs of staff, at the White House on January 16th, 1941. Then he had discounted the 'worst case' – concerted action by Germany and Japan – at 'one in five' but revealed that, if it materialized, at the outset he would stand on the defensive in the Pacific, seek to do no more than safeguard convoys in the Atlantic but, without cavil, maintain aid to Britain. As for the army's mission, it should not be committed to any offensive until fully prepared to undertake it. In the interim, he suggested, it might 'assist to a moderate degree in backing up friendly Latin American governments against Nazi-inspired fifth column movements'.

The Second World War, General Marshall might have reflected, would not be won in the jungles of Paraguay. If such a thought crossed his mind he kept it to himself, and continued to fret for lack of direction all through the spring and summer of 1941. Eventually in June he decided that the President's withholding of 'dis-approval' from Rainbow 5/ABC-1 implied, if not approval of the plans themselves, then at least permission to transform their broad outlines into detailed provisions. The necessary work, however, proceeded so slowly through the mutual misunderstanding and jealousies of War Plans Divisions, General Headquarters and the G-Divisions, particularly G-4, that the day of Pearl Harbor found little prepared that was concrete. War Plans Division numbered only thirty-nine officers on December 7th, 1941 and the time of many of them was consumed in day-to-day trivia. But the crisis demanded action. The United States at war, above all the United States at bay, expected not some ponderous, slowly unwinding strategic response, but last-man and last-round defence where the enemy was strongest and instantaneous and ferocious attack at his points of weakness. So let the Philippines, Guam, Wake, be held at all costs. And let Points X, Y, and Z be attacked at once with every man who could hold a gun.

But where were Points X, Y and Z? Where was the enemy vulnerable? Not – spare the President's springtime illusions – in Latin America. Not in Iceland, which he had sent American troops to garrison under his 'short of war' policy in July. And certainly not in iron-bound, bayonet-studded Europe. Where else then? Suddenly the fruit of the years of 'pure staff thinking', all the theoretical plans written in the academic spirit so carefully cultivated at Command and General Staff College, were at a premium, as the veterans of War Plans Division and a flood of recalled reservists scrabbled to produce anything which would stand up to the rigour of proper military analysis – Situation, Enemy Forces, Friendly Forces, Assumptions, Mission, Execution, Administration and Logistics, Command. It was this activity which confronted Stilwell on his arrival in Washington.

> I find there is no basic strategic study in existence [he confided to his diary]. For instance, shall we now go to work and prepare seriously for war ... or shall we attempt to take the offensive? ... There is tremendous pressure to do some-

thing. The Limeys want us in with both feet. So the answer is
we must do something *now*, with our hastily-made plans and
our half-trained and half-equipped troops. The next question
would naturally be, if we must take the offensive, where shall it
be? Because we are not strong enough to do anything serious in
both the Atlantic and the Pacific ...'[2]

His impression of the scenes in the army offices he visited was
even more derisive.

My impression of Washington is a rush of clerks, in and out of
doors, swing doors always swinging, people with papers
rushing after other people with papers, groups in corners
whispering in huddles, everyone jumping up just as you start
to talk, buzzers ringing, telephones ringing, rooms crowded
with clerks all banging away at typewriters. 'Give me 10 copies
of this AT ONCE.' 'Get that secret file out of the safe.' 'Where the
hell is that Yellow Plan (Blue Plan, Green Plan, Orange Plan,
etc.)?' Everybody furiously smoking cigarettes, everybody
passing you on to someone else, etc., etc. Someone with a loud
voice and a mean look and a big stick ought to appear and yell
'HALT. You crazy bastards. SILENCE. You imitation ants. Now
half of you get the hell out of town and the other half sit down
and don't move for one hour.' Then they could burn up all the
papers and start fresh.[3]

Stilwell's Washington irritations would not have much longer to
run. Within the month he would be off to China, where his heart
was, where he could give his best and where he would lead a yellow
army on a strange and terrible anabasis through the mountains of
northern Burma. His visit to Washington had not, therefore, been in
vain and his impatience with its headless-chicken bureaucrats may
even have had a salutary effect on those to whom he showed it. But
he had misread, or at least misrepresented the War Department if he
saw it as an animal entirely without senses or a central nervous
system. Amid the scurrying ranks of staff officers searching for
paper solutions to real crises, at the scale of which they could as yet
only guess, there was at least one man who had forseen what was to
come, had taken its measure and was ready with a plan for the
American army to fight its way down the road back. The man was a
recently promoted lieutenant-colonel of the War Plans Division,

Albert C. Wedemeyer. The plan would very largely determine how and where the American army would fight the Second World War.

# Wedemeyer

Wedemeyer was not unknown to Stilwell – he had served between the wars in Stilwell's old regiment, the 15th, at Tientsin – and their careers were not dissimilar. But while Stilwell was weather-worn, uncouth and angular, Wedemeyer was handsome, graceful and smooth ('thinks well of himself, that young man', was Stilwell's comment on their obvious differences) and his inclination was to win arguments by determining beforehand the terms on which they would be debated rather than trusting to the cutting-edge of his tongue in the duel itself. It was this intellectuality which had recommended him to Marshall; that, and the particular circumstances in which he had refined his mind. For Wedemeyer was that rare bird in an Anglo-Saxon army, a graduate of the German Staff College, class of 1936–8. The *Kriegsakademie* had taught him to think of war as a life and death struggle. It had also implanted in him a philosophical distaste for peripheral operations, which he suspected the British favoured. He was, via the lectures of Haushofer, now familiar with the teachings of the British geographer Mackinder, who believed that power in the world flowed from a country's place on the map. In the past the maritime states, like Britain and Holland, had exercised power out of all proportion to their populations because sea transport round the periphery of the 'world island' – Europe–Asia–Africa – moved men and guns and the wealth they won faster than land transport within it. But the technology of the twentieth century – railways, motor vehicles and the aeroplane – had begun to reverse the odds, threatening to 'enable a continental military empire to outflank the oceans' which 'in popular parlance would put America ... in the hole'. As the United States satisfied Haushofer's conditions for strategic greatness in at least two respects – it was 'autarkous' (economically self-sufficient) and controlled a 'panregion' (North and South America) – her strategic position was not irretrievable. But to capitalize on her advantages she would need in a world war to seize a foothold on the 'world island' at the earliest moment, and a foothold as near as possible to the heartland.

The 'heartland' was, roughly speaking, European Russia, into which the Wehrmacht was driving its tanks down deep corridors of conquest. So the right, indeed the only antidote to Hitler's strategy for Germany – which was not autarkous and did not yet control a panregion – was to outbuild her, tank for tank, aeroplane for aeroplane, transport the result across the ocean by the shortest possible route and get it ashore at Germany's nearest frontier. While the force was assembling, preparatory operations should be vigorously prosecuted – the sweeping of the Atlantic of U-Boats, the achievement of overwhelming air superiority, the encouragement of subversion in Nazi-occupied territories and, within strict limits, the mounting of diversionary operations. But the real task was to build an army which the Germans could not defeat. Wedemeyer, in a paper demanded by the President in July 1941 on 'a strategic concept of how to defeat our potential enemies', had calculated what manpower could be spared from industry against ratios of superiority known to be necessary for success (the three-to-one rule), and eventually decided that the army must be 8·8 million strong, and be ready by July 1st, 1943. It could not, in any case, be sent overseas until that date, since its transportation would require 10 million tons of additional shipping not yet built.

More important than the army's size, however, was its composition. It was to contain sixty-one armoured divisions, nearly a third of the total and an altogether higher proportion than that present in the German, British or Russian armies. Wedemeyer had been introduced to the idea of mass armoured tactics at the *Kriegsakademie*; he had, like all professional soldiers, marvelled at their successful application in the 1940 blitzkrieg; he was determined that the United States should have the means to outblitzkrieg Germany when the time came. And so, unlike the British army, which was building and training a host of small specialized units for raiding and diversion, the American army, in Wedemeyer's plan, was to contain only three sorts of formation: armoured divisions, a few airborne divisions to operate with them on the blitzkrieg pattern, and a mass of infantry divisions to consolidate the gains won by the tanks. It was, in short, to be an army suitable for only one sort of operation: large-scale, tank-infantry battles on the continent of Europe. In a covering note, Wedemeyer revealed that intention and his own philosophy of battle in unequivocal terms: 'We must prepare to fight Germany by actually coming to grips with and defeating her ground forces and definitely breaking her will to combat ... Air and sea forces will make important contributions, but effective and adequate ground forces must be available to close with and destroy the enemy inside his citadel.'

Though a citizen of the most productive nation on earth, and one with slack enough in its economy after twelve years of depression to display a breathtaking burst of industrial acceleration, Wedemeyer recognized that not even the United States was rich enough to disregard the most fundamental of all truths about strategy; that it is always a matter of choice. 'He who defends everything', Frederick the Great used to warn his generals, 'defends nothing.' 'He who attacks everywhere', Wedemeyer might have echoed, 'attacks nowhere.' The United States, though over twice as populous as Germany, could not at the same time build an army large enough to fight a major war against the Japanese, wage peripheral operations around the coast of Europe and attack the German heartland, while still manning the factories which made her the arsenal of democracy. Since all else depended on their output, there would have to be economies elsewhere. The Japanese could not be ignored; the Germans *must* be brought to battle; therefore the economies must be made in peripheral operations. But they could also be achieved by correct, early decisions about the way Germany was to be fought to a standstill while the Japanese were kept in play. A war in the Pacific must of necessity be amphibious, entailing the creation of expensive amphibious task forces. The

> logistics of a large-scale invasion of Europe promised on the whole to be . . . cheaper. Even if an amphibious assault should be necessary to gain entry, it would be only a small part of the whole undertaking. Once a beachhead was gained, the whole invading force could pour in . . . Transportation of the invading armies would thus become a massive ferrying operation using conventional rather than amphibious shipping. Large forces organised on a large scale meant low unit cost . . . Logistical plans could be stabilised far in advance. In essence, the logistics of task force operations was retail, that of large-scale invasion wholesale. The argument of economy favoured the latter.[4]

This retrospective judgment by the American official historian may be taken to encapsulate Wedemeyer's view. And, because held from the outset and built into the foundations of the US war plan, it determined of course that the arguments of economy would prevail.

Had another man, an 'Easterner' with Pacific obsessions, a pilot with Mitchellian dreams of victory through air power, an officer who had acquired a Mediterranean angle of vision at the *Ecole de Guerre*, a genuine American Firster, been nominated to guide the President through the maze of strategic choice, quite different arguments might have pre-occupied the War Department from the outset and taken months to be expelled from the machinery of decision. As it was, the *Kriegsakademie*, by a stroke of supreme irony, had unwittingly planted in the machinery's control centre someone to whom it had taught a philosophy of war exactly complementary to its own, a *landsinnig* strategist with no thought but that of bringing the Wehrmacht face to face with its mirror-image and little concern with how the trick was to be achieved. It thereby determined that the coming struggle between Germany and the United States must inevitably take the form of a great land battle between their two armies on the land mass of Western Europe. Presciently, Wedemeyer's plan, transmitted to Roosevelt on September 21st, 1941, was presented under the title of the 'Victory Programme'. Its conception and delivery was to be one of the decisive acts of the Second World War.

# Eisenhower

There is a surprisingly long history of junior staff officers decisively influencing the outcome of great military events – for good and ill; the role of Lieutenant-Colonel Hentsch in writing finis to the Schlieffen Plan in September 1914 is the best known. But Wedemeyer was slightly too junior slightly too late to consolidate the position of influence which chance had brought him. Internal re-organization in the War Department carried him away to Joint Planning with the Navy and Air Forces at the outbreak of the war, which brought to the War Plans Division another slightly more senior product of West Point, Leavenworth and the Philippines, Dwight D. Eisenhower.

Like Stilwell, Eisenhower received his call abruptly by telephone in California. 'The chief', said Bedell Smith, 'says for you to hop a plane and get up here right away.' Unlike Stilwell, Eisenhower had met Marshall only twice. It was not personal acquaintance which had recommended him therefore, but his army-wide reputation, as first in his class at Leavenworth, protegé of Pershing, personal assistant to MacArthur and chief of staff of one of the two opposing armies in the 1941 Louisiana manoeuvres – a graveyard and seedbed of many careers. It was his experience in the Philippines which in particular commended him to Marshall, who, as the defence of those islands hung in the balance in December, urgently needed advice as to how they might be reinforced and, with them, what remained of American power in the far Pacific.

Within two months, as a result of a re-organization for which Marshall had long fought, Eisenhower would be head of the War Plans Division. Meanwhile his weeks were to be taken up with solving day-to-day problems and telling Marshall later what he had decided. They were entirely concerned with the Pacific, whose importance he judged to be paramount. On January 1st, in a private memorial of his first two weeks in office, he wrote: 'I've been insisting Far East is central – and no other side shows should be undertaken until air and ground are in satisfactory state. Instead we're taking on Magnet [despatch of US troops to Britain], Gymnast [an attack on North Africa, mooted by Churchill at the Washington Conference of December 1941], etc., etc.' Two weeks later he was even more adamant: 'The whole Far East situation is crucial. My own plan is to drop everything else – Magnet, Gymnast, reserves to Ireland and make the British retire in Libya. Then, scrape up everything, everybody, and get it into (Netherlands East Indies) and Burma. We mustn't lose Netherlands East Indies – Singapore – Burma.' A week after writing that, his view had changed absolutely. He had had word of MacArthur's withdrawal to his final defence line on the Bataan peninsula; the news from Malaya made it clear that the colony would fall shortly to the Japanese. Accordingly, he reflected:

The struggle to secure the adoption by all concerned of a common concept of strategical objectives is wearing me down. Everybody is too much engaged with small things of his own – or with some vague idea of larger political activity to realize what we are doing – or rather not doing. We've got to go to Europe and fight – and we've got to quit wasting resources all over the world – and still worse – wasting time. If we're to keep Russia in, save the Middle East, India and Burma, we've got to begin slugging with air at Western Europe; to be followed with a land attack as soon as possible.

Five days later, in another note to himself, he was yet more emphatic, and now precise about where the United States should go to fight. 'Tom Hardy [his assistant] and I stick to our idea that we must win in Europe. Joe McNarney [a colleague] not only agrees – but was the first man to state that the French coast *could* be successfully attacked.'[5]

Eisenhower's achievement in perceiving strategic wood among the forest of trees which flowed past his War Department window in January 1942 had much to do with his carefully disguised mental ruthlessness, but also with his training and background in the army. For all the *Kriegsakademie* sneers at American military dependence on factory production – her 'pitiless industry', as Hindenburg had called it – few officers had any grounding in industrial mobilization. Eisenhower was one of them. He knew Wedemeyer's Victory Programme, had seized from it the key concept – 'offensive operations in one theater [Central Europe] and concurrently defensive operations in all others' (memo, February 20th) – had added to it arguments which sprang from his fears of Russia's imminent collapse ('We've got to do it – go after Germany's vitals – while Russia's still in the war'), had identified allies who would support his advocacy (March 9th, 'saw McNaughton – commanding Canadians in Britain – he believes in attacking in Europe. Thank God!'),[6] and at the end of February sat down to transform the thrust of the Victory Programme into a plan of action.

His plan was presented to Marshall on March 25th, just in time for the chief of staff to take it with him that morning to the White House. There after lunch he outlined its elements to the President. Roosevelt had just concluded for the benefit of his guests a strategic *tour d'horizon* of his own and a scheme for action or reaction on every sector of the worldwide battlefront which appalled Stimson, his veteran Secretary for War, as a 'dispersion debauch'. Marshall's 'very fine presentation' of a single, clear-cut, war-winning aim brought back sense to the meeting. Deflated, Roosevelt first cautiously suggested that Eisenhower's document should be sent to the Combined Chiefs of Staff – the Anglo-American strategic committee established at the Washington Conference – for its opinion. But, dissuaded by a warning from Harry Hopkins that 'it would be simply pulled to pieces' and 'emasculated' by the Committee's clever young staff officers, he then agreed that 'someone should take it directly to Churchill, Pound, Portal and Brooke ... and get it through them directly'.

As it stood, Eisenhower's paper was not persuasive enough for presentation to an ally, so in the next three days he redrafted it. When finished, it proposed two distinct operations: a full-scale invasion of the continent on April 1st, 1943 by thirty American and eighteen British divisions – almost 1·5 million men – to be landed in France between Le Havre and Boulogne and to make an advance on Antwerp. They were to be disembarked from seven thousand landing craft, which had yet to be built and, though the paper did not reveal it, were still tenth on the US Navy's list of building priorities. This operation was to be code-named Roundup. The second operation, to be undertaken only if Russia seemed about to collapse or if Germany's military position were suddenly 'critically weakened', was to be an emergency landing by five British and American divisions not later than the Autumn of 1942. It was to be code-named Sledgehammer. The Eisenhower paper itself would become known as the Marshall Memorandum. So highly had the chief of staff already come to think of its author, that he had decided to take the paper to London himself.

The party – Marshall, Hopkins, Wedemeyer, a doctor to look after Hopkins's delicate health, an aide-de-camp – embarked on April 3rd in a Boeing 314 flying boat which in stately stages, via Bermuda and Ulster, brought the party in five days to London and to an immediate succession of conferences. Few of the participants had met before. Well travelled though the soldiers were, their journeys had generally taken them in opposite directions – the British eastward to Egypt and India, the Americans westward to the Philippines and China.

Exaggerated courtesy and over-ready agreement flourished at this early stage, stimulating sudden friendships, of which the most surprising was that formed between the chilly Marshall and the extrovert Mountbatten. But Brooke and Marshall also got on well (reserving for their diaries opinions they did not show each other – 'lacks Dill's brains', wrote Marshall; 'pleasant and easy but not a great man', wrote Brooke), and under Brooke's direction the British chiefs of staff tackled the Marshall Memorandum with energy. Two meetings, on April 10th and 13th, were devoted to it, the second followed by a meeting with Churchill to 'settle final details of reply to Marshall'. On the next day the two sides reached agreement. There had been much oratory and some telling criticism. Mountbatten, for all the friendship he had shown the Americans, used

his expert knowledge to point out how short both countries were of
shipping in general and landing-craft in particular, without which
nothing could be attempted. Brooke, making MacArthur's and
King's case, had warned that Japan's Pacific victories might force the
Western Allies to bend everything to the defence of India and the
Middle East; he also shed doubt on Sledgehammer, showing that no
more than nine divisions could be landed in France in 1942 and that
the Germans could certainly destroy them all if they chose. But late
in the evening the British withdrew the vestiges of their objections.
The Prime Minister assured Marshall that the two nations would
march ahead together 'in a noble brotherhood of arms'. The more
cautious Brooke recorded in his diary 'a momentous meeting at
which we accepted their proposals for offensive actions in Europe in
1942 perhaps and in 1943 for certain', a compact made explicit by
Churchill three days later in a telegram to Roosevelt; 'our agreed
programme is a crescendo of activity on the continent'. Its receipt in
Washington only just preceded the return of Marshall, who had been
cheered by a call *en route* on an American advance guard in Northern
Ireland and arrived home confident that they and the millions in the
training camps would soon be at grips with the German army in
France. Eisenhower, *metteur-en-scène* of Wedemeyer's scenario,
recorded with satisfaction: 'Gen. Marshall returned from London
... He looks fine. I hope that – at long last and after months of
struggle by this [War Plans] Division – we are all definitely
committed to one concept of fighting.'

## Molotov

Eisenhower's hope, like so many emotions of a young friendship,
exaggerated the unselfishness of the other party. Generosity of spirit
towards the United States flowed strongly in Britain in 1942. But it
was never unmixed with calculation. At his most theatrical Churchill
could laugh with his advisers about his transatlantic sweet-talking
before the United States had 'joined the harem', of his switch to a
husbandly firmness immediately after. But he had, of course, never
deluded himself that the United States was a captive bride, and he
was still careful to cozen and beguile while so few American soldiers
and aircraft had actually arrived on his side of the ocean. He retained
realistic doubts about the feasibility of Sledgehammer and Roundup, and preferred the operation he had outlined in Washington in

December 1941, the invasion of French North Africa, codenamed
Gymnast. 'But I had', he wrote, 'to work by influence ... to secure
agreed and harmonious action with our cherished Ally, without
whose aid nothing but ruin faced the world. I therefore did not open
any of these alternatives at our meeting on [April] 14.' And Brooke,
already approving Churchill's tactics, supported them all the more
strongly because he believed he had detected in Marshall's position a
cynicism which justified a measure of their own: '[Marshall] has
found King, the American Navy Chief of Staff, is proving more and
more of a drain ... continually calling for land forces to capture ...
land bases in the Pacific ... MacArthur in Australia constitutes
another threat. To counter these moves Marshall has started the
European offensive plan ... it is a clever move that fits in with
present political opinion and the desire to help Russia.'

Brooke could fall in with Marshall's espousal of a 'Second Front
Now' because it reinforced the westward orientation of American
strategy without, as he saw it, committing Britain to any precise
location or, more important, time-table for the invasion. 'It's earlier
than you think', would have summarized the answer he would have
given Marshall if pressed to name a date, but he did not believe that
the British on April 14th had agreed to anything more than a reading
of the banns. It was with alarm therefore that he heard in mid-May
of a different interpretation of the agreement apparently conveyed
by Roosevelt to Stalin. On April 11th the President had cabled an
invitation to Moscow for Molotov, Russian Minister of Foreign
Affairs, to visit Washington for discussion of a 'very important
military proposal involving use of our armed forces in a manner to
relieve your critical western front'. Stalin had eagerly agreed and on
May 21st, after an extraordinary flight across German-occupied
Denmark, Molotov landed in England. The visit was essentially a
passing one, but the Russians sought none the less to wring some
diplomatic profit from it. Simulating a belief that the British were at
one with the Americans in the object of his mission, Molotov
demanded an announcement of the imminence of the Second Front.
Churchill, however, stonewalled and Molotov was obliged to fly on
to Washington with no more concrete reward for his effort than
Anthony Eden's signature on a twenty-year treaty of friendship. But
in Washington, which he reached on May 29th, he met a more
friendly welcome.

The Americans were acutely sensitive to the ordeal which Russia was undergoing and anxious to be briefed on the progress of the current German offensive. Molotov had a terrible tale to tell. White Russia and the western Ukraine had, of course, been lost in the previous year, the eastern Ukraine since the recent spring. These losses of territory had transferred to the German war economy the use of 60 per cent of Russia's coalfields, 60 per cent of her iron-ore fields and 20 per cent of her wheatlands. The German advance towards Stalingrad and the mountains of the Caucasus presently threatened the loss of her Caspian oilfields, without which she could not continue the war. Molotov did not reveal the extent of Russian casualties but the Americans could guess that they already numbered several million. In fact, about five million Russian soldiers had thus far met death or been taken prisoner, the latter fate usually but a brief postponement of the former. The Germans were now inflicting further heavy losses in their battle for the Crimea, which they were about to capture, had bloodily repulsed a Soviet counter-attack at Kharkov and were walking over whatever Russian forces they met on the steppe. Roosevelt attempted to keep other issues alive against the background of these revelations and the unspoken Russian question of what the United States proposed to do to help – policy towards Turkey, Iran and Finland, even the desirability of Russia's signing the 1929 Geneva Convention. But the eastern front kept breaking through and when, on the last day of the conversations (June 1st), Roosevelt infelicitously raised the proposal that Lend–Lease shipments to Russian ports be reduced from 4·5 to 2·5 million tons over the coming year so that larger stocks for the Second Front might be accumulated in Britain, Molotov's icy politeness cracked. Roosevelt then gave him his cue: ships, Roosevelt said in summarizing his argument for Lend–Lease reduction, could not be in two places at once; the Second Front was brought nearer by every ton shipped to England; the Soviets could not have their cake and eat it.

The Second Front, Molotov retorted with insulting logic, would be stronger if the *first* still stood fast. What would happen, he went on, if Russia made the sacrifices requested and then 'no Second Front materialized?' The unmistakable tone of his sarcasm outran the tongue of the translator. He had brought from London, he went on, his delivery becoming more forceful, a new treaty of friendship. 'What answer', he asked, 'shall I take back to London and Moscow on the general question which has been raised? What is the President's answer with respect to the Second Front?'

Roosevelt's political success was built on averting the posing of uncomfortable questions, usually by changing the subject or taking refuge in secondary issues. Molotov, by his patient consideration of any stray idea which had crossed the President's mind during the last week, had exhausted all evasions. Roosevelt now had to answer or keep silent. Silence was a gift he did not possess. The Russian Foreign Minister, he answered, could say that the Western Allies expected to open a Second Front and that Admiral Mountbatten was arriving from London the next day to complete the arrangements. General Marshall would make further arrangements with Mr Molotov. And a joint statement, to be published to the world over the names of Stalin, Churchill and Roosevelt, would be prepared at once for his approval.

During the next two days the State Department drafted the appropriate document. A suddenly cautious Marshall demurred at the specification of 1942 but Molotov was adamant and eventually wrote the key sentence himself. It read: 'In the course of the conversations, full understanding was reached with regard to the urgent tasks of creating a Second Front in Europe in 1942.' On June 11th, at a meeting of the Supreme Soviet in Moscow, news of Molotov's journey to the Western capitals, together with the full text of the communiqué he had brought back, were simultaneously released. The audience responded with a storm of enthusiasm which, for once, was wholly unfeigned.

## Marshall

While Molotov had been successfully winning commitments on the diplomatic front, Marshall had been fighting to hold ground on his home territory. During April and May he had been deeply perturbed by the persistent efforts of Admiral King and General MacArthur to shake the American 'Germany First' strategy. On March 29th Admiral King had fired a warning shot with a message to Marshall which, while conceding the needs of the Pacific to be 'possibly smaller than those of Europe', represented them as 'more urgent in point of time'. On May 4th he stated his case formally to the Joint Chiefs of Staff in a letter which demanded a decision. 'Important as the mounting of Bolero [The American build-up in Britain] may be', he wrote, 'the Pacific problem is no less so, and is certainly the more urgent – it must be faced *now* ... we must not permit diversion of

our forces to any proposed operation in any other theater to the
extent that we find ourselves unable to fulfil our obligation in the
Pacific . . . '

Unable to resolve the matter between themselves – the Chiefs of
Staff Committee had been set up only in February and Marshall and
King represented two-thirds of its voting strength – the chiefs of
staff referred the matter to the President. But he had simultaneously
come under pressure from MacArthur, who had dexterously
adopted Roosevelt's concern for action to keep Russia in the war as a
means towards his own strategic end. 'That [second] front', he had
urged on May 8th, 'should be in the Pacific Theater. Nowhere else
can it be so successfully launched and nowhere else will it so assist
the Russians.' In an earlier letter to MacArthur on the same subject,
the President had revealingly suggested that his own approach to
strategy was to keep all his allies 'reasonably satisfied' and avoid 'any
real rows'. And although apparently committed to Bolero,
Sledgehammer and Roundup, his placatory response to the Pacific
commanders kept Marshall on tenterhooks throughout May. On
May 6th he had extracted from the President an assurance that he
did 'not want Bolero slowed down'. But as late as May 24th he was
dealing with a request from King for reinforcements of army
aircraft, 'as rapidly as possible, giving the objective first priority
even over Bolero'.

The President was known to be soft on the aircraft issue; indeed
he had conceded King's request in principle on May 6th. What saved
the 'Germany First' strategy was the great victory of Midway on
June 4th. After Midway no admiral, no Pacific general, not even the
silver-tongued MacArthur, could plausibly represent the Imperial
Japanese Navy, reduced overnight to mere parity with the American
Pacific Fleet, as a force which retained the initiative. The battle had
made it as clear to Roosevelt's government as to the Emperor's that
the *ne plus ultra* lines of the Pacific war had now been attained and
that all future battles would be fought on the battle line of June 4th,
1942 or nearer the Japanese home islands.

This release from domestic struggle was welcomed all the more by
Marshall because much of his energy during the spring had been
consumed in an internecine conflict to reform the antediluvian
structure and methods of the War Department. In December 1941
sixty-one officers had the right of direct access to him. By March
1942 that number had been reduced to six. The displaced had fought

the re-organization at every step. If they had been beaten it was because of the extraordinary personal authority which the chief of staff had already established within the organization he had so recently come to head. Marshall, who rarely lost his temper and never raised his voice, was terrifying. Tall, spare, his heavily handsome face expressionless save for a permanent suggestion of disappointment at the world's failure to match his own Olympian qualities of mind and comportment, he had deliberately cut himself off from old friendships as he rose to the top of the army and, now that he had reached its pinnacle, appeared to subsist without any companionship whatever.

Yet he was no mere technocrat. 'The thing that stands out in everybody's recollection of General Marshall', wrote Dean Acheson, 'is ... the loftiness and beauty of his character.' Explicitly not a politician, Marshall possessed a vision of a better world which as a postwar Secretary of State he would do as much as any man in this century to realize. And in 1942 he had convinced himself that the shortest step towards it was by way of a Second Front. Hence the support he had given Eisenhower while he himself was battling to reform the War Department, hence his own embassy to London with the Marshall Memorandum in the spring, hence his relief at the tidings of Midway. And hence his sense of betrayal at, and aggress-ive reaction to, the news that the British would not, after all, stand by their promises for 1942.

The news came to him in a roundabout way. Mountbatten, whose impending arrival Roosevelt had used to convince Molotov that the Western powers were on the point of writing an operation order for Sledgehammer, had in fact been sent to Washington to warn that the British did not think it feasible. As Churchill had put it in a caveat to the Molotov communiqué, naturally not published with it, 'it would not further either the Russian cause or that of the Allies as a whole if, for the sake of action at any price, we embarked on some operation which ended in disaster ... we can therefore give no promise in the matter'. Mountbatten's explanation of the apparent double-dealing turned on the disparity of strengths and lack of suitable ships, and was convincing. He showed that by September the United States would at best field 3 divisions in Britain, that Britain had in the home islands only 13 divisions fit for action and that in any case there were sufficient landing-craft to debark only 4,000 troops (about a third of a division) at one time. Meanwhile the Germans, with 190 divisions in Russia, 15 in Scandinavia, 5 in the Balkans and 3 in the Western Desert, still kept 27 in France. And they could find 1,500 first-line aircraft to meet an Allied air force of 1,200 British fighters and less than 100 American.

'It's not on', was the brunt of Mountbatten's message. 'The British won't fight', was no doubt how Stilwell would have put it. Marshall was less corrosive. But he was not to have Roosevelt to himself for long enough to shake the doubt Mountbatten had planted in his mind on June 10th. For on June 19th, undeterred either by the risks or fatigue of another of his twenty-eight-hour transatlantic flights, Churchill arrived in Washington bearing arguments for an entirely different strategy for 1942. While he tackled the President, his persuasive military supporters kept the chiefs of staff in play. And when all met at the White House on June 21st, Marshall found that the ground was gone from under his feet. Churchill, outwardly unmoved that the day had also brought news of the humiliating surrender of the Tobruk garrison in the Western Desert, led Roosevelt with him in a running argument against the Second Front Now. And when he and his advisers had left, the President asked Marshall to stay behind, and then put it to him that the United States should plan to commit its painfully accumulated expeditionary force to the Middle East.

Marshall, finding himself at that moment as close to losing his self-control in the President's company as he ever came, declined to discuss the project and withdrew. But his sense of strategic necessity forbade him to acquiesce in what he saw as the President's surrender. The aftermath of the 'Day of Dupes' gave him no immediate pretext for a counter-attack, though reports from London, whither Eisenhower had departed on June 23rd as commander of United States Forces Europe, heightened his suspicions that the British were squirming off the hook of the Second Front. When, on July 8th, Churchill conceded as much, by signalling that Gymnast (North Africa) must now replace Sledgehammer as the Allies' main offensive endeavour for 1942, he decided to play some politics himself. Together with King, who may or may not have seen through what Marshall later confessed to be a transparent ploy, he drew up a memorandum for the President advising that, in default of 'forceful, unswerving adherence to Bolero plans', the two chiefs of staff were 'of the opinion' that the United States should 'assume a defensive attitude against Germany, except for air operations;

and use all available means in the Pacific'.

Roosevelt took fright. Rejecting the memorandum, but seeing that he could not sustain an effective alliance while his chiefs of staff and the British differed over the next – effectively the first – step of joint action, he ordered Marshall and King back to London at once, where, with Hopkins, they were to come to a final agreement over strategy for 1942. The politician in him prayed that it would be for a bold and successful operation before congressional election day (November 3rd); the stateman recognized that, in a grand alliance, the rules of Cabinet government apply; that what is agreed is less important than the fact of agreement itself. Marshall, too, in his heart accepted that. Nevertheless he was determined to try and get the British to co-operate in some sort of early cross-Channel operation. After consulting Eisenhower and his staff, who had set up shop in Grosvenor Square, he hit upon the notion of giving Sledgehammer a precise objective – the narrow Cotentin peninsula, which reaches out towards the west of England ports. His reasoning was that the physical dimensions of the Cotentin – about twenty-five miles long by twenty wide – made it a landing area which could be seized and, more important, held by the size of force which might be available in the coming autumn; and that, if held through the winter, it would provide the jumping-off place for Roundup in the following spring. Privately his calculation was that unless he could commit the British to securing a foothold in Europe in 1942, Roosevelt's need to do something, almost anything, in the current year would entail the diversion of the American expeditionary force to the Mediterranean and its effective squandering on some mission which would harm the Germans very little.

For three days, from Monday to Wednesday, July 20th–22nd, the American mission and the British chiefs of staff dissected the proposal point by point. And point by point the Americans were defeated. Ultimately Eisenhower, who remained firm in his conviction that 'we've got to go to Europe and fight', suggested to Marshall that they offer the British the sop of an American armoured division for use by the Eighth Army against Rommel in the Western Desert, so that the rest of the Bolero force could be kept in Britain and used for Roundup in the coming year. But Marshall, who recalled the attempts to use Pershing's army as cannon-fodder in 1918, was adamantly opposed. Even more strongly than wanting an American strategy, he wanted an American army one and indivisible to fight the decisive battles of the war against Hitler. Regretfully, therefore, he declined this chance to keep an early Second Front alive and, in a doleful morning in his suite at Claridge's, set himself to write a plan for 'the least harmful diversion'. Recognizing that 'we couldn't do Sledgehammer and that there was no immediate prospect of Round-up ... I started writing a proposal ... for an expedition into North Africa, with operations, limits, nature and the like'.[7] As he finished, Admiral King entered and, to Marshall's astonishment, signified that he would give it his support.

The British naturally gave it their instant support; it was exactly the outcome for which, soldiers and civilians alike, they had hoped. Some of them quibbled at Marshall's suggestion that a final decision for Gymnast – soon to be recoded Torch, under which name the North African landings would eventually pass into history – be postponed until September 15th, perhaps rightly recognizing a device by which Torch and Sledgehammer might jointly be laid to rest and Roundup revived in 1943. General Alan Brooke, recognizing victory when he saw it, overcame them, concerted Cabinet and chief of staff agreement and delivered it intact to the Americans before they left. They were a dispirited party. Marshall now recognized that the North African landings, besides scuppering Sledgehammer, probably wrote off Roundup for 1943 and committed the Allies to a 'defensive, encircling line of action for the Continental European theater'. He was yet more cast down to discover, soon after his return to Washington, that Churchill had persuaded Roosevelt, through Hopkins, to squash the idea of postponing a date for Torch and had got it fixed for October 30th.

October 30th became, in the event, November 8th. Torch entailed a passage of labyrinthine dealings with the Vichy representatives in North Africa, a murky and inept attempt to replace the intractable de Gaulle with a more pliable general at the head of the Free French Forces, and a campaign against the attenuated power of the Afrika Korps less than magnificent in many of its episodes. But Marshall, stifling every occasion which provided him with self-justification, forbore to reproach the President with following the British down the wrong strategic turning. It was now for events to prove to whomsoever would see – Roosevelt, who must, and Churchill, who might be made to – that a cross-Channel attack would not wait for ever on calculations of safety and prudence.

# Brooke

Churchill's will to combat was doubted by none, not even Marshall at his most pessimistic. Whatever disappointment the American professionals may have felt at the decision to postpone Sledgehammer in favour of Torch, they recognized that Churchill's advocacy of the North African plan had stemmed ultimately from a genuine desire to win victories over the Germans in 1942, and a belief that victory was certain there, while any invasion of France was likely to end in calamity. But their belief in British commitment to the right choice of strategy at the next stage of decision was less wholehearted. For Marshall had already detected that the guiding compass which charted Churchill's course through the war was not his own overpowering urge to march to the sound of the guns but the watchwords of caution and calculation voiced by his chief of staff, General Sir Alan Brooke. And in Brooke's attitude to the war Marshall had identified a tepidity of enthusiasm for the cross-Channel attack which he disliked and mistrusted.

Brooke's cautiousness should not have aroused surprise. For his background and experience might have been designed to school him in that mode of outlook. By training and service a gunner, he had made his name in the army by his adaptation during the First World War of French artillery methods to British practice. In particular he had taught fellow British gunners the technique of the 'creeping barrage'. The basis of the technique is in part mathematical, an application of the science of ballistics, but in part also psychological, requiring judgments about how human beings react to extreme but apparently impersonal threat. Mere 'searching forward' does not guarantee the effectiveness of a creeping barrage, since infantry may go to ground while the curtain of fire passes over their heads; 'searching back' is essential also, to catch the unwary as they emerge from cover in the belief that the danger is past. A fine judgment about human self-protectiveness in the aggregate therefore distinguishes a good from an indifferent barrage plan. Brooke possessed exactly that judgment; but its logic is the opposite of that which animated the blitzkrieg and the break-through.

Brooke's cautiousness was heightened by his experience of how additionally uncertain are operations mounted with unblooded troops. The British army's campaign in France in 1915–18 had been fought for the most part by amateurs, the Kitchener volunteers and

the millions of untrained conscripts who had followed them into the
ranks when the volunteering impulse had died. No Briton, least of
all Brooke, could fail to take pride in their courage or their ultimate
mastering of their trade. But they had learnt it at the side of a strong
ally on ground securely barricaded against sudden irruption by the
enemy, who, in any case, had chosen to stand on the defensive in
France for most of the fighting there. And when the Germans had at
last been freed to attack, in the spring of 1918, Brooke had seen with
his own eyes how quickly an apparently battleworthy army could be
broken, as Gough's Fifth was on the Somme in March 1918, by a
superior force. The Dunkirk campaign had reinforced that impression. 'There is no doubt that they are the most wonderful soldiers',
he had written of the Germans on May 23rd, 1940; it was an opinion
which did not leave him throughout the Second World War.

All the more was he moved to question the good sense of
prematurely confronting the Germans inside their own continental
fortress by comparison of their known strengths and skills with those
of the fledgling American army. He had seen some of it in training at
Camp Jackson, South Carolina, in June 1942 and, though impressed
by the look of the young soldiers, had found the demonstration
manoeuvre they had put on for him 'disappointing' and come away
with the reflection that they had not 'yet realized the standard of
training required'. His disquiet was not restricted to feelings about
the lower ranks. The high command and its methods of working also
perturbed him. Marshall's achievement in rationalizing the War
Department was admirable, but so recently completed that its
purpose had not yet been translated into the smooth and rapid staff
practice to which Brooke was accustomed at home. There politicians, civil servants and servicemen had been attuned to working
within a common organization, the Committee of Imperial Defence,
since before the First World War. Britain's power, though limited
and indeed already shrinking as the cost of the war eroded its
financial and industrial base, was thus deployed as swiftly and
effectively as thought and routine could ensure.

Brooke found the American system by contrast time-consuming
and inefficient. He envied Marshall his relationship with the President, who 'had no military knowledge . . . was aware of the fact and
consequently relied on [Marshall] and listened to [his] advice'; and
all the more because his own head of government 'never had the
slightest doubt that he had inherited all the military genius of his

great ancestor, Marlborough'. Brooke lamented the time necessary to wean Churchill from his 'wildest and most dangerous ideas'. But that diversion of energy was to be preferred to the 'slow and tedious process' of dealing with the American chiefs of staff, to whom 'all matters have to be carefully and slowly explained and re-explained before they can be absorbed'.

The particular issue which prompted his complaints of the need to explain and re-explain was his effort, at his second meeting with the Americans at Casablanca in January 1943, to reorientate their European strategy. Marshall arrived with the determination to force through a decision in favour of some sort of cross-Channel operation that year. To achieve it he was prepared to see all surface operations in the Mediterranean closed down, as soon as the German-Italian army in North Africa had been defeated, and all surplus ground troops transferred to Britain. Other resources in the area he was prepared to allot to the Pacific, where, as Admiral King was forceful in emphasizing, only 15 per cent of Allied strength was arrayed against the Japanese. Brooke had come with an argument prepared for a different strategy in the Mediterranean. He took it as given that the first task in the west was to break the U-boat campaign; not only was it threatening to starve Britain, which required thirty million tons of imports a year but could get only twenty-five, but it was actively postponing the cross-Channel invasion from month to month by preventing the transport of American troops to Britain and diverting shipyard capacity from the building of landing-craft to essential escort vessels. On land, however, the balance had swung in favour of the Allies. The Germans were no longer attacking and the defensive itself was now overstraining their resources. Rather than present them with the chance of an easy victory, therefore – and a battle on the coastline of France between the forty divisions they had in the country and the twenty-two the Allies could find for the invasion promised them a very easy victory indeed – he proposed heightening the 'overstretch' from which they were already suffering. The elimination of Italy from the war was the most obvious means to exert overstretch and it could be achieved by air and sea offensives, perhaps supplemented by amphibious operations against Sicily and Sardinia. The result would be to force Germany to replace Italian troops with her own, not only in the Italian peninsula but in the Balkans and Greek islands as well, where Italy provided much of the Axis manpower. Encouraged by this policy, Turkey might enter the war, thus providing short supply routes to Russia, whose land campaign was currently hurting Germany most, and a basis for further operations against the occupied Balkans.

Brooke had brought his British colleagues to accept this strategy by hard argument during the months since they had defeated Marshall in July; and they stuck by it throughout five days of tense and testy negotiations at Casablanca. He had much greater difficulty rallying the Americans. It was central to his argument that the poor road and rail communications to southern Europe would make any German build-up there painfully slow and difficult, while the Allies' enjoyment of free movement by sea and air would allow them to deploy rapidly wherever they chose. Marshall interpreted 'free movement' to mean 'diversion', and warned that 'every diversion or side issue from the main plot acts as a suction pump'. The 'main plot', by his lights, included the war against Japan, and he challenged the British to explain why, if they were not anxious to take direct cross-Channel action against the Germans in 1943, men and materials made redundant by their heel-dragging should not be redeployed from the Mediterranean to the Pacific.

It was the Joint Planners, that group of staff officers who prepared papers for the American Chiefs of Staff Committee, who eventually produced a compromise. Asked for a fundamental statement of strategy, they produced on January 17th a document which set 'the destruction of the economic and military power of all our adversaries at a rate exceeding their powers of replacement' as the primary aim. Little matter that this was a resort to that principle of 'pitiless industry' which the German professionals despised. It amounted to an argument for attrition, which was exactly Brooke's starting point. Like all British veterans of 1914–18 he shrank from the methods of attrition practised on the Western Front; hence indeed his reluctance to risk attrition by assault across the Channel. Attrition by overstretch – of the Germans' limited stock of divisions, equipment and fuel – was however what he meant his Mediterranean strategy to impose; the results of Passchendaele without its cost in blood. And by repetitious advocacy, concessions to American needs in the Pacific and firm reassurance of Britain's intention to transfer all her forces thither as soon as Germany was defeated, he ultimately brought Marshall round. An important indulgence of Marshall's abiding concern was an agreement to appoint a chief of staff to the Supreme Allied Commander (COSSAC) for the cross-Channel invasion force who would work to have plans ready for the Supreme Allied Commander as soon as he was appointed, so that preparations might go forward even though a date for the operation had not yet been fixed.

Marshall returned home less dejected than he had expected to be. His hopes for a cross-Channel invasion in 1943, never high either on his estimate of British will or joint Allied resources, had not really been dashed. And he believed he had set a limit, of aims if not of time, to further embroilment in a secondary theatre. Prospects for an end to dissent at the next Allied conference seemed set fair. No date for one had been fixed at Casablanca; but the imminent conclusion of the Tunisian campaign in April prompted the Prime Minister to propose a meeting in May. The President accepted and on May 11th, after a six-day crossing on the liner *Queen Mary*, the British arrived in New York. The conference itself convened at the White House next day. Its opening session immediately revealed that the divisions between the two allies yawned as wide as ever. With this difference: it was now the sensation of success in the Mediterranean, rather than fear of repulse elsewhere, which armed British arguments for further advance in that theatre. The totality of the Axis collapse in Tunisia, the first in any theatre of war, had so elated the British that they could not bring themselves to forgo the chance of repeating it by crossing to Sicily. Brooke rehearsed now-familiar arguments, Marshall his familiar warnings. His only variation was one of metaphor, from the suction pump to the vacuum. 'The Tunisian campaign had sucked in more and more troops . . . The invasion of Sicily would establish a vacuum in the Mediterranean which would preclude . . . a successful cross-Channel operation and Germany would not collapse . . . from air bombardment alone.' He foresaw a protracted European war, with calamitous effects in the Pacific, unless all available force in the theatre was transferred early to France. His swipe at the British belief in Germany's 'collapse' – though he did not tax them with their rapidly devaluing credence in the power of 'blockade and subversion' to achieve it – drew Brooke, and a good deal further than reflection would have allowed him to go. A victory in Europe was unlikely in any case, he insisted, until 1945 or 1946, 'since it must be remembered that in previous wars there had always been some eighty French divisions on our side'.

'Did this mean', Marshall countered, 'that the British Chiefs of Staff regarded Mediterranean operations as the key to a successful termination of the European war?' Caught too far out on a limb, Brooke hedged. And the two sides withdrew to consider their differences. Once again Marshall and King prepared to play the Pacific card but, sensitive to that probability, the British at the next session forestalled them by a stout declaration of commitment to an early Roundup – or Overlord as the invasion was now to be re-codenamed. It therefore remained to find an interim strategy which they might agree to pursue until Overlord could be mounted.

Eventually the Americans proved willing to discuss the Mediterranean in return for a British commitment to a firm date for Overlord, ideally April 1944. Brooke 'nimbly countered' that April 1944 would only be possible after Italy had been knocked out of the war and the Germans obliged to divert thither the divisions which otherwise would oppose the Allies in France. On those positions a compromise was achieved. The British eventually accepted a target date of May 1st, by which time seven divisions would have been transferred from the Mediterranean to Britain; the Americans assented to 'such operations in exploitation of Husky [Sicily] as are best calculated to eliminate Italy from the war'.

A year remained to fill. The collapse of the defences on Sicily, invaded on July 10th, was so precipitate and complete, the opportunities offered by the Italian request to treat for peace which it provoked so attractive, that for once the British and Americans found no difficulty in agreeing to enlarge the campaign. Marshall showed himself indeed as enthusiastic as Churchill for a full-scale assault on the Italian mainland, and as high up the peninsula as possible, even though the assault would consume almost the entire Anglo-American army in the Mediterranean and require the retention there of all the landing-craft promised for Overlord. The Quebec conference which followed in August therefore ran more smoothly than those at Washington and Casablanca. Though temperaments clashed, the issues which divided Americans and British were smaller. Brooke again felt obliged to explain to the Americans the inter-relationship, 'which they have never fully realized', between Mediterranean attrition and cross-Channel assault – a passage which drove Admiral King to 'very undiplomatic language, to use a mild term' – but the main debate turned on the size of the force to be launched into France, and an acceptable formula was worked out. It included a provision for a subsidiary but simultaneous invasion in the south of France to be mounted with the French and most of the American troops currently campaigning in Italy.

Yet, from behind the façade of common purpose, came the creak of shifting foundations. It would grow louder as the autumn drew on. For to the British the prospect of subordinating the Mediterranean campaign to Overlord now grew increasingly fraught with anxieties and disappointment. Anxieties because, as COSSAC's detailed plans approached completion, so too did the necessity to face the brutal implications of a direct assault in the teeth of German prepared positions. 'Memories of the Somme and Passchendaele and many lesser frontal attacks upon the Germans were not to be blotted out by time or reflection', Churchill wrote later of his state of mind at this time. Brooke's was similarly haunted; for him the cross-Channel operation had become 'very problematical'. He was even more afflicted by a sense of disappointment. Though the campaign of 1943 had achieved much of what he had always promised it would – the elimination of Italy, the 'attrition by attenuation' of German manpower (fifty of Germany's three hundred divisions had been drawn into Italy and the Balkans), the free use of the inland sea for inter-continental shipments, the winning of air bases close to the industries of southern Germany – he could think only of how much more might have been done, and still lay within the Allies' power to consummate if time and resources were granted.

To the Americans, who scented their ally's deepening irresolution, the explanation seemed to lie in Britain's incurable imperialism, which they suspected of seeking a focus in the eastern Mediterranean. That was inaccurate; Britain's attachment to the Mediterranean was not directly material. It was, however, deeply psychological. Not only was the sea a bridge between the homeland and the East, it was also the amphitheatre in which for two hundred years they had played grand strategy, longer indeed than they had played it in India and with quite as much personal involvement. There were families in Britain as 'Mediterranean' as others were 'Indian', who could count grandfathers born in Malta or the Ionian Isles, great-great-grandfathers in Gibraltar, and to whom the ports of the Levant and the politics of its hinterland were as familiar as the forts and dynastic intrigues of the Frontier to the servants of the Raj. Brooke belonged to neither clan; his roots were in the older garrison of Ulster. But as a maker of British strategy, which had for so long exerted one of its centres of effort in the Mediterranean, he was attuned to campaigning there and disinclined to surrender the rewards it promised. 'When I look at the Mediterranean', he confided privately to his diary on November 1st, 'I realize only too well how far I have failed.' Professionally he continued to work for a softening of the 'Marshall strategy'. The result was a Chiefs of Staff paper, significantly dated November 11th, which advanced, for what would turn out to be the last time, the anti-Marshall case.

> We must not [it ran] regard Overlord on a fixed date as the pivot of our whole strategy ... The German strength in France next Spring may ... be something which makes 'Overlord' impossible [or] 'Rankin' not only practicable but essential ... with the Germans in their present plight the surest way to win the war is to attack them ... continuously ... in every area where we can do so with superiority ... our policy is therefore clear ... we submit the following proposals for the Mediterranean ... The offensive in Italy should be nourished and maintained until we have secured the Pisa–Rimini line ... we should bring Turkey into the war ... we might form a limited bridgehead on the Dalmatian or Albanian coasts.

Second thought counselled them to suppress the last sentence. But the reference to 'Rankin' was in itself enough to inflame American mistrust. For 'Rankin' was a long-laid plan to occupy France in the event of a German collapse, entailing no need to fight at all. Its bracketing as an alternative to Overlord implied that the British were again shrinking from the knife. Brooke dissembled by arguing that he was only seeking means to reduce the rate at which the Germans could 'build up' with divisions on an Overlord front; and at Teheran in late November he succeeded in persuading the Americans that an advance to the Pisa–Rimini line in north Italy actively contributed to that end. But there he found that he had driven his ally to the sticking-point; though the mark was in fact made by the Russians rather than the Americans. This first joint meeting of the Big Three gave Stalin's military professionals the chance to fix the British, in the presence of the Americans, on fundamentals: 'Marshal Voroshilov asked Sir Alan Brooke if he could say a little more precisely whether he regarded Operation "Overlord" as the most important operation, as he understood the United States to think so.' Brooke twisted on the hook, warning again of the strength of the Germans and of the need to drain their divisions away from France by subsidiary operations. But the

Russian was remorseless: Brooke's diary records that 'he did not insist on an operation against the South of France' (Anvil, which Brooke disliked because antithetical to advance in Italy) 'but ... did insist that the operation against the North of France should take place in the manner and on the date already agreed on'.

And while Voroshilov gratified Marshall by his exposure of Brooke's ambiguities, Roosevelt abandoned Churchill to stringent interrogation by Stalin. 'Do the British really believe in "Overlord" or are they only saying so to reassure the Soviet Union?' As the conference wore on he pressed harder. He demanded a date, he wanted operations in Italy recognized as diversions from the invasion of southern France, he wanted a commander named for Overlord, if not at the conference then within a week of its closure. Abandoned by Roosevelt, who had fixed on the meeting as an opportunity to forge personal links with Stalin, Churchill could find no room for manoeuvre on any of these issues. Brooke had already been immobilized by the combined pressure of Marshall and Voroshilov. Appropriately it fell to him on November 30th to read to the three heads of government the unanimous recommendation of the Combined Chiefs of Staff, 'that we will launch "Overlord" in May, in conjunction with a supporting operation against the South of France on the largest scale that is permitted by the landing-craft available at the time'.

## Montgomery

It remained only to choose the Supreme Commander Allied Expeditionary Force. Both Marshall and Brooke, for all the latter's misgivings, had hoped to be named; both indeed had been promised the appointment, but Brooke had known since August that it must go to an American. Marshall was the obvious man; he greatly desired to leave Washington for the command in the field he had never exercised and believed Roosevelt would release him. But on December 5th – within Stalin's time limit of a week from the end of the Teheran conference – Roosevelt nerved himself to tell his chief of staff that he 'could not sleep at ease if [he] were out of Washington'. Eisenhower, therefore, would move from the Mediterranean to London. But he was not to command the ground forces in the initial stages, when air and sea operations would require two-thirds of his attention. That responsibility was to go to a subordinate who, it was easily decided, should be British. Churchill favoured Alexander, to him a paragon among soldiers, and Alex was also Ike's choice; their relationship had long been on nickname terms. Brooke insisted, as he firmly believed, that Montgomery was the better general and drove through the appointment. On January 2nd, 1944 the commander of the Eighth Army flew from North Africa to England to immerse himself in COSSAC's Overlord plan.

But he had already seen its outline and communicated his opinion of it to Churchill, 'my first impression is that the present plan is impracticable'. Not because of COSSAC's chosen landing area, quibble at it though he might. To that selected, in the Bay of the Seine between the Cotentin peninsula and the river Orne, there was no alternative. Other sections of the French coast which lay within effective fighter range were backed by high cliffs, and those nearest British ports, though closer to the exploitation route into Germany, were therefore better garrisoned as well. Not because of the air and sea arrangements either. The cross-Channel shipment of the assault and follow-up, their escorting, beaching and docking and the ship-to-shore bombardment which would cover the landings were irreproachable in conception. Over a thousand naval vessels, a thousand merchant ships and three thousand landing-craft were assembled or earmarked to sail on the day – D-Day as the plan identified it. Massive air bombardment was assured by an amicably arranged interruption of the strategic bombingg against Germany. The air 'interdiction' (denial of use) of road and rail communications in and to the Normandy front promised to be complete, indeed so generous in scale was it that by over-concentration on targets outside the 'lodgement area', as the COSSAC staff now called Norrmandy, it would significantly aassist the deceits which were to guarantee, if anything could, the success of the disembarkation. Nor could he find fault with the deception plan which would orchestrate dozens of procedures and devices to mislead and confuse the Germans as to time and place – some highly technical, like the dropping of metallic chaff to simulate the movement of an invasion fleet in the Channel narrows while German radars elsewhere were blinded, others sheer whimsy, as in the despatch of a junior officer who dubiously resembled Montgomery to impersonate hiim in his old Mediter-ranean haunts.

What aroused Montgomery's doubts was the ingredient of the plan he was best fitted to judge, the size and deployment of the landing force. COSSAC had settled ultimately for a forcee of three divisions, which were to be followed over the beaches in quick succession by twelve more. 'This would lead', he wrote to Churchill on January 1st, 'to the most appalling confusion on the beaches and the smooth development of the land battle would be made extremely difficult, if not impossible ... The initial landings must be made on the widest possible front', fifty not twenty-five miles, with a British and American army landing side by side and each deploying two and possibly three corps. And there should be a descent by an airborne division, rather than a brigade, on the eastern and western flanks, to secure them against early German counter-attack.

It was the fear of immediate counter-attack which alarmed him most, followed by concern that 'reserve formations might succeed in containing us within shallow positions with our beaches under continuous covering fire'. He rightly looked beyond the technical difficulties of the landing, to the solving of which years of thought and experiment had been given, to the invasion battle itself. And he could not forget that he would, at the outset, fight at a crazy disadvantage of numbers. Against his five divisions, all infantry, though to be supported by some swimming and ship-loaded tanks, the Germans would in theory oppose fifty divisions, of which ten were armoured. Only eight infantry and three panzer divisons were close to the landing area. But they would outnumber and outgun those he could put ashore in the first wave. It was therefore essential to drive forward on as wide a front as possible in the first days, so that room was made as quickly as possible for the follow-up divisions (of which there were thirty in England) to arrive and reverse the odds.

He convinced Eisenhower, at their first executive meeting on January 21st, of the need for the extension of the front, and their authority rapidly sufficed, as the dedicated General Morgan's technical submissions had not, to win from the Combined Chiefs of Staff the additional resources required. At great expense to the British ship-building programme, at a little cost to Admiral King's Pacific campaign, by the deferment of Anvil until after D-Day and by the postponement of D-Day itself for a month, one thousand extra landing-craft were found to add to the three thousand already earmarked; they would accommodate the two extra divisions to be disembarked and allow the use of five instead of three beaches, to be codenamed, in order from west to east, Utah and Omaha

(American), Gold (British), Juno (Canadian) and Sword (British). Admiral King also donated, late and grudgingly, enough extra bombardment ships to ensure that every yard of the beaches and the routes to them would be drenched by fire from the sea. The extra aircraft needed to fly the American 82nd and 101st Airborne Divisions to the western flank and the British 6th Airborne to the eastern, and to extend fighter and bomber cover over the larger beaching zone, were procured without difficulty; though it took firm words from Eisenhower to quash the opposition of his air deputy, Leigh-Mallory, to the airborne landings. The Air Marshal's pessimistic judgment was that losses of 75 per cent of men and aircraft were to be expected. Montgomery himself had quickly established excellent working relationships with his own subordinates: Dempsey, who was to command the British Second Army, Bradley of the American First Army, and Crerar of the Canadian First Army.

That he was able, with his abrupt and egotistic personality, to enlist their confidence is explained by the assurance he managed to communicate of understanding and equalling the task in hand. Montgomery was not a Brooke. Though he greatly admired the Chief of the Imperial General Staff (but very few other men), he had no complex or subtle strategic views. His personal military experience was bloody – he had been wounded near to death in his first campaign in 1914 – and he never shrank from confronting the ultimate truth about war: that it is won or lost with the lives of human beings. Like Brooke he had drawn from his First World War experience a conviction that the squandering of life is the cardinal military sin; and he had deliberately adopted a style of command which ensured his close supervision of all the expenditure of life that he ordered. But he did not seek for ways to avoid battle itself. Where Brooke had hoped that the octopus of Mediterranean strategy would strangle the Germans to death in its tentacles, and the COSSAC team had looked little beyond the difficulties of transporting an invasion force to the coast of France, Montgomery focused sharply on the battle that must follow its arrival. For it was in 'arranging' battles, in the old-fashioned sense, by correct disposition and 'balance', that his skills chiefly lay. 'We must blast our way on shore', he told his audience of senior invasion commanders assembled at his headquarters in St Paul's school on May 15th 'and get a good lodgement before the enemy can bring up sufficient reserves to turn us out ... We must gain space rapidly and peg out claims well inland ... then we will have the lodgement area we want and can begin to expand.'

To do so he planned to fight a large and relentless armoured battle around Caen, in the British eastern sector, so that the Americans to the west might progressively build up their strength to twenty divisions, break out into open country and turn the Germans' flank in a drive to the Seine. But it would not, he warned, be easy at any stage. For all that the Allies, deploying 12,000 aircraft, would outnumber the Luftwaffe by over twenty to one, it must be expected that the German army would still find the means to move reserves to Normandy. Their forces already there were formidable. And they were commanded by Rommel. He, Montgomery concluded,

> is an energetic and determined commander; he has made a world of difference since he took over ... He will do his best to 'Dunkirk' us – not to fight the armoured battle on ground of his own choosing, but to avoid it altogether by using his tanks well forward ... It is now clear that his intention is to deny us any penetration: Overlord is to be defeated on the beaches.

## Rommel

Montgomery's penetration of his old desert adversary's intentions was almost telepathically accurate, and oddly so because it was Rommel rather than he who preached the need to empathize with the enemy. Montgomery, it is true, displayed photographs of the enemy commanders in his command caravan and searched in their features for clues to their future actions. Rommel, out of a similar distaste for the château generalship under which both had suffered in the First World War, had also inhabited a caravan in the desert, but used it as a base to establish even more direct contact with his enemy's moods and shifts of purpose, which he believed were best detected in the front line itself. Now that the Channel intervened between him and Montgomery his antennae had temporarily ceased to function. He harboured no hunches about the timing of the invasion and was inclined to suspect the Pas de Calais would be the landing area. But his intentions towards the invasion fleet, when it appeared, were, as Montgomery had guessed, unequivocal. He would stop it and its passengers at the low-water mark.

That mark was, when he had arrived in France in December 1943, scarcely defended. The ports along his four hundred miles of Channel coast were, of course, heavily concreted and barbetted, and had been since the Dieppe raid. There were some impressive strongpoints, as at Cap Griz Nez, from which a big-gun battery regularly duelled with its twin across the straits at Dover, and there were discontinuous belts of wire and mines covering the easiest beaches. But since 1941 only 1·7 million mines had been laid – he reproached his staff with the reminder that the British had laid a million in two months at a critical stage of his offensive against them in North Africa – and they were spread far too thinly. His inquiries revealed that explosive stocked in France was sufficient to manufacture 11 million anti-personnel mines alone and he demanded in addition the delivery of 2 million a month of all types from Germany. With these he planned to create an impassable zone 100 metres deep along the whole channel coast, containing 20 million mines, and eventually to extend its depth to a kilometre by the laying of 200 million. Within weeks of his arrival, mine-laying had increased from a rate of 40,000 a month to over a million and by mid-May 4 million were in place. He also dramatically accelerated the rate at which obstacles were constructed, and by May 11th over half a million had been raised along the Channel foreshore and on likely glider and parachute landing zones behind.

But he did not count merely on passive defence to stop the enemy. Like Montgomery, he expected to have to fight a hard battle and he spent much of his time on his endless travels around the threatened zone working to raise the will of his commanders and soldiers to meet its stress. Their numbers were increasing. Since November, when Hitler had at last issued a decree – Führer Order 51 – instituting a state of pre-invasion alert in the west, the movement of troops out of France towards the ever-hungry battlefields of the east, had been reversed.

The hard and costly struggle against Bolshevism during the last two and a half years. [Führer Order 51 explained] has demanded extreme exertions ... But the situation has since changed ... a greater danger now appears in the west; an Anglo-Saxon landing! In the east, the vast extent of the territory makes it possible for us to lose ground, even on a large scale, without a fatal blow being dealt to the nervous system of Germany. It is very different in the west. Should the enemy succeed in breaching our defences on a wide front here, the immediate consequences would be upredictable. Everything indicates that the enemy will launch an offensive ... at the latest in the spring, perhaps even earlier. I can, therefore, no longer take responsibility for further weakening in the west, in favour of other theatres of war. I have therefore decided to reinforce its defences, particularly those places from which the long-range bombardment of England [with pilotless and rocket weapons] will begin.

In consequence, the total of German divisions in France rose between November 1943 and June 1944 from 46 to 55. Their aggregate quality rose as well; France had long been used as a rest area for divisions exhausted on the eastern front, those pathetic skeleton formations of 'five bakers and a doctor' over which Rundstedt, the Supreme Commander West, had lamented during 1942–3. More recently it had been used as a training centre in which divisions formed from under-age and unfit recruits could be brought gradually to battleworthiness; there were six of these in the country on June 6th, 1944, as well as two 'Luftwaffe Field Divisions', raised from ground crews superfluous to the needs of Göring's shrinking air force. A number of divisions fit only to hold trenches and strong-points had also been created specifically for service in France, and assigned to positions on the coast, which they were expected to defend until relieved or destroyed. They were numbered in the 700 series and the average age of their soldiers was thirty-seven; some of their dependent units, moreover, were composed of *hilfswillige*, prisoners captured on the Russian front who had volunteered for German service, of whom there were 60,000 among the 850,000 under Rundstedt's command. The number of 'earthrooted' (*bodenständige*) divisions were five and their fighting value was rated low even by Supreme Command West.

But, subtracting these doubtful formations from the total, there were still nearly thirty infantry divisions of reasonable quality ready to oppose an Allied landing. A number were in the wrong place. Six guarded the Mediterranean shore against the possibility of a subsidiary invasion from Italy. Another stood alone almost on the Pyrenees. Seven, including two of the Luftwaffe's excellent parachute divisions, were in Brittany, which was remote from the more probable invasion beaches, and one was in the Channel Islands, and so effectively imprisoned. A round dozen of first-class infantry divisions, however, lined the Channel coast. They were smaller than Allied divisions, and without much mechanical transport – 90 per cent of the German army was still dependent on the horse or the train for movement in 1944, because the German automobile industry lacked the capacity to build the necessary military vehicles, which the German oil industry (natural and synthetic) could in any case not have fuelled. But they were strong in fire-power and very strong in experience. Unlike the Allied formations, most of which were unblooded, they contained a high proportion of officers and NCOs who had already met the enemy, learnt the wiles of the battlefield and could pass on their skills to their inexperienced soldiers.

Behind the infantry divisions stood the reserve of panzer divisions, whose fighting power was undoubted. By June 1944 they would number eleven, with another two on temporary detachment to the eastern front. One of the divisions, the 17th SS, was a panzergrenadier formation, and so had only a single armoured battalion, equipped with assault guns instead of tanks. Two others, 116th and 21st, were newly raised, the latter to replace the original 21st lost in the Tunis disaster. Tank strength in these and in the 2nd, 9th and 11th Panzer Divisions was low, less than a hundred or so, only half that in their Allied equivalents. But the equipment was of good quality. And in the other armoured formations, Panzer Lehr and 1st, 2nd and 12th SS Panzer Divisions, not only were tank numbers up to establishment but the quality and motivation of the personnel was beyond the ordinary. Other elements of the German army in France might be content to enjoy the pleasures of garrison life. And they were considerable. The population, outside the industrial towns, were not unfriendly. The resistance movement, to any German who had been in Yugoslavia, would have seemed unobtrusive. The countryside produced more food than could be consumed by the inhabitants, who were willing to sell the surplus even at the grossly unfavourable exchange rate of franc against mark. Wine, denied an export market, was more plentiful even than in peacetime. And the climate, even along the Channel coast in winter was gentle. The élite panzer divisions were prepared to enjoy but not to be softened by these temptations. They had been raised and trained to fight. They were accustomed to victory, even against apparently overwhelming odds. Their leaders and soldiers were confident that they would deal as competently with the Americans and the British as they had consistently done with the Russians.

The outcome of the battle, however, would turn not just on morale but also on dispositions and chains of command. And here Rommel grappled with difficulties he could not resolve by instruction or exhortation. He was not master in his own house. Above him, as Supreme Commander West, Field-Marshal Rundstedt exercised control over his own Army Group B and Blaskowitz's Army Group G south of the Loire. Army Group B had the bulk of the infantry divisions, but they were disposed in two separate Armies, Fifteenth and Seventh, east and west of the Seine respectively. And the one could not be used to feed the other without Rundstedt's express permission, ultimately to be sought from the Führer. Worse, an attempt made by Rommel in March to take tactical control of the armour into his own hands had resulted in a further fragmentation of command. Rundstedt, an orthodox tactician who had never experienced the Allied air forces' power to nail mobile forces to the ground, had as early as November 1943 created a central armoured staff, Panzer Group West, to hold the six panzer divisions in northern France in deep reserve. His scheme was to commit them in a massive, classical counter-attack against the main enemy landing when its size and axis had been identified. It conflicted absolutely with Rommel's plan, based on the reasoning that success would come early or not at all, to deploy the tanks forward and fight on the beaches. But an appeal to authority, though it gave back to Rommel control of three of the panzer divisions, reserved the other three to Hitler's own use, through his operations staff at Wehrmacht Supreme Headquarters (OKW). The arrangement promised delay at the moment when speed of decision would be most critical.

When that moment would come none of the German side could guess. Weather forecasting provided the best clue, since the Allies would need the assurance of several days of calm sea and open skies to risk setting forth, but their dominance of the Atlantic made the readings Rommel's meteorologists needed for prediction as hard to come by as their control of the Channel intelligence of troop dispositions within the United Kingdom. So infrequently did German aircraft penetrate British airspace (only 129 sorties were flown in the six weeks before D-Day) and so carefully were those that did shepherded by the RAF that they reported only what they were allowed to see. Such sightings tended naturally to confirm the existence, carefully fabricated by false radio traffic, of a major Allied formation, the non-existent 1st US Army Group, in the counties opposite the Pas de Calais. And this bad intelligence confirmed the belief, now firmly held by Rommel, though not by Hitler, that the proximity of the Pas de Calais to the German frontier must oblige them to land there.

Wherever the *Schwerpunkt* should fall, however, neither man shrank from the coming battle. By May 1944 Hitler welcomed a return to the throw of the dice after two years of remorseless grinding down of his armies and people by Russian land and Allied air offensives. Gone were the days when the RAF lost more air crews than it killed civilians in raids on German territory. Since June 1943 the Pointblank campaign had regularly brought a thousand American bombers by day and a thousand British by night to drop their loads on German cities. By April 1944 the 26,000 acres which represented the centres of the 43 cities most heavily attacked had been levelled; in Hamburg, the worst hit, the population had been reduced by 30 per cent. And exaggerated though the bombing propagandists' claims were of the damage done to the German war economy, which flourished strangely in certain engineering sectors, the long-term danger to communications and synthetic oil production could not be disguised. Losses at the front were equally alarming. In the year November 1942–October 1943, the eastern army (*Ostheer*) had lost 1,686,000 men dead, wounded or missing and received only 1,260,000 replacements. Heavy engagements, as in the Dnieper bend in October and November 1943, consumed the effective worth of a division's manpower every three days; full-scale offensives, like Kursk in July, exhausted the strength of whole armies in a week's fighting. And such battles – mercifully Kursk had no parallel in 1943 – also imposed tank losses at a rate beyond the means of the factories to make good. Between January and December 1943 Germany's stock of tanks declined absolutely from 5,700 to 5,200.

The U-boat war had been lost and there was no hope of returning to the Atlantic until the improved *Schnorkel* types were ready in the autumn. But their performance was as fraught with uncertainty as that of the 'secret weapons' – V-1 flying bombs and V-2 rockets – on which Hitler now counted with increasingly desperate optimism to reverse the trend of attrition, industrial and psychological, in the strategic air war. And beyond the frontiers of formal conflict, land, air and maritime, the other certitudes of German power were also shifting and slipping. Not only had the Italian government, together with half its national territory, passed to the Allied camp; but the other satellites, even tiny but once ferocious Finland, grew less ardent in their devotion to the Axis with every yard that the Russians won towards their borders – and by May the Red Army had returned to the shores of the Gulf of Finland, begun the ascent of the Romanian Carpathians and menaced Bulgaria at a distance of two hundred miles. Intelligence from Hungary and the puppet state of Slovakia suggested that their armies, which had earlier campaigned with the Germans in the east, were preparing to open the gates to the Russians. And to their south occupied Yugoslavia teemed with guerrillas so numerous and warlike as to require the presence of twelve German divisions which could be ill-spared from other hard-pressed fronts.

Little wonder that a battle against a shipborne enemy, even one who might have learnt the secret of swimming tanks ashore with its infantry, appeared to offer Hitler almost his only chance of breaking the run of losses and regaining an initiative. On March 18th he had summoned all the generals in the west to Berchtesgaden to explain to them that,

> once defeated, the enemy will never try to invade again. Quite apart from their heavy losses they would need months to organize a fresh attempt. And an invasion failure would also deliver a crushing blow to British and American morale . . . We shall then transfer [our divisions in the west] to the eastern front to revolutionise the situation there . . . so the whole outcome of the war depends on each man fighting in the west, and that means the fate of the Reich itself.

Rommel too looked forward to the battle, and with assurance. On May 5th he had dictated to his secretary, 'I am more confident than ever before. If the British give us just two more weeks, I won't have any more doubt about it.'[8] The growing suspicion, felt by Hitler, that Normandy, not the Pas de Calais, was the threatened zone drove Rommel to fuss over its defences during the rest of the month. But on June 4th, convinced that the tides and approaching bad weather made any invasion impossible until after June 20th, he decided to leave supervision of his now almost complete preparations to his staff, and take birthday leave in Germany. The same evening, in his advanced headquarters at Portsmouth, Eisenhower read weather reports which convinced him that he must postpone the sailings he had ordered for next morning. In its early hours, fresh information indicating an unexpected break in the clouds persuaded him to change his mind. As the dusk of June 5th drew in, the thousands of ships and aircraft he commanded across the breadth of the south of England prepared to depart from their bases. As they left ports and runways behind, he scribbled for himself a note of inculpation against defeat in the battle the men he commanded must fight: 'Our landings in the Cherbourg–Havre area have failed to gain a satisfactory foothold and I have withdrawn the troops. My decision to attack at this time and place were based on the best information available. The troops, the air and navy did all that bravery and devotion to duty could do. If any blame or fault attaches to the attempt it is mine alone.'

These were the words of a great man and a great soldier; the greatness of Eisenhower as a soldier has indeed yet to be portrayed fully. But, as a soldier, he knew secretly that the outcome of all he had planned now rested not with him but with the troops who were about to land, with those who would follow them to fight the great battles inshore and with those of the enemy who would oppose them. At a distance, such as that which isolation in a Supreme Head-quarters lends, the troops, Allied and enemy alike, might easily reduce to a formless, featureless mass of field-grey or khaki. But battles are not fought by masses. Armies appear masslike, but their effective parts, the fighting units, are quite small. Of the 11 million men in the United States Army Ground, Air and Service Forces, for example, less than 2 million belonged to the 90 combat divisions of the land forces, and of those 2 million less than 700,000 represented tank crews or infantrymen. Yet the whole effort of the army, via selection, training and support, was dedicated to transforming those 700,000 into groups of comrades whose skill and loyalty to each other might overpower the skill and loyalties of similar groups on the other side.

What follows is a study of several such groups: of the parachute infantry battalions of the American airborne divisions in their first bewildering hours on French soil; of the seaborne battalions of Canadian infantry debarking from their landing-craft under the guns of the German beach defences; of the Highland and Lowland infantry who fought to open the first corridor out of the bridgehead; of the English and Scottish armoured cavalry regiments which spearheaded the charge to break the German ring around Caen in July; of the German panzer battalions which Hitler sent to the destruction in his final, foredoomed effort to win the Battle of Normandy in August; of the Polish Dragoons and Riflemen who sacrificed themselves to stem the flood of the Germans' flight home; and of the Free French of Leclerc's 2nd Armoured Division returning in triumph to liberate Paris. Together their experience makes the story of the Battle of Normandy.

# CHAPTER 2

## *All-American Screaming Eagles*

PARACHUTING HAD COME LATE to the Allied armies. Until the outbreak of the war, it had been known to the West only through the reports of British and French observers at the Soviet 1936 manoeuvres and from some shaky but unnerving propaganda film later released by the Red Army. Shot through the turbulence of the camera aircraft's slipstream, it had shown a file of wind-tortured automata climbing from the door of a giant Tupolev transport, clinging desperately to the rail along its fuselage as they breasted the chord of its monstrous wing and then, at a signal, releasing their grip in unison to be whirled away into invisibility like needles from a mountain pine in the first storm of winter. This weird footage, as if directed by Eisenstein for a Sovfilm version of *Flying Down to Rio* – whose release only briefly antedated the experiment and whose aerial gymnastics may indeed just have inspired it – still possesses the power to alarm and to mystify. In those who saw it at the time its effect was to evoke disbelief in the applicability of anything so necromantic to the operations of war.

Four years later its applicability was demonstrated all too convincingly in the skies of the Netherlands by the Germans, who in the interval had formed and trained a whole division of parachutists which they used to bypass and nullify the defences of Fortress Holland in a single day. But the aura of witchcraft continued to attach to military parachuting well beyond that. The idea of a large, homogeneous formation of soldiers descending from the skies, ready to fight on the ground as conventional infantry, seemed one which the popular imagination could not assimilate, preferring to feed on the image of the parachutist as troll or warlock. Nuns in jackboots had been one of the half-comic, half-terrifying rumours circulating in Britain in the months after Dunkirk and even in the following year, when the threat of invasion had receded, a respectable English

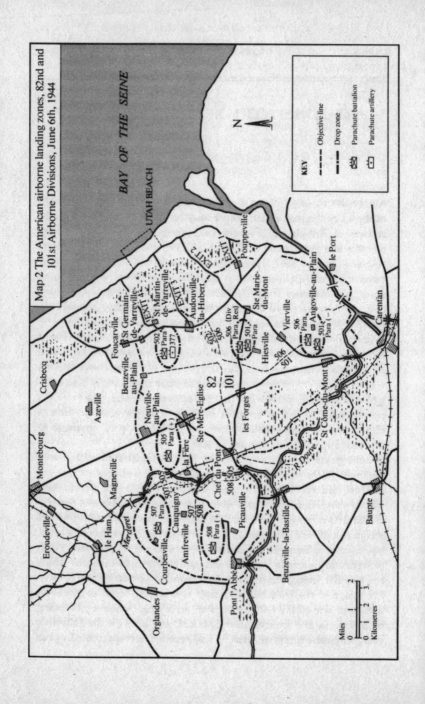

Map 2 The American airborne landing zones, 82nd and 101st Airborne Divisions, June 6th, 1944

publisher could still sponsor a book warning that parachutists might appear disguised as 'postmen with collapsible bicycles in postman's bags', policemen with grenades 'of small size under peaked cap', butchers' boys with grenades 'in meat basket covered by white cloth' or clergymen 'with machine-guns under cloak' – presumably Anglo-Catholic from their garb and therefore doubly dangerous.

Even at that moment, however, British soldiers in strange Sorbo-rubber Lana Turner turbans were learning at Ringway airport outside Manchester to fall through a hole cut in the floor of a Whitley bomber, and far away among the pines of Fort Benning, Georgia, Americans in Superman overalls were descending on steel ropes from the pinnacle of a 250-foot tower into the hot southern sand. As German parachute formations grew in numbers and confidence, so that in April 1941 they could assault and take the island of Crete over the heads of an impotent Royal Navy, the first experimental airborne units had begun to take shape in the Allied armies. Tentatively in Tunisia in 1942 and then on a larger scale in the invasion of Sicily in July 1943 British and American parachutists had jumped directly into action in the teeth of enemy opposition. Many had died by misadventure, dropped into the sea or on to windswept crags miles from their landing zones. But the survivors had kept their faith in the technique intact, had spread the word and seen the airborne arm continue to grow through the middle period of the war. While the German parachutists, though established as an élite of the Wehrmacht, lost their access to aircraft and found themselves increasingly committed to earthbound heroics, on the other side of the lines pilots, planes, specialized equipment – airportable vehicles, howitzers and even tanks – men and money came in profusion to the Allied airborne divisions.

By the spring of 1944 those ready in Britain for operations numbered four, the 82nd (All American) and 101st (Screaming Eagles) of the US Army, the 6th and 1st of the British. Under the invasion plan the first three of these were to swoop across the Channel in a single night flight, drop into darkness at the eastern and western ends of the bridgehead and seize the rivers which delimited its flanks. The bridges over them were to be blown, the approach roads mined and their banks garrisoned against all enemy attempts to pass troops across. In this way the seaborne assault waves could be assured of a little security, a diminution of the ferocity of the counter-attack they must undergo as soon as they had stepped ashore.

The parachutists were to start their rendezvous with destiny – the famous phrase was chosen by the historians of the 101st as the title of the divisional chronicle and is entirely characteristic of the romantic and rhetorical spirit of the parachute pioneers – from widely scattered billets in the Midlands and the south of England, the 82nd from the flatlands of Lincolnshire and the 101st from Devon, Hampshire and Berkshire, where its camps abutted dangerously close on the cantonments of the British 6th. Fighting for the company of the local girls had been a popular inter-Allied weekend activity in the small towns of the Berkshire Downs during the spring of 1944. But so too had been beer-drinking in the tiny villages, with names which the veterans would recall with pleasurable disbelief thirty years later – Ogbourne St George, Berwick St James, Lower Slaughter, Middle Wallop – and cautiously enlarging friendships with local families, from which the survivors would bear back across the Atlantic a small army of GI brides when the war was over.

On May 30th, however, all intercourse with the outside world had abruptly ceased for the parachutists. Those in the permanent encampments of the British army which litter Salisbury plain, the Victorian red-brick cantonments of Bulford, the First World War hutments of Tidworth, named indifferently after the victories of the Peninsula and the more doubtful triumphs of the Crimea, Talavera, Albuera, Inkerman, Balaclava, were confined to quarters. Those dispersed in civilian lodgings were formed up, packed into buses and driven away to hastily pitched tented staging areas where they were to be quarantined until take-off. A lieutenant of the 101st recalled his unconvincing attempt to persuade the villagers of Aldbourne that it was departure merely for another rehearsal. 'The English knew we were pushing off ... it got me to see them cry and take it as they did." The parachutists, too, were affected, but the mood soon passed. They were volunteers, boys in the main from the wrong side of the tracks in S.L.A. Marshall's recollection, who joined for adventure, had survived the nine-mile runs, 'Gimme twenty-five' (pushups) and endless 'Hubba-hubbas' ('hurry, hurry' in what the drill instructors inexplicably believed to be Hebrew) of airborne training, had jumped in practice by day and night a dozen times and were now ready to try the real thing. Pent up in their temporary stockades, they gorged on a high-protein diet and submerged their frustration in endless, high-stake gambling.

For the commanders and the junior leaders there was more serious preparation to be done, the fruits of which they must eventually pass on to their men. On maps, air photographs and models constructed from them, they studied the terrain of the Cotentin peninsula, the locations of the German units garrisoning it, as far as they were known, and the objectives the parachute divisions must seize. These lay within a kidney-shaped area about ten miles long on its east–west axis and five from north to south. It was bounded on the east by the sea and on the south-east and south-west by the course of the little river Douve. On the west and in the north the boundary of the airborne area ran through open country, flat and unwooded near the Douve and its tributary, the Merderet, then closely hedge-rowed on the slopes which rose gradually into the interior of the Cotentin. The river valleys had been inundated by the Germans and, because they were shallow, were flooded for a wide distance – as much as a mile in places. The floods in the valley of the Merderet were a particularly irritating obstacle, because that little waterway divided the western third of the airborne area from the main landing and dropping zones to the east, and the bridges across it, which would be called 'the Causeway', were therefore an 'important initial objective'.

Another important initial objective was the little town of Ste Mère-Eglise, through which ran Route nationale 13, the main road from Cherbourg to Bayeux in the British sector, and the only first-class road available to the Germans in the Cotentin as an axis of reinforcement. All the other objectives lay on the perimeter. First and most important were the four exits from the beach, codenamed Utah, which the American 4th Division would need when they came to move inland from their landing-places. Because the coast was low and marshy, these exits on to dry ground were each about a mile from high-water mark, at Pouppeville (Exit 1), Hébert (2) Audouville-la-Hubert (3) and St Martin-de-Varreville (4). From Pouppeville, along the estuary of the Douve, the objectives were a series of locks across the river, which the parachutists were to seize and hold so that they might be used for moving between the Utah beachhead and the Omaha beachhead to the east when the time came to join the two. The objectives along the course of the Douve were also a series of crossing places, some of which were to be destroyed to deny their use to the Germans, the others to be held either for the immediate use of the parachutists or for a break-out later by the beach-landed infantry and armour. The most important of these were, from east and west, at St Côme-du-Mont, Chef-du-Pont and Pont l'Abbé. Thereafter the line of objectives, from Pont l'Abbé back to Exit 4, ran through the open countryside and would have to be defended, if and when captured, by grit and hope.

The danger to this open flank would come, it was believed, from the two German divisions which it was known had long been stationed in the Cotentin, the 709th on the east coast and the 243rd on the west, and the recently arrived 91st, which had unfortunately been positioned exactly astride the airborne area. Moreover, while the 709th and 243rd were static formations – what the Germans called *bodenständige*, 'ground holding', a euphemistic admission of their total lack of mechanical transport and the low physical fitness of their soldiers – the 91st was composed of young men who had actually been trained in air movement. Still, between them they fielded no more than twenty-four battalions against the eighteen which the Americans could parachute. Moreover, several of the German battalions were not German at all in composition, but manned by more-or-less willing volunteers from the army of prisoners whom the Germans had taken in the east during 1941–2. They were indeed known as East (*Ost*) Battalions, for to have called them Russian would have been inaccurate. They represented for the most part the peripheral and unassimilated peoples of the Russian empire, Cossacks, Georgians, Turkomen, Armenians, Volga Tartars, and Azerbaijanis, who had swapped a tenuous sense of citizenship for the guarantee of regular meals, and might be expected to waver in their new loyalty if pressed to fight for their suppers. That prospect rather bettered the odds, which the Americans calculated to yield a more or less even fight on the first day, when most of the defenders would be pinned in their fixed positions. At worst, it was thought, the Germans would be able to find five battalions to mount a counter-attack against the parachutists, and to concentrate no armour against them until the third day. The forecast was slightly optimistic. There was also in the area a scratch panzer battalion, No. 100, equipped with old French tanks and makeshift assault guns, and the 6th Parachute Regiment, counting three battalions of highly trained soldiers, whose average age was 17½ (it was 36 in the 709th Division). But even this addition of a force so closely similar in quality to that of the American need not mean that the operation was too risky to be attempted (as Air Marshal Leigh-Mallory had argued). It did mean that the Americans would have to put forth every shred of that Red

Indian bravery which, with a last-minute sprouting of Apache haircuts and smearing of red and white warpaint, many of the young bloods in the battalions were nerving themselves to emulate if they were to come through.

The approaching moment of departure evoked other rituals, perhaps made all the more necessary by the disturbing effects on tautened nerves of the invasion's postponement from June 5th to June 6th. A rash of fights broke out, as men who had steeled themselves to leave lost their tempers over minor irritations in the resulting decrescendo. The divisional staffs hastily recalled the regimental bands which had filled the encampments with music during the recent hours, replayed over the public address systems the hit records of the moment and found new films to show. When word of the renewed order of departure came, an officer of the 377th Parachute Artillery, the gunner regiment of the Screaming Eagles, recalls that he found the men to whom he was to pass it watching a Ted Lewis movie, *Is Everybody Happy?* and reflected, as he climbed on to the stage to interrupt it, that 'this was just the way it would happen in Hollywood'. There was an element of Hollywood in the round of hand-pressings and exchange of home addresses which followed, avowals of comradeship to death and promises to visit bereaved relations if a friend should not return. There was Hollywood too in the parting speech of Colonel Wolverton, who was to be killed the following day, to his battalion of the 506th Parachute Infantry: 'Although I am not a religious man, I would like all of you to kneel with me in prayer – and do not look down with a bowed head, but look up, so that you can see God and ask His blessing and help in what we are about to do.'[2] There was even more Hollywood in the ferocious final briefing by Colonel Howard 'Skeets' Johnson of the 501st, which he concluded by whipping out his jump knife, brandishing it above his head and screaming: 'I swear to you that before tomorrow night this knife will be buried in the back of the blackest German in Normandy.'[3] His men screamed back in exultation. But many more sought consolation in quiet, personal religion, making their confessions if they were Catholic, as were so many from the big industrial cities of the north and east where the divisions recruited, or simply retreating into private prayer. One of those who prayed most fervently was the commander of the All American, Matthew B. Ridgway, whose calm and handsome features and soldierly bearing concealed a nature of the deepest romanticism. June 6th was to be the day of his first combat jump. The night before, as on other nights awaiting an ordeal, he lay with his God in the dark, listening for the words spoken to Joshua, 'I will not fail thee nor forsake thee', and, 'in all humbleness, without in any way seeking to compare His trials to mine', reflected on the Agony of Our Lord in the Garden of Gethsemane and told himself that 'if He could face with calmness of soul the great suffering He knew was to be His fate, then I surely could endure any lesser ordeal of the flesh or spirit that might be awaiting me'.[4]

# Flight

In the days before June 6th the airfields near which the tented staging camps had been pitched had gathered in the hundreds of aeroplanes needed to drop the 13,000 parachutists into action. Eight hundred and twenty-two were needed for the first drop, all C-47s, as the army called the twin-engined DC-3 airliner with which Douglas Company had revolutionized internal air travel in the United States before the war. Painted now in khaki with three broad white stripes on each wing, which was to be the inter-Allied recognition sign for D-Day and after, each could carry eighteen fully laden parachutists, besides the pilot, co-pilot, navigator and crew chief. These, the permanent crew of the aircraft, belonged to the Army Air Force but, despite the extremely risky nature of their mission, they stood low on the totem pole of its prestige. Officially they were rated 'non-combat', because the C-47 was not armed and could not carry bombs and, as most aircrews 'would rather lay an egg or shoot a gun than fly a truck or tractor', it was in the nature of things that the least qualified were assigned to the Troop Carrier Commands rather than the Bomber or Fighter Wings. The ugly ducklings' disgruntlement was heightened by their knowledge that parachute dropping was both technically demanding and operationally hazardous, since it required the pilots to fly in tight formation at heights of 600–700 feet and at low speed – about 120 mph – which made them excellent targets both for fighters and anti-aircraft guns. The crews of the 52nd Troop Carrier Wing, which had worked with the All American since the Sicily landings, had developed none the less a close and mutually trustful relationship with the division, based on some plain speaking early on after numbers of parachutists had been dropped to drown in the Mediterranean. One of its groups, however, was inexperienced and another had been withdrawn for nearly a year before D-Day to fly transport missions, a common experience for all 'non-combat' units. It had certainly been that of the other Wings in IX Troop Carrier Command, which as a result were undertrained, particularly in night flying. And the drop of both divisions was to be by night.

But night comes late in an English June and the trucks taking the men to the runways unloaded them besides their aircraft in daylight. Eighteen to each stick (planeload), they were tipped out with a mountain of packages which it seemed impossible to distribute about a human body. With each other's help, and then that of the aircrew, they began. Private Donald Burgett, of the 506th Parachute Infantry, 101st Airborne Division, contemplated his load.

> One suit of Olive Drab, worn under my jump suit – this was an order for everyone – helmet, boots, gloves, main parachute, reserve parachute, Mae West, rifle, ·45 automatic pistol, trench knife, jump knife, hunting knife, machete, one cartridge belt, two bandoliers, two cans of machine gun ammo totalling 676 rounds of ·30 ammo, 66 rounds of ·45 ammo, one Hawkins mine capable of blowing off the track of a tank, four blocks of TNT, one entrenching tool with two blasting caps taped on the outside of the steel part, three first-aid kits, two morphine needles, one gas mask, a canteen of water, three days' supply of K rations, two days' supply of D rations, six fragmentation grenades, one Gammon grenade, one orange and one red smoke grenade, one orange panel, one blanket, one raincoat, one change of socks and underwear, two cartons of cigarettes.[5]

Burgett's multiplicity of knives reflected not a particular bloodthirstiness but an anxiety, shared by all American parachutists, about ease of escape after landing from his parachute harness which, unlike the British pattern, was secured not only by a single quick release catch but by five buckles. Although in theory easily opened, in practice they all to often defeated thumbs and fingers, because the harness served not merely to support the man in descent but also to secure the enormous load of kit close to his body, was therefore strained iron-hard about him, and had to be cut if he was not to be dragged when he touched ground. Burgett was so heavily loaded this evening that he actually could not accoutre himself, even by the normal method of lying down and sucking in his stomach to fasten the last catch.

> When I tried to lie down, I found it impossible to bend at the waist and had to fall into a prone position, breaking the fall with my hands. Two Air Corps men came up and asked if I needed help. I told one of them to stand on my back while the other fastened the bellyband; after which I found it impossible even to get to my knees. The two men lifted me bodily, and with much boosting and grunting shoved me up into the plane where I pulled myself along the floor and with the aid of the crew chief got into a bucket seat.

Later he found that 'the best way to ride was to kneel on the floor' (a journalist who flew with them was to write that they knelt in prayer), 'and rest the weight of the gear and the chutes on the seat itself'.

The size and nature of these extraordinary burdens, which nearly doubled a man's weight and required for assumption something like the assistance a knight in armour received from his esquires, tells us a great deal about the nature of airborne operations. Dramatic though the immediate psychological advantages of a mass parachute drop may be, the longer-term difficulties it presented to the side which launches it are immense. By the nature of its role a parachute division confronts the first-line troops of the enemy, or very shortly attracts them to its landing zones. In the battle which must follow a conventional division of infantry or armour would be able to deploy artillery and support arms comparable in weight and quality to the enemy's, and to resupply its needs for munitions directly from its rear through a well-defined system of roads and dumps. If it suffered defeat, it would do so for military reasons alone. A parachute division's predicament is different. Its own ('organic' in militarese) artillery is little more than symbolic in character – in 1944 it comprised a single miniature artillery battalion equipped with twelve 75 mm pack howitzers, a weapon which aroused in its crews all the emotions felt for an ingenious toy, being accurate, easily dismounted into nine parachutable loads but, when assembled, 'very unlethal', as a veteran ruefully recalled. The division cannot therefore hope to match the enemy in weight of metal. But neither can it in any other respect – except that of the bravery and skill of its soldiers. It cannot look to its rear for reinforcements or for resupply. Those must come either by aeroplane, and only if landing grounds can be captured or

1 Eisenhower addressing Company E, 502nd Parachute Infantry, who are about to emplane for Normandy

2    Eisenhower and Montgomery in England before D-Day
3    Patton (left) and Bradley in the air over Normandy, July 1944

4    Rommel inspecting the defences of Normandy before D-Day
5    Anti-aircraft sentries of an SS division in Normandy, June 1944

9    A patrol of the 502nd Parachute Infantry at St Marcouf, Utah
     Beach, June 8th, 1944

10   Parachutists of the 501st and villagers of Ste Marie-du-Mont,
     June 7th, 1944

11 The aftermath of the Dieppe raid: damaged landing-craft and Canadian dead, August 19th, 1942

12 'Rommel's asparagus': German engineers scattering for cover under Allied reconnaissance aircraft before D-Day

13 German infantry practise manning beach defences before D-Day

14 Wounded of the 3rd Canadian Division awaiting evacuation on Juno Beach, June 6th, 1944

constructed within the dropping zone, or by more parachuting. And even then, until the ground troops break through to join hands, the equipment and supplies it receives will not differ at all from what was brought in the first place. And supply will be chancy.

Hence the necessity for parachutists, like mountaineers making a dash for the summit, to be self-sufficient, to carry with them all and more than the enemy's infantry will have but also token means of defence and attack against his armour and artillery. Those were what Burgett's blocks of TNT, Hawkins mine and Gammon grenade (a lump of plastic explosive stuffed into a stockinette bag) were meant to be. The Gammon grenade would, if accurately thrown, adhere to the outside of a tank and, when it exploded, cause a 'scab' to detach itself from the internal face of the armour, cannon about inside the fighting compartment and kill the crew. The bazooka, with which one man in each rifle squad was equipped, would achieve the same result, and at slightly less risk to the attacker, since its range was several times greater than a grenade throw. And the 60 mm mortar, packed in a 'leg bag' which the parachutist suspended by a twenty-foot line once he had left the aircraft, would provide the semblance of artillery support, if chiefly in the form of noise, until heavier weapons arrived by 'parapack' – the containers holding equipment too bulky to drop on the man, like the 81 mm mortar – by glider (most importantly, 57 mm guns of the airborne anti-tank battery) or by land transport (which would in any case spell relief).

That relief lay in the very problematical future. And knowledge of how fragile a shield these puny weapons offered to the advance guard of his great enterprise had decided General Eisenhower to spend the evening hours of D−1 with the Screaming Eagles. His arrival at Welford was unannounced and his appearance among the waiting sticks, sitting tensed under the wings of their planes in the gathering dusk, created a muted sensation. Corporal Kermit Latta was struck by the 'terrific burden of decision and responsibility' which showed on his face and by the sincerity of his effort to communicate with his young soldiers. He paused to speak to their group and we can detect in his exchanges something of that deft personal appeal which was to make him the United States' most popular postwar President:

'What is your job, soldier?'

'Ammunition bearer, sir,'

'Where is your home?'

'Pennsylvania, sir.'

'Did you get those shoulders working in a coal mine?'

'Yes, sir.'

'Good luck to you tonight, soldier'.[6]

As he moved among them, many of the sticks began to emplane, struggling through the fuselage door to find their places within. To those with whom he had not spoken a mimeographed sheet bearing a farewell message was passed. To all was issued the second dose of the air-sickness pills the divisional medical officers had prescribed, which had the important side-effect, intended or not, of inducing a comfortable drowsiness. Many were grateful for them as they fidgeted to find the least uncomfortable position in which to make the flight, joined sporadically in the medley of songs started by the most wakeful and tried to empty their minds of thoughts of the immediate future.

The time was 10.15 p.m. and the darkness of the night of June 5th–6th had begun to close over the long lines of C-47s, at Welford, Membury, Ramsbury, Greenham Common and Aldermaston, and at the Devon airfields of Merryfield and Upottery. At the Lincolnshire airfields of the 82nd, Fulbeck, Barkston Heath, Saltby, North Witham, Folkingham, Cottesmore and Spanhoe, the engines had already begun to turn for take-off, to carry the flight serials down to imaginary localities above the Channel bearing names more familiar to American ears – Flatbush, Hoboken, Reno and Spokane. Towards 11 p.m. the men of the 101st caught the sounds of the same sequence, 'the whine of the starter winding up; a few throaty coughs as the engine caught and finally roared into a full crescendo'. The lead pilot ran up his engines 'and then taxied slowly down the runway to a position facing into the wind. The other planes fell into single file much like soldiers assembling and followed the lead craft'. At Welford General Eisenhower raised a salute to each which passed.

> Then at 2245 [Corporal Koskimaki noted], our plane began moving down the runway, gathered momentum rapidly and gently lifted from the concrete surface. The rest of the [forty-five] planes in our serial followed at seven-second intervals until the entire group was airborne. The planes continued to circle ... until all forty-five were airborne and in formation. Our plane served as the point. The planes flew in Vs of nine planes. The centre plane of the three lead planes of each

nine-plane group served as its immediate point. Wing lights were on and it was a beautiful spectacle to behold through the open doorway.[7]

It was also the last time but two that anyone would see such a thing. Like the dreadnought fleets of 1910–20, the sight of which man-oeuvring in close formation in the narrow waters of the North Sea left ever after in those who had witnessed it something of the fascinated awe felt by travellers stumbling unawares on an elephants' graveyard, the great airborne armadas were to prove obsolete amost as soon as conceived. The naval pachyderms, nearly invulnerable to each other's attack, had been withered out of existence in a few years by the appearance of the fragile but lethal carrier-borne aeroplane. Massed troop-carrying aircraft were to enjoy an even shorter life-span. In the not-yet-planned Market Garden Operation pilots would find themselves flying directly into concentrated anti-aircraft fire and surviving only because their parachutists in many cases fell directly on the gun positions and disabled the crews. In Operation Varsity, which would be staged to cross the Rhine in the coming spring, the pilots were to discover that the odds had moved even more sharply against them; 440 out of 1,590 troop-carriers were severely damaged or destroyed and a parachutist who survived the curtains of flak would recall the horror of watching the crews of the stricken aircraft which had just dropped them at minimum altitude 'coming to the doors of blazing planes and then, realizing they were below the height at which they could hope to operate their 'chutes, turning back into the machines to wait their fate on impact'. Within a few years, when ground- and air-launched missiles would have been added to the troop-carrying aircraft's enemies, no general anywhere would consider sending formations *en masse* against prepared posi-tions, and the role of the parachutist would dwindle to that of the clandestine interloper.

But on this June night of 1944 it was at its apogee, and the great fleets of C-47s could ride the cloudless moonlit sky with all the confidence and something of the appearance of Jellicoe's and Beatty's squadrons breasting their way southward to their rendez-vous with the High Seas Fleet. The sight was 'extraordinary', 'breath-taking', 'majestic', and the naval analogy more than metaphorical for, as Ridgway recalled, with the 'V of V's only 150 feet from wing tip to wing tip, no lights to guide them except little lavender lights you could hardly see, only a thousand feet from one flight of nine aircraft to the next and with as many as five hundred aircraft flying on the same track, it was extremely easy to overrun the plane ahead'.[8] The formations were in fact controlled in exactly the same way as ship flotillas, by a show of lights from the plexiglass astrodome of the lead aircraft in each serial of forty-five. At its signal, shown when radar or visual beacons were picked up from the ground or sea, all turned on the pre-determined marking points, later switched on their internal red lights announcing the approach to the dropping zone (DZ) and finally the green light which was the order to jump.

Between 1.15 and 2 a.m. on June 6th, after half an hour flown at 500 feet to escape detection by the German radar and a shorter period at 1,500 feet to establish landfall, the troop carriers dropped to 700 feet to make their approach runs. Some aboard had slept the trip away, helped by the air-sickness pills, many had smoked it through, 'the ends of their cigarettes glowing white in the dim red light'. Some had done both. Hugh Pritchard of the 101st had given way to drowsiness, then roused himself to dig out a cigarette. 'I asked the man next to me for a match; his reply, "There will be no more smoking as we are approaching the French coast." I thought – "Oh brother, I'm a long way from home."' The same thought had run through thousands of heads, filled with memories of families – favourite sisters figured curiously frequently in the subsequent recollections of veterans – and carefully controlled fears of the coming descent. Lieutenant Richard Winters of the 2nd Battalion, 506th Parachute Infantry, had found himself soon after take-off 'making a last prayer. It was a long, hard and sincere prayer that never really did end for I just continued to think and pray during the rest of the ride.' General Ridgway, watching the men in his C-47 (it was at the heart of the parachuting ethos that generals and privates jumped together), saw little of this show on their faces. 'The men sat quietly, deep in their own thoughts. They joked a little and broke, now and then, into ribald laughter. Nervousness and tension, and the cold that blasted through the open door, had its effect upon us all.'

He had watched 'glints of yellow flame from the German anti-aircraft guns on the Channel Islands . . . curiously and without fear, as a high-flying duck may watch a hunter, knowing that we were too high and too far away for their fire to reach us'. Others had lifted the little black-out curtains which covered the windows to share the view but he looked 'straight across the aisle through the doorless exit'. And suddenly he saw land.

> No lights showed ... but in the pale glow of a rising moon, I could clearly see each farm and field below. How peaceful the land looked, each house and hedgerow, path and little stream bathed in the silver of the moonlight. I felt that if it were not for the noise of the engines we could hear the farm dogs baying and the sound of the barnyard roosters crowing for midnight.

And then the view was extinguished by

> cloud, thick and turbulent. I had been looking out of the doorway, watching with a profound sense of satisfaction the close-ordered flight of the great sky caravan that stretched as far as the eye could see. All at once it was blotted out. Not a wing light showed. The plane began to yaw and plunge, and in my mind's eye I could see the other pilots, fighting to hold course, knowing how great was the danger of collision.[9]

This bank of cloud, unpredicted and probably unpredictable by the meteorologists, stood across the approach routes of both the 82nd and the 101st. The serials of both divisions flew straight into it. And on all it had the same effect. Pilots instinctively separated, horizontally and vertically, so that the tight V's of V's dissolved and 'when after hours (actually seconds or minutes) we came out', recalled Lieutenant Harold Young of the 326th Parachute Engineers, 'we were all alone. I remember my amazement. Where had all those C-47s gone?' Ridgway's plane too emerged into sudden isolation, and at once the red light came on in the cabin which warned of four minutes to the dropping point. He and his stick stood up and clipped the hooks of their static lines to the cable. In other aircraft, however, the sticks were already standing when the pilots met the cloud and their manoeuvring threw the men off balance or even off their feet. And others emerged from the cloud to find themselves not alone but in close proximity to other aircraft and under fire from German light and medium anti-aircraft guns positioned immediately under the flight path. 'Our plane', remembered Private Donald Wilson, 'was flying low and suddenly went straight up to miss a number of others which crossed suddenly in front of us. We were all "stood up" and hooked up and it really caused quite an uproar to get back into position so we could make our jump.' Many of the aircraft were hit, numbers of the parachutists wounded in the cabins and most sticks called to jump either while their aircraft was taking evasive action or when they were short or beyond their assigned dropping point. When things went right, the sequence was as described by Corporal Koskimaki, who was in General Taylor's stick:

> Jumpmaster Lawrence Legere ... yelled, 'Get ready!' Bodies went rigid as troopers waited for the next command. 'Stand up!' Soldiers struggled to their feet with their heavy loads. Everybody was anxious to leave the confines of the plane. Next came the order to 'Hook up!' The snap of the anchor line fastener clicking into place could be heard the full length of the cabin. Each man made doubly sure he had hooked his static line to the cable running overhead down the centre of the ceiling. Next came the order to 'Check your equipment'. Each man checked the connections of the man directly in front of him to make sure all items were secure and would remain in place when he was jarred by the opening shock of the chute. Above the roar of the engines could be heard the call, 'Sound off for equipment check'. From far forward could be heard, 'Sixteen – OK', 'Fifteen – OK', 'Fourteen – OK', right on down to General Taylor, who bellowed, 'Two – OK'. Quickly followed the order, 'Stand in the door' from the jumpmaster who was crouched in the open doorway looking for landmarks. The members of the stick crowded in tightly behind him. Movement was now limited and no one would be able to react as an individual any longer.

When the order to jump came, the whole stick would leave the plane at gymnastic speed, emptying it in less than ten seconds.

If things went amiss, this smooth sequence could be severely disjointed. And much was going amiss in the aircraft General Taylor could not see. Sergeant Louis E. Truax, of the 1st Battalion, 506th Parachute Infantry, described his jump:

> The front men were jumping. The first twelve men got out pretty close together. I was running down the aisle. Suddenly the plane was hit in the left wing by flak. The wing went straight up. My left shoulder crashed into a window. With

ammo, a 1903 Springfield rifle, 12 grenade launcher rounds, 2 cans of blood plasma, 2 cans of distilled water, gas mask, helmet, K rations I must have weighed 225–250 pounds – stripped I weighed 130. I was surprised the window didn't break. The pilot was fighting to right the plane. When he succeeded, I was appalled at the view which greeted me – I was the only one standing. Four men lay in a tangled heap on the floor. I realized it was almost impossible for them to stand up with their equipment loads. Also that an absolute sequence had to be maintained or we'd have a glob of human hamburger dangling outside the door at 150 miles an hour. One man dived out the door head first. I stepped over the top of two men. The closest man to the door crawled out head first. I grabbed the ammo belt in the centre of the man I thought next and gave him a heave out nose first. The next man made it crawling on his own power. I reached up and pulled the salvo switch which released the machine gun and mortars attached to the bomb racks under the plane. Then I dived out.[10]

Worse things were happening in other aircraft. In one, carrying the headquarters of E company, 506th Parachute Infantry, a bundle of high explosives was detonated by flak and the aeroplane disintegrated with stick and crew in the middle of a formation, knocking headlong the men waiting to jump in a neighbouring aircraft. In others the door was jammed by over-large equipment bundles or even, in one, by an ammunition cart. Some lines of jumpers were interrupted when one man or several were hit by splinters, so that they had to be unhooked and left in the plane or manhandled to the door and pushed out to take their chance of medical attention on the ground. Incredibly in that highly charged atmosphere, and despite the sheer physical difficulty of standing firm in the stampede for the door, a few men 'refused' – that is, announced that they were unwilling to jump. In all, four men of the 505th Parachute Infantry, one of the 507th and two of the 508th preferred to face the savage disciplinary consequences and total social ignominy of remaining with the aeroplane to stepping into the darkness of the Normandy night. But 13,000 others, whether over their drop zones or not, whether over dry land or the flooded valleys of the Douve or the Merderet, whether over the Cotentin or already beyond its wave-lapped coast, took their courage in their hands and followed their leaders out into the tempest of their aircraft's slip-stream.

# Descent

The static line of the American T-5 parachute, a broad webbing strap hooked at one end to the anchor cable in the aircraft, tied at the other to the top of the parachute canopy, was fifteen feet long. As the parachutist emerged from the cabin of the DC-3, throwing himself outward towards the port wing with a pull of his hands on the edges of the doorway, he was flicked by the slipstream – a combination of the propeller wash and the wind of the plane's own forward movement – to the static line's end. The resulting tug ripped the cover off the pack tray, exposing the canopy of the parachute which it began to pull free by a thinner cord attached to the canopy's apex. At the same time the jumper's body, acting under the force of gravity, began to leave the slipstream and fall earthwards. In the opening sequence of the British X parachute, under which the 6th Airborne Division's soldiers had just landed at the other end of the bridgehead, this separation of jumper and canopy occurred at relatively low velocity, since the static line deployed the rigging lines, twenty-two feet long, joining canopy and jumper's harness so that he was at rest, relative to the canopy itself, when it began to deploy. With the T-5, however, separation of canopy and jumper was dynamic, the canopy itself pulling the rigging lines from his pack tray, and the resulting moment of arrest, as deploying canopy and falling body worked against each other through the rigging lines, could be extremely severe. Known as the 'opening shock', and dreaded by all, it exerted a force of up to five G on the human body and threatened to injure it if the harness were not properly adjusted. As its apogee, it broke the tie at the end of the static line and released parachutist and canopy to fall to earth together.

The sequence took three seconds and the descent, from seven hundred feet, about forty. Burgett, who landed just north of St Martin-de-Varreville, gives a vivid account of his experience:

> Doubled up and grasping my reserve chute, I could feel the rush of air, hear the crackling of the canopy as it unfurled, followed by the sizzling rigging lines, then the connector links whistling past the back of my helmet. Instinctively the muscles

of my body tensed for the opening shock, which nearly unjointed me when the canopy blasted open. I pulled the risers apart to check the canopy and saw tracer bullets passing through it; at the same moment I hit the ground and came in backwards so hard I was momentarily stunned ... The sky was lit up like the Fourth of July. I lay there for a moment and gazed at the spectacle. It was awe-inspiring. But I couldn't help wondering at the same time if I had got the opening shock first or hit the ground first; they were mighty close together.[11]

Colonel Vandevoort, dropped by a flak-wary pilot at far above jumping speed, reported that 'the opening shock popped lights in the back of your eye-balls and tore off musette bags, field glasses and anything else that wasn't tied down securely'. Lieutenant Elmer Brandenberger, of the 1st Battalion, 502nd, was cradling a rifle in his arms. 'The opening shock tore it from my grasp. I can still remember the thought flashing through my mind that it would hit some damned Kraut and bash in his head.' Private Sherwood Trotter, of the 1st/506th, lost a ·30 machine-gun to opening shock and Lieutenant Robert Matthews, of the 377th Parachute Artillery, was knocked out. 'When I got that tremendous opening shock, my chin snapped down on my binocular case and out I went. Came to just off the ground and was knocked out again when I hit.'[12]

Some of the jumpers suffered more serious wounds in the air, though few of these were the result of aimed shots. Despite the moonlight, the falling parachutes showed up poorly against the sky and only in two places, at Angoville-au-Plain, where the Germans deliberately set fire to a house, and at Ste Mère-Eglise, where a building was ignited by the Allied preparatory bombing, did the Germans see well enough from the ground to pick off individuals. One of these was Colonel Wolverton. But there was a great deal of loose metal criss-crossing the parachutists' airspace, and some of it found a billet. Private Guerdon Walthall 'saw tracer go through the fellow below me and I really started sweating about getting hit before I reached the ground', but he did so unharmed. Captain Felix Adams, medical officer of the 377th Artillery, was hit on the helmet ('good old helmet') by a piece of flak and landed unconscious, and another medical officer, Captain Hugh Caumartin, of the 2nd/506th, was hit twice, 'once on the nose – and I worried about what my wife would think when I returned without a nose' and then in the leg. He landed on his unwounded leg near St Martin-de-Varreville, in a field lined with German machine-guns which sent 'streams of tracer in cross fire only a few feet over my head ... Others were dropping into the same field and they were being hit and hurt'.[13] After dosing himself with his own morphia, he disregarded his wounds, crawled off to a hedge and set up his aid post.

# Landing

Medicine could do nothing for those injured in the way parachutists feared most – by landing with a malfunctioning or unfurled parachute. Malfunctions are always rare with a static-line parachute and, because the Americans carried a reserve (which the British then did not), even more rarely fatal. There are no surviving reports of fatal malfunctions from the 82nd or 101st on June 6th (though one gloriously unlucky private managed to open his reserve in his DC-3 as it approached the dropping zone, filling the cabin with billowing silk and driving his stick companions to flights of blasphemy unequalled even by the drill sergeants at Fort Benning). But a considerable number reported being dropped so low that their parachute scarcely had time to deploy or of seeing others whose canopies had not deployed at all. Burgett at St Martin-de-Varreville saw a DC-3, coming in low and diagonally across the field where he was struggling to unbuckle his harness, disgorge a stick of 'vague, shadowy figures ... Their chutes were pulling out of the pack trays and just starting to unfurl when they hit the ground. Seventeen men hit the ground before their chutes had time to open. They made a sound like large ripe pumpkins being thrown down to burst against the ground.'[14]

Some sticks fell to their deaths because their pilots gave them the green light when they had already crossed the east coast of the Cotentin, though at least one dropped close enough to the beach for most men in it to struggle ashore and hit a track through minefields and German strongpoints to dry ground – as hard a way of invading Europe as anyone found that day. Many who landed on the Cotentin drowned all the same, for the floods of the Douve and the Merderet, undetected on the aerial photographs and invisible from the flight path, stood two and three feet deep among the reeds and ripe hay of the water meadows. A man making the regulation sideways roll on landing finished beneath the surface and, if he could not free himself

on one lungful of air from his imprisoning harness, breathed water
and died. Private James Blue, an All American, just escaped that
fate. A North Carolina farm-boy, he was strong as well as fit, had the
good luck to find hard ground under the flood and managed to
struggle to his feet. 'Before he found his balance, his parachute
dragged him over backwards and he went under again, weighed
down by his equipment, fumbling at the buckles of his harness ...
he was half dead when he got clear, sick from the water he had
swallowed and trembling from the shock.'

All along the valleys of the two little rivers, other parachutists
were fighting their own little battles with the unexpected enemy.
Corporal Francis Chapman, of C Battery, 377th Artillery, 'landed in
water about five feet deep. Managed to stand up after a bit of
swimming. Reached down, got my jump knife from the boot top and
slashed my harness, cutting right through my jump jacket in the
process. I managed to wade towards shallow water'.[15] Father Francis
Sampson, Catholic chaplain of the 506th Infantry, landed in water
over his head, cut free his equipment and was then dragged by his
parachute to a shallow patch. He took ten minutes to free himself
from his harness, crawled back exhausted to where he had touched
first and, after five or six dives, recovered his Mass equipment. As
he did so, he saw first one and then two other aircraft crash in flames
near by, and offered prayers for the repose of the souls of the men
within. Hugh Pritchard, a radio operator with a set in his leg bag,
fell into water with 140 lbs of equipment securely fastened to his
body and a back injured by 'opening shock', lost his knife as he
struggled to cut his way to the surface and was reprieved at his last
gasp when his parachute collapsed and ceased to drag him along the
bottom. 'The terror of that first night', he recalled in 1967, 'remains
so vivid even today that sometimes I wake up in a cold sweat and
nearly jump out of bed.'

## Gathering

Other jumpers had fallen into trees, into hedges, on to the anti-glider
poles sown across the flatter fields and known to the German
defenders as 'Rommel's asparagus', one – later to be made famous in
a scene in the film *The Longest Day* – on to the steeple of the church
at Ste Mère-Eglise. But whatever their landing place, those who had
avoided the water had reason to be grateful even though a great

number were injured on impact. In one party of a hundred men assembled by the S-3 staff officer of the 501st, a quarter had sprains or breaks. Some were far too seriously hurt to move. Private Robert Barger, ironically medical-aid man in General Maxwell Taylor's party, unintentionally collapsed his canopy while swinging to avoid tracer on the way down and hit very hard; he sustained a broken pelvis, cracked hip, cracked ribs, broken arms and dislocated shoulder. Others unintentionally wounded themselves in their haste to free themselves from their harness, cutting their fingers or slashing through their clothes into flesh. Private Ernest Blanchard, at Ste Mère-Eglise, realized only after he had got free that he had sawn off the top of his thumb in the process.

But the sensation which afflicted all, hurt or whole, senior officer or junior private, was that of intense and unnerving loneliness. Almost everyone could see and hear the sounds and sights of battle, close at hand or far away. A few, who had studied their maps particularly hard and had had the luck to be dropped in the right place, could tell where they were (Colonel Timmes, commanding the 2nd/507th was one of these). The majority were lost, lonely and afraid. The cloud bank, which had broken the careful approach run of the aircraft, scattered the serials all over the south of the Cotentin, carried them far from the beacons which the pathfinders had set up to mark the dropping zones, and encouraged so many pilots to flash green light at speeds faster than those normal for jumping, was the cause of a dispersal far wider than the airborne planners had feared even in their 'worst case' appreciations. Only two of the six parachute regiments – 505th, significantly a regiment which had worked with its Troop Carrier Group, the 316th, since its first operation in Sicily a year before, and 506th – achieved 'good' drops, that is, the delivery of most of their men to the right zones (DZs 'O' and 'C') at the right time. Two others, 508th and 507th, had very bad drops, the former because it was scattered almost all over the peninsula, the latter because most of its men, though dropped tightly bunched and close to their zone (DZ 'N'), fell into the inundations along the Merderet. The last two regiments, 501st and 502nd, had mixed fortunes. In each, one of the battalions was dropped well, but the other two were scattered and had to spend hours or even days piecing themselves together.

This piecing together, with which all parachute operations began, was in theory simple. A drill, called 'rolling up the stick' taught the soldiers who had jumped first to note the direction of the 'aircraft stream' as soon as they landed and to follow it, the soldiers dropped last to move against its direction and the soldiers in the middle of the stick to stand firm until the two ends met them. But the dispersion of the aircraft serials on this night left no 'aircraft stream' for the jumpers to observe. Because many of the pathfinders had been dropped in the wrong place or had been attacked by the defending Germans, there were few homing beacons for the main bodies to form on. And the battalions' own marshalling parties found themselves often in the wrong place or without the equipment they needed to call the sticks in: the 2nd/506th, which rallied on a green electric lantern and a large bronze bell, lost both in the marshes.

Gathering therefore depended on luck, leadership and the willingness of thousands of isolated individuals to brave the darkness and look for each other. Some – in what number we shall never know – could not bring themselves to do so, or soon gave up. Corporal Kermit Latta of the 377th Artillery confessed that, on failing to find another American, he 'wandered about in the shadows for an hour, took a drink from a pond of stagnant water, found a deep ditch covered with bushes and went to sleep'.

John Urbank, a mortar platoon-sergeant in the 3rd/501st, 'strolled around in the darkness for an hour and couldn't find anybody. By then I was dog tired and so, being the country boy that I am, I found a stand of wheat, walked so I wouldn't beat a path into it, curled up under my innocence and slept until dawn.' Even when a lonely paratrooper made contact with another, sleep might still supervene. Sherwood Trotter, a machine-gunner in the 1st/506th, landed alone, eventually located a buddy with his cricket (the child's cracker toy all Screaming Eagles had been given) and then picked up another nine or ten men.

> We were headed in the general direction of what sounded like a real battle. About daylight we got into a small skirmish with our first Krauts. They were behind one hedgerow and we were across the fields behind another. Within a short time, they broke off the engagement and disappeared. We relaxed and the next thing we knew there were two GIs standing on top of the hedgerow looking down at us. Everyone of us had fallen asleep and slept for the next two hours.[16]

Even soldiers collected by a superior – and the need to collect was

the first thought which came to every officer after he had freed
himself from his harness and identified (or more probably failed to
identify) his position – betrayed this strange readiness to sleep.
Ballard, the commanding officer of the 2nd/501st, who had happened both to fall in the right spot and to recognize it for what it was
fairly quickly collected about 250 men of his three companies, one of
the best assemblies of the day. He himself, through a combination of
responsibility and severe nettle stings, found no difficulty in keeping
awake. But he was acutely worried by

> the dazed reaction of most of his men. Only the soldiers who
> had landed in the marsh seemed relatively alert; soaked and
> shivering, they had to keep moving for warmth. It was
> different with the men who had landed dry; some of them fell
> asleep standing, while Ballard talked to them, then fell head-
> long. When the formation pulled away from the assembly area,
> then paused briefly, Ballard saw men fall in their tracks and hit
> the ground with their eyes closed.[17]

The phenomenon was probably the result of nervous tension
fortified by loss of sleep and dosing with the air-sickness pills
(Drapomine), which had a sedative side-effect. But these clinical
speculations would have been of little comfort to Generals Taylor or
Ridgway or to their regimental and battalion commanders, whose
urgent need was to organize a dozen striking parties and set off for
their objectives before dawn broke. By first light a dozen parties had
been collected, but in nothing like the strengths prescribed and most
often in the wrong spot. In each division over 3,000 soldiers were
either lost or – though this was not yet realized – already dead. Only
one battalion, the 2nd/505th, had dropped both concentrated and in
its planned zone. And, because most of the radio sets had been
dropped separately from their operators in bundles which had gone
astray, few commanders at any level could communicate news of
their isolation and weakness either up or down the chain of
command. Many, moreover, were quite simply lost and could not
establish where they were either from maps, air photographs or such
signposts as they stumbled on.

An obvious thought was to seek directions from the inhabitants.
But few French people in that densely garrisoned countryside were
willing to fall for what might have been a Gestapo ruse or to help
fly-by-night raiders with retribution hot on their heels. Lieutenant

Guillot, whose ancestry stretched back to the land he was invading, had the door slammed in his face when he knocked at a farmhouse near Picauville. An old French couple who did answer near Ste Marie-du-Mont were sure that the Americans were going to kill them, and a farmer whom Colonel Sink of the 506th extricated from his cottage near St Côme-du-Mont with the phrasebook assurance, 'The invasion has begun', shook so hard with fright that he could scarcely lay his finger on the right point on Sink's map. Later, as the sheer volume of the airborne descent made its impression, the country people overcame their nervousness, began to volunteer intelligence of the whereabouts of the Germans and of hidden crossing-places in the inundations, pressed milk and cider on their liberators and lent help to the medical men who brought wounded into their dwellings. These were inevitably to include, as the battle wore on, some of their own number; Bill Kidder, an aid man of the 3rd/506th, recalled twenty years later the gratitude shown him by a French father whose six-year-old daughter had received a severe head wound and who offered 'what must have been his prize possession, his gold pocket watch' in thanks for the bandaging.

But before the dawn most French people kept to their beds or their cellars, leaving the Americans to blunder about looking for each other and their assembly points. Fortunately, until light broke, the Germans on the Cotentin showed no more willingness than the civilian inhabitants to leave the security of their known positions. And so, in the precious hiatus between landing and daylight, half a dozen parties of Americans were given the time, leadership and direction to gather themselves and their weapons and to move out on what would prove to be the vital missions of the operation.

## Action

### 1 The 3rd/505th at Ste Mère-Eglise

Ste Mère-Eglise, the large stone-built village astride Route nationale 13, had seen the first serious shedding of blood between Germans and Americans on invasion night. Two sticks of the 2nd and 3rd Battalions, 505th Parachute Infantry, had been dropped by their pilots directly over the village, in which a house had been set alight by the Allied air raid which preceded the arrival of the parachutists, and many of those floating earthward had been killed in mid-air by

German soldiers who had turned out to stand curfew guard over the volunteer fire brigade. Two, loaded with mortar bombs, had fallen into the interior of the burning house and been killed there, either by the flames or, more mercifully, by the detonation of their loads. Others had hung up on roofs or trees, to be riddled by the Germans before they could cut themselves free. Then, as those lucky enough to land unscathed were taken prisoner or made their escape, the firing had died down and the Germans had gone back to bed.

The readiness of the German defenders of Normandy to observe the normal routines of military life throughout the events of June 6th is one of the stranger features of that extraordinary day. Soldiers are incurably fond of sleep; air raids had become commonplace along the Normandy coast; but the parachuting was a novelty which makes the Germans' adherence to domestic convention inexplicable. Nevertheless, back to bed the garrison of Ste Mère-Eglise went. Thus when Lieutenant-Colonel Edward Krause, commanding the 3rd/505th, came to earth a mile west of the village, exactly in the field he had selected for his assembly, signalled the rest of his stick and took stock of his surroundings, the resistance he was expecting to encounter was already evaporating. His stick was quickly divided into four and sent in opposite directions to collect strays, with orders to be back in forty-five minutes. This netting gathered another ninety Americans, and a drunk Frenchman out after curfew, who revealed that the German infantry battalion which had garrisoned the village until a week before was now camped outside, leaving it in the hands of a transport and supply company. Krause quickly re-organized his command into two companies and marched on the village, keeping to the hedgerows. He had issued, for no good reason 'except that it sounded hard-boiled', the order that there was to be no rifle firing until daylight; 'use grenades, knives and bayonets only'. As the outline of the buildings showed through the dawn, he detached six patrols to set up blocks on all the roads out of the village except the one he planned to use himself. When he calculated that they were in place, he left what remained of his force, crept into the centre, found the cable point carrying all German communications from Cherbourg and cut it through. 'That was one he wished to boast about later.' Finally he called up his main body and sent them to search the buildings around the Place de l'Eglise. Thirty Germans were captured in or next to their beds, eleven were shot on the run, rather more made it into the countryside. At 5 a.m. he sent a runner to find the regimental commander, Colonel William Ekman, with the message, 'I am in Ste Mère-Eglise' and, Napierlike, an hour later, the message 'I have secured Ste Mère-Eglise'. But the runner went astray.

So many messages went astray that morning, or remained unsent because of the lack of means to transmit them, that the misdirection of Krause's news is entirely unremarkable. It did not in truth go entirely astray since it was passed to General Ridgway. But the runner failed to tell him for whom it was intended and Ridgway did not have a radio with which to inquire of Colonel Ekman, who was less than 1,000 yards away, if he had got the word by another route. Moreover, his mind was chiefly occupied with the fight for the bridges across the Merderet. In consequence Ekman continued to believe until mid-morning that Ste Mère-Eglise was in German hands, thus distorting what might otherwise have been a smooth deployment of his three battalions.

His 2nd Battalion, commanded by Lieutenant-Colonel Benjamin Vandevoort, had made one of the very few compact and accurate landings of the night, and by daylight had collected 575 men out of the 630 who had jumped. Vandevoort had broken a leg on impact, as had so many of the senior officers whose slightly greater age made their bones vulnerable to shocks which the private soldiers' absorbed unhurt, but had commandeered a small farm-cart and, like an eighteenth-century Spanish general miraculously endowed with a lion heart, had ordered his men to wheel him on to the battlefield. His mission was to secure the northern approaches to Ste Mère-Eglise, in particular by erecting a substantial roadblock at Neuville-au-Plain, astride Route nationale 13, down which a German counter-attack was expected. At 6.15 a.m. when almost there, he got word from Ekman, with whom he was in radio contact, that he should 'halt in place'. For an hour and three-quarters he heard nothing more, until at 8 a.m. he was subjected to one of those order—counter-order—disorder episodes so characteristic of fluid operations. Ekman first signalled, 'Have heard nothing from the 3rd Battalion'; at 8.10, 'Turn back and capture Ste Mère-Eglise'; at 8.16, 'Proceed to Neuville; I think 3rd Battalion is in Ste Mère-Eglise'; at 8.17, 'Disregard the last order; move on Ste Mère-Eglise.'[18] Vandevoort's response to this flurry of contradictions was remarkably judicious, all the more so in view of the pain he was suffering. He at once turned his force to retrace its steps, but not before detaching a platoon of forty-one parachutists under Lieuten-ant Turner Turnbull to organize a skeleton defence of Neuville.

Turnbull was half-Cherokee, known as 'Chief' in the battalion and much respected for his soldierly qualities, which he was about to demonstrate in their plenitude. Leading his men at a jog-trot, he reached Neuville within a few minutes. It was little more than a hamlet and its east–west axis short enough for the platoon to hold its whole length. On the west was an orchard bounded by open fields, on the right one of the high-banked hedges of the Norman field-system probably already old when William left to conquer England, which met the road at right angles. He put a squad of ten men with a machine-gun he had retrieved next to the orchard, its flank resting on a large manure heap, the rest of the platoon behind the hedgerow, a team of three with a bazooka – the 2·36-inch rocket-launcher with which, with luck and a great deal of bravery, an infantryman might disable a tank – in a building on Route nationale 13 and settled to await events. He did not have long to wait.

After about twenty minutes the men behind the hedge saw a long column of German infantry approaching down the road. They were a company of the 1058th Grenadier Regiment, 91st Division, about 190 strong, and they were singing – another of those bizarre flights of insouciance displayed by the defenders throughout the morning. The squad in the orchard, who were a little farther forward, had observed them also but were waiting for the range to close. When the head of the column was about level, the machine-gunner opened fire and the Germans, apparently unscathed, disappeared into the ditches. Some of them managed to return fire, for the lieutenant in charge of the squad, Isaac Michaelman, was wounded almost simultaneously.

But at the same moment Colonel Vandevoort re-appeared. He had now found a jeep, landed in one of the gliders which had flown in the division's heavy equipment three hours after the drop. It was towing a 57 mm anti-tank gun, extricated with some difficulty from the landing zone. He heard the exchange of fire, saw the German column disappearing into the undergrowth and asked the bazooka team at the road block what was happening. They assured him that the Germans were prisoners, being escorted to the perimeter by some parachutists, and Vandevoort briefly persuaded himself he had seen some American orange recognition panels among the field grey. Moreover, a mysterious Frenchman on a bicycle, who quickly made himself scarce, confirmed the story. But the swelling volume of fire exploded it. Turnbull's men behind the hedgerow had spotted Germans leaving the line of the road and moving into the fields to turn their flank. They sprang into action, bringing to bear two ·30 mm machine-guns, two Browning Automatic Rifles and fifteen rifles. Heartened by the sound, but unable to see for himself what was happening, Vandevoort sent a runner to Turnbull to ask: 'How are you doing? Do you need help?' He returned with the assurance: 'OK, everything under control, don't worry about me.'

Trusting in the Chief's reputation, Vandevoort unhooked the 57 mm to reinforce the bazooka team, and started back in the jeep for Ste Mère-Eglise. As he disappeared, however, mortar bombs began to fall along the line of the hedgerow and shortly afterwards a self-propelled gun came into view about 500 yards up the Cherbourg road. With its second shot it killed the bazooka gunner at the road block and with its fifth drove the anti-tank gunners from their piece. They took cover in the houses but then took heart again, re-manned their gun and hit the SP with two shots. Seeing a tank behind it, which they identified as a Mark IV, probably wrongly for there were few of those heavy models in the Cotentin, they continued firing and disabled it also.

The fight then settled down into one between infantry and infantry, with the disadvantage to the Americans that they were outnumbered and unsupported by heavy weapons. While they held their line, behind the hedgerow on the right and the stone wall in the orchard on the left, they were secure. But the Germans' numbers allowed them the chance to work through the open field beyond and eventually to find positions from which they could shoot into the Americans' rear. It was slow going for them, for Turnbull was vigilant, resolute and well supplied with ammunition. But by early afternoon his position was close to collapse. He had only twenty-three men still in the firing line; of the others, eleven were stretcher cases and nine were dead. Mortar bombs fell in a steady stream along the bank. A sniper had found his way into the hamlet and Private Clifford Keenan, who was posted on the right flank, was killed when he tried to pinpoint his position. Fleeting glimpses of the enemy at hedge gaps revealed that left and right pincer jaws were only 200 yards apart and threatened to close across Route nationale 13, cutting Turnbull and his men off from Ste Mère-Eglise.

His Cherokee blood stirred. 'I have heard about spots like this', he

yelled. 'We're surrounded. That leaves one thing to do. Hit them in
the centre. So we charge them.' One parachutist called back agreement. Another, Private Sebastian, who had just been out to recon-
noitre the right flank, shouted his dissent. He had seen that they
were not yet cut off and urged that Turnbull should lead a breakout
rearward. The Chief, in a fashion more characteristic of Mao's army
than Eisenhower's, asked for a group decision. It was for Sebastian.

Turnbull gathered his survivors. It would be necessary, he
pointed out, to leave the wounded. The aid man, Corporal Kelly,
offered to stay 'and surrender them if I can keep from getting
killed'.[19] Sebastian then volunteered, as the proponent of the retreat,
to stay as well and hold the Germans off with his Browning
Automatic Rifle. Two others made to stay with the wounded too,
but a German bullet killed one as he moved to take his position.
That death started the others, now numbering sixteen, into flight,
and they did not stop until they reached Ste Mère-Eglise. On their
way they passed unknowingly through the skirmish line of another
platoon Vandevoort had sent to their relief. Much earlier in the
afternoon he had fired a flare signal ordering their withdrawal, but
no one noticed it in the heat of the action.

Turnbull's stand on the high ground of Neuville-au-Plain – so
reminiscent in its essentials of one of those little dramas of the Great
Plains in which his ancestors had tested their courage against the
horse soldiers seventy or eighty years before – on the great panorama
of events of that day looks neither particularly heroic nor particularly
significant. Yet for men outnumbered more than four to one,
fighting on unfamiliar ground, at the end of a nerve-racking journey
by air, a parachute descent by night and a stiff cross-country march,
to hold up for eight hours against heavy small arms and mortar fire
and to engage and destroy two armoured vehicles into the bargain is
heroic by any reckoning. And, while they had held up, Ste
Mère-Eglise had been saved from assault from the north, precisely
at a moment when it had come under heavy attack from the south:
at 9.30 a.m. Vandevoort's block on the Carentan road had been
engaged by two infantry companies supported by five armoured
vehicles. On the safety of Ste Mère-Eglise turned that of the whole
airborne bridgehead. So Turnbull belongs not only with the brave
but also with those who saved the invasion. He did not survive to
understand what he had achieved. On the morning of June 7th he
was killed by a mortar bomb.

## 2 The 1st/505th at the Merderet

While Turnbull was fighting his Little Round Top at Neuville, a minor Alamo was being played out two miles to the south-west at the manor of la Fière. Le Manoir was a collection of strong, stone-walled buildings around a farmyard, at the eastern end of a bridge across the Merderet which carried the road from Ste Mère-Eglise into the zones of the 507th and 508th Parachute Infantry Regiments. Not only was its seizure and use essential for their security, it was also needed as a crossing place for the 4th Division, when it arrived from the beaches, in its drive to the west coast of the Cotentin.

A whole battalion had therefore been assigned to seize both it and the second Merderet bridge at Chef-du-Pont at the outset of the landing; Major Kellam's 1st/505th, and Able Company in particular, were to secure le Manoir. The company had an excellent drop 1,000 yards east of its objective, collected all but 2 of its 136 men in 60 minutes, together with their equipment bundles, and marched for the bridge. The leading files were actually despatched as the last serials were touching down, a copybook achievement which the planners had expected to be repeated all over the peninsula.

The company commander, Lieutenant John Dolan, covered the advance of the company with a strong patrol under Lieutenant George Presnell which, within 300 yards of Le Manoir, was sprayed by machine-gun fire. It touched no one but drove them all to cover, from which Presnell, after hurling a futile grenade, ordered a withdrawal. His report persuaded Dolan that the bridge was too strongly defended to be taken by *coup de main*, so Dolan set up the company's battery of 60 mm mortars in a near-by orchard and began peppering le Manoir's masonry with their ineffective little projectiles. Tiring eventually of this exercise, he decided to envelop the buildings from the rear and sent off a patrol on a long cast to the south. And he then decided on a frontal assault down the road.

Frontal assaults on defended buildings, if unsupported by artillery, verge on the suicidal and the platoon commander to whom the order came, Lieutenant Donald Coxon, listening to the volume of German automatic fire the mortaring had provoked, answered, 'Well, sir, if I must send someone out into that, I'll go myself.' Taking a scout, he crawled down the hedge beside the road for a hundred yards until a bullet killed his companion. He was almost immediately wounded himself, and began to crawl back for help, but was hit again by a bullet which tore open his stomach wall. Before help could reach him he bled to death.

Worse was to follow. The other officer in the platoon, Second-Lieutenant Robert McLaughlin, came forward to take the lead. His radio operator was hit and, when he moved to give him aid, he was hit also, the bullet passing through his thigh, buttocks and lower stomach. The battalion executive officer, Major James McGinity, who was watching the scene from the spot McLaughlin had just left, was almost simultaneously shot through the head by a sniper. Dolan, who was at his side, spotted the source of the fire before it shifted to him, drilled the sniper with his tommy gun and then crawled to tend McLaughlin's wounds. The stricken second-lieutenant begged not to be moved, because he was in such pain. Dolan therefore left him but crawled back when it began to drizzle to cover him with a raincoat. In the interval he had bled to death also.

Dolan had now lost ten dead and twenty-one wounded, almost a quarter of his company, in its first eight hours on French soil. The time was about 10 a.m. He dared not send any more men down the road, and he feared that if he manoeuvred off it he would run into the patrol he had detached under Second-Lieutenant Oakley and risk an exchange of fire between friends. So, for an hour, he lay and pondered. At about 11 a.m. he sent a runner to look for Oakley, but the man ran into the regimental commander, Colonel Lindquist, and passed to him the news of the disaster which had struck Able Company. As it happened, General Ridgway arrived at almost the same moment, heard the news and ordered Lindquist to make the battle for le Manoir his first priority.

Like Dolan, he pondered, but with rather more despatch. He already had one force, a scratch collection of men of the 507th under Captain Ben Schwartzwalder, out on the left of le Manoir, on which it had made two costly and unsuccessful attacks earlier in the morning. He now knew of Dolan's and could pinpoint it on his map. He therefore decided to co-ordinate the actions of the two and launch a pincer movement against the farm at midday.

He sent out orders accordingly. Schwartzwalder was alerted. But the messenger who should have reached Dolan got lost in the small fields which surrounded the manor and did not find him. As Schwartzwalder prepared to move off, he was departing, though he did not know it, on another of the lone missions which had already failed several times that morning.

Mischance now intervened for the third time. Dolan's subordinate, Oakley, whom he had been frightened of running into unawares, had not got lost, but merely followed a very circuitous route to the far side of le Manoir. Just before midday, he judged himself, after three hours of hedgerow-crawling, to be in position to attack. He and his platoon sergeant, Oscar Queen, braced themselves to charge from the last hedgerow to the stone wall which surrounded le Manoir's farmyard. As they emerged from cover, supported by the fire of the other members of the patrol, they were counter-charged by one of the defenders, who was firing a Schmeisser machine-pistol. He fell dead, as did two others behind him. But Queen had seen into the rear of the machine-gun position which had killed so many of Dolan's party on the main road. Covered again by the rest of the patrol, he made a short run to throw a grenade but was toppled over by a counter-throw. Recovering his senses, he heard the movements of a sniper in a tree above him and brought the man down with a shot from his carbine. He then ran back to Oakley to report what he had seen.

The patrol's machine-gun team made a dash for the spot Queen had left, saw the German machine-gunners and killed them. They were just about to make the final charge into the courtyard of the manor when fire from the opposite direction announced the arrival, quite unexpected to them, of Schwartzwalder's column. The Germans were now at last enveloped and the survivors showed a white flag. An American who stepped forward to accept the surrender was shot dead, probably by one of those involuntary trigger reflexes so common at the moment of capitulation. Magnanimously, the Americans did not take their revenge. Three Germans had been killed by Schwartzwalder. The survivors of the garrison were made prisoner.

They numbered eight. Throughout the morning circumstances exactly the opposite of those embroiling Turnbull at Neuville had prevailed at le Manoir. It was the Americans who had outnumbered the Germans, and by a very considerable margin. About 300 Americans, altogether, had tried in turn to capture the little fortified farm. It had been held throughout by a platoon of the 1057th Regiment of the 91st Division, who had turned up, apparently on an anti-invasion exercise at 11 p.m. the night before. They had roused the startled owner, M. Louis Leroux, from his bed and he had had the chance to count them. They totalled twenty eight. Good soldiers all, they had, like the 2nd Light Battalion of the King's German

Legion at la Haye Sainte, done their duty to the end. There was a
more telling parallel between the two tiny sieges. La Haye had fallen
because Wellington did not get word that the defenders were
running out of ammunition. The great clouds of smoke which
enveloped the Waterloo battlefield cut sight of it off from him at the
crucial moments of the action. Le Manoir had held for as long as it
did for a similar failure of communication. Had the Americans been
able to recover their radio sets from the bundles parachuted into the
marshes of the Merderet, Dolan, Lindquist, Schwartzwalder and
Oakley would have co-ordinated their movements from the outset
and the bravery of the German defenders would have availed them
scarcely at all.

## 3 The 2nd/507th at Cauquigny

But the consequences of the loss of the radio sets were not yet ended.
At the far end of the bridge covered by le Manoir de la Fière, a
sizeable fragment of the 2nd Battalion, 507th Regiment had been
assembled by its commander, Lieutenant-Colonel Charles Timmes.
He himself had nearly been drowned on landing in the marshes of
the Merderet, but had collapsed his parachute at his last gasp and,
when recovered, had collected men in dribs and drabs until he had
enough to march on Cauquigny, the village immediately across the
river from la Fière into which its bridge and causeway led. At Cauquigny he had been fired on by a vigilant German picket and, after
losing eight men, had fallen back to an orchard a mile to the north.

He had no radio and thus no means of discovering that Lindquist
was probing westward towards him at le Manoir, separated from
contact only by the handful of Germans in the bridge guard.
Between 9.30 and 11 a.m., moreover, he was busily engaged
encouraging his men to dig themselves in against German fire,
which was falling heavily in and around his concealing apple trees.
But he then decided that he ought to try again at Cauquigny, the
importance of which he had not forgotten, and selected Lieutenant
Louis Levy to take ten man back to the village and dig in round its
church. Their orders were to cover by fire the western end of the
causeway through the floods which terminated in the la Fière bridge,
denying it to the enemy until a stronger force of Americans could
relieve them either from the west or east.

Levy's group set off at once, armed with a Browning Automatic

Rifle and a sackful of anti-tank grenades. On the way they fell in with another party of twenty from their battalion, commanded by Lieutenant Joseph Kormylo. He had already been to Cauquigny, judged himself too weak to hold the bridge and withdrawn – but then changed his mind. He was thus on his second approach when he and Levy met. Exchanging notes, the two decided to send the bulk of the force back to Colonel Timmes in the orchard, while Kormylo and a machine-gun team joined Levy. Together they led the slightly enlarged party into the village, found it now empty of Germans and sited their machine-gun to cover the road down to the bridge. The riflemen dug themselves in behind the walls of the churchyard and, that done, settled down to lunch off K rations; a villager appeared to soften the fare with milk and cider. Shortly afterwards more Americans appeared, two lieutenants and thirty-seven men of the 508th, who offered to join them in the defence. Levy readily accepted and sent a runner back to Timmes with the news, justified by the circumstances, that he had secured the bridgehead. Kormylo, meanwhile, had gone to explore the bridge itself and, the time being midday, caught the rattle of fire which marked Oakley's and Schwartzwalder's final assault on le Manoir. Shortly afterwards he saw an American approaching from that direction, threw an orange flare to reveal his presence and not long afterwards met Schwartzwalder himself leading his troops forward to secure, as he thought, the position which Levy already held. All three officers shook hands happily. Schwartzwalder had had a little fight on the causeway, but had killed or made prisoner all the Germans there and now pronounced both it and the bridge clear. Levy therefore doubled quickly across to see Lindquist – the distance was less that a thousand yards – and doubled back to find Schwartzwalder about to move off again, anxious to reach his original objective at Amfreville. When Levy told him of Timmes's location, he decided instead to join forces with him and took all the men in the churchyard, less Levy's original patrol, Kormylo and the two other lieutenants.

Lindquist had followed Levy from le Manoir, surveyed his position and returned intending to reinforce it. Before he could do so, however, Levy's handful of stalwarts heard the sound of approaching tanks, the unmistakable and unnerving squeal of metal track on tarmac. Mysteriously an ambulance with German markings appeared and a Red Cross flag was waved from the door before it drove off. Then five shells fell a little short of the churchyard, and others beyond it along the river bank. Levy shouted a warning to expect an assault, called Kormylo and a private from his line of riflemen, and ran forward along a sheltering hedgerow towards the sound of the advancing tanks. They were preceded by infantry, a small group who passed Levy's hiding-place without seeing him. Kormylo and the private – the two officers never discovered his name – fired on them and then, as the tanks appeared opposite them in the road, ran. Levy stopped to throw a grenade at a machine-gun team who were setting up their weapon, jumped into the road to kill the survivors with his rifle, emptied the rest of the magazine on the front armour of the leading tank, and joined Kormylo and the unnamed private, who had stopped to cover his flight. Levy was helmetless, bleeding from the shoulder and 'laughing like a maniac'. The strange euphoria of combat which sometimes comes to a man, often in the most desperate circumstances, had him in its grip. He ran back past Kormylo into the churchyard where only six of their parachutists were still in position, and stood throwing grenades at the German's tanks until he had none left. Then, with Kormylo, but without their faithful private, who was killed by a bullet at the last moment of the fight, they left the field.

They were not the last to go. Private Orlin Stewart, who had been posted apart from the others, had not seen the course of the fight and was still in position when the leading tank appeared beyond the churchyard. Mysteriously it was hit by a shot from an unidentified source and burst into flames. Stewart had a supply of Gammon grenades and, seeing two other tanks behind the flaming leader, picked them up and ran towards them. When he paused to shelter in the ditch, he was joined by a sergeant and another private, strangers to him, who were also carrying Gammon grenades. The sergeant said, 'Hi!' and, as the tanks – two old French Renaults – drew opposite, he and his companion stood up and threw. Stewart, electrified by their example, stood up also and fired his Browning Automatic Rifle. The others continued to throw grenades, theirs and Stewart's. Five heavy explosions followed, the tanks slewed burning to a halt, and the crews jumped out of the hatches. A moment later another tank, accompanied by a large party of infantry, came round the corner and Stewart and his nameless comrades, taking one look, legged it into the fields to catch up with Levy, Kormylo and the other heroes of the Cauquigny fight. Decisively outnumbered, they had decided to fall back on base in the orchard and seek security with the Timmes party.

## 4 The 3rd/506th at the Douve Bridges

The lack of radio communication between Timmes on the west bank of the Merderet and Lindquist on the east had thus had dispiriting consequences. It had denied the two colonels the chance to make a concentric advance on the bridge when that vital link across the marshes might have been theirs for the asking. It had hidden from them the fact that, by mid-morning, both ends were effectively under American control which only a stretching out of hands was necessary to consolidate. And when, by happenstance and the bravery of a few individuals, the bridge had actually been secured for their use, it had blinded them to the slenderness of their hold on it and so had given it back to the Germans. The American parachutists would pay terribly in the next days to recover the disregarded prize.

Eight miles to the south-east, in the most exposed corner of the airhead, a second task force was groping to find crossings across the other vital waterway, the Douve, but in full realization of the difficulties and in the teeth of heavy German resistance from the outset. The task force was drawn from the 501st Parachute Infantry and the 3rd Battalion, 506th. Most of the four battalions had had good drops, but two, Colonel Ballard's 2nd/501st and Colonel Wolverton's 3rd/506th, had fallen on to ground which the Germans of the 91st Division had identified as a likely dropping zone and where they were lying in wait. There had been instant carnage. The 3rd/506th had suffered particularly grievously. The battalion commander, Lieutenant-Colonel Robert Wolverton, his executive officer and one of the rifle company commanders were killed on the drop zone. The headquarters company commander and the other two rifle company commanders were taken prisoner, and there were proportionate casualties among the junior officers and soldiers. Only 117 of the battalion's 800 men were to appear at the objective, and the operations for which the battalion had been trained would be commanded by a comparatively junior staff officer from battalion headquarters, Captain Charles Shettle.

Shettle, 'one of nature's silent men', had the good luck to fall on the edge of the drop zone, which the Germans had illuminated by setting fire to a petrol-soaked building, and so avoided the deadly streams of fire poured against those who fell more accurately. The light from the blaze helped him to use his compass and map, and he quickly identified the bearing of the battalion assembly area and moved on it, cutting across the fields. He found the spot empty and so began to search for lost parachutists, until he had assembled two lieutenants and thirteen enlisted men. His foundlings suggested waiting until the party was stronger before marching on the objective. But Sheettle thought differently and his voice carried a note of authority. So the sixteen set off for le Port and its two bridges, the farthest downstream on the course of the Douve, a mile from the drop zone. Their orders were of the simplest: they were to take possession and hold against all German attacks until relief came, when the crossing places would be used to connect the bridgeheads of Utah and Omaha Beaches.

Shettle reached the bridges at about 4.30, soon after dawn. On the way he had picked up another two officers and sixteen enlisted men and at the objective he was joined by another twenty parachutists, five of them officers. (This large ratio of officers to men, 10:49, was typical of the airborne operation in its early stages, leading General Maxwell Taylor to comment, 'Never in the history of human combat have so few been led by so many'). Shettle called a short conference, which decided that they would have to put a party on the far bank, and then called for volunteers. Two men stepped forward. One, Private Donald Zahn, had a light machine-gun. The other, Private George Montilio, had the ammunition. The first was ordered to race to the far end and set up his piece. He made it, though his sprint called to life at least one German machine-gun, hitherto undetected, and he reached the safety of a ditch amid a hail of bullets. Montilio also made the passage unscathed but, though they then began to return the enemy's fire, the reinforcement which Shettle sent after them – two teams each of five men and an officer – found it possible to get across only by swinging arm over arm along the girders between the treadway and the water.

During the next two hours, by aggressive use of fire and movement, Zahn's machine-gun covering short dashes by the riflemen, the fourteen men on the south bank of the Douve shot or grenaded three German machine-gun crews. But the volume of fire did not abate and Shettle, forced to recognize that the Germans had more men available than he had ammunition, decided at mid-morning to recall his men from the other side and seek help elsewhere. He had no radio and so no glimpse of how the battle was developing, and his first thought was that he might get help most quickly from the south rather than the north. He therefore sent off a brave officer and two men to break through the German lines and make contact with the American V Corps at Omaha Beach, quite unaware that at that moment V Corp's ability to leave the water's edge and find a foothold ashore hung in the balance. By mid-afternoon, without word from any direction and still more worried, he decided to leave the position and seek help from his regimental commander, if he could find him. After a good deal of searching, he ran Colonel Johnson to earth in some farm buildings at la Barquette, also on the Douve, where he was trying fruitlessly to take possession of a lock across the river. Johnson was in a furious temper. He had lost many men from his small party and the commander of his one intact battalion, Robert Ballard, had just refused a direct order – if for the good military reason that circumstances dictated otherwise – to muster on his position.

Shettle, at the best of times a poor advocate, thus got nothing for the trouble of his dangerous journey, except an order to hang on and a promise that the attached naval officer, Lieutenant Farrell, who had miraculously recovered his large specialized radio from the marshes, would pass on news of his predicament to General Taylor. Farrell, who had trained as a parachutist in order to support the Screaming Eagles and was as stout-hearted as any who jumped that night, was busy directing the 8-inch guns of the USS *Quincy* on to German positions between Carentan and St Côme-du-Mont, but found time to pass on the message. It brought no succour, for Taylor had none to offer. The arrival of forty stray parachutists in early evening helped Shettle repel an enemy attempt to recapture his end of the bridge, but they had no machine-gun ammunition with them and this last effort had consumed his reserve. As the dusk of D-Day fell, he remained in precarious and incomplete control of what he knew was one of the division's most vital objectives, but with no assurance that he would not be driven from it next morning as soon as the Germans could mount a counter-attack in strength.*

* Shettle was able under cover of darkness to wire the bridge for demolition, thanks to the arrival of some parachute engineers with their equipment, and during the next day more of the battalion appeared, until he had 150 men present. Before he could use his new strength to mount a further attack, however, American P-51 fighter-bombers appeared overhead, failed to see the orange recognition panels put out to warn them off, and destroyed both bridges by bombing. Shettle was finally relieved in his lonely outpost on D+2.

## 5 The 1st/502nd at WXYZ

Shettle's bold and brave effort to seize his objective had been frustrated by the presence of superior and well-prepared enemy forces, against which only the full battalion might have been expected to prevail. Away on the northern extremity of the airhead, however, an even smaller force meanwhile had succeeded in overcoming superior forces at a critical point, largely because of their unpreparedness and the manic recklessness of a single soldier.

He was Staff Sergeant Harrison Summers. His battalion commander, Lieutenant-Colonel Patrick Cassidy, short of men and with a variety of missions to perform, had assigned to him the task of capturing a German coastal artillery barracks, known from its map signification as WXYZ, while he set up a command post and sent the rest of his slim battalion northwards to mount road blocks at Beuzeville and Foucarville, between Neuville (Turnbull's field of glory) and the beach. He could allot Summers only fifteen men, few of whom were from the 1st/502nd, and Summers had no time even to ask their names. They followed him willingly enough from Cassidy's command post but, when he deployed them within assaulting distance of WXYZ, he detected that they had little enthusiasm for his leadership or the coming fight. He decided therefore on the most dangerous course of action a leader can adopt: to advance alone in the hope that his example would draw the others in his wake.

WXYZ was a collection of thick-walled, stone farm buildings strung out along some 700 yards of road leading to the beach at Exit 4. The nearest was a small farmhouse. Summers sprinted for the door, kicked it in and sprayed the interior with his Thompson sub-machine-gun. Four of the defenders fell dead, the rest escaped through a back door to the neighbouring house. Summers looked round. Not one of his men had followed. They were sheltering in a roadside ditch. He charged the second house. The enemy left before he entered but his example now had its first effect. One of his fifteen, Private William Burt, came out into the open and set up his light machine-gun to cover Summers's movements. This took him to the third building, fifty yards away, from which the defenders were shooting through loopholes. On his run Summers noticed that he had been joined by a lieutenant he knew, Elmer Brandenberger, but the officer was badly wounded as they reached the door and

Summers entered alone. Again he sprayed the interior, killing six Germans and driving the remainder out of the back.

Summers was temporarily overcome by the physical and emotional shock of his single-handed demonstration. He crouched beside the building he had most recently cleared to recover, and it was half an hour before he moved again. But as he rose to go he found at his side an unknown captain from the All American, misdropped by miles, who said, 'I'll go with you.' He was shot through the heart almost with the words on his lips and Summers again found himself entering an enemy-held building without company. This time he killed six Germans and the rest ran out to surrender to his followers, who had crept up the ditch to within talking distance. One of them, Private John Camien, spoke.

'Why are you doing it?' he asked.

'I can't tell you', answered Summers.

'What about the others?'

'They don't seem to want to fight', said Summers, 'and I can't make them. So I've got to finish it.'

'OK,' said Camien, 'I'm with you.'[20]

Side by side, they worked their way down the row of buildings ahead of them, five in all, pausing to rest between each and swapping Camien's carbine for Summers's Tommy gun to take turns between charging and giving covering fire. In their rear, Burt, the machine-gunner, followed along to give extra support with his heavier weapon. Between the three of them they killed thirty more Germans.

Two buildings remained untaken. Summers charged the first and kicked the door open to find inside, inexplicably deaf to the fight raging around them, fifteen German artillerymen seated at mess tables eating breakfast. He paused neither to reason why nor think of mercy; battle-crazed, he shot them all down in their places.

The last building was the largest and strongest in the WXYZ complex. Between it and the American party, which now included some of the stragglers who had been following Summers along the cover of the roadside ditch, stretched a small, flat and open field. From the cover of a bank, the attackers surveyed the objective. To one side of the building stood a shed and a haystack; Burt, Summers's lone machine-gunner, set up his weapon to fire tracer at them. Within minutes both were ablaze, the shed exploding as ammunition stored within caught the heat, driving its thirty German occupants into the open, where they were shot down. A new reinforcement to Summers's group now arrived with a bazooka and, deciding that the walls of the last strongpoint were too stout to be penetrated by its rockets, fired at the roof instead. After seven shots flames began to lick through the rafters and torn tilework and to spread downwards. As the upper storey took fire the Germans in the lower storey continued to maintain a steady fusillade from loopholes in the walls. But as the heat rose their fire slackened and the collapse of the floor above drove them out to the waiting muzzles of the parachutists. Fifty died in the open. The survivors scattered into the hedges, but their escape was short-lived. When the Americans moved forward with levelled guns, thirty-one emerged with raised hands to offer their surrender. Those who had run earlier may have made the same gesture. But now that resistance was at an end, the mood of this terrible little battlefield changed. The attackers, suddenly numerous as the noise of fighting died away, lowered their weapons and hustled the prisoners to the rear. WXYZ thus passed to the invaders, and with it the last obstacle to free movement between Exit 4 and the landing zones. The 1st/502nd had accomplished its mission.

Summers, bruised and bleeding all over his body from sharp and sudden encounters with door frames and house corners – a characteristic minor wound pattern of the street-fighting soldier – collapsed exhausted by his five hours of combat. As he lit a cigarette, a witness of his extraordinary exploits asked him, 'How do you feel?'

'Not very good', he answered. 'It was all kind of crazy.'[21]

# 6 The 3rd/501st at Pouppeville

While Sergeant Summers had been fighting his almost single-handed battle on the road to Exit 4, another group with an embarrassment of leaders had been assembling on the route to Exit 1, three miles to the south of WXYZ. The 3rd Battalion, 501st Parachute Infantry, commanded by Lieutenant-Colonel Julian Ewell, was a reserve battalion whose initial mission was to protect the drop of the headquarters party of the 101st Airborne Division. The assembly point was on Drop Zone C, near Hiesville, east of the road joining Carentan and Ste Mère-Eglise, from which it was to be moved later to reinforce other battalions which signalled that they needed help in taking their objectives.

The battalion's serial of Dakotas had been badly scattered on the run-in, however – one gallant pilot who failed to find the mark circled over the Channel for some time before picking up the beacons on a second attempt – and three were shot down by flak, with the loss of most of the passengers. Ewell was one of the few members of the battalion who landed close to the rallying position, but when light broke and he was able to count heads he found he had only 40 of his 600 men. But because the pilots of the headquarters planes had dropped accurately, his group also included most of the divisional staff, including the commander, General Maxwell Taylor, and the artillery commander, General Anthony McAuliffe (who, six months later at Bastogne, would return the immortal 'Nuts' to the surrounding Germans' demand for his surrender). Taylor had landed alone in a field of cows, searched for some time for a fellow American and warmly embraced the first one that he met, one of Colonel Ewell's riflemen. Together they had set out to look for more, picked up General McAuliffe on the way and arrived at base to discover that officers almost outnumbered men in this corner of the invasion battlefield. Besides the two generals, there were three colonels, a major and numerous captains and lieutenants waiting to command a collection of signallers and clerks. Regular riflemen and machine-gunners were in a minority.

The signallers, too, were without their radios. General Taylor's heavy command set had been dropped in two separate loads, and though one half had been brought in by its operator, the other could not be found. The divisional artillery could raise no answering call. Taylor was therefore without the means to communicate with the rest of his command or to discover how the land lay – literally, for during much of the night he had been unable to persuade himself that he was in the right place. It was only when dawn showed him the loom of the distinctive church tower of Ste Marie-du-Mont a mile to the east that he was able to convince himself that he was where he ought to be. But, without troops to lead, that knowledge did him little good. He and his chief of staff, Colonel Higgins, conferred. The map told them that the nearest point of significance was Exit 1, at the southern end of Utah Beach, through which the leading infantry of the 4th Division were due to make their way inland later that morning. The road to it ran through the little coastal village of Pouppeville, organized as a German strongpoint. After agreeing with Higgins that the division must have been badly dropped and that they could not for the time being hope to function as a divisional headquarters, Taylor decided, 'It remains for us to help the 4th Infantry Division in every way possible', and gave orders for the party to march to capture Pouppeville. A few specialists were left to man a skeleton command post. The rest, with the generals in the van, marched off towards Pouppeville. It was about 6 a.m. and they numbered about eighty.

They had about three miles to cover and their route lay first across country. When they found the road into Pouppeville they also began to draw enemy fire from scattered outposts in the ditches and fields, but pressed on to reach the outskirts of the village at about 9 a.m. The party now numbered about 150, having picked up stragglers during its approach march, but only 40 were combat infantrymen. The headquarters personnel were to prove an encumbrance in the coming fight. Some, indeed, fell asleep on the start line from nervous anticipation as they waited for the order to attack. It came as the first salvoes of onshore bombardment from the invasion fleet impacted. The parachutists advanced to discover that the landward edge of the village was covered by a network of trenches, but that these had been abandoned by the Germans, who were hiding in the houses of the village itself. They were not numerous but willing to fight and not only shot accurately as the Americans broke from one place of cover to another but pushed fire groups out to take them in flank. Major Legere, General Taylor's assistant operations officer, was badly wounded in the leg in the village street, Colonel Ewell was hit on the helmet, and a lieutenant and a private were killed as they tried to work their way forward. General Taylor almost became a casualty to one of his own men, who mis-threw a grenade which bounced off the side of the window he was trying to throw it through and exploded by their position. By relentless pressure during three hours of skirmishing, however, the parachutists drove the Germans from one house to another until only the village school remained in their hands. A bazooka was found to bring it under fire and after a few shots a German officer ran out. Ewell shot at him but missed. He was trying to offer surrender. When the facts were established he called out the rest of his men to surrender. They numbered 38, the survivors of an original garrison of 630. The Americans had lost 6 dead and 12 wounded.

A few more Germans were observed running along the causeway towards the beach and a party was sent after them. The fugitives

were found hiding under a small bridge and summoned to surrender. As they filed out, more movement was observed nearer the sea.
A tank appeared. The Senior American present, Lieutenant Luther
Knowlton, was asked by his sergeant if it was German. 'Damned if I
know,' said Knowlton. 'To hell with it, I'm firing,' said the sergeant.
The patter of his shots on its armour brought it to a halt. An orange
recognition panel was displayed from behind its turret hatch. It was
an American Sherman. Knowlton threw an orange smoke grenade in
reply and it ground forward to make contact. In its wake a line of
little orange flags showed above the lip of the roadside ditch, waved
by American infantrymen who had also made their way up from the
beach. They belonged to the 2nd Battalion, 8th Infantry Regiment
of the 4th Division and their officer, Captain George Mabrey,
walked forward the 200 yards which separated the two invasion
forces, airborne and seaborne, to shake Knowlton's hand and clasp
him in embrace. This element of the Overlord plan had worked
almost to perfection.

As the tanks and infantry of the 4th Division began to file through
Pouppeville, they passed General Taylor standing in the village
street to watch them through. 'The invasion is succeeding', he told
Colonel Higgins. 'We don't have to worry about the causeways. Now
we can think about the next move.' He had to think of strengthening
his road blocks at Ste Mère-Eglise, securing the bridgeheads across
the Douve which would give access to the Omaha hinterland, and
opening and holding the causeway across the Merderet to the
positions of the 82nd in the interior of the Cotentin. There were days
of hard fighting ahead, and it would be harder still in Ridgway's
divisional area, where Ste Mère-Eglise would be counter-attacked
heavily next day and German strongpoints continue to hold out
within the landing zones across the Merderet until June 11th.
Throughout those days and until long afterwards, the lost and
scattered parachutists of both divisions would continue to find their
way back to the now solidifying perimeter. One group 33 strong was
adrift 14 days before coming in, and lost 29 of its members in daily
skirmishes while coming in; another was lost for 17 days; some
groups, dropped as much as 25 miles south of their assembly points,
deep within enemy-held Normandy, were never heard of again. But
Taylor's snap judgment was nevertheless the right one. For all its
wastefulness, the airborne descent on the margin of the Utah Beach
was a success. The very extent of its scatter, for all that it was

unintended, had multiplied the effect of confusion in the German high command, preventing it from offering any organized riposte.

It was appropriate and characteristic that the effect should have been produced by Americans. Like pioneers in an unknown land, ignorant of its language and landmarks, uncertain of what danger the next thicket or stream-bottom might hold, confident only in themselves and their mastery of the weapons in their hands, the best and bravest among them had stifled their fears, marched forth and planted the roots of settlement in the soil that was there for the taking. Whether or not it might be held would turn on the strength and resolution of those who came later, on D-Day, on the fighting skills of the shipborne divisions who debarked in the wake of the airborne landings. It was they who must fight the battle of the beachhead which Montgomery had warned from the start would be the test of the cross-Channel strategy.

# CHAPTER 3

## *Canada: To the South Shore*

THIRTY-FIVE MILES EAST of the drop zones of the American parachutists, and five hours after they had touched earth, the North
Shore Regiment of the 3rd Canadian Division started the difficult
trans-shipment between the ships in which they had crossed the
Channel and those from which they would step out on to the beaches
of France. They had come as far as the 'lowering point', seven miles
out, in a Landing Ship Infantry (LSI), a converted cross-channel
steamer which, in peace, had carried tourists to France. Conversion
had meant no more than stripping its sides of lifeboats and replacing
their davits with a heavier-duty type, from which could be swung a
port and starboard row of LCAs. The Landing Craft Assault was the
lowliest class of vessel admitted to the books of the Royal Navy.
Commanded by a petty-officer coxswain, it provided nothing but
rough benches for thirty-five men – a platoon of infantry – and a
diesel engine just powerful enough to push them ashore at ten knots.
When its flat bottom touched ground, the bow ramp would swing
down and the passengers would catch their first glimpse of the
Continent. Now the lines of LCAs bumped and grated along the
flanks of the mother ship, pitching between the tops of four-foot
waves under an overcast sky. From some Landing Craft Infantry
(LCIs) the assaulting infantrymen slid to the waiting steel bottoms
down a canvas helter-skelter, to land with a loud thud. From most
they negotiated a painful and dangerous descent down scrambling
nets, strait-jacketed in sixty pounds of equipment, feeling for
footholds which would save them from the mincer of the two hulls or
the deep six in between.

The North Shore was a New Brunswick regiment, from the coast
opposite Prince Edward Island, a land of old settlement both by
French and Scots. An interwar amalgamation of several local militia
battalions, it had its older origins in that great surge of enthusiasm

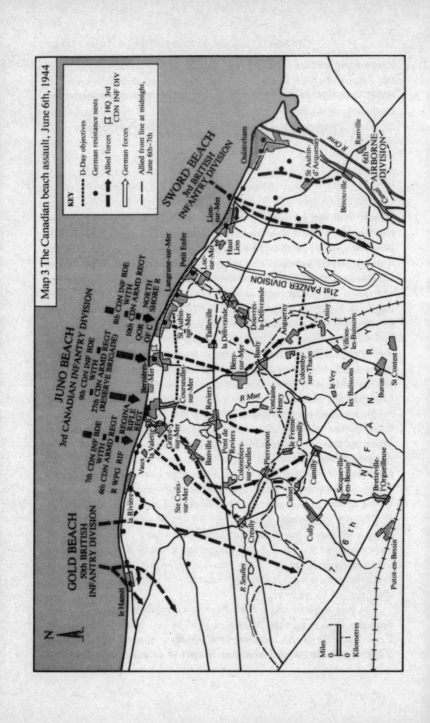

Map 3 The Canadian beach assault, June 6th, 1944

for amateur soldiering which had dotted mid-Victorian Britain and the empire with an outpost line of frustrated patriots, burning to close with an enemy who stubbornly refused to materialize. Hodden-grey doublets and stout canvas gaiters had been their livery, romantic territorial titles their trade-mark. But nowhere, not even in the English Nottingham where the Robin Hood Rifles had stood forth to defend the city against Louis Napoleon, had their titles rolled more romantically off the tongue than in Canada: Voltigeurs de Québec, St Clair Borderers, the Grey Battalion, Manitoba Grenadiers, Argenteuil Rangers, Megantic Light Infantry, Lisgar Rifles, Princess Louise Fusiliers, 48th Highlanders, Temiscouata and Rimouski Regiment – the roll call read as if by Tennyson ('Form Riflemen, form!') out of James Fenimore Cooper.

When a real enemy, the Kaiser, had at last presented himself, and Canada had responded to the challenge – 'Our answer goes at once,' Laurier, the French Canadian imperialist had trumpeted to parliament, 'and it goes in the classical language of the British answer to the call of duty, "Ready, aye, ready!"' – these titles had gone into the melting pot of a new army. The Canadian divisions which had captured Vimy Ridge in 1917, the Canadian Corps which, with the Australians, had won the great battles of autumn 1918, had been composed of anonymously numbered battalions. But the men had been the same as those who had combined to soldier for Queen Victoria – descendants of the United Empire Loyalists who had fled the United States for Ontario and the Maritimes after the War of Independence ('Historically a Canadian is an American who rejects the Revolution'), Scots in their thousands displaced by the Highland clearances or tempted from the lowland city slums by the word of a 'working-class empire' across the Atlantic, English and Irish caught by the dream of free land on the prairie,

> an infinitesimal dot on the vast expanse, a wagon drawn by a yoke of oxen, a woman and a child or two on top, a man driving the animals ... moving away from the railway, day after day, stopping at night along the trailless way, until at last it reached its destination, the long-dreamed of quarter section ... they searched until they found the surveyors' signs, three freshly dug holes and a marker ... no house welcomed them, no barn – nothing but the land and the sky.

These were the people who had made the new Canada, who had

driven the Canadian Pacific from coast to coast, strung the beads of shanty townships along its unifying thread, pushed the frontier of settlement to the edge of the permafrost and yet, however sharp the goad of poverty or intolerance which had driven them from home, volunteered in their hundreds of thousands to make the return journey in khaki and, in their tens of thousands, die for King George in the trenches round Ypres or on the long downland slopes beyond Arras.

There was another, older Canada. It too had powerful military traditions – of settlement by the Régiment de Carignan-Salières, fresh from victory over the Turks at St Gotthard in 1664, of endemic warfare against the great Iroquois confederation, of Frontenac's daring excursions into British America, of the triumphant defence of Quebec against the British in the War of the English Succession. But the central and abiding element of the tradition was threnodic. French Canada lived with the memory of Montcalm's defeat by Wolfe at the gates of Quebec in 1759, which, like Victor Emmanuel's defeat of the papal army at the Porta Pia in Rome in 1870 – there were French Canadians among the Pontifical Zouaves – had not merely imposed an alien sovereignty on a Catholic patrimony but had driven its leaders and subjects into a self-imposed internal exile. French Canada, in its heart, had never accepted the severance of the link with France. But equally French Canadians shunned association with the French of the Third Republic. They too rejected a revolution and, through their loyalty to a clerical church, semi-feudal society and narrow provincial patriotism, had isolated themselves both from their conquerors and from their historic homeland.

The outbreak of war in 1914 therefore presented their leaders with an exquisite dilemma. 'Je me souviens' is the motto of Quebec Province, and the memory is rich in associations with the land and civilization of Old France, which the German invasion of August and September violated both in fact and spirit. Memory's stirrings were powerful enough in the circumstances to tempt politicians and churchmen alike in Quebec to overcome their distaste both for the godless republic and the protestant empire and encourage French Canadians to volunteer. And the men were there. French Canada had not been immune to the volunteering impulse of the 1860s, and there were numerous French-Canadian battalions of militia – like the Carabiniers de Mont-Royal, the Battalions of Joliette, St Hyacinthe and Trois-Rivières – from which might have been drawn the nucleus of a powerful increment to the Canadian Imperial Force. But the bigotry of the Scottish and Orange Presbyterians who dominated the Canadian defence establishment determined that that should not be. Their decision had dissolved the old battalions of the militia. It also denied that French-Canadians should have their chance to serve together in the new numbered battalions. By the time the decision was reversed, enthusiasm for the adventure had waned and the firebrands of nationalism were reminding their audiences that the 'Prussians of Ontario' were not only as anti-French as the 'Prussians of Europe' but much nearer at hand and better equipped to do French Canada harm.

Thus, of 300,000 Canadians serving overseas in August 1917, only 14,000 were French, 4·5 per cent of the Imperial Force, though the French represented 20 per cent of the population of the dominion. And they were all volunteers, with few at home willing to reinforce or replace them. And, by 1917, the replacement of casualties had become the most pressing need in all the armies party to the First World War. The French and German armies had always been conscript, the British had adopted conscription the year before. It was now Canada's turn. But the prospect of conscription, even more than the menace of 'Regulation 17' which imposed English-language teaching in the French schools of Ontario, outraged the French Canadians' sense of nationhood. Their representatives fought the passage of the Conscription Bill tooth and nail through parliament, and when at last it was passed its targets disappeared to the forests and fishing grounds of the St Lawrence in numbers so large as to make it an empty measure.

So grave was the threat to the shaky unity of Canada offered by the conscription crisis that postwar federal governments determined never again to impale the country on a military issue. The right to declare or abstain from war independent of Britain was extracted from the home government in 1922 and, on the repatriation of the Imperial Force, the old militia was reconstituted with its traditional names and comfortable local loyalties. At the outbreak of war in 1939 it was the militia battalions which were called out and, as in 1914, each individual serviceman was invited to decide whether or not he would serve overseas. Mackenzie King, the Prime Minister, had delayed the declaration sufficiently to emphasize that it was made in sovereign independence – and also to allow French Canadians to reveal the undoubted support they felt for the Anglo-French cause.

Their motives were ideological rather than nationalist: sympathy for the Catholic Poles and hostility to Hitler rather as the Bolsheviks' friend than Britain's enemy. But the effect was the same. A Montreal militia battalion, the Régiment de Maisonneuve, was the first in Canada to produce a full complement for overseas service and, by January 1941, over 50,000 French Canadians were serving in the armed forces. They provided nearly a third of the strength of the Royal Canadian Navy and fifteen of the seventy-five infantry battalions. Of those, only four – the Royal 22$^e$, the Régiment de la Chaudière, the Régiment de Maisonneuve and the Fusiliers de Mont-Royal – were to find enough volunteers to join the Canadian army abroad, the rest remaining in home service. But numbers of other expeditionary units contained a significant proportion of French Canadians – like the Royal Rifles, tragically thrown away in the defence of Hong Kong – so that in general the federal government, whose Deputy Minister of Defence was a French Canadian, could congratulate itself by 1944 that it had taken Canada into the war without, as in 1914, dangerously threatening the unity of the dominion.

It was keeping to itself the anxiety that the coming battles of the Second Front threatened to inflict such losses on the First Canadian Army as could only be filled by pressed men. But all Canadians, even if they did not yet foresee how the invasion might precipitate a second conscription crisis, had special reason to hold their breath as what must be the invasion summer drew on. For Canadians had been to the south shore of the Channel once before in this war, to Dieppe in August 1942. The appalling casualties which the 2nd Canadian Division had suffered on the beaches there in a single morning, had then forced even the most optimistic advocates of a Second Front to recognize that 'Now' was certainly premature, that 1943 might still prove too soon. And neither they, nor the great mass of ordinary citizens of the dominion – English and French, Scots, Irish, Ukranians, Poles, Finns, Swedes and all the other immigrant contingents who had chosen the St Lawrence instead of the Hudson as their gateway to the new world – could be certain even in June 1944 that the 3rd Canadian Division was not bound for a second Dieppe.

## Dieppe: the Awful Warning

Dieppe, in retrospect, looks so recklessly hare-brained an enterprise that it is difficult to reconstruct the official state of mind which gave it birth and drove it forward. Churchill himself in the planning stages expressed anxiety, and was confirmed in support for the operation only by the insistence of General Sir Alan Brooke that 'if it was ever intended to invade France it was essential to launch a preliminary offensive on a divisional scale'. Churchill was moved too by the need to offset in some way the recent loss of Tobruk, to say nothing of his loss of face with Roosevelt and Stalin through his opposition to Operation Roundup. And there were the raiding successes achieved by the Commandos – his 'Tigers' – at Vaagso and the Lofoten Islands to lend reassurance. But a few Viking victories by the pick of the army over the small and third-rate garrisons of remote Norwegian fishing havens provided no basis at all for judging how a full-scale military operation against a defended Channel port would go. The Commandos, clinging to the edge of the sea mists of the far north, had always achieved surprise. The 2nd Canadian Division was to sally forth in high summer from ports only seventy miles from the German-occupied coastline and disembark on the esplanade of a French seaside resort. The justification for choosing an objective which the Germans were known to occupy in strength was that the feasibility of capturing a harbour by direct assault had to be tested. The risks were discounted by the argument that Commandos would disable the flanking batteries which bore on the beaches and harbour exit and that the close-in defenders would be overcome by tanks landed from the new Tank Landing Craft directly in the muzzles of their machine guns. And, to cap their case, the staff officers of Combined Operations Headquarters invoked the legendary fighting qualities of the Canadians, who had broken the Hindenburg Line in September 1918 after two years of abortive effort by the rest of the Allied armies.

But bravery was to count for nothing on the morning of August 19th, 1942. The Commandos, attacking up the high cliffs which march almost to the mouth of the little river Arques on which Dieppe stands, achieved their customary surprise and silenced the flanking batteries. But the battalions of Canadian infantry and the tanks they had brought with them were stopped almost as soon as they left their landing-craft, sometimes before.

The Royal Regiment of Canada, one of the three permanent battalions the dominion maintained in peacetime, was detailed to land in the mouth of a narrow gully which led into the cliffs at Puys, east of the harbour. It was defended by a company of the German 571st Regiment and some Luftwaffe anti-aircraft gunners. They had watched the approach of the landing-craft and, as soon as the ramps went down, directed the desperate fire of outnumbered men at the open mouths of the vessels. The Canadians, like the Irishmen on the *River Clyde* at Gallipoli, reeled momentarily before the storm and then burst through the curtain to find shelter under the sea wall. It was capped with wire. They blew a gap with their bangalore torpedoes. The first few scraped through to the cliffs beyond. The rest were barred by fire on the gap and killed by machine-guns firing 'in enfilade' – that is, at an angle to the Canadians' line of advance – from under the wall. Twenty minutes later a second wave of landing-craft arrived, and soon after a third, carrying a company of the Black Watch of Canada. The landing-craft drew off behind them. Fire implacably denied their advance. By 8.30 a.m. every man on the beach was dead or captive. They had begun their landing only three hours before. The party which had crossed the sea wall was, by report of the German 302nd Division, 'annihilated by assault detachment of 23 (Heavy) Aircraft Reporting Company' – a hastily assembled band of Luftwaffe technicians. Out of 554 Royal Canadians who had disembarked, 94·5 per cent had become casualties; 227 had been killed. Almost all were from the city of Toronto.

At Pourville beach, west of the town, the South Saskatchewans and Cameron Highlanders of Canada found a landing place protected from the worst of the German fusillade, fought all morning and got off with only a hundred casualties apiece. But in the centre, at the harbour and along the promenade, disaster was almost as complete as at Puys, and highly spectacular. For here Combined Operations Headquarters had decided to experiment with the direct disembarkation of a new tank – the Churchill – from a new type of assault vessel, the Landing Craft Tank. Each carried three tanks. There were ten LCTs, of which the first three were to beach with the craft carrying the two assaulting infantry battalions, the Royal Hamilton Light Infantry and the Essex Scottish. In the event they arrived late, and only five of their tanks managed to get off the beach on to the promenade. The three following waves got ten of their tanks on to the promenade. But their crew, like those in the first wave, found that access to the town was blocked by large concrete obstacles, which the accompanying sappers were unable to destroy with explosives. All the tanks were therefore confined within a zone on which heavy German fire played. At first the fire was from guns too light to penetrate the thick armour of the Churchills, and the officers aboard the landing vessels offshore listened with admiration on their radios to the 'cool and steady voices' of the tank crews co-ordinating their fire to support their infantry comrades. Gradually however the enemy brought heavier calibres to bear and, one by one, the Calgary Regiment's tanks fell silent. None was evacuated from the beach. Very few of the Hamiltons and the Essex Scottish got away; the first lost a hundred, the second two hundred dead. And, to crown the tragedy, at the last moment the force commander landed his 'floating reserve', Les Fusiliers de Mont-Royal, who were bracketed by concentrated German artillery during their ten-minute run-in to the beaches, and drenched with fire as they touched ground. The French Canadians nevertheless stormed from their landing-craft. But shortly they too had lost over a hundred men killed and were pinned to the shingle, unable either to advance or retreat.

When the badly shocked survivors of that terrible morning were got home and heads counted, only 2,110 of the 4,963 Canadians who had set sail the day before could be found. It became known later that 1,874 were prisoners, but of these 568 were wounded and 72 were to die of their wounds, while 378 of the returning were also wounded. Sixty-five per cent of the Canadians engaged had there-fore become casualties, almost all of them from the six assaulting infantry battalions, a toll which compared with that of July 1st, 1916, first day of the Battle of the Somme and blackest in the British army's history. The 2nd Canadian Division had, for practical purposes, been destroyed. Six months later it was still in the category of 'lowest priority for employment' in the Canadian army.

Strategic as well as human criteria applied in measuring the scale of the disaster. All the tanks which had been landed had been lost, 2 by swamping between ship and shore, the other 27 by enemy action or mechanical breakdown. Lost also were 5 of the 10 precious Landing Craft Tank. And, auguring worst of all for the future, the damage had been done not by hastily summoned reinforcements but by the forces already present; the 3 Canadian battalions which had stormed the central beach had been opposed by a single German company – at odds, that is, of 12 to 1 – and the tanks and landing-craft destroyed by 28 pieces of pre-placed artillery, most of medium calibre. The gunners had worked hard – their returns showed 7,458 shells fired – but they could not be expected to work any less hard on a future occasion. And though not all these details were yet known by Combined Operations Headquarters, after-action reports and prisoner interrogation yielded enough information to point to a depressing disparity between the power of the attack and the defence. It clearly could not be overcome merely by increasing the numbers of those embarked for the assault. That would be to repeat the mistakes of the First World War, when the solution of greater numbers resulted arithmetically in greater casualties for no territorial gain. It would have to be offset by a change in technique.

It is as illuminating to say of Dieppe – as it was and is often said – that it taught important lessons about amphibious operations as to say of the *ateliers nationaux* of the 1848 revolution that they taught important lessons about state intervention in the economy, or of the *Titanic* disaster that it taught important lessons about passenger liner design. In the last case no improvements could compensate the victims, in the second none could rectify an experiment which was fundamentally misconceived. Even if Canada could not do so, it was better that the planners should forget about Dieppe. And so, in a sense, they did. The Germans concluded from the experience that the Allies, when they came for the Second Front, would still land near a port but would seek to surround it. The planners decided that they would steer as far clear of ports as possible. Fighter cover – which had worked very well at Dieppe – and the maximum radius at which it could be provided would impose the only territorial criterion they would accept. Inside that line they would look for a coastline with open beaches, low cliffs or none at all and a positive absence of harbour facilities.

But one lesson was drawn, by the man best placed to perceive it and, as luck would have it, subsequently to put it into practice. Captain (later Vice-Admiral) John Hughes-Hallett had acted both as Naval Adviser to the Chief of Combined Operations, Lord Louis Mountbatten, before the operations and as Naval Commander during it. He had come back from the raid naturally impressed by the importance of air cover – the RAF had brilliantly succeeded in sparing the Canadians the crowning agony of air attack – and concerned by the need to add to the number and types of landing-craft, to rehearse their crews in a variety of simulated beach assaults and to keep such a specialized force in permanent existence. But he was above all determined to ensure that no landing should ever again take place without covering firepower sufficient not simply to hinder the enemy from using his weapons but to shock him into inaction, stun him into insensibility or obliterate him in his positions. '*The Lesson of Greatest Importance*', his report capitalized and italicized, '*is the need for overwhelming fire support, including close support, during the initial stages of the attack.*' It should be provided by 'heavy and medium Naval bombardment, by air action, by special vessels or craft' (which would have to be developed) 'working close inshore, and by using the firepower of the assaulting troops while still seaborne'.[1] He wrote while the naval events of the operation burned fresh in his memory. It reminded him of his four little Hunt-class destroyers, armed with four 4-inch guns, duelling with the German shore batteries, forced to use hastily laid smoke screens for protection against the heavier metal which their thin sides did not provide and still suffering grievous damage each time they emerged into the sunlight. Goronwy Rees, aboard HMS *Garth*, recalled that 'the manoeuvre became monotonous and repetitive, and each time harder on the nerves, especially after we had been hit twice, the second time with considerable damage and casualties'.[2] *Garth* survived (though HMS *Berkeley*, hit by German bombs, did not) but she and all the other ships of the bombarding force limped home in the knowledge that, in this latest episode of the four-century-old struggle between ship and shore artillery, they had been clearly worsted.

## Fire Support

By D-Day Hughes-Hallett had left the planning staff to get in his sea-time as captain of HMS *Jamaica*. But he had left his legacy. The fleet of landing-craft which had disembarked the 2nd Canadian Division had indeed been kept together, under his command (as J Force), had added to its complement all the specialized craft for which he had seen the need, had rehearsed incessantly to improve its approach, support and beaching techniques and, for the critical test, were actually assigned once more to embark and deliver the Canadians. It and the 3rd Division had practised together first in October 1943 during Operation Pirate, a large-scale exercise held at Studland Bay, the Dorset beauty spot, and had perfected their co-operation in Operation Trousers, held at Slapton Sands, Devon, in April 1944.

Though they did not know it, the Slapton Sands landing had foreshadowed in almost every detail that planned for D-Day itself. The sole missing element had been the full bombardment, too

destructive to be unleashed even on remote beaches which had seen
no holidaymakers since August 1939. Now, as the battalions bobbed
queasily in the LCAs alongside the mother LSIs, British and
*Acadiens* of the North Shore Regiment, Scots of the Canadian
Scottish, *Québecois* of the Régiment de la Chaudière, English of
Ontario in the Queen's Own Rifles, prairie settlers of a dozen
backgrounds in the Winnipeg and Regina Rifle Regiments, their
flotilla was enveloped on either hand and as far as the northern
horizon by an enormous fleet of bombarding vessels.

Heaviest and farthest out were two battleships, *Ramillies* and
*Warspite*; the second had fought under Beatty's orders at Jutland
twenty-eight years and four days before. They both mounted four
15-inch guns, and there were two more in *Roberts*, their accompanying monitor. Their chief task was to engage the large-calibre shore
batteries between the Orne and the mouth of the Seine, but so great
was their range – over eighteen miles – that they could in emergency
be talked in on to any target in the British bridgeheads by one of the
thirty-nine naval forward observers who would land with the troops.
Immediately port and starboard of the lowering position was
disposed a line of twelve cruisers, the smallest, like *Diadem*, mounting eight 5·25-inch guns, the largest, like *Belfast*, twelve 6-inch.
Both were covering the Canadian beaches, their guns initially
targeted on batteries at Ver-sur-Mer and Moulineaux. In front of the
Canadian lowering position manoeuvred the supporting destroyers,
eleven for the Juno sector, each mounting between four and eight
guns of 4- or 4·7-inch calibre; one was Norwegian, one French, two
Canadian, HMCS *Sioux* and *Algonquin*. And immediately ahead of
the assault-wave infantry was deployed a small fleet of support
landing-craft: eight Landing Craft Gun, a sort of small monitor
mounting two 4·7-inch guns; four Landing Craft Support, bristling
with automatic cannon; eight Landing Craft Tank (Rocket), on each
of which were racked the tubes for 1,100 5-inch rockets, to be
discharged in a single salvo; and eighteeen Landing Craft Assault
(Hedgerow), which were to fire their loads of twenty-four 60 lb
bombs into the beach obstacles and so explode as many as possible of
the mines attached to them.

That did not exhaust the provision of on-board fire support. The
fourth group of assault vessels comprised twenty-four Landing Craft
Tank, each carrying four 'Priests', a 105 mm field gun on a Sherman
chassis, of the self-propelled artillery regiments. They were to fire

at selected targets on the run-in, concentrating on four identified 'resistance nests'. Two squadrons of the 2nd Royal Marine Armoured Support Regiment would join in, firing with the 95 mm howitzers of their Centaur tanks from hull-down positions in the water as soon as they reached shore. And, of course, most celebrated ingredient of the landings, there were the DD tanks. DD stood for Duplex Drive – the term revealed the American origin of the invention – a gearing device which used the Sherman's Ford V-8 engine to drive either the tracks on land, or in water a pair of propellers. The DD Shermans' speed in the water was not great – four miles per hour was a realistic allowance – and they could not fire while afloat, since they derived their buoyancy from a canvas screen, supported on struts, which rose high above the turret. In the water, indeed, the crew were literally submariners, their seats being below sea level and the commander steering by standing on the turret top and shouting instructions through the open hatch to his driver. A small pump expelled the sea lop which found its way over the top of the screen, in moderate seas at any rate. But when the tank touched ground, the canvas screen was deflated and the gunner could at once bring his 75 mm to bear on beach targets. A DD tank regiment had been assigned to each of the two Canadian brigades which would land on D-Day, and would swim thirty-eight of its tanks ahead of the landing-craft. To compensate for their slow rate of progress, they were to be the first craft which would actually commence the run-in to the beaches, though their departure time was so calculated that they would arrive only just enough ahead of the infantry to 'shoot them in' as their Landing Craft Assault touched down.

All in all, therefore, 3rd Canadian Division could look to a weight of support for its venture to the south shore over twelve times as great as that which had covered 2nd Division's assault on Dieppe two years before. Instead of 16 4-inch guns, there were to be 198 pieces firing. Some, like the 48 'Priests', were to be rough and ready in their effect, which was to stun and deter rather than destroy. Others, like the guns of the destroyers, were to direct pinpoint fire at bunkers and batteries on the beaches and to keep on firing at them until they were silenced. The big guns of the cruisers, directed by the refined techniques of naval ballistic science, were to crack the concrete shells of the heavy coastal batteries, invisible inland. And the one-shot rocket salvoes of the specialized landing craft, were to create devastating blast waves at the main German centres of resistance. All the German defences would, in addition, have been subjected to heavy air bombing before the landing fleet came within sight of the shore, an ingredient of the offensive the German defenders of Dieppe had been spared for fear of killing large numbers of French civilians.

## The German Defenders

Yet more heartening to the Canadians, had they known the facts, would have been the knowledge that the German defenders of the Beach they were to assault – codenamed Juno – were considerably fewer than those present at Dieppe. There, on an offensive front of about four miles, which exactly equalled that of Juno, the German 302nd Division had had two battalions in line – eight companies each of about two hundred men – and two companies of combat engineers. They had been disposed, moreover, in commanding positions on the cliffs or in bunkers along the sea front, difficult to distinguish among the many buildings of the town and immune, by Cabinet fiat, from air attack. By 1944 the 302nd was long gone from France. A mobile field formation of fit and mature men, it had departed for the maelstrom of the Russian front. The soldiers whom the Canadians would meet were of a different order. They belonged to the 716th Division, one of a group of *bodenständige* organized on a weaker scale than the field divisions, equipped with older, very often foreign weapons captured in earlier campaigns, and lacking the transport to manoeuvre effectively should they be expelled from their initial line of defence. As a token of mobility, one battalion in each *bodenständige* division was mounted on bicycles. The only other mechanical, and sole automotive, vehicles the formation possessed was the divisional commander's staff car. Everything else – the guns of the divisional artillery and the supply wagons of the infantry battalions – was pulled by horses. The men were expected to march.

And they could not march well. By definition the soldiers of the *bodenständige* divisions were too old or too feeble to find a place in the first line. The German army had not yet been reduced to forming 'dyspeptic' and 'flat feet' battalions, as it was to be in the crisis of the coming winter. But the 716th's soldiers – under eighteen, over thirty-five or victims of third-degree frostbite – were not the physical equivalents of the magnificent young Canadians, hardened by two years of intensive and realistic training, who now

bobbed offshore in their landing-craft waiting for the signal for the
run-in. They lacked the Canadians' fitness. They lacked their variety
of experience. And, most important of all, there were fewer of them.
At Dieppe the Germans had opposed six battalions with two and a
half. On Juno they were to oppose nine battalions with less than one.
The 736th Infantry Regiment was one of two in the 716th Division.
Its sister, the 726th was largely absent from the divisional area,
however, only one battalion remaining in reserve behind the
defences of Juno. This allocation of force meant that General
Richter, the divisional commander, had only four German battalions
with which to defend a front of nineteen miles. He had also been
given two 'East' battalions, the 642nd, which was not in line, and the
441st, which was; its quality was believed to justify the risk of using
it in a close reserve role but, on D-Day, it was to run away all the
same. He had naturally put his Germans in the immediate front line,
a string of bunkers and trenches which closed the exits from the most
open beaches. He had also tried to retain a reserve, to counter-attack
against a break-in, choosing the II Battalion, 726th Regiment. In
consequence, each of his twelve companies of the 736th Regiment
had to hold over a mile of front. There were therefore only three
directly in the path of the Canadians, the 5th and 6th Companies and
part of the 7th, numbering in all about 400 men. And they were
about to be attacked by 2,400 men in the Canadian first wave,
supported by 76 swimming tanks and a shattering weight of air and
sea bombardment.

If they were to hope to survive, it would be through the greater
degree of protection which they enjoyed and the response of their
own artillery. The 716th Division, if weak in infantry, was officially
reckoned to be strong in artillery. The division had its normal
complement of field and medium batteries, 8 of the former and 4 of
the latter. There was also a self-propelled artillery battalion of 3
batteries belonging to 21st Panzer Division in its area and under
General Richter's tactical control. Extra to the divisional allotment
were 3 batteries of 155 mm guns and 2 of coast artillery. The total
number of pieces on paper was 83. However, 3 of the divisional
heavy and one of the field batteries had been lent to 352nd Division,
defending Omaha and Gold Beaches to the west, so the true total
was 67, including 4 Polish, 8 Czech and 5 French guns, captured in
the Wehrmacht's easy days, of very varied calibre. All the heavier
guns were supposed to be under concrete, but Rommel's accelera-

tion of the building programme had not touched everywhere in
716th Division's area, and only two battery positions – mounting the
Czech 100 mm guns – had been completed. Elsewhere the crews
were protected only by unroofed bunkers; many were in earthen gun
pits in the open fields. Unable for the most part to change their
positions while in action – it would be out of the question to bring
the horses to the gun lines during a counter-battery duel – the
German gunners were thus fated to fight where they stood against
three times their number of guns, all mobile either by sea or land,
and many of far heavier calibre than they could match.

The infantry companies were better protected. On the Canadian
beaches they occupied four 'resistance nests' (*Widerstandnester*)
at Vaux, Courseulles, Bernières and St Aubin, each centred on
one or more heavy concrete gun positions. The gun positions were
supplemented by trenches and gun-pits, usually concreted, for
machine-gunners and riflemen, and surrounded by barbed wire and
minefields. All the weapons were sited to fire along the beach in
enfilade, and their zones of fire were calculated to interlock on the
menacing array of obstacles arranged just below high-water mark.
These – lines of concrete stakes pointing seaward, backed successively by rows of wooden ramps raised six feet at their landward end,
concrete tetrahedra, iron 'hedgehogs' and finally in some places, as at
Courseulles and Bernières, by 'C Elements' (sections of massive iron
obstacles stripped from Belgium's pre-war anti-tank defences of her
eastern frontier) – were designed to tear the bottom out of invading
landing-craft as they attempted to beach on a falling tide. Many were
also festooned with Teller mines, fused to explode on touch. The
combination of fixed obstacles and enfilading fire from the resistance
nests was deemed to guarantee the destruction of any landing force.
So, at any rate, the defenders were assured. But no senior officer,
and certainly not General Richter, could feel that the beaches were
really adequately defended. The resistance nests were 2,000 yards
apart on average, at the extreme limit of automatic weapon fire from
each other, and none was occupied by more than a platoon of men.
They had a certain number of crew-served guns to supplement their
personal weapons: at Vaux, where the Winnipeg Rifles would land, a
75 mm gun; at Courseulles, the Regina Rifles' objective, 3 50 mm,
2 75 mm and an 88 mm, as well as 12 machine-guns, the largest
concentration of weapons on the Canadian beaches; at Bernières,
objective of the Queen's Own Rifles, 2 50 mm guns and 7 machine-

guns; and at St Aubin, for which the North Shore Regiment was destined, a 50 mm gun and 4 machine-guns. There were also 7 mortars, of 50 or 81 mm calibre, distributed between the strong-points and a number of electrically operated flame-throwers.

But, however the odds were counted, the human disparity remained. About 400 Germans were about to be attacked by 2,400 Canadians. The defenders were forbidden to give ground. Hitler himself had decreed the doctrine of 'an unrelenting line of resis-tance', in which he had been schooled in Flanders as a soldier of the 16th Bavarian Reserve Regiment. And even should they try, they would be prevented, for their encircling girdles of wire and mines served not only to keep – they hoped – the enemy out, but also to keep them in. Nor could they look for any large or quick reinforce-ment from the hinterland. The four reserve companies of the 736th Infantry Regiment were disposed two miles inland on average. The main reserve, II Battalion, 726th Regiment, was nearly four miles inland and in the wrong place at the far western end of the divisional area. None of these units could move faster than their feet would carry them. And the nearest mechanized reserve, the panzer-grenadier battalions of the 21st Panzer Division, were six miles away at Caen, and their half-tracks highly vulnerable to air attack on any daylight journey. Like the Goths slaughtered at Vesuvius by the Byzantines in 553 – a folk-memory increasingly favoured by Nazi propagandists as the shadows drew in over the Reich – the striplings and greyheads of the 716th Division had death before their eyes on the morning of June 6th.

## Bombardment

The weather had spared them, however, from the first instalment of destruction which the Allies had planned to deliver on their posi-tions. Two major air-bombing raids had been included in the preparatory fire-plan, a midnight attack by the heavy night bombers of RAF Bomber Command, and an early-morning raid by the Flying Fortresses of the Eighth US Army Air Force. The RAF's standard of accuracy had greatly improved in the last year, aided by the target indicating skills of the pathfinder squadrons it had added to its strength. And in weight of bombs dropped – 5,268 tons – the D-Day raid was the heaviest Bomber Command had yet mounted, the unusually short range allowing it to economize fuel against payload.

But the prevailing low, thick cloud frustrated its efforts. The results of the bombing were described as 'spotty'. The heavy battery at Mont Fleury, the target closest to the Canadians' beaches, survived. At dawn the Americans had taken up the attack. But because there were now large concentrations of Allied shipping under the overcast, the staff of Eighth USAAF had secured Eisenhower's last-minute agreement to the pathfinders delaying the release of their markers by up to thirty seconds after they had crossed their aiming point. None took the risk of releasing on time and, in consequence, the thousand Flying Fortresses all dropped their bombs well inland, 'from a few hundred yards up to three miles'. Because of the thinness of the German beach defences, very few – and none in the Canadian sector – were therefore hit, the bombs falling in the open fields to begin that great slaughter of the dairy herds of Normandy which was to be one of the smaller horrors of the campaign.

The bombing did not even alert the defenders to what it presaged, so accustomed had they become in the past weeks to the regular raids of the two air forces. Nor did warning reach them from the higher commands, since what signs Seventh and Fifteenth Armies and Naval Group West detected were so scanty and conflicting that they were not judged the basis for a firm directive. Deprived of radar cover, and with the patrol groups of E-boats and U-boats taking advantage of the unfavourable weather to lie in harbour, OB West (German supreme headquarters in France and the Low Countries) was shorn of the antennae on which it counted for long-range forecasts of danger. First news of the American airborne landings brought an order to both Seventh and Fifteenth Armies to go to the state of 'highest alert'. But that had happened before and Seventh Army did not apparently consider that the alert required the presence of the divisional commanders with their divisions, since no cancellation was issued to them of a summons to attend the army war game at Rennes the following morning. Nor did the beginning of the naval bombardment, reported by LXXXIV Corps at 6 a.m., clarify things for the higher command. At 6.45 a.m. Seventh Army's routine morning report to OB West read: 'Purpose of naval bombardment not yet apparent. It appears to be a covering action in conjunction with attacks to be made at other points later.'

By then the men in the beach bunkers were all too aware of the purpose of the naval bombardment – the heaviest, though they could not know that, ever fired from ship to shore. It was designed to kill

them. From 5 a.m. onwards they had heard the whistle of heavy
calibre shells from *Belfast* and *Diadem* arching high over their heads
to land on the concrete battery positions of the heavy guns at
Ver-sur-Mer and Bény-sur-Mer. At 6.19 the destroyers had begun
firing and the volume of their fire swelled as they moved closer to the
shore. By 7.10 it was supplemented by that of the Landing Craft
Gun, and shortly afterwards by the creeping barrage of the
embarked self-propelled artillery. While it was still possible to look
seaward, a few had seen looming through the dawn 'countless ships,
ships big and small, beyond comprehension'. After 7 a.m., H-Hour
minus forty-five, it was no longer possible to see and very dangerous
to look, for the whole of the sea front boiled with the smoke and
debris of explosions and the crash of aimed fire rang inside the
concrete of the bunkers. Few bunkers – only about 14 per cent a
target-analysis team later calculated – were destroyed, but the houses
prepared for defence along the beaches – those little brown and
yellow, half-timbered holiday cottages, *style paysan*, which summoned their owners August after August from Paris and Rouen –
were collapsed from the inside, roofs falling on to floors and the
walls subsiding to choke the streets behind with banks of rubble.
The defenders, wherever they sheltered, were stunned by the noise
and shock waves, magnified a hundredfold at the last moment by the
gigantic salvoes of the rocket ships, each discharging a broadside
equivalent to a hundred Diadem-class cruisers firing simultaneously.

'Neutralization' was the technical term which the planning staffs
used to describe the effect they hoped the bombardment would
achieve. It meant that those defenders left alive after the fire lifted
from their positions should not, through fear, shock and disorienta-
tion, be able to bring their weapons to bear on the landing parties
until they were upon them. How well the bombardment had done its
work would tell in the last few hundred yards of the landing-craft's
approach and the first minutes on the open sands of the beaches.

# Run-in

It was a topsy-turvy world in the invading fleet. Three hundred and
sixty-six ships of all sizes, from Landing Craft Assault to a 6-inch
gun cruiser, were milling about off Juno, in a sea area ten miles deep
by five wide. By 5.30 a.m. the slowest, the Landing Craft Tank with
the amphibious squadrons of the armoured regiments aboard, had

begun to make their way shoreward, shepherded by pilotage and control craft and the light support vessels. An hour after them had started the heavier support craft, with the destroyers manoeuvring on their flanks. Next came the engineering group, Landing Craft Assault (Hedgerow) armed with the bombs which would breach the beach obstacles, the embarked assault tanks of the Royal Marines and AVREs (Armoured Vehicles Royal Engineers) which were equipped to throw heavy charges at concrete bunkers and tank traps, and the flail tanks of the mine-clearing troops. In their wake came the first wave of Landing Craft Assault, filled with the spearhead companies of the infantry battalions. Each was attacking with two companies in the first wave, and two in a second wave to follow a quarter of an hour behind. Behind the leading companies the rocket ships took station and behind them the special Landing Craft Tank with the 96 Priests of the self-propelled artillery regiments, each programmed to fire 3 shells for every 200 yards covered towards the beaches.

Order, rehearsed in a dozen exercises, imposed itself on the confusion. And the spectacle of the armada, so terrifying to the Germans who could spare a glance for it, brought courage and even inspiration to the infantrymen peering over the bare steel gunwales of the LCA. But it was difficult to feel inspired in the sea conditions which the retreating bad weather had brought. The wind blew at fifteen knots, raising four-foot waves, driving white breakers on to the shore and pushing the rising tide towards the beach obstacles which the choice of H-Hour should have left uncovered. The infantry had been given anti-sea-sickness pills before they left the landing ships, but they had also been fed a warrior's breakfast and most suffered agonies of sea-sickness as their assault craft circled in the chop waiting for the signal to run in. When it came, the motion improved, but the increased speed brought wave-tops spuming over the landing ramps, soaking clothes and equipment and adding to the chill of the grey morning.

Some of the smaller craft found the sea conditions too much for their low freeboard, puny engines and heavy loads. The Landing Craft Assault (Hedgerow) found the going particularly hard. It had been decided to tow them inshore but, even so, only one out of the nine reached the right-hand Canadian beach. 'The remainder had foundered or had to be cut adrift before entering the swept assault channels, apparently because they were being towed at excessive

CANADA: TO THE SOUTH SHORE

speed for the prevailing weather conditions.' Other towed craft,
'Rhino' ferries carrying wheeled vehicles, broke their tows and some
of the landing-craft fell back with flooded engine rooms or even
swamped troop spaces. Group Captain Stagg's break in the weather
looked hard to find among the short seas of the Bay of the Seine at
7 a.m. on June 6th. Worst of all, the commanders of the DD tanks in
the second wave of landing-craft judged conditions too rough to risk
their barely amphibious cargoes in the water and, in both 7th and
8th Brigade areas, the decision was taken to beach the LCTs and
disembark the tanks direct on to dry land. After passing the 7,000
yard mark, the Senior Officer of the 7th Brigade DD tank wave
changed his mind, and the tanks were swum off close inshore,
landing barely ahead of the infantry. On the other brigade front they
actually landed behind them.

Launching tanks at sea was nerve-racking to those involved, a
mesmeric sight to spectators. The LCTs slackened speed until dead
in the water, the bow ramp was then lowered on its chains, the sea
flooded in to fill the tank deck and the four DD Shermans, engines
already running, launched into the deep, plopping off the ramp into
the waves like toads from the lip of an ornamental pond. It was not a
manoeuvre to be attempted under heavy fire from the beach unless
well out to sea and the decision to risk it testified to the discovery
which almost all the assaulting Canadians were making in the last
4,000 yards of the run-in: that fire from the beach was light and
badly aimed. The coastal batteries were not firing because they had
been silenced, if only temporarily, by the bombarding cruisers. The
field batteries inland were not hitting because they could not spot
their fall of shot. The beach guns were silent because the design of
their embrasures prevented them from bearing until the enemy was
on the beach. That left only the mortars, entirely hit or miss when
directed against maritime targets, and small-arms fire, which did not
carry farther than 2,000 yards and which most of the landing-craft
were stout enough to stop. But as the leading landing-craft passed
the 1,000 yard mark, a new hazard threatened unexpectedly to
present itself. H-Hour was timed ten minutes later on the Canadian
beaches than the British, to carry the landing-craft over the Bernières reefs. The rough sea had delayed the run-in by a further ten
minutes. It was not therefore until 7.45 on the 7th Brigade's front
and 7.55 on the 8th's that the landing-craft reached their beaching
points. And as they did so they found themselves faced with exactly

that trap which the Germans had planned for the invaders all up and down the Normandy coast and the Allies' half-tide landing hour was designed to avoid. To port, starboard and dead ahead the spikes and ramps of the beach obstacles, festooned with Teller mines and graze-fuzed shells, broke the surge of the incoming tide. It and the engines of the landing-craft bore them inexorably into the belt.

# Touch-down

In a few places where the obstacle clearance groups, first of all troops ashore, had had time to work before the tide reached them, passages had been blown and mines detonated. For these gaps the nearest landing-craft headed. Elsewhere, 'the larger landing-craft had to drive on shore in spite of the obstructions and the smaller craft worm their way through if they could'. About a quarter did not make it, blowing up either as they touched down or pulled off for the return trip. The commander of a group of five LCAs reported his experience:

> About three quarters of the troops had been disembarked from LCA 1150 when an explosion ... blew in the port side. The port side of LCA 1059 was blown in by the explosion of one of the mined obstructions after about one third of the troops had been disembarked ... Another explosion holed LCA 1137 and stove in the starboard bow ... All troops had been disembarked from LCA 1138 and the craft was about to leave the beach when a wave lifted it on to an obstruction. The explosion which followed ripped the bottom out of the craft ... All troops were discharged from LCA 1151 without loss ... but as we were leaving an approaching LCT forced us to alter course. An explosion ripped the bottom out.

But even when their landing-craft were damaged or sunk, most of the infantry struggled ashore, probably because the open troop space did not confine the force of an explosion. Equally important they found their DD tanks already landed or wading in close behind them, and with them the AVREs, Crab flail tanks and Royal Marine Centaurs – though thirty-four out of forty of the last had either foundered with the overladen mother ships or been forced back to English ports – which were to break their way through the belts of dry obstacles at the top of the beach. Almost everywhere the tanks were at once in action, for the Canadian infantry had now entered the zone on which the fire of the defences had long been arranged to bear. And those who directed it knew that they had only a few minutes in which to destroy the impetus of the landing or themselves be killed.

As they cleared the landing-craft and looked for the tanks which would support them, the Canadian infantry companies went instantly into the drills which they had practised a hundred times in England. The Regina Rifle Regiment, disembarked under the defences of Courseulles, strongest of the sector, had prepared with particular thoroughness. From aerial photographs they had divided the little fishing village and harbour into twelve sectors, each allotted to a platoon. The six platoons in the two assault companies were to take the seaward sectors, the six in the two follow-up companies those beyond. Touching down at 8.15 to the east of the village B Company met almost no resistance and quickly cleared its assigned blocks. Its neighbour to the west, A Company, had a far more difficult time. Landing six minutes earlier directly under the three guns of the harbour strongpoint, the three platoons, each carried in a separate landing-craft, ran for the sea wall. As they broke for cover, they split into their sections, three groups of ten men organized round the firepower of a light machine-gun, which would support the riflemen as they moved to suppress one strongpoint after another. They were immediately brought under attack by the German artillery, into whose zone of fire they penetrated as soon as they left the tideline, as well as by the machine-guns which had been firing at them during the last stages of the run-in. Fortunately B Squadron of the 1st Hussars had got its tanks ashore ahead of them. Nineteen had set out to swim from 2,000 yards out. Fourteen had made the beach. They now began to engage the strongpoints from the shelter of the beach obstacles, at ranges of about 200 yards. The strongpoint gun crews fired back, steadily if not accurately. No tanks were knocked out. But the 88 mm gun beside the harbour exit and the 50 mm behind it, the first of which had certainly sustained near misses from the naval bombardment, went on firing until their shields were pierced by the Shermans' shells. The 75 mm, out to the right flank, held out for a good deal longer. It had fired over 200 rounds, almost its entire ammunition stock, before a 1st Hussar tank got it with a shell straight through the embrasure. And while this gun-to-gun duel had been going on, the Canadian infantry had been working through the trenches and dugouts in between the concreted positions, killing all the Germans they could see who would not surrender; but at a heavy cost: 45 Reginas were killed on D-Day, most of them here at the head of the beach.

The Reginas' sister battalion, the Royal Winnipeg Rifles, had a landing experience which was almost exactly identical. Its left-hand company landed west of the strongpoint area and moved easily into open country, clearing a path through one of the minefields strung along the coastal dune and then capturing the little village of Graye-sur-Mer beyond it. Six days later Churchill, Smuts and Alan Brooke would land with Montgomery on Graye beach, and four days after that King George VI. But on the evening of June 6th a sanatorium west of the village was still in the hands of some Russian artillerymen who either would not or dared not surrender. It had been left by D Company of the Winnipegs, who had gone on with A and C, and their attached 1st Hussar tanks, to consolidate an outpost at Creully, four and a half miles inland.

The other Winnipeg company, B, had had a tragic ordeal. Fired on while still yards out to sea, it landed to find that 'the bombardment had failed to kill a single German or silence one weapon'. Many of the Canadians were killed 'while still chest high in water' and those who got on to the sand saw their only salvation in a direct charge at the enemy. None of the 1st Hussar tanks had yet landed – only seven were to do so after mishaps at sea – and the infantry had to wait six minutes under accurate fire until they arrived. When they did, and all moved forward from the beach obstacles among which they had been sheltering, casualties came thick and fast. By the time the company had got into Courseulles itself, it had only twenty-six men still standing and, among the ruined houses of the little port, the ghosts of Dieppe seemed close at hand.

Dieppe-like too was the landing of the Queen's Own Rifles of Canada at Bernières. Tide and wind had carried B Company's landing craft 200 yards east of their assigned landing place, directly into the zone of fire of the village strongpoint, mounting two 50 mm guns and seven machine-guns. The tanks of the Fort Garry Horse, which had not been allowed to swim off their LCTs, had not yet arrived. For several dreadful minutes therefore the soaked and shivering infantrymen crouched for shelter among the beach obstacles, while the bursts of German fire dropped one man after another into the boiling surf. Sixty-five had been killed or wounded before three, Lieutenant W.G. Herbert, Lance-Corporal René Tessier and Rifleman William Chicoski, broke for the sea wall, there ten feet high, and worked along in its shelter until within range of the strongpoint. Using grenades and Sten guns against the firing slits, they destroyed the defenders within. It had taken a quarter of an hour, during which a troop of assault engineers working to dismantle beach obstacles 500 yards to the east reported that they too had been kept under fire from the 50 mm.

Farthest east of all, on the outer flank three miles from the beaches where the British 3rd Division was landing at Lion-sur-Mer, the North Shore Regiment touched down at 7.40. Towering over the beach on the St Aubin sea wall stood a large concrete gun shelter which the naval bombardment had not touched. Swimming tanks of the Fort Garry Horse, which arrived simultaneously with the infantry, at once brought it under fire. But its 50 mm anti-tank gun was valiantly served by the crew and two tanks were knocked out in the surf. It had fired seventy rounds before it was overwhelmed by the combined effect of shelling from the 95 mm of a Royal Marine Centaur, the concrete-breaking petard of an AVRE and the high-velocity shells of two of the Fort Garry Shermans.

## Inland

Two hours after touch-down, all along the five miles of coast which the Canadians had just assaulted, little bursts of combat still flared and died. In Courseulles B Company of the Royal Winnipegs was finding Germans alive and fighting in the ruined houses around the harbour. In the Reginas' half of the village on the other side of the harbour, the enemy had filtered back into trenches and tunnels which the first arrivals thought they had cleared. The leading company was forced to turn round and do again the bitter and dangerous work of shooting and grenading from hole to hole. At Bernières there was fighting on the landward edge of the village. And in St Aubin the reserve companies of the North Shore Regiment had blundered into booby-trapped houses while taking the village from the rear.

There was also a growing toll of casualties at the beach edge. In Assault Group J2, which had brought the Queen's Own Rifles and the North Shore to land, the LCAs started to set off mines on the beach obstacles as soon as they went astern and a quarter were sunk or disabled. The Canadian Scottish, reserve battalion to the Winnipegs and Reginas, was held up on the beach while a way was sought through the minefield on the dunes, and was heavily mortared. The other reserve battalion, Le Régiment de la Chaudière, saw all but five of the landing-craft sunk under its leading company, by mines or mortar bombs. The men took off their equipment and swam ashore and, though most made the beach, they were driven by fire to shelter under the Bernières sea wall until the Queen's Own Rifles released them.

About a quarter of the landing force was thus still tied to the immediate area of the assault at H-Hour plus 2. Some of it would be there much longer. The North Shore Regiment would not finally overcome resistance at St Aubin until 6 p.m. But already it was possible to see that the majority of the two leading brigades was safely ashore, unencumbered by the enemy, and ready to move inland as soon as the way was open. Behind them the reserve brigade, the 9th, had begun to land, together with its supporting armoured regiment, the Sherbrooke Fusiliers. The beaches were clogging with men and vehicles while the flail and engineer tanks struggled to clear gaps in the minefields – 14,000 had been laid between Courseulles and Bernières – and blow gaps through the sea wall and dunes for the wheeled vehicles to exit. At Bernières a flooded area beyond the dunes complicated their task, so that it was not until noon that a crossing was built by sinking a tank in the mire and bridging across it. The infantry companies which had landed first, however, had already begun to march towards their objectives. And in their wake the rest of the division would follow as soon as it was able.

It was an almost deserted landscape through which the Winnipegs, Reginas, Canadian Scottish and Chaudières found themselves moving. The French Canadians of La Chaudière had found a few terrified natives in the ruins of Bernières to comfort in their common tongue. From the countryside beyond the inhabitants had disappeared. Some had been killed by the air and sea bombardment which had fallen beyond the strongpoint line. The rest had taken to their cellars. But, if there were no French, equally there were very few Germans. The policy – and shortage of men – which had dictated that all should be put at the very forward edge of the defended area meant that there were almost none left to hold the chain of inland villages beyond the beach. The Reginas found none in Reviers, two miles south of Courseulles, and the Winnipegs only a few half-hearted snipers in the neighbouring village of Banville. There were also snipers in Colombiers-sur-Seulles, west of Reviers, who fired on the Canadian Scottish as they approached the place through cornfields in the late morning. After they had been chased away, the advance continued and the Queen's Own Rifles on the left flank also found that, once out into open country, the worst of their ordeal was over. They met a little resistance in the village of Anguerny, but had taken full possession of it by late afternoon.

Nor was any of this in retrospect surprising. General Richter, commanding the 716th Division, later revealed that of his four German and two Russian battalions there remained at the end of D-Day only one German battalion still extant, at about 80 per cent strength. Of the rest there were only handfuls of demoralized soldiers, sufficient three days later to furnish a single battlegroup of 292 officers and men. For practical purposes, the 716th Division had been destroyed. And, unlike the Canadian 2nd Division after Dieppe, it would not rise again. Fears of comparable Canadian losses proved unfounded. Nearly 2,000 had been expected, to include 600 drowned. The actual total was 1,000, which included 335 dead. The Winnipegs, Reginas and Queen's Own Rifles had 55, 42 and 61 fatal casualties, mostly in the assault companies which had landed under the beach strongpoints. As the survivors pressed cautiously but steadily on into the Norman countryside, following their attached tanks wherever the armour had been able to get up to them, they took with them a blessed sense of release from the spectres born twenty-two months before on the beaches seventy miles to their east, a release which would ease the anxieties of all Canada when the first full news of the landing reached them the next morning.

Details had already relieved the tensions at Supreme Headquarters Allied Expeditionary Force. There Eisenhower and Montgomery had followed at a few hours' remove the progress of the fighting all along the landing zone, from the American airhead at the base of the Cotentin to the British east of the Orne. They had been content with the reports of the British seaborne landings at Gold and Sword Beaches, west and east of Juno. They had been gratified by the ease and speed with which the American 4th Division had got ashore at Utah to rescue the parachutists. They had been racked by the sufferings and near failure of the American 1st Division on Omaha, which had taken 2,000 casualties simply in the business of crossing the beach from surf to cliff foot. But nothing in the day's news brought as much satisfaction as the account of the Canadian landing. Not only had the 3rd Division extricated the Supreme Command from the danger of visiting on Canada a second national tragedy only two years after the first, but it had also won an important victory. At the end of the day its forward elements stood deeper into France than those of any other division. The North Shore Regiment was still battling near the beach to reduce the command post of the II Battalion, 736th Grenadier Regiment at 8 p.m. But the North Nova Scotia Highlanders, who had landed fresh on the beach at noon, were in Villon-les-Buissons, only three miles from the outskirts of Caen. Late that evening a patrol of the 21st Panzer Division, tardily released by Army Group B to Seventh Army for the only German counter-attack of D-Day, aimed at the gap between the British and Canadian bridgeheads and blundered into the pickets of the North Nova Scotias. Nineteen prisoners fell into Canadian hands. The rest of the Germans fled into the night. The Allies were ashore.

# CHAPTER 4

## *Scottish Corridor*

THE FAILURE of 21st Panzer Division to push its way to the coast on the evening of June 6th cast the first shadow of doubt on the confidence Hitler had always expressed at the outcome of the Second Front. 'They will get the thrashing of their lives,' he had predicted earlier in the year. 'I am convinced that when the time comes it will be a huge relief, just like Dieppe.' But his confidence had rested on his ability to hold the Allies on the beaches and destroy them there, perhaps with the assistance of bad weather but certainly with the flail of air power. '*If* only they would land half a million men,' he had mused on December 30th, 1943, 'and then foul weather and storms cut them off in the rear. Then everything would be all right.' The foul weather would come. By air power, and particularly the just 'one jet', the Messerschmitt 262, on which he counted to force them 'to take cover and . . . waste them hour upon hour' until his reserves were on their way, had not shown itself; the Luftwaffe flew only 319 sorties on June 6th, and lost many aircraft, the Allies flew 12,015, of which not one was interrupted by enemy air action.

## The Fight of the Panzer Divisions

The defeat of the landings would therefore depend on the action of the ground troops and above all on their ability to keep the Allies' still shallow footholds separate from each other. On the evening of June 6th the British seaborne infantry had joined hands with the parachutists in the 'airborne bridgehead', just as the Americans of Utah Beach had done with their parachutists earlier in the afternoon. The Canadians had made early contact with the British on their right (who had almost reached Bayeux before the end of the day), and would on the morning of June 7th close the gap between themselves and the British on their left, into which the 21st Panzer Division had

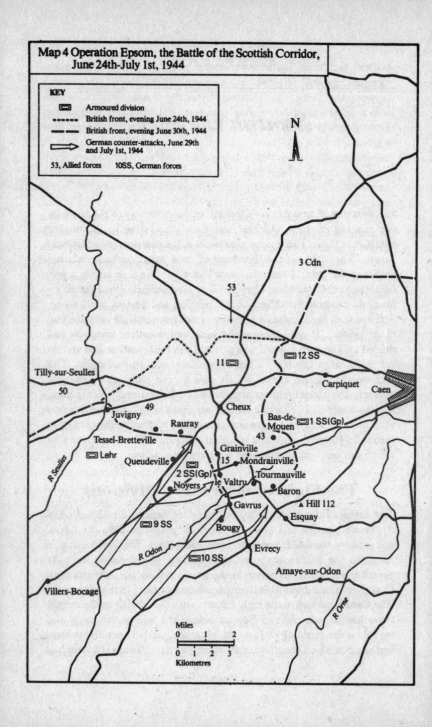

# Map 4 Operation Epsom, the Battle of the Scottish Corridor, June 24th–July 1st, 1944

## KEY

▭ Armoured division

······ British front, evening June 24th, 1944

— — — British front, evening June 30th, 1944

⇨ German counter-attacks, June 29th and July 1st, 1944

53, Allied forces   10SS, German forces

N

3 Cdn

53

11 ▭     ▭ 12 SS

Tilly-sur-Seulles

50

Carpiquet     Caen

Juvigny     49

Cheux

Rauray     Bas-de-Mouen     ▭ 1 SS (Gp)

Tessel-Bretteville     43

▭ Lehr     Grainville

Queudeville     15     Mondrainville

2 SS (Gp) ▭     Tourmauville

Noyers     le Valtru     Baron

Gavrus     ▲ Hill 112

Bougy     Esquay

R Seulles

▭ 9 SS     Evrecy

R Odon     ▭ 10 SS

Amaye-sur-Odon

Villers-Bocage

R Orne

Miles
0     1     2
0  1  2  3
Kilometres

probed and then withdrawn in the dusk of D-Day. But these interlinkings still left two holes in the Allied front, a small one between the British and American landing-places north of Bayeux and another much larger one between the American Omaha and Utah Beaches across the tidal mouth of the Douve. These gaps offered tempting prospects. The difficulty was to find the troops to insert into them. Rommel's immediate reserve, 21st Panzer Division, was already committed. The two other panzer divisions which he controlled were in the wrong place; 116th was beyond the Seine, 2nd was even farther away beyond the Somme. Panzer Lehr and 12th SS Panzer, though both in Normandy, were also at some distance from the battlefield and still 'under OKW control', which meant in practice that they could be released to the battle only with Hitler's express permission. The infantry divisions were, for purposes of immediate reinforcement, useless. Those nearest the landing places, on the other side of the Seine, could not be touched as long as Hitler believed that they might yet be called upon to repel a second invasion on their coast. Those farther away simply lacked the mobility to get up to the battlefront in time, or to manoeuvre when they reached it.

Rommel, moreover, commanded on June 7th *in absentia*. He had gone home on leave to his native Swabia on June 4th, leaving his chief of staff, Speidel, in charge, and though the two had 'thoroughly discussed ... the measures to be taken in the case of an attack', the deputy could not speak with the voice of the master. Worse, the two officers at the next level of command below were also absent from their posts on the night of invasion; Dollmann, chief of Seventh Army, which occupied Normandy, was running the war game in Rennes from which the commander of the 91st *Luftlande* Division was returning when ambushed by the American parachutists; Sepp Dietrich, commander of I SS Panzer Corps, to which 12th SS and Panzer Lehr Divisions were subordinate, was in Brussels. The German chain of command therefore ran upwards from Speidel to Rundstedt, far away in his headquarters at St Germain outside Paris, and thence to the *Führerhauptquartier*, temporarily installed in the Berghof at Berchtesgaden; downwards it ran directly to the commanders of the panzer divisions.

Speidel had been conducting a dinner party as the parachutists made their approach to the landing zones at either end of what would soon be the Normandy front. Among his guests was Ernst Jünger, the lyricist of the trench experience of the First World War, whose *Storm of Steel* offered any young German soldier who had read it – and they might be many, for Jünger was among the regime's approved writers – a terrible warning of what the coming battle held in store for each one of them. The party was still in progress when the first news of the parachute landings arrived. Speidel at once signalled Rommel to return and meanwhile tried to get 12th SS started on the road to the danger spot. A morning and afternoon of order and counter-order followed, as Hitler havered over the means to use to deal with the landings. At his morning conference he greeted Keitel, chief of his headquarters, with the optimistic summary: 'The news couldn't be better. As long as they were in Britain we couldn't get at them. Now we have them where we can destroy them.' Expecting the beach infantry to achieve that task, he cancelled the movement of the panzer divisions. When the news worsened after lunch, he changed his mind and devolved control of 12th SS to Dollmann's Seventh Army. But by then it was too late for the division to intervene that day.

Its commander, *Brigadeführer* (Major-General) Witt reached the headquarters of the devastated 716th Division during the night of June 6th–7th, with a doleful story of his journey: 'I have been on my way to you for about eight hours. I lay a good four hours in roadside ditches because of air attacks. The division's marching columns are suffering serious losses in men and material.' Shortly afterwards, however, the commander of the leading column arrived, and brought fire to the conference. He was Kurt Meyer, paradigm of the SS soldier, and a magnet of attraction to the Hitler Youth of whom the division was formed. His plan was incisive and realistic. Rather than look for yesterday's hole between the Canadians and British, he proposed to create his own and drive the 'little fish' into the sea. Battlegroup Meyer, which consisted of the three infantry battalions of his own 25th SS Panzergrenadier Regiment and a battalion of the division's Mark IV tanks, would be inserted on the left of 21st Panzer Division, and the two would drive side by side to the beach. By noon of June 7th his leading units, which had averaged only four miles an hour on their flame-licked forty-mile journey from the other side of Lisieux (the conventual home of the Little Flower of Jesus was to feature with incongruous frequency in the war reports from the Normandy front), were in place. He himself had found a commanding point of observation in one of the turrets of the Abbey of Ardenne, which overlooked Caen from the west; but about noon, while waiting for the remainder of his force to arrive, he noticed large numbers of Canadian troops – probably the North Nova Scotia Highlanders – moving about inside their lines and he therefore decided to attack at once, before they attacked him. This improvised assault shook the defenders, and took some ground and prisoners, of whom twenty-three were immediately murdered, an outrage which would be repeated and make the Hitler Youth Division the most detested formation the Allies would meet in Normandy. But the powerful Canadian artillery, supplemented by fire from the sea, broke the German attack up and allowed the Sherbrooke Fusiliers to mount a counter-attack, to such effect that as Meyer arrived to put heart into the commander of one of his hard-pressed battalions, the unfortunate man's head was struck clean off by a tank shell.

By the evening of June 7th, therefore, 12th SS had failed in the same task which the evening before had defeated 21st Panzer – which did not get back on to the offensive at all on this day. The Germans had lost thirty-one tanks, yet would be faced from now on with an ever-thickening crust of resistance as the Allies reinforced their landing troops with the follow-up divisions, and bulldozed fighter airfields into the Normandy clay. General Bayerlein, who was bringing the Panzer Lehr Division up to the front, was already re-discovering – he was a veteran of the desert – the implications of close Allied air support of their ground troops:

> By noon on the 7th my men were already calling the main road from Vire to le Bény Bocage *Jabo-Rennstrecke* ['fighter-bomber racecourse']. Every vehicle was covered by branches of trees and moved along hedgerows and the fringes of woods ... but by the end of the day I had lost forty petrol wagons and ninety other trucks. Five of my tanks had been knocked out, as well as eighty-four half-tracks, prime-movers and self-propelled guns. These losses were serious for a division not yet in action.[1]

Panzer Lehr, the strongest armoured division in the German army, was one of several which by the evening of June 6th Hitler had released from reserve to make their way to the battlefront: 2nd SS Panzer had begun the long journey northward from Toulouse, 17th SS Panzergrenadier had started from south of the Loire and, closer at hand, the 77th Infantry Division had left St Malo and the 3rd Parachute Division Brest. Rommel was now back in France, after a

breakneck car journey, to deploy them as they reached the front. He
reached his headquarters at la Roche Guyon on the Seine on the
evening of June 6th and first thing next day went to call on Geyr von
Schweppenberg, the commander of Panzer Group West, under
whom the panzers were to be grouped for the counter-stroke. The
situation map still offered attractive prospects. The American
bridgeheads were shallow and widely separated, and the larger of the
two still apparently held in the main by parachutists. The invaders
moreover were there obliged to face two ways, southwards towards
the divisions approaching from Brittany, northwards towards those
in the Cotentin. The other American beachhead, Omaha, also
tempted attack – its occupants had suffered the worst casualties of
any of the landing forces on D-Day. They might be supposed to be
still shaken and indeed had not consolidated their footholds into a
firm defensive position. It might pay to attack on either side of
Omaha, since in each case a success would tend to hold the enemy
apart. Captured documents revealed that a drive on Cherbourg was
an early intention of the Americans, making a push into the gap
between Omaha and Utah particularly desirable. But it was equally
rational to think of attacking on the other side between the British
and Americans, in the hope of levering their beachheads even wider
apart and eventually destroying first one and then the other. What
spoke against these calculations was distance. It was forty miles from
Caen to the Utah–Omaha gap, twenty to the hole between the
British and American bridgeheads. The panzer divisions, if they
could be extricated from the close fighting around Caen, could cover
the distance to the first gap in a night's march, to the second in two.
But, once arrived, there was no guarantee that they could be
recovered with any speed and, while they were away, every expectation that the British would take Caen, or break out south of the city,
or both. And from Caen to Paris was only a hundred miles across
level and unobstructed plain.

Rommel naturally decided, therefore, that while he must attack
before the enemy's numbers grew any larger, and particularly before
they had parity with him in armoured divisions, the point of assault
must be laid as close to Caen as possible. Early on June 8th he gave
orders for the three panzer divisions in place – 21st, Lehr and 12th
SS – to concentrate and drive in the Allied front between Bayeux
and Caen, where there was room for them to attack side by side. It
was easier to propose than dispose. General Feuchtinger's 21st

Panzer Division was still entangled with the 3rd British Division around Caen, its infantry fighting in the hedgerows and villages, its tanks intervening to close off gaps in the line wherever the invaders struck hardest. Meyer's Hitler Youth and the Canadians had temporarily declared quits, but the rest of 12th SS, though now arrived, was so short of petrol for its tanks that it could not manoeuvre. Panzer Lehr was still straggling up from Chartres. At Falaise its columns had experienced air attack by what the German army in Normandy would soon come to call 'Nuremberg Rally' formations (*Parteitag Geschwadern*), squadrons of Allied bombers stacked up straight and level across the open sky. A little farther on General Bayerlein had been caught on the road in his staff car by three fighter-bombers. He had been wounded, his driver killed and his aide-de-camp saved only by falling from the burning vehicle into the mouth of a concrete culvert.

Rommel was realist enough to recognize that he would not get his armoured offensive moving that day with so little to hand. As he had, however, to keep up the pressure on the bridgehead, he directed 12th SS to resume its attack against the Canadians. A day and night of murderous fighting followed – literally murderous; another forty-five Canadian prisoners were shot under the walls of the Abbey of Ardenne during its course. Early in the morning the Royal Winnipeg Rifles were encircled at Putot, on the Bayeux road west of Caen, fought surrounded all day and had to be rescued by the Canadian Scottish and the 1st Hussars that evening. Three of their four companies had suffered so many casualties while cut off that the whole battalion had to be sent out of the line. At about the same time as they were being extricated, Meyer intervened in the battle at a point nearer Caen. It was growing dark. Leading on a motorcycle, his preferred command vehicle, he drove westward down the Caen–Bayeux road with the divisional Panther (tank) battalion strung out behind him and the men of the reconnaissance battalion riding on their hulls. Just short of the headquarters of the Regina Rifles in Bretteville l'Orgueilleuse, the tanks stopped to shoot up the village. Then, when persuaded that resistance had been crushed, they advanced and drove round the Reginas' positions Sioux-style to look for a way in for the kill. The Reginas had been holding their fire and so achieved the feat, rare for an infantry battalion, of inflicting crippling losses on a tank force with their own few static anti-tank guns. Six Panthers short of the twenty-two with which he had begun his *Walkürenritt* six hours before, Meyer turned his motorcycle as the glimmer of dawn showed towards Bayeux and rode away from the burning ruins.

He expected to be back. But Rommel decided later that day, June 9th, that he would defer the counter-offensive until more of the marching divisions from the interior had arrived. Its planning meanwhile was consigned to Geyr von Schweppenberg. That officer's headquarters had hitherto played the role of government-in-waiting for, though specifically organized to prepare and control large armoured operations, the necessary troops had been withheld from it until the appearance of the Allies on the beaches, and indeed for some time after that. Now called to life, it had installed itself with some amplitude at Thury-Harcourt, twelve miles south of Caen, where Geyr and his officers lived in the château of la Caine and the clerks and signallers worked under canvas in the orchard outside. Communication was provided via four large radio trucks. As soon as they had come on the air, however, their transmissions had been picked up by the British monitoring service and the intercepts subjected to Traffic Analysis. Traffic Analysis is a technique which helps to identify where and from whom transmissions emanate, rather than what the encoded messages contain – that information was extracted by the Ultra service at Bletchley.

Ultra was to play a major and, towards the end, perhaps a decisive part in the winning of the Battle of Normandy. The reason is simply explained. The Germans, like all other major military powers, had in the years before the Second World War sought to simplify their need to transmit securely enormous quantities of military messages by encoding them mechanically. The machine they had chosen for the task was a commercial model, called Enigma. Externally it resembled a typewriter. There is indeed a famous photograph of Guderian in his command car with his Enigma operator at his elbow, whom the uninstructed for years took to be his typist. But the electrical circuits of the machine, when complexified for military purposes, enabled the 'typist' to encode a plain text in any one of one hundred and fifty million million million possible ways, any particular setting being changed every twenty-four hours. Not unnaturally, the Germans believed that messages so encoded were unbreakable.

They were, however, mistaken. The Poles, before 1939, had succeeded in reconstructing an Enigma machine, a model of which they handed over to the British. The British then assembled a team of mathematicians, cryptographers and engineers at Bletchley Park, outside London, who by 1940 had designed additional electro-mechanical devices which could sort their way through the possible variations of an encoded text – given sufficient time. Fortunately for the team, certain careless practices adopted by some German senders, mostly Luftwaffe, allowed the electro-mechanical devices, called 'bombes', a head start, thereby greatly shortening the delay between reception and decoding of enemy messages. Intelligence of the greatest strategic value thus became available in quantity; and as soon as the delay was reduced – as it was – to a matter of hours, many of the messages became of superlative tactical value. Measures to forestall an enemy attack, for example, might be taken before it was launched (as they were against the German Mortain operation in August 1944). In such circumstances it became of overriding importance to conceal from the enemy the insecurity of his com-munications, lest catching a small fish now lose one the whole shoal for the future. The choice of what Enigma intelligence (called Ultra) was to be used was therefore often of exquisite difficulty; and the most remarkable element in the Ultra story is that the choices so made never did in fact betray the source.

Traffic Analysis, at which the Germans themselves were expert, threatens no such danger, if all that is required is immediate disruption of the enemy's command structure. Early in the Nor-mandy battle nothing was desired more; the ancient convention by which commanders granted each other tacit immunity had in any case been interred much earlier in the Second World War. So, on the evening of June 10th, rocket-firing Typhoons of 83 Group, Royal Air Force, and Mitchell medium bombers of 2 Group suddenly appeared over la Caine and subjected it to devastating attack. Geyr and one of his officers escaped with wounds. His chief of staff, von Dawans, and twelve other officers were killed, the equipment of the headquarters destroyed, and the survivors transferred to Paris. For the time being, Panzer Group West ceased to function altogether and command of the armoured divisions was temporarily entrusted to the chief of I SS Panzer Corps, who decided that he did not share Geyr's belief in the feasibility of a major armoured counter-stroke.

As it happened, such a counter-stroke would have run head on into a British armoured offensive coming the other way. Montgom-ery now had an armoured division ashore, the 7th, well known to Rommel and Bayerlein from Western Desert days as the *Springmaus*

(Desert Rat). Fielding four armoured regiments, with nearly three
hundred tanks between them, manned by crews which had stood in
the Alam Halfa line, broken Rommel's position at Alamein and
chased his Afrika Korps down the long coast road from Egypt to
Tunisia, it was a proven fighting force of great strength. Montgomery knew it of old, trusted it and believed that with it he could now
begin to lever his way westward round Caen, where the panzer
divisions were pinned, and unhinge their positions from the rear.
His plan, he explained to his chief of staff, was for 7th Armoured
Division to advance through Tilly, just west of the point where
'Panzer' Meyer had made his recent night attack, 'secure Villers-
Bocage and Evrecy and then exploit south-east' (i.e. towards Paris).
Meanwhile, the 51st Highland Division, one of the 'follow-up'
divisions of D-Day, would 'attack southwards, east of Caen, towards
Cagny'. He would then 'put down the 1st Airborne Division' (still on
call in England) 'somewhere south of Caen in a big "air lock" and . . .
link up with it from Evrecy and Cagny'. The result would be to
enclose Caen in a three-sided envelope of armour, infantry and
airborne troops, which would ensure its capitulation.

A by-product of the 'Sigint' which had prompted the air attack on
Panzer Group West, however, was the warning, extracted by the
Bletchley 'Ultra' apparatus, of its impending offensive. And in that
context Montgomery, who had landed in Normandy on June 8th and
set up his headquarters at Creully, midway between Bayeux and
Caen, decided that his own would merely run into trouble – perhaps
end in the destruction of 1st Airborne Division (three months later
over Arnhem, he would be less prudent). Instead he settled for the
more modest aim of sustaining pressure on the Germans on both
sides of Caen. During June 10th–12th, therefore, the 51st Highland
Division pushed inland from the 'airborne bridgehead', menacing
Cagny but never threatening to reach it in the teeth of 21st Panzer
Division's opposition, while the 7th Armoured Division struggled
southward from Tilly towards Villers-Bocage. It was the first serious
venture into that difficult and most characteristic Norman countryside. 'Pleasantly shaded woodland', says *Larousse* for 'bocage'. The
woodland stands between small, thickly banked hedgerows, enclos-
ing fields first won from the waste by Celtic farmers who tilled the
land before the coming of the Romans, and separated by narrow and
winding lanes. Through over a thousand years of growth the roots
of the hedgerows have bound the banks into barriers 'which will

rebuff even bulldozers', while winter rains and the hooves of Norman cattle have worn the surface of the roadways deep beneath the level of the surrounding fields. The countryside is thus perfectly adapted to anti-tank defence. Tank crews which will brave it must expect a bazooka shot from every field boundary or risk ambush in lanes so constricted that they cannot traverse their turret. And if, in the hope of faster progress, they cling to the larger roads, they will be brought every few hundred yards to strong, stone-built villages in which every house forms an infantry fortress, every barn a hiding place for an anti-tank gun. Bocage, for all the soldiers of the Liberation armies, swiftly lost its pleasant sylvan undertones. Bocage came to mean the sudden, unheralded burst of machine-pistol fire at close quarters, the crash and flame of a *panzerfaust* strike on the hull of a blind and pinioned tank.

The particular stretch of bocage into which the Desert Rats were now venturing had been assigned for defence by Rommel to Bayerlein's Panzer Lehr Division. Strong though the division was, it had ten miles of front to cover, which meant that its two tank and four infantry battalions would be badly stretched if they were to be everywhere. Bayerlein's best hope was that the Desert Rat Division would attack on a narrow axis, which would allow his tanks and half-tracks the chance to counter-attack. Fortunately its commander, General Erskine, chose to do so, yielding Panzer Lehr, and an attached SS battalion of Tiger tanks, some prime targets. During four days of slow and bitter fighting, the British edged towards Villers-Bocage, but lost men and tanks at every bound forward. On June 13th the advance guard of 7th Armoured Division at last entered Villers-Bocage but, when it passed through to the countryside beyond, was ambushed by 501st SS Heavy Tank Battalion, which had been on the move from Beauvais, beyond the Seine, since June 7th. The company commander of its leading company, Obersturmführer Wittmann, was a veteran of the Russian front, where he had won the Knight's Cross, and then the Oak Leaves to it, for extraordinary skill and bravery in tank combat; his personal score of knocked-out Russian tanks was 117. Waiting in a small patch of woodland beside the road out of Villers-Bocage on the morning of June 13th, he observed the head of 7th Armoured Division's column leaving the town. It was formed of a tank battalion, 4th County of London Yeomanry (Sharpshooters), supported by the motor battalion, the 1st Rifle Brigade, in half-tracks.

Holding his fire, Wittmann allowed the leading Cromwell of the Sharpshooters to approach within eighty yards, when he destroyed it with a single shot from his 88 mm gun, thus blocking the road. Confident of the impermeability of his armour to the Cromwell's 75 mm, he then left cover and motored along the length of the column, brewing up one British tank after another and devastating the infantry vehicles with machine-gun fire. Plugged into the road by the burning Cromwell at its head, the British column was unable to advance, while the collapse of tactical control prevented an orderly withdrawal. The 8th Hussars, divisional reconnaissance regiment, advanced to the rescue but, as soon as it broke into view, was engaged by four other Tigers of Wittmann's company deployed to his rear, lost tanks and was driven off. The noise of the engagement had by then alerted another company of the Tiger battalion, commanded by Hauptsturmführer Mobius. In the best tradition of marching to the sound of gunfire – Panzer Lehr was maintaining radio silence to deny the attackers tactical intelligence – he now advanced, found the way open to Villers-Bocage and entered the town. Its forward edge was defended by the 7th Armoured Division's anti-tank regiment, with its 6-pounders positioned in the streets covering the approaches. But that excellent gun, lethal to a Mark IV Panzer, could only rarely hurt a Tiger. Wittmann, following Mobius, was an unlucky victim when a 6-pounder shot took off one of his tracks, forcing him and his crew to bale out and run for cover. The rest of the Tigers pressed on down the narrow streets. One of the British anti-tank guns was put out of action by a Tiger demolishing the house in whose shadow it stood. The rest were bypassed. It was only when over-confidence took the German tank crews too deep into the built-up area that they began to fall prey to close-range weapons handled by the British infantry hiding in cellars and on rooftops. After two Tigers had been set on fire the rest withdrew. Later that afternoon, however, the infantry of Panzer Lehr launched an enveloping counter-attack against Villers-Bocage and retook the town. The 7th Armoured Division abandoned their local gains and fell back on Tilly, having lost 25 tanks, 28 other tracked vehicles and suffered a heavy toll in human casualties.

## The March to the Battlefield

A major factor prompting General Erskine and General Montgomery to draw off from the fighting was news of the appearance among the scattered elements of Panzer Lehr of those of another German armoured division, 2nd Panzer. It was identified when some of its infantrymen were captured by the British 50th Division, which had been operating on 7th Armoured Division's left, nearer Caen. Here was a development to cause anxiety. For not only was 2nd Panzer one of the most experienced armoured divisions in the Wehrmacht, with a roll of battle honours reaching from the Polish campaign to the defence of the Ukraine in 1943; it was also the first German armoured division to have reached the Normandy front from beyond the two great rivers – Seine and Loire – which marked its military boundaries. The division's base was at Amiens, 120 miles from Caen, towards which it had been ordered on June 7th. It had therefore not averaged better than twenty miles a day on the road. But the point was that it had arrived. And there were other panzer divisions still to come; 116th from Paris, 17th SS Panzergrenadier from south of the Loire, 2nd SS from the region of Toulouse, 11th from Bordeaux, 1st SS from Brussels, perhaps even 9th from Avignon on the sunbaked lower Rhône. When and if released by Hitler's authority to join 12th SS, 21st and Lehr, how long would they take to make the journey and in what sort of state would they arrive? These were questions of overriding importance and immediacy to Supreme Allied Headquarters as the invasion battle drew into its second week.

What Allied air power had done to the French communication system was known in broad outline, and for some localities, via the networks of the resistance in which the French railwaymen were strongly represented, in greater detail. What Montgomery could not yet know was how well the German formations with orders to march to the battlefield were coping with the obstacles they found in their way and the attacks directed at their transport. Had he been able to see their side of the hill, he would have been greatly encouraged. A fair example of German difficulties were those undergone by 2nd SS Panzer Division, which started from Toulouse in the far south of France on the evening of June 6th. Some wheeled vehicles got on the road that day. The tanks, which would have worn out their tracks before reaching Normandy had they followed, were assembled at Montauban to load on to rail flat cars, but had to wait four days for trains. The marshalling yard was then heavily bombed, imposing a further delay. When the first trains reached the Loire on June 11th, having travelled on the main line through Limoges and Château-roux, they found only one bridge in use, a single-track span at Port Boulet, near Saumur. After it was destroyed on June 14th, traffic had to be diverted to another at Tours-la-Riche, which had been so weakened by bombing that it would not take the weight of a locomotive. The cars had therefore to be uncoupled and pushed over singly and the train reassembled with a new locomotive on the far side. Not until June 23rd did the last of the division's rail elements reach the battlefront, having been seventeen days on a journey of 450 miles. In normal times it would have taken five.

The wheeled elements had made the journey faster but not without trouble, though of a different sort. News of the landings had sounded the tocsin to local resistance groups, which were strong south of the Loire in the old unoccupied zone, and their franc-tireurs had kept up a regular fusillade on the columns of 2nd SS from long range. The I Battalion, Panzergrenadier Regiment 'Der Führer' lost its commanding officer, apparently kidnapped when he stopped his car in a village, and his men spent a day and two nights fruitlessly searching for him. The IV Battalion of the same regiment, when it lost an officer to a sniper in the same area, reacted quite differently. The nearest village, Oradour-sur-Glane, was selected for an exemplary reprisal, its 642 inhabitants, including 207 children, herded into the village church, which was set on fire, and all fugitives shot.

North of the Loire the Germans encountered little activity by the resistance, but suffered comparatively worse from the Allied air forces. On June 11th Rommel reported to Keitel, at Hitler's headquarters, that 'the enemy has complete control of the air over the battle area up to a distance of about a hundred kilometres behind the front, and with powerful fighter-bomber and bomber formations immobilises almost all traffic by day on roads or in the open country'. The experience of one of the infantry divisions which was making its way to the front – a vital reinforcement if the panzers were to be got out of close combat and concentrated for a counter attack – emphasizes how immobilizing this air attack was. A Battle Group of 275th Division had been ordered to Normandy from its station at Redon in south Brittany on June 6th. Unlike a panzer division, a German infantry division had no mechanical transport, so the orders entailed marching or taking the train. The first three trains, after suffering much interference from air attack, got away from Redon on the morning of June 7th and one actually reached Avranches, on the outskirts of the battle zone, at 2 p.m. that day. A little farther down the line it was attacked by Allied aircraft and destroyed. The next train, close behind it, was halted by cuts in the line just short of Avranches and, while stationary, also attacked by Allied aircraft. The engineer battalion aboard, which had suffered numerous casualties, was then detrained and instructed to proceed on foot. It was still sixty miles short of the front. The rest of the divisional trains were thirty miles behind the leaders when these mishaps struck, and had been halted because of news of three breaks in the line ahead. Re-routed, they were then halted again by reports that the alternative line was cut in nineteen places and spent twenty-four hours waiting for orders. These, when they came, were for a detour via Fougères, which was then almost immediately reported to be blocked. The rail backlog by then amounted to twelve trains to which the military railway staff declared themselves unable to guarantee onward movement. Higher command therefore decided to disembark all passengers and equipment and send them forward by road. They had taken two nights and three days to cover less than thirty miles and had at least another three days before them on the road. First to arrive at the battlefront, on June 11th, were two infantry battalions which had covered the distance on bicycles. In these circumstances the headquarters of Seventh Army decided that dependence on the use of the railways for military movement was vain, and closed down the office it had set up on D-Day to organize traffic.

For all but the panzer divisions, therefore, the road to the battlefield was to be long and hard – and necessarily all the longer while Hitler forbade the movement of the nearest infantry divisions from Fifteenth Army across the Seine. Even for the panzer divisions, chronically short of fuel and starved of resupply by Allied air attack on the staging areas, the journey was to be marked by interruptions and anxiety. For the footslogging *Landser*, tramping up from south of the Loire in his nailed 'diceboxes', leaning on his chinstrap and sweating his tunic black in the long hot June days, it was to be an anabasis of pain and fatigue, the toll of the miles to be borne only by an endless repetition of the songs to which German armies have route-marched since the Seven Years War, '*Ein Schifflein sah ich fahren*', '*Schlesien, mein Heimatland* . . .' (Far to the east, the armies of Konev and Rokossoviski were massing for the offensive which would make Silesia German no more.)

# The Fall of Cherbourg

On June 10th the American First Army intelligence became aware
that another of the German divisions from south of the Loire, 17th
SS Panzergrenadier, had succeeded in crossing the river and was
now at the battlefront, the first German armoured formation to
appear opposite their front. It was not, for a panzergrenadier
division, very heavily armoured; a single battalion of assault guns
provided its spearhead (and those, on June 10th, were still on their
rail flat cars). But its infantry were mobile, well trained, young and
dedicated. First Army looked to its defences.

Since the first two days of the beachhead battle, its situation had
been much improved by a firm junction of the two beachheads.
Under the goad of Eisenhower's dissatisfaction, the commander of V
Corps in the Omaha beachhead had driven his flank as far as the
river Vire by June 9th. In the Utah beachhead VII Corps had a far
harder time breaking out across the floods and streams to join hands,
partly because the brunt fell on their airborne troops, who lacked the
heavy equipment to crack German resistance. Carentan, the small
but strong town which blocked advance southwards towards St Lô
and eastward towards Isigny, where V Corps vanguards were
waiting, was not taken until the morning on June 12th. It had been
held by the German 6th Parachute Regiment under Colonel von der
Heydte, a veteran of Crete. The regiment had fought with as much
skill and determination as the attackers, and disengaged just when
the fight became unequal. Its soldiers then formed a new line of
resistance south of the town, ready to hold up any further American
advance. First Army was indeed anxious to get on in that direction,
since thither lay the route towards Brittany. But it was temporarily
more concerned to thrust forward the positions of V Corps, alongside the British, so as to equalize the depth of the beachhead in the
centre, and to break westward out of the constricted foothold at the
base of the Cotentin peninsula towards its other shore. While 17th
SS Panzergrenadier Division and 2nd Panzer Division, which had
now appeared on the American front, were kept in play, therefore,
the main weight of VII Corps was concentrated on the task of
crossing the flood belts and driving towards the Atlantic shore.

In the vanguard marched the parachutists who had been the first
to land there. But they had now been reinforced by the seaborne 4th
Division on D-Day itself and since then two more, the 9th and 90th,

had landed, with a fourth, the 79th, to follow. Opposite them were four German divisions, of which the 91st had lost 4,000 of its 10,000 men since June 6th, the 709th and 243rd were 'ground-holding divisions' of low mobility and the 77th was one of those which had suffered in the march up from its pre-invasion base in lower Brittany. The VII Corps Commander, General J. Lawton Collins, was a veteran of the bitter fighting on the Pacific island of Guadalcanal the year before, where casualties had been suffered at every yard of the way through dense jungle, and was inclined to drive his subordinates and their soldiers with a disregard for casualties more typical of an American Civil War than a Second World War general. When the commander of 90th Division did not get on fast enough for his liking, he was dismissed and 9th Division, which had fought in North Africa, was leapfrogged through to take the lead. On June 13th the parachutists appeared across the Merderet, to the consternation of the Germans both there and in Rommel's headquarters, and next day were discovered to have built a bridge behind them. While this move distracted Rommel's attention to the probability of a drive out of the peninsula south-westward to Coutances, Granville or Avranches, Collins in fact was driving his men straight ahead. On June 17th 9th Division made a six-mile advance which brought it to within sight of the sea and on the following day, after a night of fighting against desperate German rearguards, its leading infantry arrived in Barneville on the Atlantic.

Collins immediately reorganized his command. The two airborne divisions, 82nd and 101st, together with the superseded 90th, were re-aligned to face south. The others, which had crashed across the peninsula, 4th, 9th and 79th, were swung into line facing northward and directed to advance on Cherbourg. Collins thus confronted Hitler, who the day before had arrived in France to confer with Rundstedt and Rommel, with what in pre-invasion days he had always regarded as the most dangerous threat to the security of Fortress Europe, the loss of a major port. He had already brought that danger closer by issuing orders to keep open the neck of the peninsula after any chance of doing so had been lost. He now further hastened the end by insisting that the defence of the port be organized in open country, far outside the shelter of its fixed defences, where Allied airpower and armour could wreak their worst on his unprotected infantry. A dawn attack by the American 4th Division on June 19th cracked the Channel flank of the line on which he had decreed his men must stand, and by nightfall of the same day it had advanced as far as Valognes, last major town on the Cotentin before Cherbourg itself. Next day all three divisions were lined up outside the fortifications of the city. All that Hitler's 'stand fast' order had achieved was to ensure the loss of half the soldiers needed to man them – though, so broken were the four German divisions now on the Cherbourg *Landfront* that their commander, von Schlieben, did not in fact know how strong or weak each was.

But the fight for the city and port was to prove bitter none the less. Strongly fortified in the nineteenth century, the defences had been thickened by the Germans, who, anticipating a Singapore, had studded the approaches with concrete pillboxes. Collins paused for two days to bring up his artillery and prepare the assault. When he struck on June 22nd, the initial blow cracked the outworks on the three ridges which controlled access to the port; but then the Americans found themselves in the pillbox zone and were able to get forward only by fighting with bazookas and demolition charges from point to point. The Germans impressed the 'useless mouths' of the garrison – sailors, clerks and Todt Organization construction workers – into the ranks and von Schlieben freely distributed Iron Crosses, which he had parachuted into the perimeter. By these means he delayed the Americans' entry into the centre of the city until June 26th, but on that day the resistance he had organized fell apart. That evening, having just signalled to Rommel that 'further sacrifice cannot alter anything', and received the reply: 'You will continue to fight until the last cartridge in accordance with the orders of the Führer', he surrendered to the commander of the American 9th Infantry Division at the mouth of the tunnel in which he had taken shelter.

## The Great Storm

The utter destruction of the port and its unloading facilities, achieved before the capitulation and revealed to the Americans over the next few days, spared Hitler the immediate consequences of its loss, but it did not assuage his anger. He had radioed to von Schlieben on June 21st that he expected him 'to fight this battle as Gneisenau once fought in the defence of Colberg' – one of Prussia's epics of the Napoleonic wars. News of its imminent surrender provoked him into ordering courts martial for all those who had contributed by fault or omission to the disaster, and the threat drove the commander of Seventh Army, General Dollmann, in whose sector it lay, to take poison on June 28th. The true nature of the blow was psychological. Hitler and all his commanders, had persuaded themselves that while the Allies, with their now considerable experience of amphibious operations, could not perhaps be kept from setting foot on the open beaches of France, they would not be able to develop any major offensive out of so precarious a foothold and so would eventually be defeated. The battle for Cherbourg had been a major offensive and it had succeeded, even though during its course the Allies had suffered exactly that mishap in which Hitler had always trusted to undo their reckless amphibious enterprise, a summer storm on the southern shore of the Channel coast.

On June 17th Admiral Ramsay, commanding the naval element of the invasion force, felt encouraged enough by the prevailing spell of good weather to order that the last and most fragile component for the great artificial harbour works under construction at St Laurent and Arromanches should begin their journey across the Channel. This was the floating roadway, which would eventually provide seven miles of flexible wharf within the waters of the Mulberry harbours. A few lengths had already been installed. On June 19th sections amounting to two and a half miles were towed out of southern English ports. Within sight of the Norman coast, they were assailed by onshore winds which quickly whipped up heavy seas and all foundered. That by no means completed the damage to the Mulberries. Each, the product of two years of imaginative design and costly preparation, consisted of five main components. Three were breakwaters: Bombardons, a chain of inflated rubber bags intended to absorb the force of offshore waves; Phoenixes, hollow concrete barges the size of a five-storey building; and Gooseberries, obsolete merchant and warships, sunk to the sea bed when correctly positioned. Gooseberries and Phoenixes formed the walls of the two Mulberries proper. Through the gaps between them landing ships entered to discharge their cargoes at Lobnitz pierheads (the realization of Churchill's idea of 'piers which float up and down with the tide' which had given the original impetus to the whole conception). From the pierheads, the floating roadways, or Whales, led onshore.

The storm soon tossed the Bombardons from their moorings, and all twenty-four at the American harbour were driven on shore. When the seas found their way through the harbour entrances into the interior, the very flexibility of its elements ensured their destruction. Several of the pierheads broke from their moorings early on and drifted about, damaging the sections of roadway which had been put in place. Then the Phoenixes, which had been sunk to the sea bed, began to shift from their places – by the third day only eight of the thirty two in the American harbour were still in place – and through the breaches this movement produced the seas thundered in, rising six feet high as the winds gusted to force eight on the Beaufort Scale. The small craft at mooring or anchor could not stand the extra strain and their cables parted, transforming them into haphazard battering rams which charged about the harbour, damaging whatever they met and holing themselves in the process. Most eventually were driven onshore, some ending up above high-water mark, where they would remain until the next spring tides brought the sea to refloat them. Amid the havoc, the navy and the shore parties did their best to keep supplies moving. But there was little that they could do.

> Here and there [remembered an eye witness], the wonderful little DUKWs [amphibious trucks] wallowed like hippopotamuses between the coasters and the shore. They carried ammunition mostly. In places, from time to time, a few landing craft beached. Some broke their backs, crushed by the surf as a dog crushes a bone ... Someone said, 'I reckon this will be the most famous gale since the Armada' ... Any engine failure meant certain disaster. A destroyer struck a mine and drove on shore, and as night fell a big coaster grappled by two tugs bore down on us. Next came the signal, 'If the ship on your port bow is No 269 she contains 3,000 tons of ammunition'; but the tugs held her like terriers all night and she was saved.

Unloading came almost to a halt. From 22,000 tons a day, before June 18th, tonnages landed declined during the four days of the storm to 12,000 tons altogether. When, on June 22nd, the wind's 'shriek dropped to a long drawn sigh ... and in the west a rent in the sky revealed a streak of blue', the reappearing sun shone on a scene of apparently irreparable damage.

At the American Mulberry,

> nearly a hundred small landing craft had been lost, [eight hundred had been sunk or driven ashore along the whole coast]

in addition to a large number of tank and larger landing craft. Of twenty Rhino ferries only one remained operational. All types of craft were strewn along the entire beach, partially blocking every exit. Exit Three was complete disorder. A tentative check revealed that eighty craft, including 35 LCMs [Landing Craft Mechanized], 11 LCTs, 9 Rhino Ferries, 3 LCIs and various smaller craft were piled opposite the exit. Nearby an LCM straddled the deck of an LCT, a coastguard cutter had cut into a nest of LCMs and wound up sideways on the sand, and four LCTs were piled together deck to deck. The Mulberry was a total loss, with the exception of the blockships, and even these had pulled out of line and half of these had broken their backs. Many of the Phoenixes had likewise broken, and one had piled on the cliffs at the western end of the beach. One of the piers was completely ruined. The other was bent in a great arc.

The Americans decided that the damage was indeed irreparable. Many of their logistic experts had felt from the start that 'piers which floated up and down with the tide' was a romantic rather than a practical solution to the problems of ship-to-shore supply and had been restrained from saying so publicly only by the august authority of its advocate. Now that the gale had made him a Canute, they saw no point in persisting in methods which did not convince them, and persuaded their commanders that the straightforward trans-shipment of stores by beaching craft was to be preferred. Their opinion was borne out by results. Landing directly on to the open beaches, in the coming weeks the Americans were to achieve daily delivery totals which exceeded those made through the elaborate machinery of the artificial port. The British, whose port had not been so badly damaged and who remained under the immediate impress of Churchill's interest in the matter, made good the harm the storm had wrought and continued to trans-ship on to the floating roadways and so into the waiting convoys of trucks which fed the fighting divisions. By June 29th their deliveries reached the record total of 11,000 tons; but in the same week the Americans were receiving 7,000 tons a day at Utah and 13,500 tons at Omaha, respectively 124 and 115 per cent of planned capacity.

Thus the Allies had weathered what Hitler had always assured his commanders would be their downfall, a spell of 'foul weather and

storms' which would 'cut them off in their rear' making 'everything
... all right'. But they had not weathered it without setback.
Montgomery's strategy of keeping the Germans stretched, so that
they should not assemble a reserve for a counter-attack, had been
successful enough to see him through the days when his artillery had
starved for ammunition and the armies had survived only by living
on their hump, both of supplies and manpower. But it had
prevented him from decisively taking the initiative, as he had
planned to do in the week the storm had raged. The setback inflicted
by Panzer Lehr and 2nd Panzer on the Desert Rats at Tilly had been
grave enough to raise murmurings of doubt about his leadership
among his critics, always numerous, at British, American and Allied
headquarters. The further postponement, imposed by the great gale,
of firm offensive action would strengthen their voices, besides giving
comfort in the quarter that really counted, OKW, OBW and Army
Group B.

## Epsom

No one was more conscious of that, though for the least of
self-serving reasons, than Montgomery himself. He could feel, if he
could not directly see, the renewed efforts the Germans were making
to gather their forces for the counterstroke aborted by the air attack
on Panzer Group West. They were urgently in hand. On June 17th,
the day before the great storm, Hitler had made a journey to France,
his first since that to meet Franco at Hendaye in October 1940. He
had flown as far as Metz in his Focke-Wulf Condor, down an air
corridor from which the rest of the Luftwaffe had been banned for
fear of an accidental engagement, and then driven to Margival, the
underground headquarters near Soissons he had built as a command
post from which to oversee the invasion battle. It was to be his only
visit. Its purpose was to hearten Rommel and Rundstedt, whose
nerve he rightly believed to have been shaken by the power of the
Allied attack, and to outline counter-measures. 'Don't call it a
beach-head, but the last piece of French soil held by the enemy,' he
began. 'They require seven million tons of shipping space,' he went
on – the use of unchallengeable statistics was one of his favourite
methods of dealing with doubters – 'and cannot last longer than
through the summer.' Seated on a stool, with the field-marshals and
their chiefs of staff standing before him, he described how the next

stage of the battle was to be fought. A *Schwerpunkt* (centre of effort) was to be created with four SS panzer divisions – two, the 9th and 10th, were on their way from Russia – and a new drive was to be launched at the junction of the Allied armies.

Meanwhile the flying-bomb attack on London, which had begun five days before, was to be intensified. The resulting combination of pressure against the Allies' military front and their civilian rear would quickly break their resistance. The field-marshals listened. They were visibly impressed, an observer noticed, by the report from the Luftwaffe representative of the progress of the flying-bomb campaign. But they remained pessimistic about the course of the Normandy battle. Rommel insisted on emphasizing the power of the Allied tactical air forces, now reinforced by that of their naval gunnery, and proposed a withdrawal into the heart of the bocage country, beyond the range of the ships' guns, where natural cover would allow the infantry to form a strong defensive line. Even though the proposal promised to release more armour for the offensive, Hitler would no more hear of it than of any other move entailing the voluntary surrender of ground. 'He seemed to agree,' recorded Blumentritt, Rundstedt's chief of staff, 'but made no decision and then changed the subject.' After lunch, when he spoke and his generals listened, the conversations were renewed. Rommel now raised the forbidden topic of coming to a political agreement with the enemy in the west and, when Hitler tried to cut him off, insisted on knowing his real opinion of the chances of continuing the war. 'That is a question which is not your responsibility,' bellowed Hitler. 'You will have to leave that to me.' It was a cardinal principle of his management of the war that he divided the direction of the eastern front from that of the western, and kept the fighting generals ignorant of both diplomatic and economic matters. Rommel, though he tried to sustain the argument, therefore lacked the means to do so and was dismissed at about 4 p.m., with the promise that Hitler would visit the headquarters of Seventh Army with him next morning. That evening, however, one of the flying bombs in which the Führer now placed such hopes ran wild after launching and impacted within the Margival compound directly above the command bunker. Hitler, protected by twenty-two feet of concrete, escaped injury. But the mishap decided him to return to Germany at once. He cancelled his programme of visits and left France that evening, never to return.

It was on the following day, as the great gale began to drive the Channel seas into the breakwaters of the Mulberries, that Montgomery issued a directive designed to quieten the criticism of his failure at Tilly and forestall the building of the *Schwerpunkt* for which Hitler had just laid plans. He emphasized how well the Allies had done so far, in establishing their lodgement area -- the linguistic obverse of Hitler's 'last piece of French soil held by the enemy' – and exhausting Rommel's mobile reserves. But he predicted, correctly, that the enemy would now attempt an armoured counter-attack and prescribed the antidote. 'We must now capture Caen and Cherbourg as the first step in the full development of our plans.' Cherbourg was a plum clearly about to fall, and he did not therefore elaborate plans for that half of the scheme. For the drive to capture Caen he proposed an envelopment east and west of the city, that on the east by troops in place, that on the west by new divisions which were only just coming into the battle, the 11th Armoured Division, the 43rd Division, infantry from Thomas Hardy's Wessex and the 15th Scottish Division, which was to make the main effort. 60,000 men in all were to be engaged, supported by 600 tanks and 300 guns, with a heavy-gun monitor and three cruisers standing offshore to provide long-range fire. The objective was to be the high ground east of the Orne, in its bend between Caen and Falaise, and the advance was intended to sweep up the German positions on the flanks of the corridor as it was pushed southward, bringing in particular possession of Carpiquet and the Abbey of Ardenne, Meyer's pirate lair on the heights above the city. The attack was to begin on June 22nd and was to be code-named 'Epsom'.

## Scotland the Brave

The great gale imposed an immediate postponement of the starting date; and meanwhile the uncertainty of supply diminished the impact of the subordinate operation east of Caen – originally intended to be the main thrust – and of a preparatory attack near Tilly. Not until June 23rd did Montgomery therefore decide that June 26th should be the day for 15th Scottish Division to attack. Domestically the delay was welcome. On June 18th, when he had issued his directive, the division was still disembarking. As a result of the gale, the last elements did not arrive until June 24th, and had to move directly from the beaches to the assembly area for the attack.

June 26th was therefore the earliest day it could have been ready for the battle – which was to be its first.

Its first in actuality. But war is part of the spiritual climate of Scottish life. Scotland's history is bloody with battles, against the English, against each other, and her national heroes – Wallace, Bruce, Montrose – are men of the sword. The military ingredient of Scottish life goes deeper than that. For to the Scots, as to the Swiss, Swedes, Albanians, Prussians and other peoples of Europe's margins and infertile uplands, war has been something of a national industry. Scots had soldiered in the service of foreign kings – the 'nearest guard' of the French Kings were Scots – since the Middle Ages, and the officer rolls of the armies of Austria, Russia and the German kingdoms are thick with Scottish names from the seventeenth to the nineteenth centuries; did not von Mackensen claim Scottish ancestry until the battle of Mons made it no longer politic to do so? And bands of Scottish mercenaries had hired themselves from one military marketplace to another throughout the wars of dynasty and religion, changing sides whenever pay called but always bearing with them the reputation, first framed by Joan of Arc, as 'men who made good war'. Hepburn's Regiment had served as mercenaries to the kings of Sweden and France before it returned to the Stuarts as the Royal Scots, and when the British crown began to raise Scottish regiments of its own, from the Black Watch in 1739 onwards, they instantly proved themselves among the fiercest and most dependable of its soldiers. In Canada and America they had played much the same hard-bitten, foot-loose role as the Hessians hired into British service to war beside them against Redskins and rebellious colonists. In the Peninsula and the Low Countries their military staunchness and the barbaric allure of their dress had made them an object of fear to their enemies, and of a romantic cult to the populations among whom they campaigned and the students of the picaresque who followed the progress of the armies. 'Wild and high the Cameron Gathering rose/The war-note of Lochiel's, which Albyn's hills/Have heard and heard, too, have the Saxon foes/How in the noon of night that pibroch thrills/Savage and shrill.'

But in the long run it was not to be Byronic poetasters who most eagerly consumed the myth of the Highland warrior – nature's gentleman soldier, 'a lion in the field, a lamb in the house', brave, stern, frugal, obedient, frighteningly respectable – but the Scottish people themselves. 'Balmorality' defines that extraordinary transmutation of the barefoot cattle thief of the eighteenth century into Queen Victoria's John Brown, the tamed savage whose sharpest weapon was a stare of disapproval at almost everything not wee, free and teetotal (give or take a dram or two). 'Balmorality' nowhere put down deeper roots than in the Scottish regiments of the British army and the adoring attitude towards them of the Scottish public. We can catch its effect in the marmoreal gravity of Roger Fenton's highland faces, photographed on the steps of the Scutari hospital at the end of a Crimean winter, faces which imply resistance to every human frailty, moral as well as physical. We can trace its progress in the enthusiasm the Scottish public manifested for amateur soldiering when the Volunteer craze struck the kingdom at the end of the 1850s. Scottish recruitment was twice the national average and, under the influence of the Free Church and Gladstonian politics, Scottish Volunteering shortly took that sharp, self-contradictory twist into what has been called 'liberal militarism'. Soldiering in the rest of Britain was regarded as shameful if professional and slightly comic if amateur. Soldiering in Scotland, full- or part-time, was held to be serious and commendable, providing an opportunity not merely to wear tartan (invented if necessary) but to demonstrate the qualities the Victorian Scots most admired, companionability, steadiness and decent self-respect. Highland regiments with all the panoply of kilts, sporrans and pipes, were created by the Scottish Volunteers in the most lowland of the new industrial cities, where their appearance was a force for resistance against the creeping anglicization of Scottish urban life. By a natural extension, Scottish Volunteer regiments became part of the impedimenta of the national diaspora, appearing as a focus of exile nostalgia, along with the ritual of Burns Night, Hogmanay and Caledonian Ball societies. Not only in London (the London Scottish was founded in 1859) but in whatever corner of the empire to which Scottish ambitions and enthusiasm for the imperial idea had carried the race during the nineteenth century. By its end there were Scottish Volunteer regiments not only in abundance in Canada but also in Australia (the Sydney Scottish Rifles and the Melbourne Scottish), in New Zealand (the Canterbury Scottish), in South Africa (the Transvaal Scottish and the Cape Town Highlanders), and even in India, where the existence of the Calcutta Scottish denoted the peculiar ability of the Scots abroad to combine commercial association with some lofty public purposes, in this case the defence of the Raj.

Many of these colonial regiments were to turn up on one or other of the far-flung fronts opened by British empire against its enemies during the First World War. The domestic Scottish regiments were all to appear. And, to the extant Volunteer – now Territorial – regiments, the upsurge of Scottish patriotism in 1914 added a new wave of amateur formations, the Kitchener battalions. They took their name from the appeal made at the outbreak by Kitchener, the newly appointed War Minister, for 'a hundred thousand men' to serve for three years. And so strong was the response in Scotland that it provided the earliest complement of numbers sufficient to form a whole division, the 9th, quickly sacrificed in the slaughter at Loos in September 1915. A second Scottish complement swiftly furnished another, the 15th, which also suffered at Loos but made its greatest sacrifices later in the war.

Both were disbanded at the armistice. But in 1939 the 15th was one of the divisions raised again for the new war. This time it was to be composed for the most part of Territorial regiments, later reinforced by a few regular battalions, and as the war crept on its ranks would be filled out by conscripts; the urge to service and sacrifice which had produced the Kitchener volunteers was a phenomenon of time and place which could not be repeated. Its composition, when it landed in France in June 1944 for its first battle, nevertheless encapsulated the whole of Scottish military history as well as much of the ordeal which all of Britain had also undergone in the war thus far.

Seven of its nine battalions were Territorial, three from the Lowlands, three from the Highlands, one, the 2nd Glasgow Highlanders, a product of that Romantic nationalist revival which in the nineteenth century had brought the kilt into Lowland streets from which a hundred years before its wearers would have been hissed and stoned. One of the Lowland battalions, the 8th Royal Scots, belonged by association to Hepburn's Regiment which had tramped the campaigning fields of Germany in the service of France during the Thirty Years War. The 6th King's Own Scottish Borderers was descended from the government regiment which had fought the Jacobite army at Killiecrankie in 1689, and the 9th Cameronians from the Jacobites' religious enemies, the Puritan Covenanters of the south-west. In memory of their persecuted past, all Cameronian battalions still held their church services in the open air, with sentries posted to warn of attack. The two non-Territorial battalions,

the 2nd Gordon Highlanders and the 2nd Argyll and Sutherland
Highlanders, belonged to the division as a result of a more recent
ordeal. Originally Territorial too, they had in May 1942 taken on the
identity of the regular battalions of their regiments which had been
forced to surrender at Singapore two months earlier to the Japanese.
Thus it was that the 15th Battalion, Argyll and Sutherland Highlanders found itself invested overnight with all the weighty traditions of
the old 93rd Highlanders, Tennyson's 'line of scarlet tipped with a
streak of steel' of the battle of Balaclava, the 'thin red line' of popular
paraphrase.

None of these regiments had ever smelt powder in earnest. For
four and a half years they had guarded the coasts against invasion
and the inland counties of England against parachute descent,
trained in endless divisional 'schemes' and regimental manoeuvres,
and fired their weapons at paper targets and squares on the map. A
few of the most senior officers had been juniors in the trenches of the
First World War. Their subordinates were solicitors, schoolmasters,
bank clerks, business executives who had given their pre-war
weekends to the Territorial army, or schoolboys and university
students whom the war had swept into the Officer Cadet Training
Units. A few of the sergeants were old sweats, with a North-West
Frontier medal to sew on their battledress blouses. The rest, and the
men without exception, were innocents to war inasmuch as Scots can
ever be. Epsom was to be their initiation.

## Finding the Enemy

The countryside into which the 15th Scottish Division began to
move on the morning of June 26th was the beginning of the true
Norman bocage. On the previous night it had concentrated north of
Route nationale 13, the road from Caen to Bayeux down which
Meyer had ridden his motorcycle to the attack of Bretteville
l'Orgueilleuse eighteen days before. It had crossed that road to form
up in the early hours, and at 7.30 a.m. began to move forward
through thick corn towards the dense woodland and small enclosed
fields which led down towards the Orne and its tributaries. Of these
the Odon was the first objective.

The division was attacking 'two brigades up', which meant that six
of its infantry battalions were in the first wave, the other three
waiting in the rear to support the leaders. As each brigade also

attacked 'two up', however, there were in fact only four battalions in line, each strung out on a front of about 1,000 yards. And since the battalions, about 750 men strong, likewise kept one or two of their four companies in reserve, the true number of men who started forward into the cornfields was probably no more than 700. They are best pictured, as they would have looked from the cockpit of any passing spotter aircraft, as 24 groups of 30 riflemen, separated by intervals of about 150 yards across the mouth of the funnel which was to become known as 'Scottish Corridor'. Each of these groups, a platoon, consisted of three smaller groups, called sections, which were led by a corporal and centered on the light machine-gun which gave them their firepower. Their task was of the simplest. As soon as the barrage fired by the hundreds of guns behind them began to play on the ground to their front, at a distance of 500 yards or so, they were to shoulder their weapons and walk forward. The soldiers were, in short, being asked to do exactly what their fathers might well have done in the same battalions during the First World War – the 6th Royal Scots Fusiliers on the left flank of the advance was the battalion Winston Churchill had commanded in the trenches, its officers certainly the counterparts, perhaps the relations of the 'young Scots of the middling sort' he had found when he entered their mess in January 1916. They were to 'follow the barrage'. But with this difference: each of the brigades was accompanied by a regiment of tanks, which marginally decreased the danger of the operation; but the path of the advance, far from presenting the bare and open appearance of the First World War trench landscape, on which the positions of the enemy stood clearly revealed, was covered by dense vegetation which concealed every trace of his defences from view. The barrage followers would know of his presence only when they stumbled over his entrenchments or were dropped in their tracks by his fire.

The enemy, who had now had nearly three weeks to prepare the defence of the banks of the Odon, had made the most of the natural advantages it offered him. The embanked hedgerows, sunken farm lanes, woods, coppices, streambeds, ditches and strong, stone-built barns and farmhouses which lay beyond the cornfields had been integrated into a barrier nearly five miles deep. Its foremost tier formed what was called the Battle Outposts, a honeycomb of machine-gun nests in hidden positions sited to command broad fields of fire down which the British infantry had to advance. There

were at least twenty-eight separate nests on the 15th Scottish
Division's front of departure, as well as eleven larger trench-systems
for German riflemen. And although the defensive belt was not
continuous, as a First World War trench system would have been, its
elements interconnected along well-reconnoitred tracks and covered
ways. Defenders expelled from one position would therefore easily
be able to fall back on another, and so maintain their resistance.

Beyond the line of Battle Outposts, the ground fell gently towards
the course of a small waterway, the Mue, and then rose again to the
crest of the ridge which formed the north bank of the Odon.
Following the flank of the ridge ran a line of orchards, small woods
and tiny villages, of which the largest was Cheux, where the north–
south roads in Scottish Corridor converged. The Germans had made
it the centre point of their second defensive belt, or Advance
Position. About two miles south of the Scots' startline, it consisted of
the same elements as the Battle Outposts, thickened by wire
entanglements and minefields (though there were also mines sown in
the forward belt), and reinforced by batteries of heavier direct-fire
weapons and mortars. There were twenty-six machine-gun nests and
at least fifty heavier weapon positions in this second belt. Its infantry
garrison, which consisted largely of the engineer battalion of the
12th SS Division – an example of the Germans' readiness to make do
and mend with other troops when no ordinary infantry were
available – were dug in and were not expected to give ground under
any circumstances.

To the rear, about another three miles to the south, ran the Main
Position. In Scottish Corridor it followed the line of the Odon,
which there flowed in a deep trench, but was an assembly area rather
than a fortified zone. Selected spots of high ground – here Hill 112 –
formed its key points, around which were concentrated whatever
reserves the German commander could find. For 'Epsom' they were
few enough. The 12th SS Division had already suffered heavy
casualties in the defence of Caen, its front was twelve miles wide
and, in order to cover the ground at all, it was having to deploy its
anti-aircraft regiment in line as if it were an orthodox artillery unit; it
provided the engineer battalion at Cheux with most of its close
support fire. Weight for weight, therefore, all the advantages were
with the British in the attack: nine infantry battalions against two,
one of which was really an engineer unit; twenty-three artillery
regiments against two, both of which were deficient in tanks. To

offset this disparity, 12th SS must depend upon the tactics its officers and NCOs had learnt on the eastern front:

> to hold fire until almost point-blank range so that the first shots would obtain a kill. Then, before the British artillery could range in and bombard the position, to choose a new location and open fire from a new direction. Used by both grenadiers and panzer men, these tactics would reduce the British superiority in numbers and cause them to believe that the defenders were more numerous than they really were.

How effective these tactics were to be the Cameronians, Scots Fusiliers, Glasgow Highlanders and Royal Scots in the leading wave were shortly to find out. They had come up to the start line jauntily enough, here and there with a piper to play them forward to 'Cock o' the North', 'Highland Laddie', or 'Blue Bonnets over the Border'. But the morning of June 26th was dispiriting. It had rained heavily all night, the thick, leafy countryside dripped from every twig and the sky was so overcast that the promised bombing programme and fighter patrolling had to be cancelled. At 7.30 a.m. the barrage burst forth, 'hurling itself over strongpoints, enemy gun areas, forming-up places, tank laagers and above all concentrated into the creeping mass of shells that raked ahead of our own infantrymen, as thousands of gunners bent to their tasks. Little rashes of goose flesh ran over the skin', recalled an officer in the 6th King's Own Scottish Borderers. 'One was hot and cold and very moved. All this "stuff" in support of us. Every single gun at maximum effort to kill; to help us.'

Alas, on the right, where the 9th Cameronians were waiting to advance, a company commander had just discovered that the transparent map overlay on which gunners draw their barrage plans had slipped in the tracing, so that his outer flank would now have to advance through its own artillery 'help'. He spent some time wirelessing to effect a last-minute change; when he found it was impossible to arrange, he walked back to say his goodbyes to the battalion commander. He expected to be killed in the cornfield into which he was shortly to advance. When the moment came, he was indeed hit together with many of his riflemen. Their comrades paused for a moment to mark their positions in the standing corn with a down-thrust rifle and bayonet, helmet balanced atop, then proceeded towards the source of the fire. 'It was poignant to gaze on these rifles surmounted by their tin helmets, looking like strange fungi sprouting up haphazardly through cornfields,' remembered an observer. The sight, a universal of that Normandy summer and soon all too familiar to veterans, was particularly unnerving to the innocent, like the Borderers waiting in second line who would find the first wave's wounded. 'We felt nervously energetic. Officers and sergeants preserved calm exteriors ... The Jocks felt the moment. Some joked – goodness knows what about, but it didn't matter. Some stood silent, smiling apart as they just listened to the enormous effort of the guns. All were joined by an under-current of emotion that obliterated rank. All were smoking. It was steadying to smoke.' The word to advance came over the wireless.

> We arose ... The wide fields of ripening corn rolled away before us, the mist already lifting to an overcast sky of grey cloud ... There were periodic stabs of small-arms fire, con-fused, some way off in various directions. Isolated elements of the Hitler Youth, having crawled to ground under the barrage and stuck it out, were attempting to fight, often lying low to let the leading battalions pass over them in the corn, and bobbing up in the rear. There was a shout over in Eight Platoon. They had stumbled on a position. But the SS defenders, still stunned from the guns, had no time to collect themselves Their hands were up. Someone was detached to escort them back. Others were stumbled upon: things in the corn that would never bob up again – and a thrill of revulsion when yet others were in all too familiar khaki.

A little farther on, where the countryside began to change from the corn of the Forming-Up Place to the bocage of the battlefield, the Borderers thought that they had met the real enemy. 'There were some pale objects in the ground by the opposite hedge, like human faces. I told a bren gunner to fire a few bursts over them, taking no chances, and watched for reactions. I raised by binoculars. Sick, I told the gunner to stop. We had been firing at our own dead.'[2]

Farther on, the Cameronians and the Glasgow Highlanders were meeting a living enemy, who were 'all around – in the standing corn, on the right flank, on the ridge in front, in the ruins of Cheux itself'. Cheux had been battered to pieces by the weight of the land and sea bombardment. But on the way down into it, the Highland Light Infantry, advancing under 'rain and a lowering sky', found 'control

15 Follow-up troops of the Canadian First Army prepare to advance inland

16 The great storm: a petrol barge and three Rhinos driving onshore, June 21st, 1944

17 The Normandy Scene
    1 : British infantry holding the front line, June 1944

18 Tradition: the 9th Cameronians hold an open-air service before
    Operation Epsom, June 23rd, 1944

19    Operation Epsom: Highlanders of the 7th Seaforths waiting on the start line, June 24th, 1944

20    D Company, 2nd Argylls, being piped forward to the Epsom battle, June 25th, 1944

26   German infantry counter-attacking, July 1944

27   Caen after the battle: a British soldier escorts a survivor, July 10th, 1944

28    Tank and infantry officers confer before Operation Goodwood

29    Men of the 4th Dorsets waiting to advance during the Goodwood battle

30   The loneliness of the battlefield: infantry following tanks during Operation Goodwood

31   Operation Goodwood: a Cromwell tank of the 11th Armoured Division crosses the Caen canal for the start line

32   The exposure of the battlefield: infantry crossing the skyline during the Goodwood advance

difficult and direction lost in the orchards'. There was a sniper scare and 'a lot of indiscriminate firing in all directions'. They passed through Cheux, whose defenders had been destroyed or driven out by gunfire, then 'struck trouble. Machine-guns opened up at the leading companies which, shocked by the suddenness of it, went to ground. Our supporting tanks replied, the tracer ricocheting in all directions, a source of fear to all. Each time the leading companies tried to advance, they were met by heavy fire, and the advance petered out.'

It should now have been pressed by the tanks of the 11th Armoured Division, which were supporting the Scots, and by the attached Churchills, the heavy infantry tanks of the 31st Tank Brigade. 'But as soon as one of them showed itself over the crest it drew fire, and there were already three or four in flames just in front of us', noted an observer. Meyer's tanks and anti-tank gunners were reacting vigorously to the threat to their front, despite distractions. An unwanted and unheralded visitor to divisional headquarters in mid-morning was

> the adjutant of the German foreign minister, von Ribbentrop. The official reports had dissatisfied his chief. He wanted to know why the Allies made steady progress though we had destroyed hundreds of their tanks. The adjutant was still talking when a panzer officer broke the news, 'British tanks and infantry have entered Mouen' – half a mile north-west of our divisional headquarters. Almost at the same moment, tank shells exploded in our immediate vicinity. All members of the staff who could be spared were ordered to defend the village.

Ribbentrop's adjutant disappeared in a twinkling, while Meyer departed to oversee the response to this break-in. He had formed the mobile elements of his division into two battlegroups, called Grainville and Mouen, taking command of the latter himself, and was now trying to pinch off the head of Scottish Corridor by concentric counter-attacks from those two places towards Cheux. And thus far he was having considerable success. The Scottish Division's attack had gained a good deal of ground. But it was on a very narrow front, not much more than 2,500 yards, while behind the point of the advance there stretched a dense traffic jam, six miles long, from which it was becoming increasingly difficult to develop any really powerful thrust. The defenders, still largely invisible, were so few in

number that, could the British high command have counted them, it
would have ordered a headlong assault to brush them aside. But

> the sniper fire all over the area, greatly intensified by wildly
> aimed retaliation in all directions, was not recognized for what
> it was; not snipers at all, not a thin screen out in front of the
> main German battle line; those scattered shots, with the
> occasional burst of machine-gun fire, *were* the main German
> position – all that was left of 12th SS Panzer Division on that
> front, a handful of determined teenagers, toughly arrogant at
> the havoc they were causing.

Their success was an example of a curious but familiar military
paradox: that, where confusion reigns, small numbers often achieve
more than great. Two factors had contributed most to the confusion
which undoubtedly reigned on the first day of Epsom – the density
of the countryside into which the British had driven their corridor
and the weight of men and armour they had thrust into it, against
unreduced defences and down unreconnoitred routes. By the end of
the day, many of the British units were simply getting in each other's
way and either doing nothing at all or else jobs which were not theirs
– the artillery commander of the division had been gravely wounded
while manning an anti-tank gun he had happened on in the course of
a visit to one of his forward observation officers (a visit he should not
have had to make). The armour in particular was largely serving no
purpose at all; 'what little space was left in the lanes seemed to be
filled by our own tanks, closed down and deaf to all appeals. None
who was in Cheux that morning is likely to forget the confusion.'
Little wonder that the Hitler Youth, merely firing into the brown,
had sown such havoc.

## Across the River

More by luck than judgment the divisional command now, however,
hit upon the correct antidote to the diffused resistance the Germans
were offering its advance. It decided to extricate one of the reserve
battalions from the ruck behind Cheux, pass it through the village
and race it southwards towards the Odon with orders not to reckon
for the safety of its flanks. The weak were to fight the weak. At
5.45 a.m. on June 27th the commanding officer of the 2nd Argyll
and Sutherland Highlanders was called to headquarters for orders.

At 6.30, as the Highlanders were warming themselves with breakfast after a miserable night in the open, he returned to start them on the road. Their objective was the bridge over the Odon at Tourmauville two and a half miles to the south. The marching columns were assembled with a shout and hurried off towards Cheux. The battalion vehicles – trucks carrying ammunition and light armoured carriers towing anti-tank guns – joined their tail. By the time these had 'literally fought their way' through Cheux, where shut-down tanks were still sitting sluglike in the ruins of the main street, the infantry were crossing the designated start line. Fortunately, they got on so fast in the early stages that the anti-tank guns were not needed at the point of the advance. And when tanks were eventually met at Mondrainville, halfway to the Odon, the guns had been manhandled through Cheux and were up with the leaders. A quick shot destroyed one of the two German tanks – identified, as all enemy tanks were by inexperienced infantry, as Tigers, which they were certainly not – and the other drew off. The Argylls were now less than two miles from the Tourmauville bridge, and they set off for it at the run. Short of the village they burst out of orchards and hedgerows into open cornfields across which three machine-guns opened fire at them, but their dash and training-school tactics carried them across the danger zone 'with miraculously few casualties'. Within a few minutes they had crashed across the bridge and posted pickets in a little 200-yard circle on the far bank.

The tiny foothold was large enough. Word of its winning brought the motor battalion of the 11th Armoured Division pressing down the road from Cheux, and close behind it the division's tanks. By 7 p.m. the bridgehead was secure and the road opened for a new advance across the bridge towards the Orne and open country. The Argylls spent the night on the alert, though they had the reassurance of tanks between them and the threat of a German counter-attack.

To their rear, however, the Tourmauville–Cheux road was still under small-arms fire, from Hitler Youth who refused to give up the fight, and the divisional command still could not co-ordinate its units effectively enough to silence them. Rather than risk a repetition of the first day of the offensive, therefore, it decided next day not to feed more units down the corridor, but to direct the Argylls westward from their bridgehead at Tourmauville to the next bridge at Gavrus. That manoeuvre would draw a base-line across the bottom of the corridor, the interior of which could then be cleaned up at comparative leisure. Early on the morning of June 28th, therefore, the Argylls were ordered to send patrols along the river bank to Gavrus. At 4 p.m. they reported to the Argyll headquarters that they had found the bridges undefended – the Odon divided at that point and was crossed twice by the same road – and that the rest of the battalion should follow.

> It set off at once through the thick woods lining both banks of the Odon. All-round defence in such country was impossible. The going was vile, and at one place the whole march was held up for over an hour while the anti-tank guns were manhandled over a sticky patch. Any well-planned ambush might have proved fatal; but fortunately there were only a few false alarms of snipers and the Battalion arrived intact and complete at the Gavrus bridgehead before dark.[3]

It had taken them five hours to travel a little over a mile.

The commanding officer, Lieutenant-Colonel Tweedie, had four rifle companies, each of about 150 men, with which to hold Gavrus and its bridges; a complicated spatial problem. The two branches of the river were about 150 yards apart and separated by flat meadowland. The road down to the bridges from Scottish Corridor descended a steep escarpment, doglegged round a mill and a quarry, in which Tweedie established battalion headquarters, ran straight across the meadows and climbed into Gavrus village through a steep cutting. From the quarry to the forward edge of the village, marked as so often in Normandy by the thick hedges of a cider-apple orchard, was about 1,000 yards. Because there were Germans both to front and rear, the battalion had to be strung out along the whole distance. The commanding officer's eventual solution of this tricky tactical situation was to keep one company north of the river, two by the bridges and the fourth in the village itself. There, after a quiet night, the Argylls were visited by 'various strange Frenchmen, who claimed to be members of the maquis and to be possessed of vital information'. They were 'received with the deepest mistrust'. Soon afterwards they received far more sinister visitors. At 3.10 p.m. following a period of calm in which nothing had been observed to the front of the battalion and nothing heard from the rest of 15th Scottish Division to its rear (the division was weathering a last effort by the Hitler Youth to cut the corridor), the right-hand corner of B Company's position in Gavrus orchard received a fierce and sudden attack from fresh German infantry.

It was to be the first of many delivered over the next five hours, sometimes by infantry, sometimes by tanks, sometimes by the two arms working together. They belonged to a division which had not intervened before on the Normandy front, had come all the way from Poland and had been a long time on the journey. Though the Argylls could not realize it, they were on the receiving end of an order which Hitler had given as long ago as June 11th and which he had intended to bring about the defeat of the invasion. On that day, convinced by the news from Normandy that the armour in place was too weak to mount the decisive counter-stroke he had long planned to launch against a landing, he directed that II SS Panzer Corps, comprising 9th and 10th SS Panzer Divisions, should start westward from the location in Poland where they had been resting after defeating a Russian offensive at Tarnopol in April. The journey was a return trip for the two divisions, since they had been brought to the eastern front from France especially for that mission; but its course was to be nothing like as smooth as the outward journey. Entrained on June 12th for a passage expected to last under a week, the first elements reached Lorraine four days later. There, like the divisions stationed south of the Loire, they found the French railways so devastated by Allied air attack that the wheeled units were off-loaded and sent forward by road. But the tanks, with their curiously limited mobility, had to be left on their flat cars, which, moving by night and with endless detours, were to take another ten days to reach their assembly area. Tanks and panzergrenadiers were thus reunited only after Epsom had got under way. And the counter-stroke for which Hitler had intended them had therefore to be transmuted into a local counter-attack of which the Argylls were the first victims.

Much of the rest of 15th Scottish Division and its supporting armour to their rear also felt its weight, for Panzer Lehr, 2nd SS Panzer and 1st SS Panzer – the latter a new arrival from Belgium – also intervened in the battle on June 29th. But no body of men stood so exposed as the Argylls. They could call on no tanks of their own to meet the Panthers and Mark IVs of 10th SS. They could call down artillery fire by radio from beyond the river, and it came in plenty when demanded, but it could not drive off the German tanks. They had therefore to depend upon their own small-arms fire to deter the panzergrenadiers, and their 6-pounders and Piats to strike at the German armour. The 6-pounders could punch a hole if positioned to find a shot; but they were immobile. The Piats were highly portable, and could be brought into action wherever the two-man crew could find space to lie. But the Piat round was a chancy tank-killer. It worked on the 'shaped charge' principle, which concentrates the explosive force of a warhead – but only if it impacted at a right-angle. If not, it glanced off, but with enough commotion to threaten doom to its operators, for the Piat's short range required them to attack from very close quarters. Two tanks, over-bold enough to venture down the sunken lane which ran through the centre of Gavrus, were attacked by Piat gunners hiding in the bank and one was actually knocked out. Three tanks which appeared on the other side of the position were engaged by Piat gunners in the hedges of the orchard and menaced to a halt. The tank commanders apparently chose not to risk pushing the advance without infantry to protect them. But these successes could not be sustained. As the afternoon wore on, panzers and panzergrenadiers began to work together with increasing effectiveness, nibbling into the weak spots of the Argylls's defences, cutting one small group off from another and gradually eating their way towards the river and the bridges. The commander of B Company, Major William McElwee, in civil life a seventeenth-century historian, led a number of counter-attacks with what riflemen he could gather from the defence of his orchard perimeter. But, as the evening began to draw in, his superiors decided that the position could no longer be held. His company was called back to the immediate vicinity of the bridges, where it dug in for the night in a thick wood.

There it stayed until the afternoon of the next day, when fresh troops arrived to relieve it. During June 29th the interior of Scottish Corridor had at last been cleared of the enemy, while its occupants, given a clearly identifiable enemy to fight by the arrival of the 9th SS, had defended the flanks with great determination. Hausser, commanding II SS Panzer Corps, was indeed forced to report to Seventh Army that he had not been able to begin his main attack, north of the Odon, until mid-afternoon and that then 'murderous fire from naval guns in the Channel and the terrible British artillery destroyed the bulk of our attacking force in its assembly area [the guns had been alerted by a very timely Ultra decrypt]. The few tanks that did manage to go forward were easily stopped by the British anti-tank guns.' Behind this screen of fire Montgomery had fed a new division, the 53rd, down into the corridor, and withdrawn the most exposed of his units, not only the Argylls, but the tanks of the 11th Armoured Division which had been holding Point 112 beyond Tourmauville ever since the Argylls had captured the bridge there on Epsom's second day.

The SS panzer divisions did attack on June 30th, though late in the day, and returned to the offensive on July 1st. But the opportunities which had offered themselves only three days earlier were spent. Small though its strategic value was, Scottish Corridor was now too strong to be destroyed by the force the Germans had at last assembled. Epsom had not been a victory. It had certainly not achieved its objectives, which lay not across the Odon but the Orne, five miles to the south. Yet it had achieved, in a roundabout way, an important purpose. Hitler's strategy, conceived long before the invasion and implemented as soon as it began, was to use his armour to drive a wedge between the Allies and drive them both eventually into the sea. The necessity of stopping 15th Scottish Division's march down the 'Corridor' had diverted his armoured reserve from that mission and so damaged its units that days would be needed to restore them to an offensive state. Montgomery would not allow the Germans that time. And so the Scottish division's losses – 2,500 men in five days – had purchased an important advantage. And the little battle of Gavrus exemplified the nature of the transaction. Unspectacular, muddled, wearisome and intermittently terrifying, it had blunted the assault of one of the most formidable fighting formations in the German army and stood fit to rank with those other small epics of Argyll and Scottish stubborness, the destruction of the 93rd at the battle of New Orleans and the stand of the 'thin red line' at Balaclava.

# CHAPTER 5

## *Yeomen of England*

CAEN, FIRST-DAY OBJECTIVE of the British Liberation Army, still lay on July 6th just beyond its grasp. It had been outflanked to the east, where the 'airborne bridgehead' ran along the shallow valley of the Orne under the commanding chimneys of Colombelles, since D-Day itself. And to the west, where in late June the Scots of the 15th Division had clawed their way to the left bank of the Odon and where the Canadians on July 4th had driven their outposts to the open plateau of Carpiquet airport, it was now overlooked by the Allies from the high bocage. Its necklace of outlying villages, St Manvieu, Norrey-en-Bessin, Villons-les-Buissons, Anisy, Périers-sur-le-Dan, Blainville, Ste Honorine-la-Chardonnerette, now marked the forward positions of an almost complete encirclement. But the *chef-lieu* of the *département du Calvados*, capital of the province of Basse-Normandie and seat of the duchy from which William I had taken ship to add England to his lands, still lay in German hands.

Its month-long isolation from the battlefield had not meant its escape from the reach of the fighting. At 3 p.m. on D-Day, after leaflets had been dropped to warn the inhabitants that the railyards and electrical generating station were going to be bombed, 600 aircraft of the Eighth USAAF had run in over the city and released their loads on to its historic centre. The medieval quarters of St Pierre and St Jean had been reduced to ashes and rubble, the distinctive houses *à pans de bois* burnt, the stone buildings tossed to pieces and the enormous blocks of the white *pierre de Caen* of which they were built thrown down to choke the roadways. Fires took hold among the ruins and raged for eleven days, during the first of which the survivors who remained were tortured by the cries of hundreds entombed in the cellars of their collapsed houses. Piecemeal destruction continued meanwhile. Standing far out to sea, the heavy ships

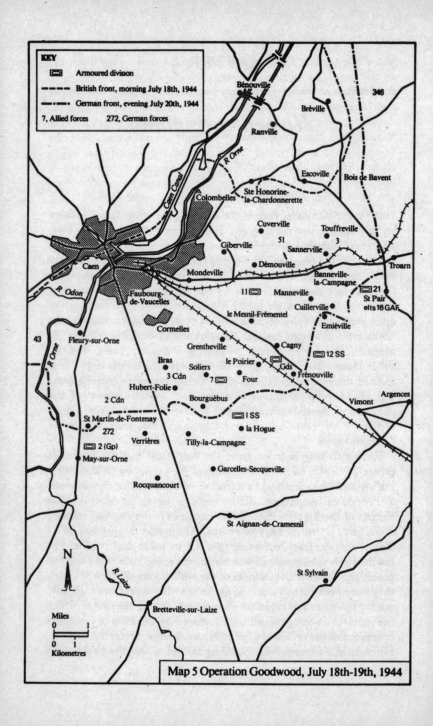

Armoured division

British front, morning July 18th, 1944

German front, evening July 20th, 1944

7, Allied forces    272, German forces

346

Bénouville

Bréville

Ranville

R Orne

Caen Canal

Escoville

Bois de Bavent

Colombelles

Ste Honorine-
la-Chardonnerette

Cuverville

Touffreville

Giberville

51

3

Sannerville

Démouville

Troarn

Caen

Mondeville

Banneville-
la-Campagne

R Odon

Faubourg-
de-Vaucelles

11

Manneville

21
St Pair
elts 16 GAF

le Mesnil-Frémentel

Cuillerville

Cormelles

Emiéville

Fleury-sur-Orne

Grentheville

Cagny

12 SS

43

R Orne

Bras

Soliers

le Poirier

Gds

Frénouville

3 Cdn

7

Four

Hubert-Folie

Argences

Vimont

Bourguébus

2 Cdn

1 SS

St Martin-de-Fontenay

272

la Hogue

Verrières

Tilly-la-Campagne

2 (Gp)

May-sur-Orne

Garcelles-Secqueville

Rocquancourt

St Aignan-de-Cramesnil

N

St Sylvain

R Laize

Miles
0                    1

0          1
Kilometres

Bretteville-sur-Laize

**Map 5 Operation Goodwood, July 18th-19th, 1944**

of the bombarding force were constantly called on to lay down fire on the city. 'Interdicting fire' was the technical term, designed to deny the use of the routes through the city to the enemy. But most of the routes were already impassable and the shelling merely added to the destruction. On June 9th the spire of the church of St Pierre, to which Pugin had brought fellow Gothic Revivalists to study the original in its most perfect form, was hit by a shell from HMS *Rodney* fourteen miles offshore, and felled. Sixteen direct hits struck the near-by convent of le Bon Sauveur, a mental hospital in which 400 nuns cared in normal times for 1,500 women patients. Their number was swelled in the first week of the invasion by 4,000 refugees who believed that its status would protect them from bombardment. When the shelling continued the Mother Superior led the occupants in a mass exodus from the city. The sane found refuge with the 10,000 other fugitives who had taken shelter in the caves of Fleury, from which Caen stone had been quarried by the Norman kings for Westminster Abbey and the Tower of London. The nuns' charges, the senile, the demented, the congenitally insane, were led in a straggling column, the Blessed Sacrament at its head, westward along the line of the fighting towards the daughter house at Pont l'Abbé, forty miles distant in the Cotentin. Blundering at times into the ragged and indistinct no man's land which separated Germans from Americans, and shocking both into unofficial armistice by their macabre intrusion from a third world of the mind, these aliens were at last got to safety.

Behind them le Bon Sauveur burned to the gable-line. But still there were *Caennais* who refused to leave – those who dared not, those whose property held them more fiercely than the fear of death repelled them, those bound by responsibility to others who could or would not move. There were still nuns, priests, doctors and teachers in the city on July 6th, many attending the inert crowd of a thousand homeless who had camped on the flagstones of William's abbey church of St Etienne, eerily untouched among the surrounding acres of devastation. On June 29th the Germans, expecting hourly a final assault on the city, had ordered their evacuation, together with the occupants of the Lycée Malherbe – that severe classical spirit too was a *Caennais* – and the sick and wounded who had been reaccommodated in the cellars of le Bon Sauveur. The hour passing, they had relented, though urging everyone to go while there was still time. Some had heeded the warning. But thousands, hidden in the broken corners of the Conqueror's city, stopped their ears and shut their eyes, perhaps believing that no future agony could exceed that which they had already survived.

They were wrong. On June 30th General Montgomery had decreed that Caen must be taken (and the sooner the better). He clung to his original strategy, that of holding as much German armour as possible at the Caen end of the battlefield, so as to allow the Americans a clean punch into their weakened lines south of the Cotentin. But he was now anxious that Bradley should make his punch quickly. 'First US Army', he directed, 'will pivot on the left in the Caumont area and swing southwards and eastwards to the general line Caumont–Vire–Mortain–Fougères', to face, that was, east instead of south. These operations were 'to be carried out with the greatest drive and energy' and were to begin on July 3rd. Bradley now had the strength to set the manoeuvre in train. Since June 6th his forces had risen to fourteen divisions, against which the Germans on a fifty-mile front could oppose only six, of which three were remnants mangled in the battle of D-Day – 91st, 77th and 243rd forming one division, 265th and 275th another, 352nd a third, although only in regimental strength. The intact divisions, 3rd Parachute, 353rd and 17th SS Panzergrenadier, were strong, but had little counter-attack edge. The 17th SS, armoured in name, had no more than the panzergrenadier's standard allotment of a single armoured battalion. But the terrain, assisted by skilful inundation, favoured the defence. On the Americans' left, the deep valley of the Vire nudged constrictingly at their elbow, and the German garrison of St Lô sat immovably on the junction of all the roads to the south and east. In the centre the flooded water meadows of the Taute and the upper Vire, death traps for the parachutists on D-Day morning, made the ground untankable. On the right, a line of steep wooded hills around la Haye du Puits was so entrenched and gun-studded that Bradley's staff dismissed it as a feasible sector for attack. That left only a narrow corridor of dry ground in the centre through which to funnel the offensive. But when measured it proved so narrow – only a mile and a half at the choke point – that it too had to be rejected. Bradley pondered, bit the bullet and decreed that the attack would after all have to go in against la Haye du Puits, in the full knowledge of its strength and the prevailing German policy, enforced by the Führer, of yielding not an inch in defence.

Many Americans, it was clear, would die in the effort to break out of the Cotentin. Their number would increase with every unit and formation which the Germans were able to shift westwards to strengthen the la Haye du Puits line. Montgomery had foreseen that danger – hence his intention to take Caen 'the sooner the better', since he could guess that Hitler's policy of unyielding defence would apply equally there and therefore guarantee the continued presence in and around it of the mass of German armour he had pinned there since June 6th. This appreciation was correct. On July 1st Rundstedt had signalled OKW from Supreme Headquarters West to advise that Caen should be evacuated, supporting the view with an endorsement by Geyr von Schweppenberg, commander of Panzer Group West. Hitler replied by dismissing both – in Rundstedt's case with a *pourboire* of Oak Leaves to his Knight's Cross, for he could not bring himself to disgrace the old warlord whose sin was cynicism not disloyalty – and then telexed to Rommel that 'the present lines are to be held. Any further enemy breakthrough is to be prevented by tenacious defence or local counter-attacks'.

How seriously his order was taken emerged during the fighting for Carpiquet on July 4th, when the Queen's Own Rifles of Canada, the Chaudières and the Fort Garry Horse struggled all day to wrest the airfield from a garrison later revealed to be no stronger than fifty young soldiers of the 12th SS Division. And there were more of these fortress-like villages facing the British and Canadians across all the approach routes to the city, Franqueville, Gruchy, Buron, Galmanche, Epron, Lebisey, each threatening hours of combat and dozens of casualties before the ruined suburbs themselves were reached. Montgomery flinched from the prospect. He had already been encouraged by Eisenhower in a signal of June 25th to 'make maximum demands for any air assistance that can possibly be useful to you'. Now seeing a 'legitimate opportunity to blast the enemy with everything we have', he arranged with Sir Arthur Harris to borrow half of RAF Bomber Command to drop 2,000 tons of bombs on to the northern outskirts of Caen.

In the planning of the bombardment, however, the risk of blasting the Allied infantry as a by-product of blasting the enemy made itself strongly apparent to the joint air-ground staff at Montgomery's headquarters and an adjustment was made to the target zone. Originally drawn to overlay the chain of defended villages, its boundary was pushed southwards to move the 'bomb line' an

unshakably safe distance from the British front line, until for
convenience it was made to coincide with the three map squares
which began 6,000 yards south of its forward edge. This rectangle
actually excluded the villages, and ran well into the northern half of
the city. Moreover, the pathfinders of 625 Squadron, who were to
lay the bombing markers, had been emphatically instructed not to let
the aiming point 'drift back', the natural tendency when every crew
was anxious to release its load as early as possible and turn to safety,
but to keep putting down target indicators throughout the raid as far
forward as possible. The counter-tendency would therefore be to
overcorrect and to push the bomb-line deeper into the city, towards
the university quarter, thus far not badly damaged, and the 'island of
refuge' around St Etienne.

Coming in over the coast on the evening of July 7th, a pilot of one
of the Lancasters saw exactly that result. There was 'tremendous
concentration right on the markers' and in the headsets of all the
converging aircrew boomed the voice of the Master Bomber shouting, 'Back up the reds [target indicators], back up the reds!' A
rifleman of the 2nd King's Royal Rifle Corps, watching from the
fields across which he was to advance next day wrote 'colossal raid on
Caen. Marvellous and awe-inspiring sight. Terrible to watch. Dust
obscured the sun.' But inside the city a refugee mother, pressing a
pillow over the face of her son to protect his eyes from the flying
glass which had blinded two of her neighbours' children, felt 'the
whole earth shudder. It went on and on for fifty minutes with a
single break of five minutes.' And at le Bon Sauveur, a nun also felt
the earth 'shake with the storm of falling bombs . . . in the basement
the "Hail Mary" could be faintly heard above the diabolical fury of
the bombardment. Evidently the complete destruction of Caen – or
what was left of it – had been decided upon.' When towards 8 p.m.
the last of the Lancasters and Halifaxes turned away very little
indeed of the northern half of the city still stood. It had received in
an hour as many bombs as had Hamburg, a city of twenty times its
population, in each of the great fire-storm raids of a year before. One
of the British soldiers who entered on July 9th, after another day of
heavy fighting for possession of the ruins, found 'just a waste of brick
and stone, like a field of corn that has been ploughed. The people
gazed at us without emotion of any kind; one could hardly look them
in the face, knowing who had done this'. And, wrote one of the
heroic doctors who had stuck out the month of Caen's Calvary, 'the

bombardment ... was absolutely futile. There were no military objectives ... All the bombardment did was [further] to choke the streets and hinder the Allies in their advance through the city.'

It had not even achieved its objective of delaying the transfer of German divisions from the British to the American fronts. Hitherto all reinforcements, which by Hitler's orders had had to be found from within the resources of Supreme Commander West, had gone to the British front. Because of Hitler's injunction against touching the neighbouring Fifteenth Army's capital, amounting to seventeen infantry divisions, Rommel had had first to commit his panzer divisions, which at least had the means to march up to the battlefield independently of the shattered railways, and follow them with infantry divisions from farther afield, the 16th Luftwaffe from the Netherlands, the 708th from the mouth of the Gironde, the 276th from the Biscay coast and the 272nd and the 277th from the Riviera. Their journey had necessarily been slow and, while they were plodding west and northwards the panzer divisions had had to sacrifice their highly trained riflemen and their almost irreplaceable tanks in small-scale hedgerow fights quite inappropriate to their counter-attack role. The first infantry reserves, however, had now arrived and, in response to Bradley's pressure on the la Haye du Puits corridor, two panzer divisions, the ferocious 2nd SS and Panzer Lehr, once the strongest armoured formation in the Wehrmacht and still a formidable force, had slipped westward from the British front to put a finger in the dyke. And it stopped the hole. In six days of fighting, between July 3rd and 8th, the Americans were able to advance only five miles, on some of those days only a few hundred yards and always at very heavy cost. A secondary push to unlock the road-block at St Lô made even less ground, and on July 10th Bradley decided that he must pause to rest his formations and replace their 40,000 casualties.

## Planning a Break-through

Checked at the foot of the Cotentin, and stalemated at Caen, where the Germans still held the little Stalingrad of factory suburbs south of the city, Montgomery now had a strategic crisis on his hands. The appearance of the four fresh German formations from First and Nineteenth Armies south of the Loire revealed not only a German capacity to pass unwieldy troop columns across unbridged rivers in the teeth of air interdiction; it also presaged the arrival of up to ten more, if Hitler decided to cut his losses and abandon the Mediterranean coast to a secondary Allied landing. Montgomery urgently needed therefore to sustain his offensive initiative, forcing the Germans to commit whatever reserves they could find to battles already in progress, at places of his choosing, and so deny them the chance to make a considered counter-punch of their own at some weak sector of his line. The junction of the British and American armies between St Lô and Caumont was an obvious point of attraction for them, one indeed to which Hitler's eyes had been drawn as early as June 20th. But where to kindle the fires? Immediately south-west of Caen, in the angle of confluence between the Odon and the Orne, stood Hill 112, against the long flanks of which the tide of Operation Epsom had washed and broken three weeks before. South of Bayeux, where the bridgehead was deepest, the countryside marched away in a succession of steepening ridges, thickly wooded, in places densely forested, cut by river trenches and criss-crossed by sunken lanes, towards the gorges, cliffs and castle-crowned outcrops of *la Suisse normande*. The Germans would welcome a battle in that narrow countryside and would be waiting. Between Bayeux and St Lô the way into open country was barred by the course of the Vire. And west of that sector began the American front, away from which it was the whole point of Montgomery's strategy to move the focus of heavy fighting. Nor indeed could he stand heavy fighting for its own sake. The Americans had disembarked all the infantry divisions they had ready to hand in England and would, during the rest of August, be transporting the armoured divisions which should at this stage of the invasion have been needed for the expected exploitation into Brittany. The British had no more infantry to send. Very soon their losses would have to be made good by disbanding junior units and using their soldiers as replacements. Montgomery from now on would live with the knowledge that his army was getting smaller with each passing week. And in the second week of July he was acutely conscious of another debility: a sudden ebbing of confidence at Supreme Allied Headquarters, in Downing Street, and in Washington, that he could sustain the momentum of attack; hence his mile-by-mile analysis of the map of battle westward from Caen to Carentan and back again, rejecting one point of pressure after another until, by a rigorous process of elimination his finger came to rest east of the city.

As a starting place for a large operation, the 'airborne bridgehead' east of Caen looked highly unpromising. Only four miles by three, it was sandwiched between the steep and heavily wooded Troarn heights, held at great cost by the Commandos of 1st Special Service Brigade since June 6th, and the Orne river and canal. The only way into it lay across three pairs of bridges, from the main bridgehead on to the mesopotamic strip between the two waterways and thence into the airborne bridgehead itself. Four of these bridges were new, laid by sappers since June 6th. The other two had been the target of Major John Howard's daring glider assault in the darkness of D-Day morning itself. Jealously protected ever since from attack – and the Germans had constantly struck against them with aircraft and even once with frogmen – they provided the only means of supply and reinforcement to 6th Airborne Division in its private world of battle beyond the lodgement area. And, given its light scales of equipment and consequently low requirements of fuel and ammunition, the bridges had sufficed. But did they provide a practicable route for three armoured divisions and the enormous impedimenta of guns, ancillary equipment and stores which they would need to support them in their attack? That was the crucial question, for it was with a force of no smaller size that Montgomery now felt impelled to make his effort at regenerating the offensive.

On July 12th he wrote to stay the anxieties of his most important doubter, Eisenhower: 'Am going to launch a very big attack next week ... VIII Corps with three armoured divisions will be launched to the country east of the Orne. Note change of date from 17 to 18 July'. To Alan Brooke two days later he wrote a longer letter of explanation:

> we are fighting in ideal defensive country. *We* do the attacking and the Boche is pretty thick on the ground. I would say we lose three men to his one in our infantry divisions ... The Second Army ... will in fact get weaker as the manpower situation hits us ... But [it] has three armoured divisions, 7, 11 and Gds [Guards]. They are quite fresh and have been practically untouched ... And so I have decided that the time had come to have a real 'showdown' on the Eastern flank and to loose [them] into the open country about the Caen–Falaise road.

The object which he sent his military assistant to explain personally to the War Office, was to 'muck up and write off enemy troops . . . all [is] designed to help the [American] forces in the west while ensuring that a firm bastion is kept in the east'. But 'at the same time', he added, 'all is ready to take advantage of . . . the enemy . . . disintegrating'. Much would be made later of this apparent hedging of his bets; a break-out if the front collapsed, if not, sound documentary evidence that all he had intended in the first place was a battle of attrition. His operation order to the divisions which would bear the burden revealed the same dual intention: 'Object . . . To engage the German armour in battle and "write it down", to such an extent that it is of no further value . . . Generally to destroy German equipment and personnel, as a preliminary to a possibly wide exploitation of success.' The tactical opening to either end was to be an advance from the 'airborne bridgehead along the eastern bank of the Orne to the area Bourguébus–Vimont–Bretteville'. Meanwhile, the Canadians were to capture the defended zone south of Caen. 'When [that] is done, then VIII Corps can "crack about" as the situation demands.'

The Canadians could form a clear picture of what their coming battle held in store for them, since the ground over which it was to be fought resembled all too nearly the fortified zone they had just cleared. But the ground beyond the 'airborne bridgehead' into which the armoured divisions were to penetrate was unknown territory. Geometrically it formed a long narrow corridor, three miles by six, if Bourguébus were taken as its terminus, between the Orne and the long range of wooded heights which ran from the Bois de Bavent southwards to Vimont. The eastern edge is an exceptionally pretty prospect, a drift of beech woods rising gently from a small country-side of lanes and tree-girt fields. The western boundary is hideous, a jungle of industrial chimneys and cooling towers which follows for four miles the banks of the Orne. The landscape in between is an almost uninterrupted plain – it was that which recommended it to Montgomery as a stamping-ground for his armour – curiously un-Norman in its lack of hedges and streams. Few features rise to break its long horizons, which appear to stretch inland as far as a tank could drive in a day. But the appearance is deceptive. The plain rolls southward in a succession of shallow swells, and a point of vantage, like that provided by the embankment of the Caen–Vimont railway, reveals a chequerboard of small villages – Cuverville, Démouville, le Mesnil-Frémentel, Cagny, le Poirier, Hubert-Folie – all no more than a mile apart, each sunk in thick orchards and centred on a stoutly built manorial farm.

An attack down the corridor was not therefore to be a stretch of easy motoring but a complex navigation between strongpoints, overlooked at a distance by commanding heights, natural or man-made, still in enemy hands. Montgomery did not underrate the menace which the tight German hold on the boundaries offered to the flanks of his armoured units as they passed by. And so he had arranged once more to call on the resources of Bomber Command and the USAAF. Sir Arthur Harris, who believed that the effort of his 'heavies' had been wasted the week before at Caen, was reluctant to help but eventually agreed to lend the whole of Bomber Command, 1,056 Lancasters and Halifaxes, to drop 5,000 tons of bombs on the shoulders of the corridor's entry point, the villages below the Bois de Bavent on the east and the Colombelles steelworks along the Orne on the west. The bombs were to be delayed-fuse, which would crater the ground but also crush the German defensive positions in each of the thousand-acre aiming points. Cagny, regarded as the toughest of the defended villages in the corridor, would also be hit by 650 tons, the ration in a normal operation for a sizeable town target, but the bombs would be fused instantaneously to avoid cratering the tanks' avenue of advance. The neck of the corridor and its exit at Bourguébus would likewise be hit with fragmentation bombs, dropped by 1,021 heavy and medium bombers of Eighth and Ninth USAAF. It was to be one of the largest air raids of all time and certainly the 'heaviest and most concentrated ever attempted in support of ground forces'.

## The Waiting Armour

'We were told, and fully believed', wrote Lieutenant Roden Orde of the 2nd Household Cavalry Regiment, 'that we were on the threshold of great events.' His regiment, the Corps Reconnaissance Unit of VIII Corps, could expect by reason of its role to be in the forefront. But the whole division which it should lead forward was also excited by anticipation. For this operation was to be 11th Armoured's first big battle. It had taken a minor part in Operation Epsom. Operation Goodwood, the codename chosen for Montgomery's push down the corridor, would offer it the chance to display in plenitude the 'Cavalry dash' for which it had been formed and trained. The 2nd Household Cavalry – a wartime amalgamation of the Life Guards and Royal Horse Guards – preferred to call the coming event the 'Goodwood Meeting', a good betting man's equation of warfare with the second most fashionable event of the racing season, and its officers had braced themselves for it as if Ascot were recently behind them. Driving through London to embark for Normandy, one of the subalterns had wistfully recorded that the smart crowd were just leaving the Four Hundred Club as their armoured cars passed in the small hours, and a latecomer to lifeboat drill on their converted cross-Channel steamer arrived loudly demanding to be shown to the 'officers' raft'. He was the sort of young man whom the pre-war troopers, still burnishing their blanket serge battledress to the consistency of thick cardboard, knew and understood. 'The officers', wrote a corporal-of-horse (sergeant to the rest of the army – not for nothing did the most senior regiments of the British army cherish their reputation for eccentricity), 'although suffering the worst they have yet suffered as far as rough living is concerned, still manage to look pretty comfortable.'[1] And D Squadron had indeed settled in cheerfully at the château of Brécy, recently evacuated by a *grande horizontale* of the Comédie Française. They had been fed pineapple and fresh cherries on their way across the Channel, were now looking forward to eggs and fresh butter from the farm in the shadow of the château's 'consequential little gateway' and were regretting that Calvados, though excellent for lighting fires, was easier to come by than wine.

The 2nd Household Cavalry, being equipped with armoured cars, would not, however, be called upon to advance until the crust of the German defences had been broken by the tanks of 11th Armoured. They belonged to four different regiments, typifying in their different ways the varying traditions which had gone to make up the contemporary Royal Armoured Corps. The 23rd Hussars was a war-raised regiment but a resurrection of an older one, which had campaigned with Wellington in the Peninsula. It had resumed its ancestor's battle honours, the horsed cavalry's habit of calling its tank sub-units 'sabre squadrons' and the jovial, everyday manners of the hunting field. The hunting field was the natural habitat of its sister regiment, the 2nd Northamptonshire Yeomanry, which provided divisional reconnaissance. In peacetime it rode on parade to the strains of 'John Peel', pitched its annual camp in the parks of the great houses of the Midland hunting shires – Althorp, Boughton and Rockingham – and chose its commanding officers from Masters of the Pytchley. As a yeomanry regiment it had in peacetime only a part-time existence, drawing its soldiers and officers from the ranks of civilians who felt their place in county society required them to play a military role in its life, farmers' sons, estate workers from the big properties, local solicitors and land agents, landed gentlemen from the broad acres round Kettering and Towcester. When war came, it formed ranks and marched away from Northamptonshire for the duration, in 1914 to France and then to Italy, in 1939 first to guard the south coast against invasion, then to train in Wiltshire for the return to Europe, ultimately to take ship for Normandy.

The third armoured regiment in the division, the 2nd Fife and Forfar Yeomanry, represented something of the same strain in Scottish military life. Tenuously it could claim a link with the Fife Yeomanry Cavalry, raised to defend the kingdom during the Napoleonic wars and kept in being to preserve established order during the times of the Chartists. But its sounder origins were in the Volunteer movement of 1859, that strange mid-century upsurge of enthusiasm for amateur soldiering, which had brought into being the Fife Light Horse. Twinned with the cavalry volunteers of neighbouring Forfar, the regiment had flourished, to send a mounted infantry company to the Boer War, ride with the Desert Mounted Corps in Egypt in the First World War, and after 1918 surrender its horses for armoured cars under the command of the descendant of the chieftain who had raised the Napoleonic regiment, Carnegy-Carnegy of Lour.

The fourth regiment represented the antithesis of all for which the other three stood, and was the single solid element of experience in the divisional armour. The 3rd Royal Tank Regiment had fought at Calais in 1940, when it had left its first complement of tanks behind at the evacuation beaches; in Egypt and Greece, where it had lost all its tanks again in desperate rearguard action; in Libya, in the defence of Alexandria at Alam Halfa; in the victory of Alamein and in the pursuit of Rommel to Tunisia. Few of the soldiers with whom it began the war now remained with the regiment. One – G.P.B. Roberts – had been promoted away and now commanded the 11th Armoured Division. Many had found graves on one of its numerous battlefields. The survivors were harrowed and hardened men. But their outlook from the first had partaken of little of the light-hearted, improvising, all-right-on-the-night attitude which had always allegedly characterized the British cavalry's approach to combat. The officers of the Royal Tank Regiment, the Tank Corps of the First World War, had known the hostility of the whole horsey half of the army – cavalry, gunner and polo-playing infantry regiments – in the decade after 1918 when its fodder bills had been weighed in the balance against their petrol by a cheese-paring Treasury. They had listened with clenched teeth to their opponents' arguments that the tank had reached the limits of its potential development and would never be more than an ancillary to the infantry. They had seen the means of demonstrating a rejoinder, the Experimental Mechanized Force, disbanded after a single season of trials, to the ostentatious satisfaction of Lancers, Hussars and Dragoons. In the privacy of their unfashionable messes and the cinder-block classrooms of the Bovington Tank School they had sustained each other's spirits with repeated reassurances that time and events would punish the reactionaries for their flippancy and lack of professionalism. They had not enjoyed the interwar years, and when war had come they had seized on the opportunity it offered to evangelize the new army of civilians with their message and to push leaders with their ideas into the places so long held by devotees of the antiquarian. It was not coincidence that the celebrated second badge worn by Montgomery – most abrasive and innovative of the new generals – was that of the Royal Tank Regiment.

But they had not been tactful, either before the war or after its outbreak. They had made it clear that they sought not the mechanization of the cavalry, but its disbandment and replacement by a larger Tank Corps. And so it said much for the improvising spirit of the cavalry which they affected to spurn that, when confronted with the inescapable requirement to bid horses farewell and to take to tracks, the old regiments had responded not merely uncomplainingly but with the enthusiasm of the born-again. In its heart, the cavalry had known that armour was an idea whose time had come. And cavalrymen too had felt a secret shame at the secondary, oversafe role to which trenches and barbed wire had consigned them in the First World War, from which so many of the bolder had escaped to ride steeplechase around the wide skies of France and Flanders. Their regular officers had also therefore grasped at the opportunity offered by the Second World War to remake the reputation of their arm. Recognizing their turn to listen, they had learnt all they could of the doctrine which the tank men preached, made it their own and resolved to infuse it with that dash of cavalier temper which they believed no plus-fours-and-puttees soldier could ever properly simulate. To some of the converts, the Royal Tank Regiment professionals quickly conceded their respect. Towards the cavalry as a whole they sustained their guard of doubting watchfulness. Perhaps in time they became over-watchful; some senior commanders had begun to feel that by 1944 the Tanks had made themselves the prisoners of their own orthodoxy, keener to adhere to the letter of their cherished doctrine than to win the rewards a violation of it might bring.

## Moving Up

Yet there was sense in the veterans' caution. Recklessness could lose a regiment half its tanks in a few minutes; there were even instances of units ending a day of battle with no tanks running at all. And an armoured regiment without its armour was exactly as useful as a fleet without ships. Hence the Tanks' obsession with maintenance, in their view the cavalry's weak spot, since in the early days of tank operations it was mechanical breakdown rather than enemy action which caused the majority of casualties. The balance had now swung the other way, and with the arrival of the Sherman from the United States to replace the misbegotten British designs of the early war years, mechanical breakdown was now the exception. The Sherman was a magnificent expression of American mass-production engineering, and indeed a great deal of the American motor-car industry had been re-tooled to produce it as a standard design. Built round a Ford engine, which could be removed and replaced with a spare in a few minutes, it had 2·5 inches of cast armour on the turret and front plate, stowage for seventy rounds of main-armament ammunition, and a 75 mm high-velocity gun. It had its defects. It caught fire too easily and, when it did so, burnt fiercely, for it was petrol rather than diesel fuelled. Its gun was now outclassed by the 75 mm of the German Panthers, and also of course by the 88 mm of the Tigers. And its profile was high, so that it was seen sooner than the British Cromwell, which equipped the divisional reconnaissance regiments. But some of these defects had already been taken in hand, notably by the re-arming of one tank in four with a long 17-pounder gun which made it a match for the Mark IV Panzer and the Panther.

And it was comfortable to live in. The five men who made up its crew – commander, who was trained to ride standing with his head out of the turret hatch; gunner, who sat by his right leg with his eye close to the rubber-padded telescope of his gunsight; loader/operator, who 'netted in' the radio to the frequency of the other three tanks in the troop or to that of the regiment for talk to the rear, and otherwise manhandled the heavy brass-cased shells into the breech and the empties out; driver, a level below them in the bow of the tank; and co-driver-machine-gunner at his side – looked on their tank as home. In the spaces between the ammunition they stowed socks, sleeping-bags, letters from home, and all the canned food, tea and cigarettes that smooth talk and light fingers could win from the lines of supply. Illegally, they would light solid-fuel cookers on the tank's floor in quiet moments to produce stew or hot chocolate and, when the ground was dry enough to assure that the tracks would not sink in during the night, they would sleep under it in summer, wrapped in the tarpaulin covers of the engine hatches. These comforts and the tank's thick walls endeared it to the troopers, who looked with pity on the shelterless infantrymen. 'You could hear them squealing like rabbits when the machine-guns caught them round our tanks,' a sergeant of 3rd Royal Tank Regiment recalled. 'They couldn't touch us. There was only one thing that could and there weren't many of them.'

The 'one thing' was the high-velocity, armour-piercing shot fired by another tank's gun or the specialized weapons of the *Panzerjäger* (anti-tank units). But, when such a round hit solidly home, the effects were instantaneously horrible. At best, if the shot lodged but did not penetrate, the blow to the face of the armour detached high-speed fragments from its rear into the interior, which inflicted multiple small wounds on the crew. If the shot penetrated, it would retain some of its velocity but be confined by the armoured skin and so ricochet about inside, smashing all it touched, metal or flesh. At worst, it would ignite ammunition and fuel – which first was immaterial, since they burnt together – incinerating whoever could not reach the hatch.

Tanks burn in a way that has its own grotesque poignancy. The flames are explosively fierce and yet are tightly contained in the hollow steel shell: so, the smoke rushed out with

tumbling fury ... From the turret, black smoke alternating
with intense flame thunders forth in a monstrous jet. But then
from time to time the smoke is forced into huge expelled puffs
by the exploding shells within. Each black puff, from the
circular turret hatch becomes with grotesque perfection a
rolling smoke ring. Such a smoke ring we associate with quiet
reflective moments – old men showing their skill with a pipe in
the chimney corner, to admiring children. The perfect black
smoke ring shooting up from a burning tank suggested some
grotesque devil's game in the thing, a derisory joke of the
fiends, over dying men. A burning tank, because of this,
looked like a monster, a dying dragon, vomiting up the life
within it in black gouts, and blowing aloft ghostly rings which
mounted, curling in on themselves, high into the air. Beneath
these sad signals, a red and white glower would roll in the eyes
of the dead monster, the hatch holes, through which the crew
had entered, never to emerge again.[2]

All crews, whatever sang-froid they cultivated, lived with the knowledge of their tanks' dual nature – preserver and destroyer. Many in
3rd Royal Tank Regiment had had tanks shot underneath them:
drivers had escaped from beneath a shambled turret, commanders
had jumped clear of a flaming hull. Some whole crews could think
with gratitude of an old friend which had lost its track to a winging
round or absorbed a killer in the body and let them get safely away;
but they were in the minority. So there was a flicker of apprehension
in all the armoured regiments of the three divisions – 7th, Guards,
and, leading, 11th – as they jostled their way down to the bridges of
the Orne. Each contained 3,500 vehicles and, although much of the
wheeled transport was not to cross until later, it was imperative to
pass over the river the 300 White half-tracks of the motor battalions,
the infantry's 680 tracked carriers and the 870 fighting tanks, on time
and in the right order. Each of the three pairs of bridges was fed by
two lanes, one for wheels, one for tracks, and all movement was
forward. No return journeys were allowed. First across on the night
of June 17th was the tank brigade – 29th Armoured – of the 11th
Armoured Division. The Guards and the 7th waited on the west
bank for the 11th to clear its assembly area and move through the
gaps which had been cleared in the defensive minefields. Following
the front columns, a troop leader of the Household Cavalry passed

soldiers around the bridge at Bénouville, the target of the D-Day *coup de main*, who were 'comfortably housed in the old shells of the 6th Airborne Division's discarded gliders – washing was hung out on the lines between crashed planes and the now returning French peasants were gleaning among the heaps of twisted aluminium'. Ahead 'tanks were passing us on a taped track as we drove alongside on the road. We drove down and over a canal bridge and up the steep side beyond. Notices everywhere. "Dust brings shells" – it did. Others, "Tracks Left", "Bridge Class 40". Up the hill, the ominous notice saying simply "Mines".'[3] The mines were British and the plan required fourteen gaps to have been cleared through them. The senior officers of 29th Armoured Brigade, whose vehicles when deployed covered a square mile of ground, wondered how quickly they could funnel them through the three gaps which were their allotment.

# Bombardment

At about 1 a.m. on June 18th, 29th Armoured Brigade reached its start line and the tank crews, tired by two days on the road, thought of sleep. H-Hour was 7.45 a.m. Long before that moment, even the heaviest sleepers had woken. 'For at 0500', wrote a Grenadier waiting across the Orne,

> a distant thunder in the air brought all the sleepy-eyed tank crews out of their blankets. A thousand Lancasters were flying in from the sea in groups of three or four at 3,000 feet. Ahead of them the pathfinders were scattering their flares and before long the first bombs were dropping. After a few minutes the area was a turmoil of dust and smoke with the Ack Ack tracer soaring above. Occasionally an aircraft would fall like a swaying leaf, flaming to the ground.

Only six were eventually counted to have fallen to the German anti-aircraft batteries, which themselves were under devastating attack from the artillery of the corps and divisional artilleries, about 400 guns in all, supported by the fire of two cruisers and the venerable monitor HMS *Roberts*, whose monstrous 15-inch pieces had last been in action at the Battle of Jutland. Heavy bombardment from the sea was the experience the Germans had learnt to dread most since June 6th. But neither they nor any other soldiers who had ever lived had stood in the way of the hurricane of high-explosive

which now blew down from the Lancasters upon the shoulders of the
'armoured corridor' and the defended villages on its floor.

A company of the 22nd Panzer Regiment of 21st Panzer Division
was located in the left-hand shoulder target area, directly under the
heaviest of the bombing, and one of its tank wireless operators,
Werner Kortenhaus, described the agonizing ordeal. It had begun,
as for the British, with the 'droning of approaching bomber squadrons', what a Welsh Guardsman had heard as a 'faint and steady hum
– growing into an insistent throbbing roar until the whole northern
sky was filled with aeroplanes as far as one could see – wave upon
wave, stepped up one above the other and spreading out east and
west until it seemed there was no room for any more'. The sight and
sound had brought all the Guardsmen 'out of their vehicles staring in
awed wonder'. In Kortenhaus's company the warning noise had the
opposite effect. 'The men got into the tanks and closed the flaps, or
crawled underneath for protection. We saw little dots detach themselves from the planes' (on the other side the Welsh Guards saw
'hundreds of little black clouds puffing round the bombers as they
droned inexorably towards their targets'), 'so many of them that the
crazy thought occurred to us; are those leaflets? We could hardly
believe that they could all be bombs. Then began the most terrifying
hours of our lives. It was a bomb carpet, regularly ploughing up the
ground. Among the thunder of the explosions, we could hear the
wounded scream and the insane howling of men who had been
driven mad.'[4]

'Mad' was no exaggeration. In Captain von Rosen's company of
the 503rd Heavy Tank Battalion, a neighbouring unit to Kortenhaus's, one man was driven 'insane from the effects of the
bombs' and two more, unable to stand the terrible apprehension of
waiting for what seemed the inevitable, committed suicide during
the course of the bombardment. Fifteen of the company's complement of a hundred were killed, either by fragments or by blast,
which was strong enough to turn one of the company's Tigers,
weighing sixty tons, upside down. Three others were destroyed. In
Kortenhaus's company the lighter Mark IV's were bounced up
and down by the roll of concussion and later, when the storm had
passed on to engulf the panzer battalions on the floor of the corridor,
the surviving tanks had to be dug out with bare hands from the
mounds of soil which had been thrown up round them. Every
opening in the hulls had been clogged with earth – gun-muzzles, air

filters, engine grids, exhausts. The sighting telescopes had been thrown out of alignment and the engines, when they caught, ran roughly with the mistreatment they had suffered. Yet it had been worse for the infantry who did not have armoured vehicles under or in which to hide. The survivors of the 16th Luftwaffe Field Division, ground crews remustered as riflemen from Göring's shrinking Luftwaffe, who had already undergone the bombardment of Caen ten days before, were found in the reploughed ruins of Colombelles shaking uncontrollably from the noise, blast and internal terror which they had suffered. Many were unable to co-ordinate their limbs and, when collected to be marched off to the prisoner-of-war cages, had to be allowed to sit by the roadside until sufficiently recovered to walk in a straight line.

In the middle of the corridor the attack of the American Havocs and Marauders of Ninth Army Air Force was particularly effective. It had hit the positions of two of the German units best equipped to do 11th Armoured Division harm, a battery of 21st Panzer Division's Assault Gun Battalion 200, equipped with 75 mm and 105 mm guns on converted French tank chassis, and part of its I Battalion, 125 Panzergrenadier Regiment. All of the guns in the first and most in the second had been put out of action. This boded well for the advance which was about to begin, for British intelligence reckoned on the presence in the immediate vicinity of only two battered German infantry divisions – 16th Luftwaffe and 346th, both in the wrong place and too weak to offer resistance – and the single panzer division, 21st. Continually in action since D-Day, it had lost many men and much material, leaving it by British calculations with only a thousand or so riflemen in its two panzergrenadier regiments, 125 and 192, and fifty tanks in its panzer regiment, 22. It was also reckoned to deploy not more than thirty or forty anti-aircraft and anti-tank guns of 50 mm up to 88 mm. The nearest reserves, 12th SS and 1st SS Panzer Divisions, were not exactly located on British intelligence maps, but were plotted south of Caen. Both were expected to resist strongly when encountered – 1st SS still had a hundred tanks – but neither was expected to come to the battle. The British tanks should therefore have only a few of their own kind to meet, and some static anti-tank guns, which the cavalry expected to blanket or outflank. Older tank hands, had they been able to count the number which had escaped the aerial bombardment, would have crossed their fingers.

# Into the Corridor

As the monstrous drumming of the bombardment gave way to the drone of the departing bombers which had laid it, intermittently audible through the detonations of the artillery barrage, the tanks of 29th Armoured Brigade started their engines and motored forward towards the neck of the corridor between Escoville and Ste Honorine-la-Chardonnerette. On their left, the division's infantry got up from their waiting positions and moved forward also, to clear the flank of German weapons which might impede the tanks' advance. The first obstacle they met, however, was man-made, the gapped minefield. The 3rd Royal Tank Regiment and the Fife and Forfars had negotiated the gaps while the bombardment was in progress. The 23rd Hussars, stacked up behind them, had had to wait. Swollen by a half-track company of infantrymen and a self-propelled battery of artillery, the regiment was a lengthy column and, by the time it was through, the Tanks and the Fife and Forfars, still in line ahead, had left them well behind. This extension was tactically undesirable, since the plan was that the Tanks and Fife and Forfars should deploy abreast as quickly as possible, and the Hussars close their rear as an immediate reserve. The advance had thus already begun to straggle. But little of that was apparent to those at the point. Captain Lemon, in a flimsy Honey tank of the 3rd RTR's reconnaissance troop, 'rather enjoyed the first few minutes as I think most of us did ... "MOVE NOW". These two words echoed throughout the Regiment and the tanks slowly surged forward. Then suddenly about a hundred yards in front of the leading tanks the earth started "boiling" all along the front as the rolling barrage from the 25-pounders began.'5 In a Fife and Forfar tank to his rear, Lance-Corporal Cox was watching the view through his periscope. He saw the sun come out from behind the Saharan dust storm which the bombers had raised, and recalled 'moving forward some distance behind a creeping barrage, then we stopped. I remember opening a new tin of jam and spreading it thickly on innumerable biscuits and passing them round the crew. We exchanged banter; I think the humour was a bit forced and had a slight hysterical touch to it for we were all aware that this was going to be something rather big.' This pause was imposed by the line of the Caen–Troarn railway, only a narrow-gauge industrial track, but just enough of an obstacle to waste twenty minutes of the brigade's time as the Tanks and the Fife

and Forfars clambered across, each tank doglegging to avoid exposing its belly, and then jostled into line side by side. There were now
sixty-four tanks in the leading wave, with a second and third of equal
strength behind, but the delay had still not allowed the Hussars to
close the gap behind.

Following behind came the division's infantry brigade, the 3rd
Monmouths, 1st Herefords and 4th King's Shropshire Light Infantry, all Territorials from the Welsh borders who had spent the
preceding four years training in England, much of the time within
travelling distance of their homes. The Shropshires had heard
enemy fire at close hand for the first time on June 29th, had suffered
their first fatal casualty the next day, had never before been in battle
– true too of their sister battalions – and were now moving forward to
the essential task of clearing the surviving enemy infantry from the
first villages of Cuverville and Démouville. With them came the
divisional reconnaissance regiment, 2nd Northamptonshire Yeomanry, which lost four of its Cromwell tanks to uncleared mines in
the minefield gaps. Beyond the minefield the leading waves of the
infantry began to come under shell fire from German guns hidden in
the ruins along the Orne and south of the river beyond Caen.
'Nothing could have been more inspiring', a proud Shropshire
eye-witness recorded, 'than the sight of the sections doggedly
advancing in open order, dropping on their faces as each salvo of
shells landed, and immediately rising to their feet and continuing the
advance.' Their luck was in. Next day a shell would land in the
middle of Corporal Lavender's section and kill or wound every one
of his eight men.

The Monmouths found their way into Cuverville by 8.30 a.m.
and began looking for Germans who wished to surrender. The
Herefords entered the orchards south-east of the village a little later,
where they quickly took the surrender of fifty. But ahead loomed the
ruins, choked streets and gap-toothed church of Démouville, from
which bursts of fire warned that its possession would not be so easily
gained. The brigade gathered its force for a deliberate assault. It
would take time to prepare and deliver. But with every passing
quarter of an hour their sister tank brigade moved farther away from
them, pressing deeper down the corridor into a belt of villages which
its own Greenjacket motor battalion (8th Rifle Brigade) would not
have the men to skirmish through.

The tanks had not yet quite entered the danger zone, though they were approaching the point where their supporting artillery, most of which was marooned the wrong side of the Orne, could no longer give them covering fire. Yet so far Captain Lemon of the 3rd Tanks had

> rather enjoyed [things] as I think most of us did. There was very little opposition and one had a wonderful feeling of superiority as many Germans, shaken by the preliminary bombing and shelling, gave themselves up. As time passed though, they grew more aggressive, having overcome the effects of the bombs and shells ... Targets kept appearing in the hedgerows and [beyond] the villages of Cuverville and Démouville there were a couple of embankments to cross which proved awkward obstacles.

The first of these ran athwart the line of advance of the whole armoured brigade. Carrying the railway between Caen and Vimont, it stood in places ten feet high with steep sides. To cross, the tanks would have to fan out, slow down and individually pick a way over the top. That would be a dangerous moment for each crew, as it exposed itself on the skyline to a high-velocity shot from any anti-tank gun that was waiting to strike on the far side. But as the squadrons motored down towards their pinnacles of decision, sharper and more immediate danger suddenly unmasked itself in the foreground.

## Battle Group von Luck

The bombing had killed, wounded or demoralized a very large number of the Germans in the armoured corridor, and destroyed or disabled much of their equipment. Most of the infantry of the 16th Luftwaffe Field Division had been knocked out of the battle, and the I Battalion Panzergrenadier Regiment 125 had been broken into fragments. But the bombing had not destroyed everything and everyone. A man it had not touched at all was the commander of one of the Battle Groups of 21st Panzer Division, Oberst Hans von Luck. It had not touched him because he was still on his way back from three days' leave in Paris while the bombs were raining down and reached his headquarters in Frénouville, on the Caen–Vimont railway line, at about the time the British tanks were passing Cuverville and Démouville. His deputy briefly reported the events of the last hours and advised that there seemed nothing left of the Battle Group with which to fight. Von Luck, who had the Polish, French, Russian and Western Desert Campaigns behind him, and was not in any case a colonel at the age of thirty-three for nothing, swallowed the report and went to see what he could find.

He headed first for Cagny, the substantial village just north of the Caen–Vimont railway which the route of the British tanks would leave on their left hand. As he got into it, he saw from the orchard on its forward edge the mass of Shermans wreathed in their dust cloud moving to pass between Cagny and its neighbouring village to the north-west, le Mesnil-Frémentel. But they did not seem to be accompanied by infantry (thought each regiment with it had a company of Greenjackets in half-tracks, they were not up with the leading armour), nor did they seem to be bothered about flank security. Here was an opportunity, all the more firmly to be snatched because von Luck, fresh back from leave, had no picture of the general tactical situation and believed that the remains of his Battle Group were all that stood between 11th Armoured Division and the open country beyond the bridgehead perimeter. On his way through the village he had seen one of his Mark IV tanks, miraculously untouched by the 650 tons of bombs which had been Cagny's particular dose, an 88 mm anti-tank gun of the divisional *Panzerjäger* battalion, and a battery of 88 mm anti-aircraft guns. The 88 mm had long been adapted for the dual role of fighting both aircraft and tanks, but these belonged to a specialized Luftwaffe anti-aircraft unit and still had their barrels pointed towards the sky from which they had vainly been trying to shoot the now departed heavy bombers. The tank and anti-tank gun commanders briskly obeyed von Luck's command to get their weapons up to the edge of the orchard and open fire on the British tanks. The Luftwaffe officer demurred. His task, he explained, was to shoot down aircraft, not puncture armour, whatever the capabilities of his weapons. Von Luck drew his pistol and replied that the airman could 'either die now on my responsibility or win a decoration on his own'. The pistol, or the Knight's Cross round von Luck's neck, dissolved bureaucratic rigidities on the spot.

By the time the leading British Shermans, which on the Cagny side of the armoured column belonged to the Fife and Forfar Yeomanry, came opposite the orchard, presenting their thinly armoured side-plates to the waiting Germans, there were five

88 mm guns deployed on the bearing. Choosing individual targets, the gunners crashed out their first salvoes.

> The first tank to be hit was Major Nicholl's. A moment later Captain Miller's was destroyed. The rear troop of 'B' Squadron, which had responsibility for flank protection, was next involved. The strength of the opposition came as a swift and unpleasant surprise. The land laid waste by the bombers seemed like a piece of devastated territory which could scarcely conceal a living thing. Trees were uprooted, fields pitted and littered with dead cattle, and theoretically nothing could be left alive on this lunar landscape. Yet suddenly there came evidence [ruefully recalled the Fife and Forfar's historian] that the enemy was there and very aggressive too.

Twelve tanks, most belonging to 'C' Squadron, had been destroyed in what to an observer looked like 'a matter of seconds'. To their rear, the 23rd Hussars were brought to a stop by the sight of so many tanks bursting apparently simultaneously into flames. Soon towards them across the corn came the survivors of the crews, blackened by smoke and burns and running with the energy of men fleeing a volcano.

Von Luck, however caught only the rear of the Fifes – more argument from the Luftwaffe officer and they would have got clean past – and none of the Royal Tanks. Five intact tank squadrons, a hundred Shermans in all, had left Cagny to their rear and were advancing towards their goal of Bourguébus. He had no way of stopping them, so his thoughts now turned to the rest of the front his Battle Group was supposed to defend. East of Cagny the 'armoured corridor' quickly gave way to hedgerow country, dotted with small woods, the out-liers of the forest along the Troarn ridge. Here lay the route through which the Guards Armoured Division, when it had emerged from the 'airborne bridgehead' and got into the tracks of the 11th Armoured Division, was to take in its exploitation of the offensive. But dotted about in the orchards and enclosures of the area were isolated tanks and squads of infantrymen, which had survived the bombing and might be activated, von Luck hoped, into an effective anti-tank screen. The 22nd Panzer Regiment, 21st Panzer's tank regiment, had about nine Mark IVs still battleworthy, around Frénouville and farther away near Emiéville was the Tiger company of 503 Heavy Tank Battalion. The crews of the surviving vehicles had worked frantically to start motors and free armament from clogging earth. The Mark IVs were the first to get into action and trundled forward to engage the 23rd Hussars as they followed the Fifes towards Cagny. Outnumbered and still half-crippled, however, they failed to deliver a concentrated blow and all but one was knocked out.

The Tigers were a more formidable threat, Captain Freiherr von Rosen, commanding 3 Company of 503 Heavy Tank Battalion, had got six of his eight tanks back into running order by midday and probed forward from his battle station in the Emiéville orchards to see what he could find. What he found was the Guards Armoured Division. At last clear of the 'airborne bridgehead' and through the gaps of the minefields, the Guards were pushing hard to get south of Emiéville, where they were scheduled to wheel left and drive towards Vimont and the open country. In the lead was the 2nd Battalion Grenadier Guards, which, 2,000 yards short of Cagny, was stopped by anti-tank fire, emanating it believed from the village. The battalion commander, therefore, decided to edge away nearer Emiéville, leave a squadron there as flank guard, and send another to take the anti-tank guns in Cagny from an unexpected direction. As soon, however, as the Guards' Shermans strayed from the 'armoured corridor' into the more broken country from its edge, they met fire from another source. It was rapidly identified as coming 'from Tigers', but that did not save nine of the Grenadier crews, whose tanks were soon burning. In their wake came the 2nd Battalion Irish Guards, who were also held up for a long time before Cagny and eventually diverted leftwards by the resistance from the front. An enterprising troop leader, Lieutenant Gorman, nosed forward through tall hedgerows to see if he could identify whence the enemy fire was coming, and was startled at the top of a small rise to find two Tigers and two other German tanks on the other side less than 200 yards away. His gunner fired at the leader but, to Gorman's dismay, he saw 'the shot bounce off and go sizzling up into the air. I ordered the gunner to fire again, but a hollow voice came up from the bowels of the tank, saying "Gun jammed, sir".'6 Seeing the Tigers' lethal 88 mm guns training on to his bearing and remembering that he had been trained to advance when in doubt, Gorman ordered his driver to accelerate and steer for the enemy. Fortunately, the Tiger turret was notoriously underpowered and so, just before its gun was aligned, the Sherman hit the Tiger amidships. Both crews took this as the signal to bale out and look for cover. The Irish Guards' wireless operator found himself in the same ditch as the Germans, where, under heavy shelling, the two sides declared a local truce. Gorman ran back to where he had left the rest of his troop, collected another Sherman, a 'Firefly' armed with a tank-busting 17-pounder, and with it set the rammed Tiger on fire.

Out on the opposite flank, yet another element of Battle Group von Luck had been making itself a menace to the armoured advance while this little battle had been going on. The German army in France was a make do and mend force, which had had to supplement the unsteady flow of equipment from the domestic arms factories with jury rigs of its own. One such makeshift was a self-propelled anti-tank gun produced by marrying a German 105 mm to a captured French Hotchkiss tank chassis. Assault Gun Battalion 200 had five batteries of these weapons, each of six guns, and was under the command of their designer, Major Becker. One of the batteries had been destroyed by the bombing in Démouville, another was intact in the outskirts of Caen but beyond the battle zone. The three remaining were in the path of the armoured charge, Battery 3 at Grentheville just beyond the second railway line and Batteries 4 and 5 in le Mesnil-Frémentel.

The 3rd Royal Tank Regiment, which had orders to bypass all points of resistance and keep going for the summit of Bourguébus ridge, had not been hurt by von Luck's press-ganged 88 mms in Cagny, from which it had been shielded by the mass of the Fife and Forfars. It lost only one tank to the batteries in le Mesnil-Frémentel, drenching the village with a regimental broadside as it passed. But beyond the railway it began to pay the price of leading an armoured charge. Its designated route lay across the angle of the Caen–Troarn railway and the very steeply embanked Caen–Vimont line, which ran south-east. The angle was commanded by Becker's Battery 3 and as soon as the British appeared over the first railway line and man-oeuvred to find the way under the second – it ran through a tunnel – they crashed out. The range was short and the guns hit home. Major Close, commanding 'A' Squadron, recalled seeing

> several anti-tank guns among the trees and ... the gunners
> frantically swinging their guns round towards us. In the
> cornfields around us were many multi-barrel mortar positions,
> which were already firing over our heads. They were quickly

dealt with, in some cases simply by running them over with the tank. But the anti-tank guns were a different matter. Opening fire at almost point-blank range, they hit three of my tanks [out of nineteen], which burst into flames; and I could see that the squadron on my left also had several tanks blazing furiously. My orders were still to press on and bypass the village.

Racing for the tunnel, and taking it in turn to give covering fire, Close's tanks got through to the far side, where the high embankment hid them from fire and view. There they were 'joined by the rest of the regiment. Our objectives, the villages of Bras and Hubert-Folie lay ahead, over some 3,000 yards of very open ground, on a very prominent ridge. It looked comparatively quiet and we could see no signs of enemy. (But) as there was practically no cover, it was impossible to move as we would have wished, bound by bound.'[7]

# Counter-attack

Major-General Roberts, commanding the 11th Armoured Division from his Cromwell headquarters tank behind the leading regiments, could now feel some satisfaction at the progress of the battle. The Guards Armoured Division was moving up to assume responsibility for the eastern edge of the 'armoured corridor.' His western flank was now clear of the suburbs of Caen and so beyond the reach of what German defenders still remained in the ruins of the factories and industrial villages. At the back of the battlefield, 7th Armoured Division was crossing the bridges over the Orne and would soon be flooding forward with 250 fresh Shermans and Cromwells. Of his own armoured regiments, the 23rd Hussars and the Northamptonshire Yeomanry were still intact and, though the 3rd Royal Tanks and the Fife and Forfars had each lost about a squadron's worth of fighting vehicles, each still had forty running Shermans. They were now abreast of each other, beyond the Caen–Vimont railway, with only the four little villages of Bras, Hubert-Folie, Soliers and Four standing between them and their objective of Bourguébus on the summit of the final ridge line.

But this, from their points of observation on the ridge, was also an appreciation which the Germans could make. While von Luck had been struggling on the floor of the plain during the morning, in the belief that nothing stood between the Germans and collapse but his own handful of anti-tank batteries and fragments of tank companies, the German higher command had in fact assessed the situation and put in hand measures to contain the extent of the damage. If the German army prided itself and excelled in one activity of war, it was snatching stability from the jaws of potential disaster. The great holes torn by the Russians time and again in the Eastern Front since the winter of 1941 had regularly been filled by makeshift units hastily cobbled together from the personnel of the rear areas. Anzio, the Allies' surprise descent on the coast of Italy south of Rome in January 1944, had failed to unhinge the whole German line across the ankle of Italy only because Kesselring had been able to activate the well-tested expedient of forming *Alarmeinheiten* – mainly battalions collected at the railway stations from men returning off leave – faster than the Allied commander could get his battalions off the beaches. And regular German units were not given to quibbles about functional demarcation. Von Luck's Luftwaffe officer was an exception to a pattern of remarkable flexibility, in which clerks and cooks would turn out as riflemen in an emergency and engineer battalions down tools to man the front line. That was exactly the shift which the commander of 21st Panzer Division had organized. The crest of Bourguébus ridge was now manned by his divisional engineer battalion, thickened up by the motorcyclists and scout-car crews of the divisional reconnaissance battalion (in German, *Aufklärungsbataillon*, an odd evocation of the Enlightenment which recalled university days to the donnish staff officers of the intelligence branch at 21st Army Group). Behind them stood his three battalions of artillery, far beyond the range of the British guns back on the wrong side of the Orne, and well placed to lay down an offensive barrage along the foot of the ridge as soon as 11th Armoured Division's tanks reached it.

More important, however, for the integrity of the German front, Panzer Group West, the higher headquarters responsible for the defence of the eastern end of the bridgehead, was setting in motion a counter-attack. Flare-light photographs taken by the Luftwaffe on the night of July 16th–17th had revealed the weight of traffic crossing the Orne bridges and certain precautionary moves had been ordered as a result: 12th SS Panzer Division had positioned a battle group near Lisieux (exactly the right place were Goodwood to succeed) and all units around Caen had been alerted. On the way back from the meeting at which these decisions were taken, Rommel, overall commander of the bridgehead battle, had been gravely wounded when his staff car was attacked by a roving British fighter. But the command structure had continued to function despite this numbing blow, and, when Eberbach at Panzer Group West had satisfied himself on the morning of July 18th that the attack into the 'armoured corridor' was the real thing, and not a feint to draw German strength away from the west side of Caen, he had signalled 1st SS Panzer Division to move from its position south of the city and prepare to intervene. The *Leibstandarte Adolf Hitler* (Adolf Hitler's Life Guard) was one of the most experienced armoured formations in the German Army. Blooded in Poland, it had fought in France in 1940, with Army Group B in Russia in 1941, taken part in Manstein's attempt to relieve Stalingrad in 1942, been sent to Italy in August 1943 to meet the Allied invasion and had, of course, recently helped to blunt 15th Scottish Division's offensive on the other side of Carpiquet. It enjoyed the Führer's warmest favour; as a result it was usually up to strength. The heavy fighting of the last weeks had reduced it, but it still had forty-six Panthers and Mark IVs, as well as some assault guns.

During the morning, dodging from one patch of cover to another, these tanks had worked their way from the southern suburbs of Caen to the western edge of the 'armoured corridor'. By 2.30 p.m. the Panthers of the divisional panzer regiment had installed themselves between Bras and Bourguébus, while the assault guns had pushed on to line the ridge beyond. From their position, at an elevation of 150 feet above the floor of the plain, the German crews looked down directly on to the path of the oncoming British tanks. But while the attackers stood naked in open country, the Germans could take advantage of the network of sunken roads which ran east–west along the crest and the shelter of the small woods and villages on its slopes. Trees, buildings and steep banks combined moreover to deny the roving fighter-bombers of 2nd Tactical Air Force a clear view of their targets. In such circumstances, they should have been talked on to them by the RAF forward ground controller, operating with the leading waves of armour, but his tank had been among those knocked out in the morning and he had gone off the air. When, a little later in the battle, 'C' squadron of the 23rd Hussars urgently needed air support to drive off a German tank thrust, he was unable to call it in and had to wireless the self-propelled guns of 11th

Armoured Division on the BBC frequency, with a request to transmit it onward. It is therefore not altogether fanciful to compare the situation at Bourguébus ridge in the early afternoon of July 18th, 1944, with that at Waterloo at the same time of day 129 years and one month earlier. The attackers enjoyed enormous superiority in the mobile arm. The defenders were battered and short of offensive power. But they still retained hold of some key defensive strong-points standing forward of their main position – Bras, Soliers and Cagny here playing the same role as Plancenoit, la Haye Sainte and Hougoumont on Wellington's front – and the main position itself was emplaced on perfect defensive territory, including a 'reverse slope' for the protection of the reserves. Any ascent of the ridge promised to be a bloody enterprise.

It was towards that ascent that the 3rd Tanks and Fife and Forfars were now moving, the first west of the Caen–Vimont railway towards Bras and Hubert-Folie, the second on the other side towards Bourguébus itself. 'It was just as the leading tanks were level with Hubert-Folie when the fun began', reported an officer of the 3rd Tanks. 'I saw Sherman after Sherman go up in flames and it got to such a pitch that I thought that in another few minutes there would be nothing left of the Regiment. I could see the German tanks milling about just behind Hubert-Folie and over to the left.' These were the Panthers of 1st SS. 'A tank battle was in full swing and the Germans unfortunately had the commanding ground.' First to go was the tank of a troop leader in 'A' Squadron, Major Langdon, hit as it passed between Bras and Hubert-Folie, which stand only 500 yards apart. Just before it caught fire, he and the crew managed to jump clear, dragging with them the badly wounded gunner. Next went two more tanks of 'A' Squadron, and that of the commander, Major Close. An old campaigner, with a fierce determination to get forward, he ran across to the tank of a sergeant troop leader and ordered him to dismount. Equally determined to get forward, the sergeant ignored the order until Major Close, like von Luck, also drew his pistol and so put himself back in the battle. It was then going disastrously. Close could see 'the rest of the Regiment heavily engaged, at least seven tanks blazing, and baled out crews making their way back to the embankment'. Major Langdon's crew, shelter-ing in a ditch with their wounded gunner, observed 'a mass of tanks brewing up', which was 'B' Squadron taking the impact of solid shot from Panthers which outranged them, while 'other tanks of our squadron had also been knocked out and the remainder were withdrawing off the ridge'. Major Langdon's tank had begun to explode as the flames reached its ammunition storage chamber and he and the crew had to leave their ditch close by, 'and move away without delay. At least two hundred yards to the nearest cover, uncut corn, the ground between completely open and covered by enemy fire from Bras and Hubert-Folie. We picked up the wounded gunner [who was shortly after to die at the dressing station] and carried him away across the open ground.'[8]

They were not fired on; a parting mercy, for it is not a convention of armoured warfare, as it is of war at sea, that a stricken crew are immunized from battle when they leave their protective armour. As they made their way back, they saw beyond the Caen–Vimont railway that the Fife and Forfar were also in trouble. Its 'B' Squadron had got as forward as Four and Soliers, the two defended villages overlooked by Bourguébus, when

> they found themselves up against massive opposition. Both villages were occupied by German infantry of excellent quality and through the storm of metal the Fife and Forfar men could see the Panthers near the village of Bourguébus. Captain Hutchinson, with two troops of 'A' Squadron, went over to the east flank to counter the fire coming from Four. Here he bumped into some Panthers and though he was able to destroy two of them the fire from the others held up any further movement. From Cagny through Four and Frénouville to Soliers tank fought tank in inconclusive action.[9]

To their rescue came the 23rd Hussars, whom the various delays in the advance had now allowed to close the distance. They had halted just the other side of the Caen–Vimont railway when they saw the telltale pillars of black smoke, interspersed by the circular puffs from exploding ammunition, begin to rise from the foot of the ridge. Ordered forward by Brigadier Harvey, commanding the 11th Armoured Division's tanks, they motored as far as Soliers, where the mass of the Fife and Forfar were stopped, before discovering that there was no rescuing to be done. The Fifes had been destroyed. One of their officers ran out of the circle of blazing tanks which represented 'A' Squadron to shout that all but four of the regiment's tanks had been knocked out. Like most reports from the heat of battle, this was an exaggeration. But it squared closely enough with the visual evidence, reinforced by a salvo from some Panthers which suddenly appeared on the ridge above them and set the four tanks of a troop of 'B' Squadron ablaze, to convince them that they must withdraw. With the anvil chorus of solid shot on high-tensile armour ringing in their ears, the Hussars put their Shermans in reverse and dropped back from the foot of the ridge. As they went, a final broadside from the village of Four caught 'C' Squadron, which had arrived to support the leaders but not soon enough to recognize their predicament, in flank. 'With no time for retaliation, no time to do anything but take one quick glance at the situation, almost in one minute, all its tanks were hit, blazing and exploding,' wrote the regimental historian.

> Everywhere wounded or burning figures ran or struggled painfully for cover, while a remorseless rain of armour-piercing shot riddled the already helpless Shermans. All too clearly, we were not going to 'break through' that day. It was going to be a matter not how much we should advance, but whether we should be able to hold on to what we had gained. Out of the great array of armour that had moved forward to battle that morning, one hundred and six tanks now lay crippled or out of action in the cornfields.[10]

This was not quite the end of the armoured charge. At about 5 p.m. the Cromwells of the Northamptonshire Yeomanry were ordered to make a final attempt on the ridge from the west, crossed underneath the Caen–Vimont railway and got to within 1,000 yards of Bras. There they were stopped by high-velocity shot and limped away, leaving sixteen of their tanks behind. On the other side of the battlefield, the 2nd Welsh Guards, reconnaissance regiment of their division, were probing into Emiéville at about the same time. Held up by enemy fire, one of the troop leaders left his tank to confer with his squadron commander. As he moved across open ground, he was hit by a fragment from a mortar bomb and died shortly afterwards. He was Rex Whistler, whose charming transplantation of the spirit of the eighteenth century into contemporary art had made him one of the best-loved painters of his generation. His last work had been to decorate a room in the Prince Regent's Pavilion at Brighton, where the Welsh Guards were billeted, with a highly characteristic capriccio of George IV as Prince of Pleasure. It had been completed on the eve of the invasion, its light-hearted grace betraying not a fraction of apprehension about the fate which might await the author on the other side of the Channel.

# Repercussions

The news of Rex Whistler's death travelled in small waves of grief through the circle of his friends in the regiment and beyond, overlapping and intermingling with others tripped by word of the passing of obscurer and more private men. The fatalities, given the storm wrack of ruined armour which strewed the slopes of Bour-guébus ridge, were curiously few in total. The Fife and Forfar Yeomanry had lost 36 killed, the 3rd Royal Tanks 18, and 23rd Hussars 22, the Northamptonshire Yeomanry 5. The infantry had suffered even less. The 3 infantry battalions had lost 16 men altogether and the 8th Rifle Brigade, whose half-tracks had followed the armour throughout the day, only 4. It was the loss of tanks which was so dramatic and strategically disruptive. The division had lost altogether 126, over half its strength, and the two spearhead regiments, 3rd Tanks and Fifes, had each lost over 40. During the night new tanks would be got forward to make good some of these losses, so that the regiment would next morning be ready to move back into action at something like two-thirds strength.

But by then a storm would have broken about the head of the general who had directed the battle which matched in figurative intensity the hurricane of shot his soldiers had faced during its course. Montgomery's ambiguity about its object – 'writing down' or 'breaking out' – had led him during the afternoon of July 18th, when stale news filtering back from the front line led the staff to suppose that German resistance was diminishing rather than increasing, to issue an ill-judged communiqué. 'Early this morning', it read, 'British and Canadian troops of the Second Army attacked and broke through into the area east of the Orne and south-east of Caen. Heavy fighting continues. General Montgomery is well satisfied with the progress made in the first day's fighting of this battle.' Canadian troops had certainly not broken through, even then. They spent the day fighting at heavy odds in the ruins of the industrial suburbs. 'The first day's fighting' was accurate, for on July 19th the armoured regiments, materially somewhat restored if spiritually much bat-tered, were again to motor forward from what was becoming known in the emotional geography of 21st Army Group as 'the second

railway line' to renew the assault on the ridge. But the characterization of the battle as a 'break-through' was so quickly shown to be at
variance with the facts that all those in the higher command
structure of the Allied Expeditionary Force who did not esteem or
like Montgomery – and they were many, British as well as American
– saw in the disparity their opportunity to humble that supreme
egotist. The newspapers lent grist to their mills. On July 19th *The
Times* headlined its story, 'Second Army Breaks Through –
Armoured Forces Reach Open Country – General Montgomery
Well Satisfied'. Later in the week its Normandy headline read, 'Lost
Momentum of Break In', while the leader writer was reflecting that
'the word break-through used in early reports can only be said to
have a limited meaning. The German defensive ring around Caen
has been broken but the German armour has not ... Possibly the
offensive was too much boomed when in its initial stages. It is always
better to do the booming after complete success has been secured.'

By that stage, the newspapers were taking up ideas which had
filtered through to them from Montgomery's enemies and hints of
the direct displeasure expressed to him by his senior critics. First
among these was the airman who acted as deputy to the Supreme
Allied Commander, Air Marshal Tedder. He actually alleged to
Eisenhower that Montgomery did not really want to break through
and had deliberately misled him. 'An overwhelming air bombardment', he wrote on July 20th, 'opened the door, but there was no immediate deep penetration whilst the door remained open and we are
now little beyond the immediate bomb craters. It is clear that there
was no intention of making this operation the decisive one which you
so clearly indicated [it should be].' Eisenhower himself appeared
at Montgomery's headquarters on that day – Butcher, his personal
aide, says ready to act on a recommendation of senior British officers
that Montgomery should be removed because of a 'serious lack of
fighting leadership' – and next day wrote to complain that 'when
armoured divisions of Second Army, assisted by a tremendous air
attack, broke through the enemy's forward lines, I was extremely
hopeful and optimistic. I thought that at last we had him and were
going to roll him up. That did not come about.' The British War
Cabinet was itself alarmed enough to send its own liaison officer to
Montgomery's headquarters, with orders to report on the progress of
operations. Montgomery gave his staff orders to freeze the intruder,
but it was not until July 24th, when he was able to spend two hours

with the Prime Minister, that he began to restore something of the credibility of his leadership which he had lost through Goodwood.

Yet, had Eisenhower, Tedder and Churchill been able to eavesdrop on the secret communications of the enemy high command in the aftermath of the offensive, they would have been heartened rather than discouraged. The battle had, in strictly theoretical terms, gone well for the Germans. After four years of tactical experimentation their methods of dealing with armoured offensives were well tried. In the Western Desert they had perfected a system of drawing the British armour down on to their anti-tank guns by flirtatious hithering-and-thithering with their own tanks. When the enemy had passed beyond the uttermost range of their own artillery, the eight-eights were unmasked, the British tanks destroyed by high-velocity fire and their accompanying infantry, had they been bold enough to keep up with the armour, counter-attacked by German tanks emerging from the protective screen. Things had not quite worked that way on July 18th. It was the anti-tank guns which had stood in the front line, and the tanks which had delivered the *coup de grâce*. But the effect had been the same. Ground had been lost – during July 18th and the day of continued fighting which followed the Canadians had cleared the whole length of the eastern bank of the Orne to add to the enlargement of the 'airborne bridgehead' won by 11th Armoured Division – but the perimeter of the bridgehead had been maintained.

Between theoretical success and objective achievement, however, there yawned a nerve-stretching gulf. Academic strategists on the German side might be able to explain the failure of the British offensive in terms of an outmoded but none the less relevant Jominian concept; that an attack should always be mounted, as near as possible, 'at right angles to the base of operations'. Montgomery had flagrantly disregarded that sensible rule. The axis of Goodwood ran at the shallowest angle to its base of departure and the difficulties of sustaining the initial impetus could be attributed largely to that fundamental if unavoidable defect in planning. But even though it had meant that the three armoured divisions had attacked in succession (the 7th Armoured Division, last across the bridges, had not really attacked at all) instead of side by side, the defenders had been terribly battered in body (if not in spirit) and their longer-term strategic prospects gravely compromised. They too had suffered a heavy loss of armour. Between them, 1st SS and 21st Panzer

Divisions had lost 109 tanks on July 18th, and about half the anti-tank guns which had crippled the British onslaught had gone too. A whole infantry division, 16th Luftwaffe Field, had been consumed in the cauldron of bombs and shells, a net debit as there was none to take its place. The rational disposition of reserves had been disrupted. Two panzer divisions which had been earmarked to stand behind the American half of the front, where an offensive *masse de manoeuvre* was clearly assembling, had been diverted to the British front where they would have to stay while the menace of a resumption of Goodwood still threatened. And the confidence of the German high command in the west had been shaken to its foundations.

Writing to Hitler on July 22nd, Kluge, Supreme Commander West, warned:

> In the face of the enemy's complete command of the air, there is no possibility of our finding a strategy which will counterbalance its truly annihilating effect, unless we give up the field of battle. Whole armoured formations, allotted to the counter-attack, were caught in bomb carpets of the greatest intensity ... The result was that they arrived too late. The psychological effect of such a mass of bombs coming down with all the power of elemental nature upon the fighting troops, especially the infantry, is a factor which has to be given particularly serious consideration. It is immaterial whether such a bomb carpet catches good troops or bad, they are more or less annihilated ... the moment is fast approaching when this overtaxed front line is bound to break. And when the enemy once reaches the open country a properly co-ordinated command will be almost impossible, because of the insufficient mobility of our troops. I consider it is my duty as the responsible commander on this front to bring these developments to your notice in good time, my Führer.

But before the letter was written and despatched, Hitler himself would have suffered the effects of direct bomb attack which would locate the German *Generalität* at the centre of his personal demonology and disastrously strengthen his temptation to compel the German people along his own path to immolation.

# CHAPTER 6

## The Honour of the German Army

THE DYING GASPS of the Goodwood offensive should have sounded sweet in Hitler's ears. But his ears, on July 20th, were ringing with different sounds. At 12.30 p.m. on that day he had entered his conference room at Rastenburg in East Prussia – the Wolf's Lair – where the *Führerhauptquartier* was currently installed. The time of the first daily briefing had been advanced by half an hour because he was to receive Mussolini in the afternoon. The setting had been changed also. Usually he met his officers in an underground concrete bunker; but fears that the British might use their new blockbuster bombs against it had brought the Todt Organization to Rastenburg to thicken its roof and he had transferred meetings while work progressed to a near-by hut. When he entered it a little before 12.30 he found twenty-one men present. Most he saw every day: Jodl, the operations officer of his personal command staff, the High Command of the Wehrmacht (OKW); Warlimont, Jodl's deputy; Jodl's adjutant, with six of his own, drawn from the army, navy, air force and SS; the permanent representatives at *Führerhauptquartier* of the army, navy, SS and ministry of foreign affairs; and the duty stenographers. The rest were visitors: Heusinger, the head of the operations branch at Army Headquarters (OKH); Korten, chief of the air staff; Bodenschatz, Göring's personal staff officer; and Brandt, Heusinger's staff colonel.

The conference began at once, though Keitel, the head of OKW, was not yet present. He arrived a few minutes later, with his adjutant, their lateness explained by the disabilities of their companion, a colonel with a patch over a missing eye and a heavy briefcase clutched in the three remaining fingers of his one arm. Hitler had seen him recently twice before, but Keitel nevertheless formally presented him: Colonel Count Claus von Stauffenberg, the representative of the training and replacement command (*Ersatzheer*),

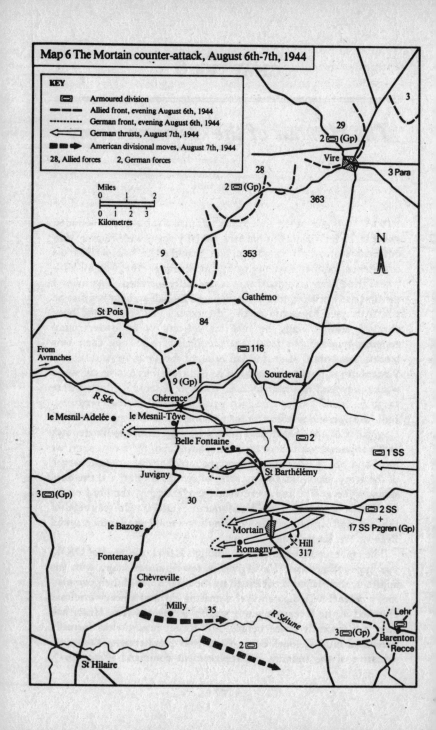

# Map 6 The Mortain counter-attack, August 6th-7th, 1944

**KEY**

Armoured division

– – – Allied front, evening August 6th, 1944

········· German front, evening August 6th, 1944

⟵ German thrusts, August 7th, 1944

▰▰▰▶ American divisional moves, August 7th, 1944

28, Allied forces    2, German forces

Miles
0    1    2
0  1  2  3
Kilometres

N

29

2 ☐ (Gp)

3

Vire

3 Para

28

2 ☐ (Gp)

363

9

353

Gathémo

St Pois

84

4

116 ☐

From Avranches

9 (Gp)

Sourdeval

R Sée

Chérence

le Mesnil-Adelée    le Mesnil-Tôve

Belle Fontaine

2 ☐

1 SS ☐

3 ☐ (Gp)

Juvigny

St Barthélémy

30

2 SS ☐
+
17 SS Pzgren (Gp)

le Bazoge

Mortain

Hill 317

Fontenay

Romagny

Chèvreville

Milly

35

R Sélune

Lehr ☐

3 ☐ (Gp)

Barenton
Recce

2 ☐

St Hilaire

who had come to report on the raising of new divisions. Hitler directed at him the famous, light-blue stare of encounter, then turned back to his maps. Stauffenberg, whose report was to be made next, moved to the end of the long map table, placed his briefcase under it and, explaining to a neighbour that he must telephone, slipped out of the room. After a moment, Keitel began to fret about his absence. Stauffenberg had already slid away once before that morning and the moment for him to make his report was approaching. Heusinger was drawing to the end of a dispiriting summary of events on the eastern front: 'The Russians are wheeling west of the Duna in great strength towards the north. Their advance guards are already south-west of Dunaburg. If the Army Group is not at once withdrawn from Lake Peipus, then a catastrophe ... ' At that moment, it seemed to Jodl, a great chandelier descended on his head. A 'blinding sheet of dazzling yellow flame' filled the room and Hitler, six feet from its flashpoint, heard 'a distinct double crack – probably the initial blast, and then the noise of his own eardrums bursting'.[1] Outside, eyes drawn by the crash of explosion saw the hut engulfed in a cloud of dust and smoke, through which after a few moments airborne sheets of paper began to drift earthward.

Figures appeared. Keitel's adjutant picked himself up from underneath a window through which he had been blown. Warlimont climbed out after him. Brandt, to whom Stauffenberg had whispered his explanation, was seen struggling to follow, and was helped out; he had left his foot behind in the room. Then, through the central door of the hut, Keitel emerged, supporting the Führer, whose face was cut and bleeding, his trousers in shreds and still smouldering from the flame. 'Somebody must have thrown a grenade', Hitler remarked to his bodyguard as he was led back to his quarters. His immediate thought had been of an air raid, then of a parachute attack. After his doctors had undressed him and treated his wounds – they found a hundred splinters from the map table in his thighs – he thought again. Four years before he had narrowly escaped the explosion of a bomb hidden in a wall at the Munich Bürgerbräukeller. Events, he decided, had repeated themselves: 'Probably one of the Todt Organization workmen installed a bomb.'[2] He sent a party to search for the cable which would have triggered the fuse. But their inspection revealed that the explosion had taken place under the table, not in the structure. He ordered investigations to continue and that the incident be kept a complete secret.

An effort was made to restore the normal and curiously banal pattern of *Führerhauptquartier* life. Hitler prided himself on his imperturbability and, though Jodl and Keitel could remember acute nervous crises from earlier in the war, he revealed no sign of one now. Immediately after the explosion he had taken his own pulse; when his wounds had been dressed, he donned a fresh uniform and summoned his female secretaries for the usual midday collation of vegetables and *schwärmerei*. He had been saddened by the news of the injuries to his entourage; a larger fragment of the table which had peppered him had impaled General Korten, and General Schmundt, his chief and favourite adjutant, had lost both legs; they were in their death throes. But the sadness was momentary. His own escape had induced in him a euphoria and sense of confidence, of a turning point in his fortunes, which he had not felt since before Stalingrad. When Mussolini, a pathetic husk of the superman whom he had once so much admired, arrived at the railway station at 2.30, Hitler babbled to him of his good luck and, at the door of the ruined hut, spoke of his belief that his 'great destiny' would 'transcend its present perils and ... be brought to a triumphant conclusion'.

He now awaited the arrival of Göring, Himmler and Kalten-brunner, head of the Reich Main Security Office, whom he had summoned before ordering the outgoing telephone lines to be disconnected to preserve the secrecy he wanted. He expected the latter to identify the '*Schweinhunde*' who were responsible for the outrage. Suspicion had already begun to centre on Stauffenberg, for the investigators were finding fragments of his briefcase – it had been of a distinctive yellow leather – all over the conference room. Moreover, it was remembered, he was an aristocrat, a Catholic and a regular officer of the *Reichsheer*, the pre-1933 army, all categories vaguely suspect to practising Nazis and, in combination, almost an indictment of guilt. He had disappeared from the central compound, was known to have talked his way through the guarded gates in the security fences and to have reached the local airfield. Perhaps he had fled abroad. Defection and aeroplanes had been neurotically connected in Hitler's mind ever since the Hess episode in 1941, and the threat of military treachery was an obsession which grew with every broadcast from Moscow by the 'Seydlitz group' of turncoat German officers. Improbable creature of the Bolsheviks though Stauffenberg looked to be, complicity with the 'Free German Committee' seemed the most obvious explanation of his motives and of the outrage.

It was simplest to think of the act, moreover, as an aborted tyrannicide. *Führerprinzip* so dominated his own outlook that he might expect it to dominate that of his enemies, believing them to think that his removal would in itself achieve their ends, whatever those might be. About 4 p.m., however, news began to percolate to the *Führerhauptquartier* which suggested a far more complicated plot. An automatic teleprinter link to the headquarters of the *Ersatzheer* started to chatter out copies of orders which were being issued to Military Districts, announcing a state of emergency. Prefixed with the codeword Valkyrie, they were familiar as stock-piled instructions against the eventuality of a raising by the millions of foreign forced labourers inside the Reich. But that was clearly not the purpose of their transmission now. At about 5 p.m. this was finally and unequivocally revealed. The circuit from the *Ersatzheer* headquarters, at the Bendlerstrasse in Berlin, began to provide a print of a telegram announcing that 'an unscrupulous clique of combat-shy Party leaders' had seized power and 'the Reich government' had appointed the signatory Supreme Commander with absolute executive authority. The signatory was Witzleben, a field-marshal retired by Hitler in 1942 and long suspected of hostility to the regime. The telegram was countersigned by Stauffenberg. It was the proclamation of a military *coup d'état*.

The disadvantages of his isolation from domestic surroundings and everyday events which Hitler had been at such pains to create and maintain ever since the start of the Russian war now began to accrue very rapidly. Rastenburg was two hours' flying time from Berlin, where the airfields might in any case be in the hands of the conspirators; Stauffenberg had landed there, not at Moscow. The great bulk of the army, under commanders who could be trusted, was at close quarters with the enemy, in Poland, the Balkans, Italy and France. Such units as remained inside the Reich proper were few and the loyalty of their officers unascertainable. Even if a majority remained outside the conspiracy, they could be led as easily by Witzleben and Stauffenberg as by Keitel and Jodl, for there was nothing to validate the authenticity either of orders or information, least of all the crucial information that Hitler was alive, angry and out for blood, reaching their headquarters in the form of teleprinted messages. Keitel did his best with the telephone, which had now been reconnected, but his voice was not Hitler's, and the con-spirators were instructing Military District commanders to disregard orders issued from the *Führerhauptquartier*: it did not strengthen Keitel's hand that Hitler had appointed Himmler, from whom even the most *Führertreu* soldier would accept orders with reluctance, as temporary commander of the *Ersatzheer*. Hitler might have come to the telephone himself. But until 7 p.m. he insisted on fulfilling his duties as a host to Mussolini, whom he entertained with tea and cream cakes, while Göring and Ribbentrop quarrelled and the generals and admirals competed in loud protestations of their services' devotion. The Berlin radio station, which the conspirators had not secured, had broadcast the news of the attack and its failure at 6.30. But as Mussolini said farewell to Hitler half an hour later – they were never to meet again – the conspirators remained in possession of the Bendlerstrasse headquarters and of other key points in the capital, and the coup was no nearer suppression.

A few minutes later, however, some more of that luck in which Hitler so earnestly believed once more came his way. Goebbels, to whom he had already spoken on the telephone with news of his survival, called again to report that he had at his side a Major Remer, the commander of the Guard Battalion *Grossdeutschland*, the only combatant unit in the capital. The major was confused by the conflicting orders he was being given – by the Bendlerstrasse to restrict the movement of all government ministers, by Goebbels to arrest Witzleben and Stauffenberg; perhaps the Führer would speak to him? The conversation was one-sided, for as yet Hitler could hear very little. But it was the sound of his voice which counted, and it was decisive. 'I am speaking to you as your Supreme Commander', said Hitler. 'You are to restore order in Berlin ... Shoot anybody who tries to disobey my orders.' Four hours later, the coup was at an end.

The dimensions of the conspiracy had still to be estimated. Its principals stood identified: Stauffenberg, his superior Olbricht, colleague Mertz von Quirnheim and adjutant von Haeften; all four had been shot by Fromm, the *Erstazheer* commander, on the evening of July 20th (it did that semi-conspirator no good – 'just covering his tracks' was Hitler's dismissal on hearing the news). They were serving officers. Three other leaders were on the retired list, Witzleben, Hoepner and Beck; the last attempted suicide twice on July 20th and succeeded the second time. Quickly arrested with the former were most of the other inner conspirators, some military, some civilian. Under interrogation they revealed more names, and others came from the conspirators' teleprinter messages to the Military Districts, appointing liaison officers and political representatives. The bones and sinews of the plot now began to stand out.

Some branches of the army had been extensively penetrated, particularly the Signals, parts of the high command (OKH), and the headquarters at Paris; the staffs of the Military Districts had been only patchily, hence their general failure to act decisively on Witzleben's orders. There was some penetration of the *Abwehr* (the tri-service counter-espionage organization); none of the navy or the air force. A few senior civil servants were compromised and many of the old party politicians of Weimar days were later found to have been included in lists of provisional ministerial appointments; that they had often not been consulted was not to spare them. And later in August there was a mass round-up of former members of parliament and party officials, which has given currency to the round figure of 5,000 for the number of conspirators.

The round-up, however, had long been planned by the Gestapo and its timing was essentially an expression of police frustration at their inability to establish whom exactly the plot comprehended. Hitler already had his own certainties in the matter: von Stauffenberg, von Haeften, Mertz von Quirnheim – the dead of July 20th; von Tresckow, von Freytag-Loringhoven – the suicides of the immediate aftermath; Yorck von Wartenburg, von Schwerin, von Kleist, von der Schulenberg – the subordinates arrested in the Bendlerstrasse; von Trott zu Solz, von Schack, von Oertzen – accomplices arrested in the first week. The names, to say nothing of the titles so many bore, were indicators enough. He had been attacked by his hereditary enemies, the military aristocracy of north Germany and their Swabian and Balt running-dogs, the servants of the old house of Brandenburg and of the little monarchies of the south he detested even more strongly. Their ancestors belonged in the pantheon of German nationalism; Stauffenberg was descended from the Gneisenau whom Hitler had recommended as an example to von Schlieben at Cherbourg. Their fathers were the unimaginative generals and civil servants who had thrown away the victories of the First World War. The conspirators themselves were a vain, empty, snobbish clique, rooted in the values of their feudal estates and nostalgic for the glittering Kasino life of the vanished *Leib-Husaren* and *Garde-Kürassiere*.

There was a grain of veracity behind Hitler's furious contempt.

The dramatis personae of the plot does read as if taken from
Benrath's *Ball auf Schloss Kobolnow*, where Graf Solduan-
Schömschö, Friedrich Schönfeld-Wöllendorf, Blanche von Berry
and the Prinzessin Maud Satulin tremble at the thought of a tour of
inspection by the self-appointed priestess of their circle, the terrifying Fürstin Kaatzenstein ('mit zwei a') and Baron von Elsenburg
fumes, 'in Ton der Garde 1900',[3] at the caste treachery of a
neighbour who has taken the citizenship of the new Poland, where
his estates now lie. Many of the conspirators had made their first
tentative affirmations of commitment at Kreisau, the Silesian
Kobolnow of the conspirator Helmuth von Moltke, and many of the
soldiers in particular were secret monarchists and social reactionaries. But not Stauffenberg – and it was on him, in the end, that
everything turned. He shared his fellow regular officers' distaste for
the majority of professional Nazis. Far from seeing their elimination
as an end in itself, however, as necessary to put a stop to the war in
the west, or to preserve Germany from another Versailles, or to
restore a 'decent' domestic society, or to cleanse her reputation
among nations, some or all of which aims motivated the other
conspirators, he was bent on nothing less than revolution. As
revolutions go, it was to have been an oddity among those of the
twentieth century; economically distributive, diplomatically inter-
nationalist, ideologically neutralist, its basis Christian, its ethos
fraternal and its precipitating act the assassination of the Antichrist
whom the profoundly religious and romantic Stauffenberg had
persuaded himself that Hitler was. But it was revolution all the
same.

Those who shared his vision were chiefly young officers who had
come under his considerable personal spell. And that was appropriate, for to Stauffenberg the army was a key institution, a force for
social good as well as a means of national defence. He was disgusted
by the self-serving of so many generals, their political timidity and
their ability to ignore or even condone atrocities committed in their
areas of command, and hence believed that the honour of the
German army required the cathartic blow to be struck by one of its
officers. It was at that point, and perhaps only that point, that his
outlook and Hitler's touched, even if they did so back to back. Both
accepted the unique and supreme importance of military action
against the head of state. But, just as Stauffenberg saw it as a duty of
honour, Hitler saw it as the ultimate treachery. Taught by the failure

of his *putsch* at Munich in 1923 that the domestic power of the army was absolute, he had scrupulously avoided all further conflict with it in the years before the seizure of power and afterwards carefully exempted it from the policy of nazification. All other institutions of German state and society – civil service, police, local government, trade unions, employers' federations, schools, universities, youth movements, even the national churches – had been *gleichgeschaltet*, which meant their absorption into some parallel party organization or the replacement of their leaders by party nominees or, at the very least, the enrolment of those leaders as Nazis. None of those measures had been visited on the army.

Hitler had indeed emasculated the one party organization which might have, which indeed had, sought to take the army's place, the *Stürmabteilungen*, and, though he had at times used his ultimate powers to alter the composition of the high command, he had always filled the vacancies he created with men acceptable to their brother officers. And, Hitler further calculated, to a relationship founded on the observance of constitutional properties, he had added the sweetening of rearmament, mass professional advancement and victory. In his public dealings with the army – whatever his private *arrière-pensées* about its attitudes, whatever the nature of his camouflaged blows against his enemies in its ranks – his conscience was clear. Clear too, therefore, was the stage for a parade of outraged emotion against the traitors, dupes and ingrates in field-grey. For the ordinary soldiers, the *Frontkämpfer* with whom he had identified himself from the beginning of his political life, he continued to express total, if quite impersonal, admiration. In 'his' generals – Model, Schörner, Wenck, who shared his own memories of the trenches and ready willingness to shed blood – he maintained complete confidence. On the traditional officer class, tainted not only by obsolete politics but by cosmopolitan connections and intellectual pretensions – Helmuth von Moltke was half-English, Stauffenberg's mother had been a friend of Rilke and he himself was a member of the circle of Stefan George – he vented a tide of passionate vindictiveness. 'We'll be taken prisoner and get decent treatment, particularly we who are of noble families', was his mocking characterization of the plotters' attitude to the defeat he affirmed their success would have entailed. For those who fell into his hands he accordingly prescribed imprisonment of the harshest severity and execution of savage cruelty. For their relatives he

decreed *Sippenhaft*, arrest because of kinship, sanctioned the detention of every member of the thirty-one leading families involved and
allowed Himmler to threaten that 'the Stauffenberg clan will be
exterminated down to its last member'.

Prosecution of the war required some public moderation of this
private mood of vengeance. On July 24th Bormann, the Führer's
right-hand, published a directive to party officials which forbade
every 'attack [on] the officer corps, the generals, the nobility or the
armed forces as a body'. It was arranged that a military court of
honour should be convened by the army itself to expel the guilty
from its ranks before they were handed over to the Gestapo. And
there were ostentatious reaffirmations of loyalty by the senior ranks,
which Hitler accepted at face value, even the demeaning offer to
adopt the Nazi 'heil' in place of the military salute the armed forces
customarily exchanged. But both parties to the uneasy relationship
knew that its equilibrium had been altered for good. The patriotism
of the army had never before been questioned because patriotism's
central issue in a totalitarian state – for or against the leader – had
never been put to the test. In consequence, and despite the arbitrary
risks entailed, officers of sufficient stature and boldness – Manstein
was one, Guderian another – had always in the last resort been able
to question the Führer's military judgment and argue with him for
an opposite point of view. That freedom had gone. Henceforth the
generals would be bound to the wheel, as tightly as their brave,
obedient and uncomplaining soldiers who bore the consequences of
the decisions taken at noon and midnight in the air-conditioned
isolation of the *Führerhauptquartier*.

# Break-through

A decision of the greatest importance – for Hitler, for Germany, for
the generals, for their suffering divisions at the front – now
confronted the high command almost before the immediate shock
waves of the coup had died away. Early in the morning of July 24th
the forward infantry of Panzer Lehr Division, manning the front
opposite the Americans west of St Lô, reported that the enemy were
leaving their positions and retiring across the line of the St
Lô–Périers road, without apparent reason. Shortly afterwards they
reported the approach of heavy bomber formations, which they
could not observe through the overcast, and then the impact of a

dense bombardment, falling in but also forward of their positions. Later during the day the American infantry returned to their positions, fighting for their re-occupation where the Germans had infiltrated troops forward to take the abandoned ground.

This passage of events puzzled the staff of LXXXIV Corps, since it seemed uncharacteristic of the American method of making war. Early next morning, its explanation was made only too plain. Once again the rumble of approaching aircraft formations was heard in the German lines and this time, the day being clear, the aircraft was soon revealed. They were Flying Fortresses, in hundreds upon hundreds, flying straight and level at 12,000 feet and more. As soon as they reached the line of the St Lô–Périers road, they again began to dump their enormous bomb loads on and behind the German positions. The effect was catastrophic. General Bayerlein, commanding Panzer Lehr, described how

> back and forth the bomb carpets were laid, artillery positions were wiped out, tanks overturned and buried, infantry positions flattened and all roads and tracks destroyed. By midday the entire area resembled a moon landscape, with the bomb craters touching rim to rim ... All signal communications had been cut and no command was possible. The shock effect on the troops was indescribable. Several of my men went mad and rushed round in the open until they were cut down by splinters. Simultaneously with the storm from the air, innumerable guns of the American artillery poured drumfire into our field positions.[4]

The guns in fact numbered 522, the combined artilleries of four infantry and two armoured divisions and that of VII Corps, which had them under command. Its mission was to attack and break through the German line between the rivers Vire and Lozon and, pivoting on St Lô, drive south and west towards the gateway into Brittany. Originally the attack had been scheduled to begin the day before but the bad weather had obliged the recall of the bombers while they were in flight. Those which had dropped their bombs had not received the cancelling signal. The clear weather of June 25th had given them the sight of their targets they needed and, even though a number bombed short, killing over a hundred of their own soldiers (more excusably, bombing through cloud, they had killed

twenty-five the day before), the disorganization caused in the
German lines far outweighed in tactical importance that inflicted in
their own. Two American units, a regiment of the 9th Division and a
battalion in the 30th, were unable to move off at the prescribed hour
because they were still evacuating casualties (many of them
psychological). But, promptly at 11 a.m., the three leading divisions
of the six under command of VII Corps crossed the startlines and
moved off into the 'moon landscape' the 1,500 Fortresses of the
Eighth Air Force had just created.

The attack, codenamed Cobra, was Bradley's third attempt to
escape from the constricting neck of the Cotentin peninsula. The
first, begun on July 3rd, had been checked by the hard fighting of
the enemy's infantry along the floodline of the Douve. The second,
begun on July 13th, had after five days resulted in the capture of the
crucial communication centre of St Lô, but only at the cost of 11,000
casualties. Cobra promised better. The preliminary operations had
carried the American line to the outskirts of easier country, for
though on the inner flank the line of advance still stretched into the
bocage, on the outer it reached towards the coastal plain, over which
armour could make rapid progress. Now, too, there was more
armour than Bradley had had before, and it had been ashore long
enough for the infantry to have practised with it the tactics of
co-operation essential for a clean break-through. The tactical air
force, of which after some early mishaps the ground troops had
grown wary, had also greatly improved its technique of close support
and would in future be eagerly summoned to remove points of
resistance in the way of forward movement. But, above all, there
were now numbers on Bradley's side. The fall of Cherbourg, which
had corrected his facing-both-ways posture, had released three
divisions to the bocage front. The steady process of reinforcement,
from an army with reserves still at home besides others nearer to
hand in Britain, had brought more, so that he now had fifteen
divisions in line, against nine German, many of them remnants, and
750 tanks against 110. Faced with this evidence of a remorseless shift
in the balance, Rommel had written to Hitler ten days before to warn
that 'the moment is fast approaching when our hard-pressed
defences will crack'. On July 25th the moment had come.

The sounds of the break were muted at the start. The three
infantry divisions, 9th, 4th and 30th, assigned by Bradley to
spearhead the advance, had the two small towns of Marigny and

St Gilles as their immediate objectives. Each was about three miles inside German territory, just beyond the strip, six miles square, which the air force had devastated that morning. Their capture would, as in the Epsom operation a month before, open the neck of a corridor into the German positions down which Bradley planned to pour his armour as soon as the crust of German resistance – their nests of machine-guns and anti-tank guns, infantry strong-points and tank lairs – was broken. Progress at first was slow. For all the sound and fury of the bombing and despite Bayerlein's dramatically pessimistic assessment, many of the German infantry had survived the holocaust and, as soon as they found themselves alive and faced by the visible presence of their tormentors, manned their weapons and opened fire. The Americans, obstructed by their own crater fields, found it difficult to make progress, and were not helped by the assistance of some of their medium bombers, which again dropped their loads short. By the evening of the first day, only two miles of ground had been won at the deepest point, and the objectives still lay beyond the bivouacs of the vanguard. The day, indeed, had passed much like the first of Epsom, with the advancing infantry unable to identify the sources of fire which struck them from time to time, or to make use of the armour which would have neutralized the opposition they met because of the narrowness of the front on which they were advancing.

But the anatomies of Cobra and Epsom fundamentally differed. Not only was Bradley attacking with far greater force than Montgomery had been able to muster four weeks earlier. He was also confronted by an enemy who was critically weaker. Realize it though they could not, his infantry had on the first day very largely destroyed the resistance which the bombing had left untouched. And behind the outer crust, far from there being a surplus of fresh and strong panzer divisions to shore up the front and stop up the holes the attack opened, there was almost no reserve at all. The two panzer divisions on the front, 2nd SS and 17th SS – the latter only a panzergrenadier formation, with a single armoured battalion – were fully committed to the defence of the line. Lehr, though still in place, had effectively been destroyed in the bombing and the fighting which immediately followed. And the intact infantry divisions – 243rd, 353rd, 91st and 5th Parachute – were all immobile and seriously under strength. If the Americans could but sustain the pressure and progress of the first day, they would shortly and inevitably find themselves clear of the obstacle belt and out into open country.

Moreover, their armoured divisions were now coming into line. Advancing behind a pattern of high-explosive laid by medium bombers on the morning of July 26th, the 1st Armoured Division drove southwards all day towards Marigny while on the other flank of the corridor the 2nd, which had learnt the hard facts of combat in the North African campaign, outstripped it to reach St Gilles and press through it to the next objective, Canisy. Sensing that there was now little to stand in his way, the commander of the forward Combat Command of the division, General Rose, decided to brave the risks of night movement and ordered his tanks forward through the dusk and gathering darkness to seize the high ground beyond. When the next day dawned, he had established positions on the eastern flank of the corridor which would guard the advance of the rest of the Cobra force between it and the sea.

July 27th saw the advance pushed with ever greater energy. The 2nd Armoured Division continued to lengthen the defensive flank it had established south of Canisy. To its west, the 3rd Armoured and 1st Infantry Divisions, working in tandem, hurried towards Coutances at the junction of the St Lô and Cherbourg roads, their object being to cut off the retreat of the German divisions still trying to hold the line on the coast. The panzer divisions, 2nd and 17th SS, were hastily switched to menace their flank and, by hard fighting did prevent the Americans from entering Coutances on that evening. Next day, July 28th, however, the appearance of two new armoured divisions, 4th and 6th, drove them off and put the town in American hands. Chasing a cloud of stragglers before them, the victorious columns of Shermans and White half-tracks pressed on through to reach, as evening fell, a new phase line as much as fifteen miles south of that from which Cobra had been unleashed four days before.

# Patton

Reporting the state of his force to Supreme Command West three days later, Hausser, the commander of the German Seventh Army, wrote of this period:

A large proportion of the divisions which had been fighting continuously since the invasion began disintegrated, as a result of the enemy armoured break-in on the Army's left flank, into small groups which fought their way back through the enemy lines on their own. Whether acting on proper rallying orders, or on unconfirmed verbal instructions, most of these groups were without officers or NCOs and roamed at random through the countryside, heading east or south-east ... The stragglers are for the most part in very bad state.[5]

On July 28th Bradley had as yet no inkling of the extent of the damage he had inflicted on Seventh Army, nor was he able to foresee what advantage he could wring from his success. His thinking before the opening of the offensive had been for a pause at this stage, while such gains as he had made were consolidated. Whatever the obscurities, however, he now grasped that he had won a great victory and, rather than settle for the safety of a conventional tidying up, decided to maintain the pressure and thrust fresh troops into the gap he had opened. Fresh troops were available to him in abundance. More important, he had a man to hand who, if anyone could, would transform the break-through into a break-out. The man was General George Smith Patton.

Patton had been allotted hitherto in the invasion campaign a calculatedly obscure role. The 'Patton Army Group' of forty-five fictitious divisions, allegedly located in the south-eastern counties of England opposite the Pas de Calais, was the principal means by which the Allied deception organization had kept alive in the mind of German intelligence the chimera of a 'second invasion' down the short route to the Rhineland. News at the end of July of the first movement from across the Seine of infantry divisions of Fifteenth Army – the 326th and 363rd Divisions completed the journey on July 30th – somewhat relaxed the need to maintain the pretence. But Eisenhower nevertheless remained anxious to camouflage the personal intervention of Patton in ground operations.

For the name could mean as much to the Germans as it did in the American army, where it stood for 'an extraordinary and ruthless driving power ... at critical moments' capable of 'getting the utmost out of soldiers in offensive operations', as Eisenhower had characterized him to Marshall the year before. In an army which laid supreme emphasis upon logistics, had brought to the making of war the techniques of the Harvard Business School and actually maintained, alone among the armed forces of developed states, a staff college dedicated to the study of industrial mobilization, Patton was a soldier who represented the Napoleonic tradition. Rich in his own right, richer by marriage, he had used the security wealth gave him to cultivate the high-born and well-placed in American society and politics and to pursue his real military interests – the literature of generalship and derring-do, the techniques of the new warfare of aircraft and armour – with a disregard for routine which humbler officers dared not risk. Like the rest of his military generation, he had known the thrill of dizzy promotion in the First World War, when for a blissful moment he had been a full colonel at thirty-three, but he had not been soured by the inevitable descent to substantive rank which peace brought. Nor had he been made professionally cautious by it; from his first re-encounter with the German army, at Gabès in Tunisia in March 1943, he had shown all that willingness successfully to bend the orders of superior officers which is so often the mark of the truly talented soldier. In Sicily, by then head of Seventh Army, he had pushed his dramatically personal approach to war too far, when he had physically chastised a pair of soldiers who did not meet his own exacting standards of physical courage, and been removed from command.

But, even in an army ruled by the puritan intolerances of General Marshall, his talent bulked too large to be neglected for long. Eisenhower had determined to make a place for him in the invasion force. Bradley, once his subordinate, had uncomplainingly accepted the notion that it should be within his sphere of command. The place had taken time to find. Now, as a new Third Army controlling all the reinforcements which July had brought into Normandy came into being, Patton emerged from the shadows to direct its operations. He was a new name to the majority of the young conscripts who filled its ranks but, with his brass buttons, pearl-handled revolver – relic of his days as Olympic pentathlete and champion army pistol shot – burnished helmet and glittering riding-boots, not a figure they would need to see twice to remember. And his troops would see him often. Patton led from the front.

His double mission, proposed to him orally by Montgomery on July 27th and confirmed in writing by Bradley on August 1st, was to take Third Army out of Normandy and into Brittany, as far as Rennes, the Breton capital, in the centre of the peninsula and to Brest at its western point. An armoured and an infantry division were allotted to each objective – 4th and 8th to the first, 6th and 79th to the second – while he kept 5th Armoured, 83rd and 90th Divisions in reserve to exploit their success. Even as Third Army became operational, the 4th Armoured Division captured the key exit point from Normandy, the coastal town of Avranches, after an advance of twenty-five miles in thirty-six hours and by the following evening, July 31st, was in Brittany proper. Its crucial achievement was to have seized intact the bridge at Pontaubault, which carried the road from Avranches southward across the river Sélune, since that provided the only ready route towards the objectives Bradley had given to Patton. He now made assurance of its fullest use the overriding concern of his staff, sending clusters of senior officers out to the feeder routes which led to it with orders to keep the vehicles rolling without regard for strict sequence of units; at the other end, the bunched columns were unscrambled by the simple means of marking each of the roads which fanned from it for a separate division. In this way, which defied every rule of staff college logistics, his seven divisions were got into the new theatre of operations in seventy-two hours.

As the tail of the army crossed the bridge, its spearheads were already eighty miles beyond. The interior of Brittany was empty of German troops, who had either already left for the Normandy front or were even then concentrating on the Atlantic coast for the defence of its ports. Nothing, therefore, stood in 4th or 6th Armoured Divisions' paths; for several days the only armed men they met were those of the resistance, now appearing along the roads of the province to guide the Americans forward. By August 4th Rennes had been captured and 4th Armoured Division had crossed Brittany to reach the south coast at Vannes, where it stood poised to take the important naval port of Lorient. The 6th Armoured was halfway to Brest on that date, while in their rear the units of First Army manoeuvred to consolidate the Avranches corridor and drive the Germans eastward from its inner flank. The capture of Mortain by the 1st Division on August 3rd anchored the Army's line on high ground which dominated the routes the Germans must use if they were to attempt a counter-attack against the break-out. So little did Bradley count on that possibility, however, that on this day he issued orders to Patton to close down his drive into Brittany – a major revision of the long-laid Overlord plan – and turn east with all available strength. On August 4th Montgomery amplified these instructions. The shape of his bridgehead had changed dramatically in eleven days. The L of the coastal strip and Cotentin had now sprouted at its angle a ballooning appendix, the outline of which enclosed a great tract of empty country west and south of the German defensive zone in Normandy. From it the First and Third American Armies might turn to take the German Seventh Army and Panzer Group West in flank and rear, with incalculable consequences for the outcome of the campaign. 'Everyone', he therefore instructed, 'must now go all out day and night. The broad strategy of the Allied Armies is to swing ... towards Paris and to force the enemy back to the Seine.' The Battle of Normandy looked within weeks, perhaps days, of its end.

## The Will of the Führer

The need for decision with which the unleashing of Cobra had confronted the German high command suddenly admitted of no compromise. Six weeks before, the German army in the east had suffered a catastrophe at the hands of the Russians. Timing their summer offensive to coincide with the third anniversary of Operation Barbarossa, the Red Army had launched 118 infantry divisions and 43 tank brigades against Army Group Centre in its positions along the Dnieper in White Russia. Within a few days its front had been riddled to a pepper pot, its strong points surrounded and its mobile elements chased pell-mell westwards towards the stop-gap safety of the old Polish fortified frontier of 1920. When ten days later the fatigue of the chase brought the Soviet Fronts to a halt and Field-Marshal Model, the 'Führer's Fireman' sent to stop the stampede arrived to take stock, it was found that a 250-mile gap had been torn in the German line and 28 irreplaceable divisions had disappeared. The disaster was worse than Stalingrad, Kursk or the Crimea, and had come at a worse time. For Germany was now running out of manpower. Before the Bomb Plot the *Ersatzheer* was supplying the army with only 60,000 new soldiers a month – in the destruction of Army Group Centre 350,000 were lost in ten days – and though Himmler, Fromm's replacement after it, quadrupled that figure, their incorporation into fresh fighting divisions would take until October. Until that date Germany could not afford to pursue any strategy which set the possession of territory above the preservation of fighting formations. The disintegration of the left flank in Normandy was therefore a clear warning to Hitler that the time had come to defend the west on different ground.

This was a warning which the Supreme Commander in the West had given him even before the crack had occurred. For the first six weeks of the fighting the various headquarters in France had managed to sustain a strange normality in their way of life. Seventh Army and Panzer Group West had been gripped by daily crises, unavoidable to staffs at close quarters with the enemy. But Rundstedt, the aged and world-weary Supreme Commander, had continued to reside at his château at St Germain outside Paris, only rarely visiting the front and still finding time during his day for the detective stories which were his escape from a reality he had long before decided to sublimate. Rommel, too, had maintained his command post in his château at la Roche Guyon on the Seine, and though he spent his days on the road, shuttling frenetically between Seventh Army, Panzer Group West and their subordinate corps, sometimes travelling 400 miles between breakfast and dinner, he made dinner a fixed engagement, at which he and his staff would reminisce about better times gone by and round off their evening with a tour of the battlements of the ruined castle above their mess. Ruge, his naval staff officer, had had the shrubbery cleared up there so that Rommel could enjoy the 'mother-of-pearl' vistas of the Seine from his favourite bench, where the two would muse into the twilight on what the future held, and Ruge would calm his chief's anxieties with a résumé of *Gone with the Wind*, his current reading, its 'endless parallels with our time' and reassurance that 'rebuilding was possible after a total defeat'. The appearance of Kluge to replace Rommel after the latter's wounding somewhat modified this agreeable pattern of mess life. The new commander of Army Group B, who was also Supreme Commander West since Rundstedt's unguarded expression of pessimism had taken him into retirement on July 5th, banished Rommel's cronies from meals, which he took with his operational staff. But he, too, was always home for dinner when, for all that his anxieties for the future were soon even sharper than Rommel's had been, he sometimes relaxed his regime enough to entertain guests.

His ability to banish the cares of the day from his evenings may have been due to a belief that Hitler, with whom he always enjoyed special favour and who had singled him out for the special responsibility of the western command, would in the end heed his advice about the proper strategy to be followed there. On July 12th, only a

week after he had arrived at Rommel's headquarters glowing with
confidence transfused by Hitler at their leavetaking, he had telephoned the *Führerhauptquartier* to stress that though 'no pessimist',
in his view 'the situation couldn't be grimmer'. On adding direct
command of Army Group B to his responsibilities, he had discovered the last situation report which Rommel had written for
Hitler; in it the old Desert Fox had forecast that 'the unequal
struggle is reaching its end' after five weeks of fighting in which his
formations had lost 97,000 men and received only 6,000 replacements. Far from suppressing it, as a more timorous general might
have done, he ordered its transmission, with a covering letter of his
own which warned that, though 'I came here with the fixed
determination of making effective your order to stand fast *at any
price*', the fact had to be faced that 'the moment has drawn near when
this front will break'. On July 31st, as the Americans rolled through
Avranches, he had signalled his doubt 'whether the enemy can still
be stopped', and then raised with Jodl, Hitler's operations officer,
the question of withdrawing from Normandy and seeking to defend
a line nearer the border of the homeland.

Hitler, curiously, showed none of his doctrinaire objection to the
notion at his midday conference. By evening, however, he spoke in
more familiar voice. Kluge could not grasp the whole picture, and
could certainly not solve the problems which would be raised by a
break-through. Therefore he should be told that 'first, he must fight
here in all circumstances, secondly that this battle is decisive,
thirdly, that the idea of operating freely in the open is nonsense'.
Warlimont, Jodl's deputy in the operations section of OKW, was to
leave for France at once to convey these instructions to Kluge in
person.

No sooner had Warlimont arrived than he found his mission
overtaken. On August 2nd he conferred briefly with the field-
marshal. Next morning he was summoned to hear the news that the
Führer had ordered a counter-attack 'from the area east of Avranches
in order to re-establish positions on the coast and so once more close
the ring in southern Normandy'. He was flabbergasted. Kluge was
equally at a loss. 'As he knew from his visit to Berchtesgaden, it had
been recognized at the end of June [when Hitler had had his last
conference with Rommel and Rundstedt] that there were no further
possibilities of conducting an offensive defence ... As far as I was
concerned', testified Warlimont, 'I had no new instructions ...

There could be no doubt that once more Hitler had taken a snap decision ... it looked as if this must have been taken the previous night.'

So it had. But the kernel of the idea had been germinating for a few days. Reports of the arrival in Normandy of fresh Allied troops and fighter squadrons previously, though wrongly, identified as belonging to 'Army Group Patton' and earmarked for the 'second invasion' had alleviated Hitler's fears of a landing north of the Seine. The situation map, which highlighted the tenuousness of the Americans communications through Avranches, graphically presented the prospect of an out-trumping blow. 'We must strike like lightning', he had suddenly declared. 'When we reach the sea the American spearheads will be cut off ... We might even be able to cut off their entire beachhead. We mustn't get bogged down with mopping up the Americans who have broken through' – blind optimism; he would have needed the 'iron broom' he had threatened to wield against the 'Augean stables' in the officer corps after July 20th – 'their turn will come later. We must wheel north like lightning and turn the entire enemy front from the rear.' The failure of a British attempt, launched simultaneously with Cobra, to break out of their end of the bridgehead, had persuaded him that the rest of the front was stable. He had therefore concluded that he could strip parts of it of divisions and play again at the war of manoeuvre of which he believed the German army alone to be the master.

## Operation Lüttich

The operational verve of the German army would have been denied by no soldier in any of the armies which opposed it, in the east or west. Its quality rested in part on its equipment, some of which, even by the standards of 1944, was still splendidly designed and engineered. The Panther was better than the equivalent medium tank in the Russian and American armies, the Tiger had no equal, and even the ageing Mark IV could still stand confidently in the line of battle. Certain specialized weapons were the fearful envy of those who faced them, notably the lethal and highly versatile 88 mm, which could appear as a tank, anti-tank, assault or anti-aircraft gun, the *nebelwerfer* multi-barrelled rocket projector and the MP 40 machine-pistol. Quantity of weapons, too, counted for much. Though the number of tanks in the panzer divisions was in decline,

numbers of other weapons in the infantry divisions had been
increased during 1943-4 to provide great superiority in automatic
and mortar firepower over their American equivalents. Some of this
superiority was offset by the altogether lower mobility of German
formations, still dependent on horses and boot leather for getting
about the countryside, but immobility mattered little in the sort of
static defensive battle to which most German divisions were now
consigned by the run of the strategic tide. The same tide tended also
to minimize the disadvantage of operating without air cover to which
the catastrophic decline in the fighter strength of the Luftwaffe – it
could oppose only 300 to over 1,200 Allied fighters in France –
condemned it.

It was not, however, either in quality or quantity of equipment
that the excellence of the German army ultimately lay. Traditionally
it had always rather scorned the belief that technology provided the
means to victory. For, though sensitive to technical change, and
generally ready to incorporate new weapons and equipment into its
order of battle (its failure to recognize the significance of the tank in
the First World War was an uncharacteristic lapse), it rightly took
the view that weapons are no more formidable than those who use
them. And it was therefore upon the training and motivation of the
users that it had always concentrated its corporate energies. Much
effort had been given to the implantation in the mind of the
Germans – a nation only since 1871 – of the idea of military service
as natural and honourable. And with astonishing success. In the
thirty years between 1850 and 1880 the patchwork of tiny German
armies had been rewoven into a single garment, the old allegiances
commemorated only in a parenthetical sub-title to that of the new
imperial units – 115th Kaiser Wilhelm's Infantry Regiment (1st
Archducal Hessian) – and personal loyalties firmly focused on the
Prussian king and German emperor. In the process, astonishingly
and unprecedentedly, military service had actually been made
popular with those who had to perform it. For three hundred years,
all over Europe, the appearance of the recruiting sergeant had been
the signal for a district's young men to take to the woods and hills.
The army of united Germany, symbol of nationhood and vehicle of
its triumphs over the pride of older states, was conscripted almost
without coercion, its recruits reporting for registration as if for the
beginning of the school-year – which in a sense they were – and
departing on discharge with sentimental trinkets of their service to

decorate the family parlour. The débâcle of 1918 dampened but did not extinguish this national military enthusiasm. 'Heerlos, Wehrlos, Ehrlos' (no army – no defence – no honour) was one of the catch-phrases of the Versailles years and Hitler's abrogation of the military terms of the treaty was as widely popular as the economic measures by which he demobilized the armies of the unemployed. Within five years of his coming to power, hundreds of thousands of young Germans were once more not only wearing field-grey but demonstrating that apparently instinctual readiness to bond them-selves to comrades, heed orders and interpret them intelligently which had made the German army of three earlier wars the world's -paradigm of military efficiency.

Even higher in the German army's scale of values than the nurture of the warrior spirit in its conscripts, however, stood the cultivation of 'operational' talent in their leaders. *Operativ* is an adjective which does not translate exactly into the English military vocabulary. Lying somewhere between 'strategic' and 'tactical', it describes the process of transforming paper plans into battlefield practice, against the tactical pressures of time which the strategist does not know, and has been regarded by the German army as the most difficult of the commander's arts since it was isolated by the great von Moltke in the 1860s. Taught, in so far as it can be taught, in his famous staff college courses, its traits were eagerly looked for in the performance of general staff candidates and its manifestation in practice, in wartime, was rewarded by swift promotion. Manstein had the skill in abundance, Guderian too; in the previous war, Hoffmann, Luden-dorff's chief of staff, had been reckoned a supreme exponent. And so also had his master, who had rebuilt a compromised career by his swift and courageous display of decision at the taking of Liège in 1914.

During the years when he had stood at the head of the German army, Hitler had not at first tested himself against the exacting standards by which 'operational' skill was matched. Encouraged, however, by clear evidence of the occasional superiority of his strategic judgment over that of the professionals at OKH – his preference for the Ardennes route in 1940 was the first example – and then persuaded that radio and teleprinter had abolished for him his disadvantage of distance from the front, he had begun during 1941 to take day-by-day control of his campaigns, and at an increasingly lower level. When things went wrong, he alleged insubordination (and came increasingly to suspect treachery). When things went right, as they did during the Kharkov counter-offensive of 1942 or the sealing-off of the Anzio landing on January 19th, 1944, his trust in his 'operational' judgment grew. Because of his insistence on rigid defence, he in practice met little call to exercise his powers of quick decision, since the inevitable collapse of the fronts he refused to adjust led to situations too fluid for him to influence. But he continued to believe that he possessed 'operational' ability, and would make the decisive intervention when circumstances presented it. The break-through at Avranches was just such an occasion.

But Kluge's talent, too, was *operativ*; he was one of the Wehrmacht's great battlefield commanders, an ex-paladin of the Eastern Front. And when he came to discuss Hitler's alarming new order with the emissary, Warlimont, he declared that he had of course detected the same opportunity at Avranches as the Führer saw, but, believing that it would yield no more than the time and tactical advantage necessary to disengage Army Group B from the line of battle and retreat into the interior, he had dismissed it from his mind, since he knew that a retreat would be forbidden. If, however, Hitler was now ready to sanction the movement of armour from the eastern end of the bridgehead, opposite the British, to the western, in order to strike at the Americans, he would of course issue the necessary orders. But it would be on the understanding, for his part, that the object was to restore the front for just as long as was necessary for a new line of defence to be completed nearer the German frontier.

That was not, however, an idea which he could discuss with Hitler – for two reasons. The first was general. Since July 20th no battlefield commander could risk suggesting retreat: dishonoured in Hitler's eyes, his generals could now only demonstrate their loyalty to the regime by unswerving obedience to orders. The second was personal. Kluge himself had had foreknowledge of the plot, was to some extent implicated in it, and knew that his complicity must eventually leak out; in fact, a hint of it had already been extracted from a member of the inner circle on August 1st. He was therefore condemned to play the super-loyalist for the sake of self-preservation. The ambiguity of his position was to have bizarre results. He now pressed on at all speed with the mounting of the attack, which entailed the concentration near Avranches of four divisions, 116th, 2nd, 2nd SS and 1st SS Panzer Divisions, the last of which had to come clear across the front from its battle station opposite the British at Caen. By August 6th they were in position just east of Mortain and ready to move off to the assault under the cover of darkness. During the day, however, Kluge was called several times to the telephone to hear Hitler, who now spoke not of accelerating the counter-offensive – hitherto apparently his only thought – but of actually delaying it. Other panzer divisions were on the way from the south of France, he explained – the 9th, which he had promised to Kluge on July 27th, and the 11th, which had not yet begun to move. To those he also wanted to add the weight of the 9th and 10th SS and so, with eight panzer divisions in line abreast, inflict on the Allies a defeat from which they would not recover. The operation, after all, was codenamed Lüttich (Liège), the place at which Ludendorff in August 1914 had, exactly thirty years before to that day, opened the way for the great German march of encirclement across the rear of the French army. It was an 'operational' coincidence too striking to be missed, a portent too fortuitous to bode anything but good for the outcome of his own great counterencirclement plan.

Four days earlier Kluge would have welcomed the news both of the reinforcement and of the postponement. Now he was obliged to argue for the same urgency which Hitler had wished upon him in the initial directive. The tactical situation had changed, and much for the worse. American spearheads were driving towards Le Mans, far to his south, threatening an ever wider envelopment of the whole of his force; the British were pressing so hard at Caumont, west of Caen, that any disengagement of 9th and 10th SS was unthinkable. His own preparations were so advanced that they could not now easily be cancelled. And he had good reason to suspect that the Allies had scented his intentions. Should that be the case, any delay would ensure that their air forces – for all that the Luftwaffe had promised 300 fighters to protect the panzer spearheads – would catch his tanks in their concentration areas and destroy them.

His suspicions fell short of actuality. The Allies had not scented, but documented his intentions. On the night of August 5th–6th Ultra, product of the decrypt service at Bletchley, had alerted Montgomery and Bradley to the movement of the panzer divisions westward. At midnight on August 6th–7th, as the attack began, Ultra was forwarding to France the timings of the attack and its

immediate objectives, Brécey and Montigny, between Mortain and
Avranches; but that news was less important than the earlier
transmission, which had allowed Bradley the time so to re-align his
forces as to ensure that the 'Mortain counter-attack', as the Allies
were to call Operation Lüttich, would run into a solid wall of
resistance just beyond its start line. Three divisions of the American
First Army, the 3rd Armoured, 4th and 30th, had been fighting
their way southward during the first week of August. On the evening
of August 6th they were disposed on either side of the valley of the
river Sée, down which the Germans planned to drive to Avranches,
3rd Armoured and 4th on the north bank, 30th on the south in and
around Mortain itself. And another armoured division, the 2nd, was
bound thither posthaste.

Whichever timetable, Hitler's or Kluge's, the Germans adopted,
Lüttich was therefore compromised from the outset. But, in the
circumstances, the latter's urge to begin made better sense than the
former's desire to wait. And, when it came to it, Kluge had his way.
Harried by news of the difficulties of assembly – the detachment of
1st SS, *en route* from Caen since August 3rd, had lost 30 per cent of
its strength, the 116th Panzer Division had failed to detach a
promised tank battalion to 2nd Panzer – he allowed his subordinates
to postpone H-Hour to midnight of August 6th but insisted that that
deadline was final. Meanwhile he signalled to OKW for the Führer:
'I am pressed for time and have no guarantee that the infantry will
hold the position [north of the assembly area] for long against the
British and American tanks. I must attack as soon as possible.' On
schedule, therefore, but in much smaller strength than planned,
Lüttich departed from its start line in the early dark of the summer
night. Down narrow corridors towards Avranches, twenty miles
distant, drove three armoured columns, two from 2nd SS Panzer on
the south bank of the Sée, one from 2nd Panzer on the north bank; a
fourth column which 2nd Panzer should have provided was left to
wait for the arrival of the tanks of 1st SS. No artillery barrage
preceded the jump-off. It was hoped thereby to heighten the
surprise on which Kluge still counted.

The southern columns did achieve some surprise. The American
30th Division had not been reinforced and most of its road blocks on
the approaches to Mortain were quickly overrun. The divisional
operations officer refused to be panicked by the attack, however,
which he characterized as a move by 'unco-ordinated units attempt-

ing to escape rather than aggressive action' – so much for the dread reputation of *Das Reich*'s storm-troopers – while the lower echelons behaved with even greater sang-froid. Recognizing that they were surrounded, the infantrymen of the foremost battalions withdrew to the high ground of Hill 317, overlooking Mortain, dug in for all-round defence and called down their own artillery on to the fringe of their positions. Its heavy salvoes at once brought the onward movement of 2nd SS to a halt, and while some tank crews settled to battle things out with the divisional tank-destroyer battalion – fourteen were to fall to the American guns – many of the others drove off the roads to drape their vehicles with camouflage nets against the air attack which they knew must come as soon as they were caught when stopped.

The northern column was not opposed by American force in such strength, and should have made better progress. At first it did, despite the non-appearance of a tank battalion from 116th Panzer Division to bolster its strength. But soon after daybreak, and three miles short of its objective for the day, it ran into the American 9th Division's line of resistance and halted. Soon afterwards the rest of 2nd Panzer, which had delayed its departure to await the promised detachment of 1st SS, was also brought to a stop and further reinforcement by 1st SS could not restart the advance. Hausser, Kluge's immediate subordinate as chief of Seventh Army, then tried to unstick things by calling on 116th Panzer Division to intervene, as it should have done already. But its commander, von Schwerin, insisted that he was too hard pressed where he stood to take the risk of disengaging; this verbal formula may have concealed an unwillingness to act, for he was a committed conspirator and had been driven into the plot by his loss of faith in victory. Hausser, the senior SS officer in Normandy, relieved him at once for dereliction, but the moment had passed when 116th Panzer could have altered the course of events.

Events were now principally influenced by the air forces, which had been alerted to engage the multitude of ground targets which Lüttich was expected to present. Far way from the battlefield, Allied combat air patrols established a barrier around the Third Air Fleet's runways near Paris and prevented any of its 300 promised fighters reaching the Mortain area. In the area itself American medium bombers struck hard all day at German movement on the roads to the front, while British Typhoon fighters of Second Tactical Air

Force engaged pinpoint targets with salvoes of 60-pound rockets. Between noon and dusk they flew 294 sorties, the majority against a concentration of 2nd Panzer Division's vehicles north of Mortain. 'We could do nothing against them', reported General von Lüttwitz, the divisional commander, 'and make no further progress.' About thirty of his remaining sixty tanks were knocked out by air attack on August 7th. But he also lost vehicles to the fire of the American 2nd Armoured Division which, thanks to Ultra, seemed 'to materialize out of thin air', as the American official historian – writing when it was inter-government policy still to conceal that source of wartime information – coyly described its calculated re-deployment at high speed from Vire to the banks of the Sée. Having done its worst against Lüttwitz's division, it disengaged during the night and turned up on the morning of August 8th on the other side of the battlefield, where it went into action against the 2nd SS.

By August 8th, however, the Americans had no further call for reinforcements. Operation Lüttich had failed. 'I command the attack to be prosecuted daringly and recklessly', were the words reaching Kluge from the *Führerhauptquartier*. 'Greatest daring, determination, imagination must give wings to all echelons of command. Each and every man must believe in victory.' But victory had gone palpably to the defenders. They had not been driven from their main line of resistance. They had even regained some of the ground lost in the initial German onslaught. Hitler chose to disregard the facts and even persuaded Kluge and his subordinate, Eberbach, to make plans for a renewal of the offensive with extra divisons under the latter's command. The renewal was postponed on August 9th and finally cancelled on August 11th. By then Kluge had a crisis on his hands even greater than that presented by the collapse of his left wing at Avranches. If he had launched Lüttich to demonstrate a German general's conformity to Hitler's narrow and selfish standard of military honour – little good it had done him: 'the attack failed because Kluge wanted it to fail', was Hitler's judgment to Warlimont – he had now to fight for the salvation of the whole German army in Normandy.

# CHAPTER 7

## 'A Polish Battlefield'

UNTIL THE END OF JULY Hitler's management of his armies in France, whatever its cost in day-to-day losses, had left him with a reserve in hand. Better, with two reserves: west of the Seine his panzer divisions, clustered against the British front; east of the Seine his cordon of coast-watching infantry divisions under Fifteenth Army which, as late as mid-July, still numbered fifteen. Both reserves, moreover, were so placed as to cover ground vital to him; the crossings of the Seine and the plains of northern France, which led by the shortest route to the frontier with Germany.

As British and Canadian pressure around Caen had grown, however, he had been driven to feed his infantry reserve from Fifteenth Army across the Seine, necessarily slowly because of the Allied air forces' destruction of the bridges, but steadily enough to ensure that by August 7th only three remained where there had been five times that number a month before. And, as they arrived to hold ground on the British and Canadian front, the panzer divisions had been shifted westward to mount Lüttich. Its disastrous outcome therefore found the German situation map radically and perilously changed. Along the coast between the Seine and the Zuider Zee only five divisions still stood to repel the 'second invasion' in which Hitler, too late, had at last ceased to believe. In the interior of Normandy seven divisions were at close quarters with the British and Canadians. Scattered before the advancing Americans between Le Mans and Paris were another five. But the bulk, nineteen in all, were now bunched close together along the edge of the original bridgehead, in between the rivers Vire and Orne. And their relative positions had been completely reversed. The ten nearest Caen were all infantry divisions. The nine westernmost were all panzer, terribly damaged by their effort to deliver the 'decisive blow' of which Hitler had insisted they were capable and so constricted in their ground

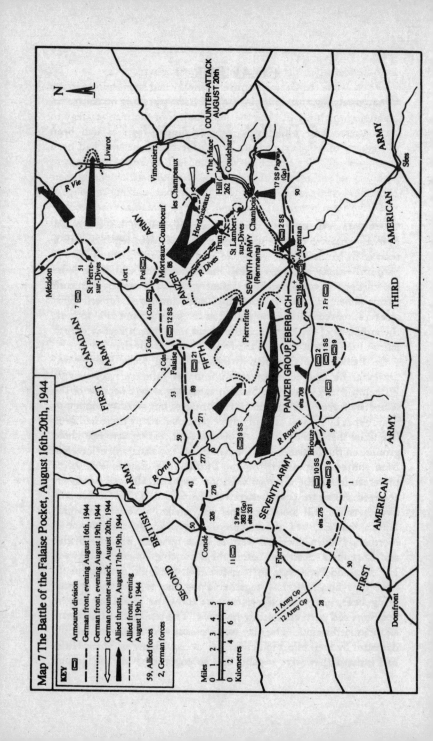

Map 7 The Battle of the Falaise Pocket, August 16th–20th, 1944

KEY

▭ Armoured division

--- German front, evening August 16th, 1944

--- German front, evening August 19th, 1944

·········› German counter-attack, August 20th, 1944

► Allied thrusts, August 17th–19th, 1944

-·-·- Allied front, evening August 19th, 1944

59, Allied forces

2, German forces

Miles
0  1  2  3  4  5

Kilometres
0  2  4  6  8

as to be scarcely capable any longer of manoeuvre.

Thus, while the German centre of gravity had been shifting in the wrong direction, that of the Allies had been travelling on course, to positions which it had been the main object of German strategy to deny them. And while the Germans' liquid reserves had been mortgaged to daily expenditure, the Allies' bank balance had been steadily rising. The British, it was true, had no fresh formations to commit; indeed, they would shortly begin cannibalizing part of their Liberation Army to make good losses in the rest, chilling evidence of what five years of war had cost them. But the Canadians had recently brought an armoured division, the 4th, to join their 2nd and 3rd Infantry Divisions, which now formed the First Canadian Army. Two émigré formations, the Free French 2nd and Polish 1st Armoured Divisions, were also arriving. And American strength had decupled in two months. It now stood at fourteen infantry and six armoured divisions, recently reorganized into two Armies, Patton's Third and the First, now commanded by Hodges in place of Bradley, who oversaw them as chief of 12th Army Group. So preponderant had American strength become that direction of the land battle must soon in propriety pass to Eisenhower, who had already established a small command post in Normandy, which he used as his forward headquarters on his frequent visits from SHAEF to the bridgehead.

Conduct of the battle nevertheless remained with Montgomery. And his situation map, transformed in the three weeks since Bradley had unleashed Cobra, scintillated with opportunity. It was now a much larger map than that which he had pored over during the nerve-racking weeks of attrition in June and early July, when a gain of half a mile anywhere between Caen and St Lô had been a matter of significance. Caen and St Lô were now well within his lines, which had reached out beyond the boundaries of the departments of Calvados and Manche to embrace nine more, Ille-et-Vilaine, Morbihan, Côtes-du-Nord, Finistère, Loire-Atlantique, Maine-et-Loire, Sarthe, Eure-et-Loir, Orne and Mayenne – about a tenth of the land surface of France – and to reach towards those which bordered the Seine: Eure, Seine-et-Oise and Yonne. In these departments all main roads led towards Paris and on every one of them a British, Canadian or American division now stood. Nearest Paris and at greatest liberty to manoeuvre were those of Patton's army. But it would not be safe to hurry them onward, nor would it be possible easily to supply them, even by air – though the air forces promised to deliver 2,000 tons of supplies a day – until the hard knot of German panzer and infantry divisions had been driven farther from Mortain, so enlarging the Avranches corridor through which all Patton's supplies still moved. On the other hand, the situation map presented another and even more spectacular solution to the problem of establishing liaison between the questing spearheads of the Patton army and the beaches over which they were still supplied. And that was for the Canadians to crash through the crust of German defences still intact south and east of Caen and join hands with them directly. It would have the additional and priceless side-effect of encircling the bulk of Army Group B between 21st and 12th Army Groups and crushing it out of existence.

'Should this be a success', wrote a diarist at First Canadian Army Headquarters, 'the war is over. The rest will be a motor tour into Germany.' Montgomery had already greatly altered the broad Overlord conception, in particular by his decision of August 4th to endorse Bradley's order, issued a day earlier, for Patton to clear Brittany with 'minimum forces' and use the surplus in a turning movement round Fifth Panzer Army's flank. He hesitated for a while over the decision to launch the Canadians out of the bridgehead towards Falaise, where they might link hands with Patton, perhaps influenced by the sturdy German resistance shown to a British southward drive on Caumont between July 30th and August 2nd (Operation Bluecoat). He was also deterred by the losses the Canadians themselves had suffered in their attacks out of the old Goodwood Corridor into the German positions on the crest of Bourguébus Ridge and beyond, on July 25th and later. On August 7th, when the Canadians opened a new and very powerful drive southwards (Operation Totalize), he was still thinking in terms of their swinging eastward when they reached Falaise and making for the Seine, which he intended to be the backstop against which the Germans would eventually be driven. On August 8th, however, as Operation Lüttich sank into the sand, he was telephoned by General Bradley, who had Eisenhower with him. The two had been conferring and Bradley had pointed out to the Supreme Commander that a 'short hook' by Patton, from Le Mans towards Falaise, would achieve exactly the same object as a 'long hook' from Le Mans to the Seine, but in quicker time and with less risk of the Germans getting men or equipment out of Normandy in any quantity. Montgomery expressed anxiety about the intentions of the Panzer force remaining

at Mortain, but agreed that 'the prospective prize was great' and left
Bradley to issue the necessary orders to Patton. On August 9th
Patton turned his two foremost armoured divisions, the 5th and the
Free French 2nd, northwards from Le Mans. Athwart their line of
advance lay the nucleus of a new German command, Panzer Group
Eberbach, formed purposely to oppose them, and two large wooded
areas, the Forêts d'Ecouves and de Perseigne. But the panzer
divisions composing Eberbach's force were already overstretched
and were unable to make use of the natural obstacles the countryside
offered them. On August 13th a French patrol entered Argentan,
only thirteen miles south-east of Falaise, towards which the Canadians were pushing from the north. The outlines of what would soon
be called the 'Falaise Pocket' had now begun to stand out on the
maps and on the countryside of southern Normandy.

About thirty miles long and fifteen broad, its southern edge was
commanded by the American Third Army, its tail by the American
First, its northern edge by the British Second, whilst on the British
left the Canadian First Army was working to close the upper jaw of
the mouth of the pocket towards the lower at Argentan. The
Canadians were working with great force. Operation Totalize, in
which they had broken out of the old Goodwood Corridor on August
7th, had been a new type of armoured operation. For the first time in
the history of warfare, the attacking infantry had been mounted in
heavily protected armoured vehicles, which had been formed up
close behind the tank spearheads and had followed them on to their
objectives. These armoured vehicles were improvisations, American
self-propelled artillery chassis from which the guns had been
removed to provide accommodation for ten soldiers. But they had
done what was expected of them, which was to deliver their
passengers unscathed to their objectives: while the four infantry
battalions engaged in the attack had lost sixty-eight killed, the three
mounted had lost only seven. Totalize, however, had not really
achieved its object. Despite the power of the ground force committed, and the support of 500 bombarding Fortresses, the front of
attack was too narrow and was once again blocked off by well-
handled German defenders, the familiar 12th SS, supported by a
Tiger Battalion. The most notable, if unperceived, success achieved
by the Canadians was to bring to an end the career of Hauptsturmführer Wittmann, whose Tiger fell to a co-ordinated salvo fired by
five Shermans on which he was making a single-handed attack. It

was a fitting end for the leading tank ace of the Second World War. But it did not count in the scales against the losses inflicted by the Hitler Youth on a wayward Canadian column they managed to cut off and surround. At the end of this tragic little action on August 9th, the British Columbia Regiment had lost forty-seven of its tanks, effectively its entire strength, and the accompanying Algonquin Regiment two companies of its infantry. It was an awful warning of the dangers inherent in cornering first-class German formations, however battle-worn and whatever the odds stacked against them.

On August 11th, nevertheless, Montgomery resolved to try again, and all the machinery of an armoured drive was reassembled for a final advance on Falaise, now only seven miles distant from the line won in Totalize. The new operation was codenamed Tractable, was to begin on August 14th, and was to muster the Canadian 3rd Infantry and 4th Armoured Divisions in parallel columns on as narrow a front as before. It was also to be preceded by the massed bombing attack which, since Goodwood, had been the standard prelude to advance on the ground. Eight hundred British bombers took part, dropping nearly 4,000 tons of bombs, of which enough fell within friendly lines – this too was becoming gruesomely familiar – to kill 150 Allied soldiers. But when the armoured columns entered the enormous dust cloud which the bombers had raised, 'steering for the sun which showed only as a red disc through the haze', they found the Germans on this occasion much less ready to resist. The 12th SS *Hitlerjugend* had been withdrawn into reserve behind the front, which was held by two weak infantry divisions, 85th and 89th, the latter recently arrived from the backwater of Norway. Those of their soldiers who had survived the bombardment surrendered eagerly, and though the 501st Tiger Battalion – the dead Wittmann's unit – re-appeared to bar the way the bombing had opened, its companies were now so weak that half-repaired tanks had to be driven out of the battalion workshops, only a mile behind the lines, to reinforce the remaining serviceable tanks. Ominously, too, some of the Tigers had to drop out of the action for want of fuel, which was not coming up the line of supply. Wherever the Canadians pressed hard, therefore, they took the ground they wanted. And so the advance which had begun on the morning of August 14th with the 'unforgettable sight of hundreds of armoured vehicles massed on the plains of rolling corn in the Orne valley' drew to a close on the evening of the following day within sight of the castle at Falaise in which William the Conqueror had been born. The pocket was about to close.

## 'The Worst Day of My Life'

The sensation of encirclement was one with which Kluge had now lived for over a week, if not longer, but certainly since the failure of Lüttich on August 7th. It was all the harder to sublimate for his inability to convey to OKW that the situation was growing daily more grave or to extract from Hitler any decision which offered the prospect of escape. For some days after Lüttich he had acquiesced in Hitler's discussion of plans to renew the offensive, perhaps half-convinced that his panzers might still inflict a reverse on the inexperienced Americans flooding past his left flank. Thus on August 9th he had pondered with every appearance of genuine absorption Hitler's proposal that Lüttich should be renewed two days later. When events overtook that scheme, he debated other dates, even one as far forward as August 20th, when the waning moon would give Panzer Group Eberbach the longer hours of darkness it needed to assemble a striking force.

But the speed of Patton's movement towards Le Mans quickly brought him up short against the 'incredibility ... of a large military force of twenty divisions blissfully planning an attack while far behind it an enemy is busily forming a noose with which to strangle it'. Realities now so alarmed him and his immediate subordinates – Eberbach, Sepp Dietrich (Eberbach's replacement at the head of Fifth Panzer Army), and Hausser, now commanding Seventh Army – that he actually managed to persuade Hitler on August 11th of the need to use the panzer divisions against the American spearhead before a second Lüttich was considered, a step in the right direction because it at least meant bringing them a little nearer to safety. Hitler, however, bemused by analogies with the eastern front, where the extreme rigidity of Soviet methods had often in the past allowed unforeseen advantages to be won from a Russian break-through, had then negated the prospect of escape by decreeing that such an attack should be aimed not at Patton's spearhead but at its lines of communication, in other words at much the same target as the abortive Lüttich. It was a case, as the disenchanted chief of staff of Seventh Army put it, of 'a command ignorant of front line conditions taking upon itself the right to judge the situation from East

Prussia', and hoping, via the right verbal formula, to frame orders from which a successful offensive might yet be conjured from the results of an unavoidable defensive withdrawal.

Military logic nevertheless wrung from Hitler the concession that the most exposed of the panzer divisions should be pulled out of the extreme western end of the pocket, to permit their regrouping for his conjuring trick – what he called 'a minor withdrawal of the front between Sourdeval and Mortain' – and Kluge at once used it to rescue them from imminent disaster. Far from this freeing them for a counter-stroke, however, he found that growing pressure by Patton's XV Corps around Alençon obliged their piecemeal engagement simply to hold the front. First 116th, then 1st SS and 2nd SS Panzer Divisions were drawn into a defensive battle, getting down to the threatened sector as best they could along the three roads still remaining open inside the pocket. Even though trying to confine their movements to the hours of darkness, all three suffered heavily from air attack, and sometimes from ambush by roving Allied armoured columns, so that when their units were eventually assembled north-west of Alençon on August 13th their strength had dropped far below the level necessary for any attack: 1st SS had only thirty tanks still running, 2nd Panzer twenty-five, 116th fifteen. The 9th Panzer, which had tried to follow in their wake, had been all but annihilated in the Forêt d'Ecouves: it reported twelve tanks and 260 men present that day.

Hitler's permission to regroup *pour mieux sauter* had also been exploited by Eberbach, Dietrich and Hausser to bring other divisions eastward. Their movement was accelerated on August 14th when the Canadian Tractable operation bore down again on the mouth of the pocket at Falaise. Totalize, which had preceded it on August 7th, had frightened Kluge badly enough – 'a breakthrough ... such as we have never seen' was how he had described it to Hausser on August 8th – and this second instalment worried him more, but now he was harried by messages from Hitler even less realistic than those of a week before. There was a 'danger that Panzer Group Eberbach, which was committed much too far to the north, will again become involved in a sterile frontal fight' (it was struggling to stay in being); 9th and 10th SS and 21st Panzer Divisions 'can and must be employed' for an attack on the Americans (they were locked in mortal combat with the Canadians at Falaise); the 'destruction of the enemy near Alençon' was Kluge's immediate mission (he was at his wits' end to keep his own army supplied with day-to-day necessities).

On the night of August 14th he set off on a tour of inspection around the perimeter of his shrunken battlefield, along 'roads clogged with traffic and dispirited troops'. At the headquarters of Fifth Panzer Army, Dietrich warned that the Falaise sector was ready to collapse. The Führer's former chauffeur was not a man to panic; Kluge would describe him in his last letter as someone 'whom I have come to know and appreciate as a brave incorruptible man in these difficult weeks', warm words from a field-marshal of an old beerhall brawler. If he warned of real danger, it was imminent. Next morning Kluge set out early to get news of the southern edge of the pocket from Hausser and Eberbach. Their rendezvous was fixed for 10 a.m. in the village square at Nécy, midway on Route nationale 158 between Falaise and Argentan, and so exactly in the eye of the gathering storm. It was forty miles from Dietrich's headquarters at Bernay and the field-marshal's command convoy was conspicuous – a motor-cycle, a staff car and a radio truck. Its progress along clogged roads was also painfully slow. Before half the journey was done, but with only thirty minutes left to the meeting, an Allied fighter-bomber made a single pass out of the sun and destroyed the radio truck, killing its four occupants. Kluge took to a near-by ditch. After he had recovered his composure he set off again, but Allied aircraft drove him constantly to cover. By midday he was in an agony of frustration and sent his aide-de-camp ahead on a bicycle. When the aide at last arrived at Nécy, Eberbach and Hausser had returned to their headquarters. Kluge therefore set off after the latter, dodging fighters all the afternoon. It was not until after midnight that Seventh Army was able to signal Supreme Headquarters West at la Roche Guyon word of his arrival.

Blumentritt, his chief of staff, at once transmitted the news to the *Führerhauptquartier*. It was one of many exchanges he had made during the day, which Hitler was to describe two weeks later as 'the worst ... of my life'. He had woken to the news of the Allied landings in the south of France, which he had long recognized would require its immediate evacuation. He was much more alarmed by the disappearance of Kluge. The day before Himmler had brought him further confirmation of the field-marshal's complicity in the July 20th plot – mere allegations, we now know, but seemingly authenticated by the presence during 1943 of so many of the real conspirators at his Army Group Centre headquarters in Russia – and he now heard at his midday conference of an intercepted Allied transmission asking of Kluge's whereabouts. The origin, even the actuality of such a transmission remains mysterious; there is no record of it in Allied files and it may have been a German misinterpretation of a casual and low-level inquiry between intelligence officers inside the bridgehead. But it instantaneously revived all Hitler's neuroses about military disloyalty and betrayal. Later he would describe his fears thus: 'Field-Marshal Kluge planned to lead the whole of the Western Army into capitulation and to go over himself to the enemy ... It seems that the plan miscarried owing to an enemy fighter-bomber attack. He had sent away his staff officer, British-American patrols advanced, but apparently no contact was made ... Nevertheless, the British reported being in contact with a German general.'¹ At the time he kept his anxieties to himself, but ordered hourly reports from Supreme Headquarters West until Kluge should reappear.

By 6.30 p.m. he had still not done so and Jodl, in conversation with Blumentritt, was told that 'the situation west of Argentan is worsening by the hour' and that, in the opinion of Dietrich, Eberbach and Hausser, 'an overall decision had to be made'. Jodl well understood this as a veiled demand for a withdrawal. He countered with what he knew was Hitler's determination to 'solve' the situation by attacking again. 'I am in duty bound to point out the state of the armoured divisions', riposted Blumentritt. They were desperately short of petrol. If the intention of the proposed attack was to win room for the evacuation of the pocket, all well and good; if it was a preliminary to some more ambitious offensive, that was now out of the question. And someone must take the decision at once. 'As Kluge is absent ... it can only be Hausser, Dietrich or Eberbach', he advised. 'He must be given a clearly stated mission without any strings attached ... As far as I am concerned,' he went on, 'I am as cool as a cucumber. But,' he warned, 'I must say that the responsible people at the front contemplate the situation as being extremely tense.'

This Moltkeian understatement apparently impressed Jodl, who at once recommended to Hitler that Hausser should take over Army Group B. Hitler had never liked that general's 'crafty little eyes', but recognized that as an SS officer he was to be trusted and so agreed. But he also telephoned both Kesselring, his commander in Italy, and

Model, his 'fireman', and requested their advice on a permanent replacement for Kluge, whom he had now written off. In all probability his decision was already made. He intended to appoint Model, the worker of miracles on broken fronts. Meanwhile he directed Jodl to re-emphasize the need for a panzer attack at Argentan and sketched out further grandiose schemes for co-operation between forces, either broken or non-existent, which would turn events to his advantage.

His 'worst day' ended with his most acute fears unrealized. The army in the west had not been led into capitulation. It had not even surrendered much ground, though Fifth Panzer Army had reeled under the Canadian attack at Falaise. But he felt nevertheless that he had been led to the edge of the abyss and, whether he could prove anything against Kluge or not, was determined never to trust him again. Model got his orders to go to France shortly after Kluge had reappeared, and arrived on August 17th not only with full powers to replace him but with instructions that he was to be kept out of the pocket. Yet, curiously, having decided to rid himself of the agent of his nightmares, Hitler accepted from him as parting advice the very solution to Army Group B's besetting dangers which he had insisted on rejecting all the previous week. 'No matter how many orders are issued,' Kluge told Jodl in his last message from the pocket in the early morning of August 16th, 'the troops cannot, are not able to, are not strong enough to defeat the enemy. It would be a fatal error to succumb to a hope that cannot be fulfilled . . . That is the situation.' He then proceeded to issue orders for a withdrawal in anticipation of Hitler's endorsement, which in fact arrived late that afternoon. The realities of the pocket had at last made themselves felt at Rastenburg: 'Roads virtually impassable, tanks repeatedly immobilized for lack of fuel, ammunition supplies erratic, troops hungry and exhausted, communications almost non-existent'; a staff officer of Army Group B, his thoughts on the retreat from Moscow, described what he saw as having a 'Napoleonic aspect'. And as the remnants of Army Group B, released at last from their pointless struggle, turned to look for crossings over the Dives and the Orne, they were indeed facing nothing less than a disaster of the proportions of 1812. For, at exactly the moment that Hitler signalled his *laissez-aller*, Montgomery and Bradley between them decided to use all force at their disposal to close the Argentan–Falaise gap and squash the pocket for good.

# Command Indecision

That they had not done so already was the outcome of a curious
passage of inter-Allied discord. Kluge, flying homeward from the
western front towards what he knew would be a Gestapo reception,
penned before taking poison a final letter of exculpation. 'My
Führer, I think I may claim for myself that I did everything within
my power to equal the situation. Both Rommel and I . . . foresaw the
present development. We were not listened to.' The Allied commanders, Montgomery, Eisenhower and Bradley alike, had not
foreseen it. Their strategic view had been shaped by the cossac plan
of 1943, which had expected the Battle of Normandy to take the
form of a succession of linear offensives, from one line of natural
obstacles to another, until the whole of the 'lodgement area' between
the Seine and the Loire had been occupied. The cossac plan had
assumed a steady rate of advance, from the D-Day 'phase line' to one
embracing Caen and Avranches in twenty days and thence to the two
great rivers in another seventy. The time-table had not worked out
like that in practice. Because of Hitler's insistence on Army Group B
fighting for every hedgerow, the real 'phase lines' had lagged weeks
behind those projected: cossac's 'D+20' had not been achieved until
D+55. Because he had stripped the interior to defend the front, the
American break-through had then made much faster progress than
anticipated, so that in some places the planned and actual D+65
phase lines had coincided, notably along the Loire. Orthodox
military thinking – and the cossac plans were highly orthodox in
theme – would presume for the Germans a prudent surrender of
threatened ground at that stage. But, inexplicably except in terms of
Hitler's mistaken correlation of Western with Soviet vulnerability to
shafts of 'operational' brilliance, the Germans had not retreated; had
indeed not merely stood their ground but driven hard back against
the 'phase lines' of three weeks before.

The Allies had made some strategic adjustment to take account of
the erratic shifts of their time-table, notably by turning Patton away
from a full-scale drive into Brittany on August 3rd. That had been
Bradley's decision, and a good one, taken in that spirit of leaving
inessential garrisons to 'wither on the vine' which currently animated
MacArthur's strategy in the Pacific. But thereafter Bradley's imagination had failed him; and so too had that part of his conscience
which should have prompted him to make his intentions clear to

Montgomery. Apparently concerned that his soldiers might, if they pressed northwards from Argentan towards Falaise, fall into a 'battle between friends' against the advancing Canadians, he ordered Patton on August 14th not to take advantage of the insane mistake which Hitler had made, and was persisting in, over Lüttich, but to head for the 'D+90' phase line on the Seine in a 'long hook' against Army Group B's ultimate line of escape. He was to leave at Argentan only as much of his force as was necessary to make it a 'hard shoulder' against enemy counter-attacks. This Nelsonian independence would have been forgiven if right-headed; even though wrong-headed, it might still have been forgiven if frankly explained and justified to Montgomery. But Bradley chose not to explain. As a pretext for his omission, he cited the existence of an inter-Allied boundary north of Argentan which he claimed it not proper to cross; but to himself he argued 'if Montgomery wants help in closing the gap ... then let him ask for it. Since there was little likelihood of him asking, we would push on to the west.'

Later he would claim that he doubted the ability of four divisions to hold a gap through which nineteen German divisions, weak in men and material but strong with the desperation of the trapped, were struggling to escape. Events would subsequently prove that doubt plausible. But when the doubt took him the Germans were not flooding eastward, but waiting immobile inside the pocket for some word which would release them from their agony. Word did not arrive until forty-eight hours after he had sent half Patton's Army towards Chartres and Orleans. The consequence was to make the closing of the gap, when the decision to attempt it was taken, a race against time instead of the deliberate military manoeuvre it might have been. Montgomery telephoned the decision on the afternoon of August 17th. Its timing was inspired by an Ultra intercept of Kluge's last appeal to Hitler for permission to disengage and it had therefore to presume that, by the time the Allies began to move, the Germans would already have started eastward. The projected point of junction between the Americans and the British army groups had thus to be set some miles beyond the Argentan—Falaise line, to ensure a firm encirclement; and the drive towards it made, in Montgomery's words, 'at all costs and as quickly as possible', even though the force available to plug the hole was one-third smaller than it had been three days earlier. Chambois, on the more southerly of the two roads still in German use, was the point chosen. The formation nominated to pay the price of Bradley's temporization was the most recently arrived and least experienced under Montgomery's command, the 1st Polish Armoured Division.

# General Sikorski's Tourists

The Poles had been long on the road, however. Their story was one of the most tragic and romantic of the Second World War. Devastated in September 1939, the Polish army had fallen to pieces. Its greater part had been taken prisoner by the Germans in the mighty encirclement of the Bzura river, and much of the rest had fallen into the hands of the Russians after their cynical intervention at the tail-end of the campaign. Fragments none the less had escaped, to internment in Lithuania, Latvia, Romania and Hungary, and with them had gone the leaders who would form the Polish government-in-exile. Later in 1942 the government would arrange for Russia's Polish prisoners, those who had survived starvation and mistreatment, to make their way into Persia, whence as the Polish II Corps they would journey to the Western Desert and Italy to fight at Alamein and win the fourth and last battle for the strategic fortress of Monte Cassino.

In time II Corps would come to be recognized as one of the great fighting formations of the war, its spirit charged, Harold Macmillan would recall, with a light-hearted disdain for danger the like of which he had met in no other. But there was a second, if smaller and less conspicuous, army-in-exile whose return to the fight had been almost as painful as that of II Corps and whose chivalric zeal was to become as notable. Formed from the 100,000 refugees who in the winter of 1939 reached France from the Baltic and Balkan states, it had already provided the French air force by the following spring with a sizeable contingent of pilots, plus a mountain brigade earmarked for the Narvik campaign, and the French army with three divisions of infantry and one of cavalry. Poles and Frenchmen were old comrades in arms; it was in part the contribution of General Haller's legion of émigrés to the victory of 1918 which had prompted Clemenceau to espouse the cause of Polish renaissance at the peace conference and to send them in 1920 equipment and advisers to help them defeat the Bolsheviks in the Battle of Warsaw, called by Major-General J.F.C. Fuller 'the eighteenth decisive battle of the world'. But they could do little to help their old allies in the nineteenth, little indeed to help themselves. Driven before the gale of the German advance, only 17,000 of the western army-in-exile reached Britain after the capitulation.

The pilots were at once re-employed; forming 4 out of the 56 squadrons of Fighter Command, they accounted for 15 per cent of German aircraft destroyed during the Battle of Britain. The soldiers were found a role less easily. Having brought with them to Britain, via the Mediterranean or Biscay ports, even less than the British army had salvaged from Dunkirk, they were a charge upon the very limited stock of armaments available, and it was only for calculated, if understandable, purposes of propaganda that enough weapons were found by the British to fit them out as fighting men once more, and then only for simple coast-defence duties in a remote corner of Scotland. The measure was naturally temporary. It was expected that, when weapons became more plentiful, the Polish formations would be brought up to normal standards of equipment, probably as conventional infantry. This, as far as British thoughts went in 1940, was the intention.

The Poles thought differently. Conscious of their restricted numbers and the near impossibility of expanding them – though patriotic appeals would bring in Polish emigrants from as far away as Latin America during the next two years – they were determined that such formations as they could raise would be of a sort to maximize the effectiveness of their personnel. Conscious too of unspoken doubts of their capacity to evolve as soldiers – 'lancers charging tanks' made for good press pieces but bad professional opinion – they were as anxious as the British cavalry to shake off any lingering reputation as hippomaniacs and embrace from the outset of their third start in combat against the Wehrmacht the most modern methods of making war. General Sikorski, their commander-in-chief (and Prime Minister), accordingly set his heart on forming his contingent in England – derided by the German radio as 'General Sikorski's tourists' – into an armoured division, fit to fight on equal terms the panzers which had overwhelmed the Polish army in its homeland in 1939. By persuasion he brought the British army to agree to the principle; by manipulation of the government-in-exile's Lend–Lease facilities he found the money for the equipment from the Americans; from the ranks of his officers he plucked the one leader with the abilities and experience necessary to transform aspiration into reality.

Stanislaw Maczek was an odd-man-out in the hierarchy of the Polish army. Like many of his generation an Austro-Hungarian subject by birth, he had fought the First World War not in the ranks of Pilsudski's Legions, from which the future high command would be chosen almost without exception, but as a *Kaiserjäger* of the orthodox Habsburg army. Through great natural ability, and a glittering reputation won in the defence of his native Galicia against the Bolsheviks in 1919–20, he had overcome this false start to his career and in October 1938 gained command of one of the only two armoured brigades maintained by the army. Long an apostle of mobility, he was dejected to discover that his new command had all the drive of a 'village fire-brigade'. In the year remaining to him he worked unceasingly to transform it into an arm of modern warfare and to such effect that in September 1939 it actually counter-attacked the future Field-Marshal Schörner's mountain division outside L'vov and won ground back from it. But its isolated successes could not alter the course of events even in its own Carpathian sector, let alone that of the campaign, and by September 19th Maczek found himself a refugee in Hungary. Re-united with some of his veterans in France, he reformed his 10th Cavalry Brigade just in time for it to be broken again in the German invasion of the west, and thence found his way via Algeria and Morocco to Scotland.

Painfully the pieces of the 10th Cavalry Brigade were put back together and in April 1942 sufficient other units joined to it to form the armoured division General Sikorski wanted. And for the next two years, while II Corps fought its way across the Mediterranean and the Home Army constructed its underground network of resistance cells in the fragmented territory of the homeland, it followed the weary round of training set to all elements of the invasion army. Its organization was consolidated on the British pattern; but the proud Polish titles of its regiments retained, 10th Mounted Rifles as the reconnaissance regiment, 24th Lancers and 1st and 2nd Armoured Regiments as the tank battalions, 10th Dragoons as the motor battalion, Podolian and 8th and 9th Light Infantry as its infantry battalions. For the division was not a King's German Legion, a formation of émigrés enlisted in the British army. It was a constituent element of the army of the Republic of Poland, on to whose territory Maczek looked forward to leading it from the beaches in triumphant return.

Even before the invasion year had dawned, his prospects of doing so had been cast into shadow. Stalin had quickly made it clear to his allies that he intended to repossess the zone occupied by his troops in 1939, Poland's right to which, established by conquest in 1920, Russia had never conceded. Though Sikorski knew that its Polish population was a minority, he could not of course negotiate such a re-adjustment while in exile. And since the Russians recognized that he would be even less likely to do so once he returned to Warsaw, Stalin took steps to foster an alternative government-in-exile inside Russian lines which was pliable to his wishes. The accidental death in July 1943 of Sikorski, a magisterial figure whose force of character even Stalin seemed to respect, removed all chance of settling Russo-Polish differences on a personal basis, and the return in January 1944 of the Red Army to the occupied zone of 1939 obliterated any motive Stalin might have had for keeping relations with his successor alive. Official relations had, indeed, been broken off the previous April, since when the Polish Home Army had been pressing on with its preparations to rise against the German army of occupation as soon as the prospect of an interregnum was glimpsed. Its hope, like Tito's, was to welcome the Red Army to a country already liberated by its own efforts, and so avoid the imposition of a government of Kremlin nominees. But the partition of the national territory effected by the Nazis made military co-ordination difficult to the point of impossibility.

The former zone of Soviet occupation was under German military administration. The western provinces had been incorporated into the Greater Reich as the *Gaue* of Wartheland and Danzig–West Prussia, the border to the east closed and the Polish middle classes domiciled there expelled or deported to concentration camps. The Home Army might therefore only organize itself with any degree of coherence inside the 'General Government', the core of the old Polish republic east and west of the Vistula which the Germans administered as a colonial territory. Of volunteers to the Home Army there was no lack; by 1944 Bor-Komorowski, the Home Army commander, reckoned there were nearly 400,000 enrolled members, a remarkable total in a population of ten million depleted by the exile of many of the younger males to forced labour in Germany. Of weapons and warlike stores there was a crippling dearth. So complete had been the collapse of the national army in 1939 that very little of its equipment had been smuggled into hiding and such arms as the patriots had were largely defective, or poor things of makeshift manufacture. In Warsaw itself 40,000 Home Army members disposed of only 1,000 rifles and 25,000 home-made hand-grenades.

On July 26th the Red Army had crossed the 'Curzon Line', that proposed by the British Foreign Minister in 1919 as an ethnically logical division between Russia and re-emergent Poland, and one for which Churchill and Roosevelt were prepared to give the Poles their support in negotiations with Moscow. Like the Germans, however, the Polish government-in-exile, which was now treating with Russia only as 'an ally of allies', counted on the inherent 'contradictions' of the Soviet-Western relationship to work out to their advantage and would not budge from the 1939 frontier. Mikolajczyk, Sikorski's successor, though actually in Moscow at the end of July, insisted on negotiating with Stalin as if from strength and would give nothing away. At one and the same moment Stalin gave his recognition to the authority of the 'Lublin Committee' of communist Poles in the liberated eastern territories, and the Germans in Warsaw seemed to be preparing to evacuate the city at the approach of the Russian vanguards, now within a few miles of eastern suburbs beyond the Vistula; the high command of the Home Army therefore decided that it could postpone striking no longer. On July 31st, the day on which 1st Armoured Division had crossed the Channel from Tilbury to Arromanches, Bor-Komorowski issued the codeword *Burza* (Tempest) for the seizure of Warsaw. On the following evening the uprising had begun.

By August 16th the battle for the city had already started to go badly for the Home Army. The Russians had halted at the outskirts of Praga, Warsaw's suburb on the east bank of the Vistula; they would later claim that they had outrun their lines of supply. It was certainly the case that, after an initial show of withdrawal, the Germans had not merely halted their retirement but brought up reinforcements – including the Hermann Göring Panzer Division – which threatened with defeat any Russian effort to cross the river and at the same time provided the detachments necessary to reduce the strongpoints held by the Poles. Those seized at the outset had given the Home Army control of a large sector of the inner city. But it had been too weak to drive the enemy garrisons of the prisons, police stations and military buildings from their positions, which had long been fortified against an uprising, and so found difficulty in arranging communication between one sector and another except through the sewers. While the surrounded Germans, who between them occupied 194 city blocks, engaged the efforts of the Home Army detachments in the Old Town and its neighbouring districts, German reinforcements outside began a systematic reduction of the approaches to the insurgent-held areas. From August 4th the Luftwaffe undertook continuous bombing raids along the axes which their ground troops were following, with such success that by August 15th the Home Army had been forced out of the main cross-city arteries.

This turn of events gave back the German high command use of the bridges across the Vistula and so the means to reinforce its field units standing before the Russian outposts on the far side of Praga. To these Bor-Komorowski was now transmitting appeals for help via his radio link to London, but without response. Stalin put a succession of difficulties even in the way of efforts by the British and American air forces to drop supplies to the embattled patriots. Warsaw being too far from English bases for their aircraft to make the flight in a round trip, with a useful payload, they had petitioned the Russians for permission to land at their forward airfields. Not until September 11th would Stalin agree to provide facilities. Meanwhile a Polish bomber squadron attached to the Royal Air Force undertook a number of missions, but their effect was symbolic and losses very high; missions flown by British and South African squadrons were even more costly. At the price of a critical worsening of relations with their Polish allies – the Polish parachute brigade in Britain, which a month later was to drop into Arnhem, declared a hunger strike on August 13th – the British therefore put relief flights on a low priority; the Americans eventually flew two strong missions, but managed to drop only about 10 per cent of their loads into Polish-held areas.

Conditions of existence within those areas – normal life had ceased from the outbreak of the rising – deteriorated from day to day. Communication with the outside world, except by radio, was broken off. Food had been too strictly rationed by the authorities for large reserves to be accumulated beforehand, and stocks began to run short within the first days; 'spit soup', so called because it was eaten to a regular rhythm of spitting out the husks of the unmilled grain from which it was boiled, became the standard diet, and was latterly consumed with all the appetite which had revolted against it when

first served. The wounded could not be evacuated or properly
treated in the makeshift underground hospitals; and surgical operations, conducted from the outset in grossly septic conditions, were
soon undergone even without anaesthetics. It was not surprising
that, as in Dublin during Easter Week, many of the civilians trapped
in the area of fighting should have developed a fierce hostility to the
Home Army soldiers, whose resistance subjected their infants and
old people to lingering starvation when it did not bring death by fire
or entombment in the collapsed buildings.

But, once embarked on their struggle, the insurgents had no way
out. The Germans shot all whom they captured – many ordinary
Poles were shot simply for being male (the SS shot women too).
Hence the desperate search for means with which to prolong the
struggle. Any unexploded shell or bomb among the thousands
dropped into the city was prized by the Home Army's engineers as a
source of explosive for their hand-made hand-grenades, and pains-
takingly dismantled despite the danger of its fuse operating during
the process. Suicidal attacks were made with bricks and clubs on
German positions in the hope of winning a few functioning firearms.
The flaming fuselage of a crashed Allied bomber, shot down on a
supply run, was invaded by insurgents seeking to strip it of its
machine guns before it exploded. And frantically urgent appeals
were broadcast to anyone who might hear for the supplies needed,
above all for ammunition. One, which was become famous among
the émigré communities, went in verse from the Home Army
transmitter, Lightning, to the government-in-exile: 'Hello ... here
is the heart of Poland! ... Hear Warsaw speaking!/Throw the
dirges out of your broadcasts;/Our spirit is so strong it will support
even you!/We don't need your applause!/We demand ammunition!!!'[2]

That particular broadcast was not made until August 24th. But
already all Poles in the diaspora hung upon news of the rising. 'Day
after day the crews [of the British-based Polish bomber squadrons]
would return from operations over France and Germany, dirty and
tired – often after desperate air battles – and their first question was
invariably, "What news from Warsaw?"'[1] For one crew, its captain
remembered, 'listening to the loud speakers, the only vital question
was: Warsaw is fighting – when do we fly to help them?'[3] By air,
Warsaw was only eight hours away, and the frustration of being
forbidden to fly thither to bomb the German besiegers, or at least to

take the supplies for which the Home Army clamoured, was violent and bitter. The soldiers of the 1st Armoured Division, also hourly alert for the broadcasts from the city which was home for many of them, could not even comfort themselves with the thought that they might give help if allowed. The signposts they had raised along their divisional supply route read 'Caen–Warsaw'; but they well knew that two German armies lay between them and their brothers-in-arms. There was no hope of breaking the ring which the *Ostheer* had thrown round the Old Town. But at least here in Normandy they had the chance to turn the tables, to complete the encirclement of what remained of the *Westheer* and so, if only in bitter symbolism, to bring succour to their comrades fighting and dying on the banks of the Vistula. The order to drive on Chambois brought – as attack orders rarely do – jubilation to their ranks.

## Contact at Chambois

The veterans of the 1st Armoured Division are growing old today. Once a year each unit, Lancers, Dragoons, Mounted Riflemen, congregates at the London Sikorski Institute for its regimental day, under the canopy of the great Turkish tent, booty from Sigmund III's victory over the sultan's army in 1621, which crowns the staircase to the regimental shrines. The standard – scarlet and white, gold-fringed, embroidered with the words 'God, Honour, Country', heavy with battle honours, Warszawa 1920, Narvik, Francja 1940, Francja 1944, and painted with the images of St Stanislaw or the Blessed Virgin of Czestochowa, to whom all Christian Poles pray in the hour of their country's need – is reverently uncased and escorted down Princes Gate to stand before the altar at Brompton Oratory while mass is said and the aching hymns of a people long oppressed are droned into the gloom of the dome. Later, over vodka and smoked ham at the Polish Hearth Club, the mood changes. Heads grey with the years of exile lift at the sight of old friends, once tank-gunners or platoon leaders, now in import–export or retired from the lower ranks of the British civil service. Faces light at the news of children established in the professions of their adopted country – the new generation of Poles, through the dedication and self-sacrifice of their parents, have become the most successful immigrant community ever absorbed into British life – and brows clear at the thought that the years between have not been so bad after all. Next year in Warsaw? The Return is not difficult for individuals. Vindictiveness has ceased to be the policy of the communist government. The Poles of the West come and go with little concern or formality. The fires of the army-in-exile have sunk into embers.

How fiercely they burnt in August 1944. Each soldier of the 1st Armoured Division wore as a symbol on his sleeve a miniature of the high feathered crest which had nodded over the helmets of the knights of the Polish kingdom in its great campaigning days. Kiev had been Polish then, as it had again for a moment in 1920, and a Polish garrison had once even wintered in the Moscow Kremlin. No Pole doubted the military prowess of his country or that the disaster of 1939 had been an aberration, produced by Russian treachery and temporary German technical superiority. Technically they were now the Germans' match and they had already thrown their tanks against German infantry north of Falaise with all the verve shown by the German panzers on their territory five years before. They had paid a price. At St Aignan-de-Cramesnil the 2nd Armoured Regiment had lost twenty-six tanks in a desperate fight with the Hitler Youth Division, nine to a single 88 mm gun. But the plentiful maw of Allied equipment reserves had replaced the wrecks, while casualties could now be made good from the ranks of Poles resident in the Warthegau and Danzig–West Prussia, conscripted into the Wehrmacht and taken prisoner in France. The episode had also taught prudence. Maczek had warned that, while losses must be borne, they were not to be suffered merely for effect.

So eager were his soldiers for the honour of closing the gap, however, that when Montgomery's order to depart reached them on the evening of August 17th, effective for 2 a.m. next day, the units detailed to form the point – the 2nd Armoured Regiment, carrying the 8th Light Infantry on their tanks – decided to set out without waiting for their re-supply of fuel and ammunition. Their route lay almost due south from their start line, abreast of Falaise, and was angled to cross the last two roads out of the pocket still in German hands, both of which led from the bridges over the Dives at Trun and Chambois to Vimoutiers. The Poles' route lay athwart the grain of the country, here as thickly wooded and sharply contoured as any in Normandy. The Pays d'Auge, home of the Camembert – the village where Madame Harel invented the illustrious cheese lay just to the left of the divisional axis – is the most obviously picturesque of all the Normandy landscapes and, lying along the valley of the Dives

33  American infantry shelter from German gunfire during the Mortain counter-attack

34  German prisoners taken by the Americans in the great break-out of July 25th, 1944

39    Paris, August 25th, 1944 : the tank Ste Anne-d'Auray leads the 2nd
French Armoured Division down the Champs Elysées

40   A German prisoner in the hands of the Resistance

41   Liberators at the Lion of Belfort, symbol of French resistance to the Prussians in the war of 1871

42 Armoured cars of the 2nd French Armoured Division in the Place de l'Hôtel de Ville, August 25th, 1944

43 German officers await the prison camp in the Hôtel Majestic

which leads eventually to Cabourg, Proust's Balbec, one of the most visited and best loved by those equipped to celebrate the beauty of the French countryside. But those who write guide-books do so without an eye — why should they have one? — for military exigencies. The Auge is dreadful country through which either to retreat or to advance — narrow, steep, deep, wriggling, overgrown, hedged, banked and densely watercoursed. The Germans at least knew where they wished to go, though the constriction of the pocket, now only six miles wide by seven long, reduced movement along their two roads to a snail's pace and drove many of the fugitives out into the open fields. The Poles, moving by night into unknown territory, soon lost their way.

> Half an hour after we moved off [wrote Ensign Stanislaw Gunther of the 2nd Armoured Regiment], the French guide who had been leading our column disappeared. Complete radio silence had been imposed, and the terrain was very difficult for tanks. We knew that at a road junction we had to take the wider of two tracks, but in the darkness it was easy to be deceived; the turning we took looked wider, but soon narrowed to such an extent that to turn some sixty tanks and twenty various vehicles would have been courting disaster. We had to press forward.[4]

The road they had taken led not to Chambois but to les Champeaux — Polish pronunciation may have confused the French guide from the outset — a place through which the Germans had to pass but only after they had escaped from the pocket proper. But the mishap had an odd and not altogether disadvantageous outcome. The regiment's advance brought it to a crossroads which an enemy column was using astride their path and the German traffic-controller actually halted it to allow the Poles through. Koszutski, the regimental commander, believed that the German recognized them for who they were and pretended otherwise to avoid a disastrous close-range encounter. It was a pretence in which he was happy to acquiesce for the chance to get forward and, though when day dawned he discovered that he had arrived at the wrong place, he also found a prize target he would have missed if he had stuck to the right route. It was a cluster of vehicles of the 2nd Panzer Division, the same fought by the 10th Cavalry Brigade in the Carpathians in 1939. In the paybooks of the prisoners taken in the fracas which

followed, veterans read the names of skirmishes – Wysoka, Nap-
rawa, Myslenice – which had left their vehicles riddled and burning
under the summer sky five years before.

The little battle decided, Koszutski swung his tanks south-west
towards Chambois, six miles away. To their right the 10th Mounted
Rifles were heading towards the same place on a more direct route,
while the 24th Lancers followed a parallel course down the valley of
the Dives to Trun. A little short of Chambois, Trun actually lay in
the 4th Canadian Armoured Division's zone of operations and was
still in German hands. But little good possession of it did them.

> The small narrow roads of Trun met at the Grande Place in the
> centre of the town and into this square, from all the traffic-
> choked side roads, oozed carts, armoured personnel carriers,
> tanks, soft-skinned lorries, staff cars and foot columns. Thanks
> to the determined efforts of their junior officers the SS vehicles
> [which Model was husbanding to hold the shoulders of the
> pocket or counter-attack to clear its mouth] were swung left out
> of the town and reached the Vimoutiers road. There the
> congestion was if anything worse ... all the time the Spitfires
> of the Royal Air Force rose and swooped over the columns,
> cannon guns supplementing the work of destruction which the
> Typhoons had earlier carried out with rockets and bombs.
> Slowly, inch by inch, the German columns, four-deep, inter-
> mingled with groups of men, guns, horses and vehicles, strove
> to achieve the Mount Ormel heights, pursued by the Royal Air
> Force, harried by the artillery, unaware that very soon they
> would be under attack from the Poles.[5]

The weather, so contrary during much of the bridgehead battle,
had now set blindingly fair in the Allies' favour, and all day the
squadrons of the 2nd Tactical Air Force commuted with relentless
and gruesome regularity between their airstrips and the choked
roads of the pocket. 'It seemed', said a local farmer caught in the
inferno, 'as though I was on the stage in the last act of the Valkyrie.
We were surrounded by fire.' A pilot who two days later examined in
a secondary road near Trun the effect of one of the 1,200 sorties
flown that day found

> destruction ... complete and terrible to the last detail ...
> under semi-darkness of the arching trees in full August leaf. It

was obvious what had happened. Typhoons had spotted the column ... and had destroyed the leading and end vehicles, in this instance two armoured cars. They had then passed up and down the lane using rockets and cannons. The vehicles were jammed bumper to bumper and each bore the sign manual of the Second Tactical Air Force – a gaping hole in the side or turret. It was quite impossible to move past them and almost impossible to clamber over them. Grey-clad, dust-powdered bodies were sprawled everywhere – propped against the trees, flopped over driving seats or running boards – the once crimson stains on their uniforms already turned the colour of rust. I gave up trying to walk over this mile of utter destruction and we made a wide detour only to reach another lane, also impassable. It was grimly guarded by four German privates crouching against a high bank, their hands to their heads, pressing them down in a gesture of futile concealment ... Beside them a mill stream rippled over their upturned vehicle.[6]

Since on the night of August 14th–15th Army Group B had ordered the withdrawal of all anti-aircraft artillery from the pocket, while the Luftwaffe simply could not find the aircraft to contest control of the skies above it with the Allies, the broken and intermingled divisions on its floor had no means with which to defend themselves against aerial attack and no hope for survival but to press ever more urgently towards Trun and Chambois. Disaster had now dissolved all distinction of rank, as in Warsaw it had between civilians and those who claimed the status of soldiers of the Home Army. There senior officers made their way through the filth of the sewers on their tours of inspection from one sector to another. West of Trun and Chambois the staffs of Seventh Army and Panzer Group Eberbach trudged the farm tracks in the anonymous ranks of their soldiers, diving for cover to the shelter of the ditches when Allied aircraft appeared overhead, hurrying onward in the short intervals of relief. The night of August 18th brought a pause to the air attacks and some coherent eastward movement was achieved by the twelve of the twenty trapped divisions still operating as entities: 3rd Parachute, 84th, 276th, 277th, 326th, 353rd, 363rd Infantry Divisions, 1st, 10th, 12th SS, 2nd and 116th Panzer. But August 19th dawned clear again. The Allied air forces appeared early overhead. And on the far bank of the Dives the hands of the

Americans advancing from the south and the Poles descending from the north reached out to touch each other.

Maczek had now divided his command into two. Towards the high ground east of Chambois, separating and dominating the roads from it to Vimoutiers, he detached his 1st and 2nd Armoured Regiment, Podolian, 8th and 9th Light Infantry battalions and an anti-tank group. Towards Chambois itself he launched the 24th Lancers and the 10th Dragoons in their half-tracks, with the rest of the divisional anti-tank guns. Each group had orders to seize and hold. The second, under the staff of the 10th Cavalry Brigade, departed from its start line near Trun in early afternoon. The 10th Mounted Rifles joined as brigade reserve.

Almost immediately the advance point bumped some Panther tanks but, taken by surprise, the Germans were quickly overcome. A hot afternoon of deadly, small-scale fighting followed, the infantry of the 10th Dragoons dismounting from their half-tracks time and again to engage small pockets of resistance, while the Lancer tanks worked round the flank to take the enemy in rear. 'From our hill', recorded a French-Canadian officer of an artillery regiment giving the Poles fire support, 'there was a panoramic view of the combat zone. At our feet the battle raged for the possession of the villages of St Lambert and Chambois. We could see the Shermans advancing, blazing away with their guns and machine-guns. The attacking tanks and infantry exploited the folds in the ground for cover.' At about 4.30 p.m. the leading infantry passed from his sight as they reached the orchards and hedged enclosures on the outskirts of Chambois itself.

Second-Lieutenant Karcz, a troop leader in the Dragoons' 4th Squadron, received orders to enter the village a little before 5 p.m.; for fear of hitting the Americans, whose patrols were reported approaching from the far side, supporting artillery fire was stopped. He 'decided to leave the road and to advance through the gardens above Chambois to the east, and so descend upon the centre ... We were able to advance without incident and to ambush so many Germans that my sixty men soon found themselves hampered by two hundred prisoners.' On his right, Lieutenant Kintzi, commanding the 2nd Squadron, found the same encumbrance.

The village was delivered to the flames ... Our men winkled out prisoners from everywhere. In the keep of the old castle overlooking the plain alone they captured forty. I was surprised to see them on the tower with their hands raised. It would have been simple to fire on us as we approached. One of the prisoners later gave me the explanation for his conduct. They knew who their opponents were and were terrified of reprisals.'

Karcz, consigning his prisoners rearward, pressed on. Working through the orchards, he reached the road which entered the village from Vimoutiers and had a short battle with a German machine-gunner, in which he was slightly wounded. The eastern approach secure, he despatched a runner to make contact with Kintzi's squadron at the western end and moved towards the centre. 'The place was on fire', he recalled later. 'The roads leading to it and the side streets were jammed with German armour already alight or smouldering, enemy corpses and a host of wounded soldiers. No civilians were to be seen.'⁸ Suddenly his second-in-command shouted news of the approach of a battalion of enemy infantry attacking across the fields in open order, 800 yards away. Karcz radioed for immediate reinforcements, deployed what men he had to defend the village against recapture and had rapid fire opened on the enemy formation.

At once it stopped and went to cover, from which after a moment white flags were waved. Karcz wondered whether he was about to add to his bag of prisoners. Then signs were made for a parley. As the group approached his lines under a white flag, a sense of embarrassment grew in Karcz's breast. The soldiers' helmets, so clearly German at a distance, changed silhouette as the range shortened. Suddenly he could mistake them no longer. They were American.

'Feeling rather crestfallen I jumped onto the road and waved my hand. An American captain ran towards me, and, still running, caught hold of me and lifted me in the air as if I had been a child ... That was the precise moment when the Falaise Pocket was closed. It was nearly 1800 hours and the American's name was L. E. Waters.'

## The Mace

The American advance, undertaken by the 90th Infantry Division and the 2nd Free French Armoured Division, had also been made in

the teeth of desperate resistance. Despite the support of forty-five
batteries of artillery, they had had to fight every foot of the way and
eventually achieved Chambois only because their superior weight of
armour allowed them to bypass German road-blocks by moving
across country. The Canadians, west and slightly to the rear of the
Poles, had had perhaps the most difficult battle of all. At St
Lambert-sur-Dives, between Trun and Chambois, a mixed collection of tank and infantry units, which the only surviving senior
officer present, Major D. V. Currie, had taken under command,
struggled throughout August 19th first to take and then to hold the
village; though not on either of the two roads to Vimoutiers, its
bridge provided a crossing which the Germans were desperate to
retain and, when they lost it, they counter-attacked repeatedly,
though without success, to regain it.

These counter-attacks were local. One of Model's first acts on
relieving Kluge, however, had been to give orders for larger and
better co-ordinated attacks on the Trun–Chambois sector from both
directions: from the east by the 2nd SS and 9th SS Panzer
Divisions, which had managed to get clear of the pocket, from the
west by the best of the formations still trapped. Nominally under the
command of Hausser, effective leadership there had passed to
Meindl, a parachute general, whose excellent young infantrymen
still retained the will to find a route of escape for the rest.

When Model's orders were issued on August 18th the mouth of
the pocket had not yet been closed. When his subordinates were
ready to implement them on August 20th Trun and Chambois had
both been lost. The operation therefore took on the character not of
a holding but of a break-through battle, which could succeed only if
the light Allied blocking elements on the two roads to Vimoutiers
could be driven from their positions before they were reinforced.
Almost as soon as the 10th Dragoons and 10th Mounted Rifles had
begun to celebrate with the 359th Regiment their joyous meeting –
Karcz happened on some Polish vodka in an abandoned German
staff car with which to toast Captain Waters – the Poles and
Americans in Chambois had therefore to put the village into a state
of defence. The attacks from within the pocket began almost at once
and were pressed home with desperation. But those from the other
direction, launched from a prepared line of departure and with more
deliberation, were yet more serious. They fell, however, not upon
the Dragoons and Mounted Rifles but on the other half of Maczek's

division, now located farther to the east.

This group, consisting of the 1st and 2nd Armoured Regiments and the three light infantry battalions – Podolian, 8th and 9th – had arrived in their positions on the morning of August 19th. Not without difficulty: the light infantry had to make a formal attack to drive the German defenders off the high ground which was their objective and the tanks which followed found the steep incline a strain on their engines. When they reached the crest, however, Maczek's reason for directing them thither was made immediately apparent to all ranks from the highest to the lowest. They were occupying a 'long whale-like ridge' which dominated the surrounding lowland and its valleys for several miles in each direction. Maczek had called it, after a glance at his map, 'The Mace' and, with its round head lying north of the Chambois–Vimoutiers road and narrow tail crossing it to the south, its contours did indeed resemble one. And the contours were steep; so that the Poles were not only positioned to deny movement to the Germans along the road below but also secure against assaults to drive them off. All they needed was a regular supply of ammunition to ensure that any Germans still managing to filter across the Dives between Trun and Chambois were turned back or stopped in their tracks. They had reasons then for confidence, even though they were in the most exposed position of all the Allied units striving to keep the pocket closed and – though at the beginning this was not obvious – completely isolated, within territory still German, from contact with any others.

The dangers of their isolation dawned slowly. The troopers of the 2nd Armoured Regiment and riflemen of the 8th Light Infantry – the group which Colonel Koszutski had led on the false trail to les Champeaux in the dark of the morning of August 18th – had had no sleep for three nights and spent much of the morning of August 19th – a Saturday, they would later recall – dozing in and around their vehicles. But by midday material considerations awoke their officers to some of the facts of their situation. They were short of food, water and ammunition, and very short of petrol; they were also encumbered with hundreds of prisoners. Supply columns should have brought them their necessities and relieved them of their useless mouths. None – either from their own Canadian echelons or from the Americans – arrived. At 1 p.m., moreover, the road from Chambois to Vimoutiers which ran immediately below their points of observation began to fill with German troops and equipment making the dash from the Dives valley towards safety. More Germans were spotted filtering around the ridge to the north. The two armoured regiment commanders, Koszutski and Stefanewicz, hurriedly conferred. Their 1,500 infantry and 80 tanks were obviously cut off and surrounded behind German lines and, they knew, lacked the fuel to break out. On the other hand, as long as they stayed where they were, they could reasonably hope to hold their positions, and by using their weapons and calling down the fire of their own and the Canadian artillery could arrest all German movement they could see. They had become, as it were, the cork in the neck of the pocket. Captain Sévigny, their attached observation officer of the 4th Medium Regiment, Royal Canadian Artillery, was at once instructed to concentrate a regimental shoot on the enemy traffic jam and within minutes they were able to watch salvoes of 5·5-inch shells falling into the 'moving mass. What a massacre. I could see several vehicles alight', recalled Captain Sévigny, 'terrified horses trying to break out of their harness, men trying to flee. It was useless. Shells soon found them and I saw bodies fly in the air . . . Ten minutes later the whole road was ablaze.' The machine-guns of the Polish tanks on the ridge joined in, 'exacting payment for the great extermination battle in the bend of the Bzura river where the mass of the Polish army had been trapped and annihilated in just such a situation . . . five years before'. The execution went on until smoke from the burning mass of material below (thickened by a sudden rain squall) rose to obscure the target. 'The tanks ceased fire and allowed those Germans who wished to surrender to be collected, those who were wounded to be dressed and those who despaired of fighting their way through the ring of steel to flood back again towards Chambois.'

Koszutski, the senior officer, nevertheless recognized that the respite was temporary. The Germans below were too numerous and too hard-pressed to be deterred from another attempt to break out simply by indirect fire. Shortly they would be bound to make a deliberate assault on the Mace itself (in Polish, the *Maczuga*, a word of peculiar significance because the weapon was the symbol of sovereign power ceremonially accepted by heads of state at the moment of their installation). He gave some essential orders. 'The northern peak of Hill 262 [the Mace] soon became a fortress', recorded Captain Sévigny. 'Our only hope lay with the Americans coming up from the south who were to join us during the night. But the Americans had been halted at Chambois. There was no hope of help – the Poles could only count on themselves.'

Koszutski called a conference of his officers. 'Gentlemen, the position is serious. Our brigade is completely cut off. The enemy is still fighting. His only retreat routes are those which you can see to the left and right. No one except us can stop them. That is what we are trying to do. No question of surrender. I speak as a Pole.'[9]

That evening in Warsaw the commander of the garrison in the Old Town also took a momentous decision. He recognized that his battle had reached a climacteric. The Royal Palace and the Cathedral of St John, twin symbols of Polish national sovereignty, had been reduced to ruins. Nine hundred of the thousand buildings in the Old Town – cherished by Poles as the most easterly expression of the Baroque movement in European architecture – had been destroyed. Two hundred thousand citizens had been driven by concentric German attacks into the cellars under the rubble, while the Home Army garrison, about 10,000 strong at the outset, had suffered casualties of between 50 and 80 per cent. Bor-Komorowski therefore determined that, with the assistance of relief attacks by Home Army units from outside the Old Town, he must lead his men in a break-through to safer positions from which to carry on the fight.

August 20th was thus to be a momentous day of struggle for the Home Army and the army-in-exile. For both the object was survival; but while Bor could at best hope to survive with a crown of honour, the 1st Armoured Division might through survival consummate the destruction of the German army in the west. All night the men on the Mace had heard the rumble of German transport moving across country at the foot of their fortress. Early in the morning Koszutski accordingly sent a small-tank infantry force to seize the tail of the Mace, where the Vimoutiers road ran across it, intending to form a block there, but before it could establish itself he was forced to order its recall. A sudden and heavy German attack, supported by armour, had started to come in against the northern edge of the Mace and reinforcements were needed to beat it off. After an hour and a half of fighting, between 9 a.m. and 10.30 a.m., the position was restored; one of Meindl's parachute battalions had been badly hurt in the proceedings. What Koszutski did not realize, however, was that the tanks his men had driven off came not from within the pocket but without; they belonged to the 2nd SS Panzer Division, which had laagered overnight near Vimoutiers and was now beginning the counter-offensive which Model and Hausser had agreed on two days before.

Soon after the opening of this assault on the northern edge of the Mace, more German movement was spotted on an adjoining hill, Point 239, from which the enemy could bring the crest of the Mace under observed fire. Koszutski therefore despatched another tank-infantry group to drive them off. But the opposition was found to be too strong and the group had to return, pursued by artillery and mortar salvoes which destroyed five Polish Shermans. Allied air power should have made this dangerous sortie unnecessary; but a break in the weather, of which the previous afternoon's cloudburst had been a prelude, obscured targets and was to do so throughout the day. The German artillery was accordingly freed to build up a steady play of fire on to the summit of the Mace and, under its cover, a series of direct assaults were launched up the slopes from noon onwards.

> Every combination of tactics was used: conventional infantry assaults, combined panzer and grenadier, unsupported Panther attacks, savage bombardments or no barrage at all. Against each and every assault the Poles held firm. Some of the slopes of the Mace were so steep that the SS climbed them bent double and pulling at bushes to bring themselves forward; at other places the ground formed a natural hollow and into this killing ground poured the grenadiers driving for the summit, only to be shot down by machine guns on the tanks and blown apart by their shells.[10]

The assaults reached a climax at about 7 p.m., when the German infantry supported by tanks did at last break into the north-eastern sector of the perimeter. They were eventually driven out only when the men of a mortar platoon, who had expended all their bombs, came forward with rifles to strengthen the line of the 9th Light Infantry, which was bending under the pressure.

Behind this furious, day-long activity, Meindl had succeeded in achieving some of his purpose. The Polish lines had been forced back a little from the commanding position above the Vimoutiers road and, with the skies clear of Allied aircraft, some thousands of the press of men still inside the pocket managed to wade or ford the Dives and get away to open country; they included Generals Meyer, of 12th SS, and Hausser, Seventh Army commander, both wounded, Hausser very seriously. Koszutski had also been wounded, by a shell splinter in the chest. Late in the evening he summoned his surviving officers to his bedside. They were very few; casualties in the battalions approached 30 per cent and the hunting-lodge and farm buildings on the plateau were crowded with wounded. 'Gentlemen,' he began, 'all is lost. I do not think the Canadians can come to our rescue. We have ... no food and very little ammunition ... Fight all the same. There is no question of surrender. Tonight we shall die.'[11]

The night in fact passed without incident. But early in the morning of August 21st the attacks started again and at noon there was a 'suicidal' assault off the Vimoutiers road towards the Polish lines on the southern lip of the Mace. So fierce was it that the last reserve, a troop of anti-aircraft tanks, had to be called forward to repel the massed waves of German infantry which, with the final bursts from their twin machine-guns, they ultimately did. But the effort seemed to be the last of which the garrison was capable. A flight of American Dakotas which should have resupplied them with ammunition by parachute dropped its load in error five miles away and Stefanewicz, describing the condition of all, signalled Maczek at divisional headquarters that he could 'no longer stand up from physical exhaustion'. Shortly after midday and the ebbing of another German assault, however, sounds of tanks were heard to the north, the distinctive engine note of Shermans. Sévigny, asleep on his feet, was shaken awake by his signaller. 'Captain, I can hear our tanks.' But was it only a patrol? Might it not be driven off? A troop of the 2nd Armoured Regiment under Second-Lieutenant Niewinowski was hastily assembled and launched down the slopes of the Mace to make contact. A mile and a half beyond the perimeter, it met the forward echelon of the Canadian Grenadier Guards, who had set out that morning to bring relief. An hour later the Canadian tanks were within the perimeter. 'The scene', the Grenadiers' war diarist recorded, 'was the most savage the regiment had ever encountered. The Poles had received no supplies for three days; they had several hundred wounded whom they had been unable to evacuate; they held eight hundred prisoners, carelessly unguarded in a field. The road was jammed with burnt out vehicles, theirs and the enemy's. There were corpses everywhere, unburied and dismembered.' Amid these horrors, 'the Polish commander received us shaking with emotion and his soldiers told long stories in Polish to the Canadians, who did not understand a word but roared with laughter all the same.'¹²

There was no laughter in Warsaw. The 1st Armoured Division had held the ring; so too had the Germans around the Old Town. Perhaps 70 per cent of the survivors of the *Westheer* had been prevented by Maczek's men on the Mace from escaping to renew the fight on the Siegfried Line. The whole of Bor's garrison had been driven back into their bunkers and foxholes among the ruins, from which they would be released only when, at the beginning of October, the Germans tired of the effort to break their resistance and offered them recognition as combatants if they would surrender. The Home Army, on the evening of August 21st, knew therefore that it was doomed to defeat. Maczek could celebrate a victory. Next day in the square at Chambois, in the presence of representatives of the British and American armies, he accepted an Iron Cross taken from a German prisoner who had won it five years before in the Carpathian battle where the 10th Cavalry Brigade had been destroyed for the first time. The trumpeters of the 10th Dragoons sounded the ceremonial march of the Polish army. A telegram from the commander-in-chief in London was read to the assembled officers and men. It declared, with uncertain optimism: 'Your sacrifices will enable the rights of Poland to be established on an indestructible foundation.'

During the next days the bodies of 325 Polish soldiers killed in the Battle of the Falaise Gap would be found makeshift graves near the positions where they had fallen. On the summit of the Mace itself sappers of the Royal Canadian Engineers, in tribute to their comrades-in-arms, raised a makeshift signboard. It bore, in English, the simple inscription, 'A Polish Battlefield'.

# CHAPTER 8

## *Free France*

HITLER'S SCHEME to devastate the Allied armies in their beachhead had not merely failed; it had ended in disaster. During 1943 his direction of the war had lost him Armies. In 1944 it had begun to lose him whole Army Groups. Army Group Centre had gone in the great encirclement battle in White Russia in June. In August Army Group G had been scattered before the Franco-American landing in the south of France. The Battle of the Falaise Gap had completed the destruction of Army Group B, the largest in the order of battle of the German army. Fifty-six infantry divisions had fought under its command during the Battle of Normandy. Of these, 15 had been formally dissolved or were besieged in the coastal fortresses behind Allied lines; the remaining 40 were remnants or shadows, now flitting eastward from the battlefield to find a way across the Seine between Paris and the sea. Its 11 panzer divisions, the rock of the German defence, had suffered proportionately. Two – Lehr and 9th – had lost all their tanks and units of infantry. The other 9 varied in strength from 4 infantry battalions, where there should have been 6, and 15 tanks, where there should have been 150, in the case of the 116th, to one infantry battalion and no tanks in the case of the 2nd. The 2nd SS, which had battled so hard against the Poles to break into the pocket, reported its strength on August 23rd as 450 men, 15 tanks and 6 guns. The equipment lost, amounting to 1,300 tanks, lay burnt or broken in the narrow lanes and hedgerow corners of the bocage and the Pays d'Auge. The missing men were prisoners – 200,000 had been shipped out of the beachhead or were waiting for transport in improvised stockades – or dead; at least 50,000 German soldiers had been killed or died of wounds in the ten weeks since D-Day. Thousands lay unburied in the confines of the pocket and their bodies, decomposing under the August sun beside the thousands of horses slaughtered with them, raised a stench against

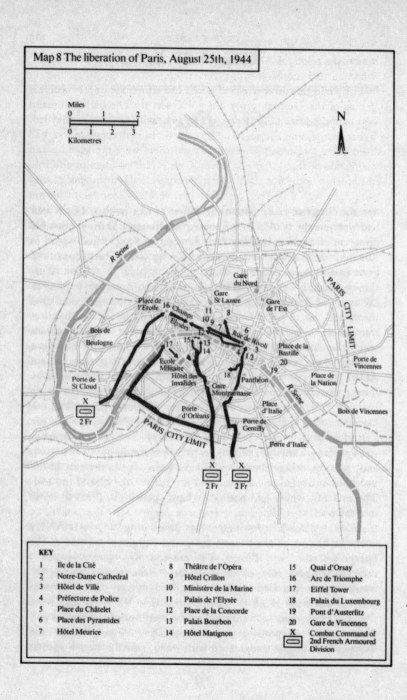

Map 8 The liberation of Paris, August 25th, 1944

Miles
0      1      2
0  1  2  3
Kilometres

N

R Seine

Gare
du Nord

Gare
St Lazare

Gare
de l'Est

PARIS CITY LIMIT

Place de
l'Etoile

Champs
Elysées

Rue de Rivoli

Bois de
Boulogne

Place de la
Bastille

Porte de
Vincennes

Ecole
Militaire

Hôtel des
Invalides

Panthéon

Place de
la Nation

Porte de
St Cloud

X
2 Fr

Gare
Montparnasse

Place
d'Italie

Bois de Vincennes

Porte
d'Orléans

Porte de
Gentilly

PARIS CITY LIMIT

Porte d'Italie

X
2 Fr

X
2 Fr

KEY

| | | | | | |
|---|---|---|---|---|---|
| 1 | Ile de la Cité | 8 | Théâtre de l'Opéra | 15 | Quai d'Orsay |
| 2 | Notre-Dame Cathedral | 9 | Hôtel Crillon | 16 | Arc de Triomphe |
| 3 | Hôtel de Ville | 10 | Ministère de la Marine | 17 | Eiffel Tower |
| 4 | Préfecture de Police | 11 | Palais de l'Elysée | 18 | Palais du Luxembourg |
| 5 | Place du Châtelet | 12 | Place de la Concorde | 19 | Pont d'Austerlitz |
| 6 | Place des Pyramides | 13 | Palais Bourbon | 20 | Gare de Vincennes |
| 7 | Hôtel Meurice | 14 | Hôtel Matignon | X | Combat Command of 2nd French Armoured Division |

which the pilots of Allied light aircraft, surveying the devastation, wrinkled their noses at 1,500 feet.

But, amid this utter wreck of hopes and effort, the improvisational genius of the German army did not desert it. The high command had paid the price of Hitler's strategy as heavily as the men they led. Three corps commanders and twenty divisional commanders had been killed, wounded or captured, and there were the suicides and dismissals of the Army and Army Group commanders to add into the score as well. But the lower staffs continued to function, as they would do with unshaken resolve to the very last months of the war (in the Battle of Lake Balaton in Hungary in March 1945 the tank recovery company of the 1st Cavalry Division would be commanded with complete efficiency by the senior medical officer, co-opted by the divisional commander because he was his last pre-war regular). Their current task was to convey the remnants of Seventh and Fifth Panzer Armies across the Seine, without the use of permanent bridges and under the Argus eye of the Allied air forces which had destroyed them. They tackled it with the skill learnt in a hundred retreats across Africa, Italy and Russia. Between August 20th and 24th they brought into operation, by later British calculation, twenty-three ferries between les Andelys, south of Rouen, and Quillebeuf, on the estuary, and a pontoon bridge at Pont de l'Arche. During the day the ferries and pontoons were hidden under the river bank; after dark – three days of bad weather interrupted night flying from Allied airfields – the boats were swung out into the waterway and men and equipment flung across to the far bank. The return of daylight caught many vehicles massed on the wrong side waiting for a crossing, and these the Allied air forces destroyed in thousands. But, at the end of five nights of ferrying, 300,000 soldiers and, more remarkable, 25,000 vehicles had reached the north bank.

Their route lay onward towards the line of the Somme, along which Hitler yet hoped to construct a second line of resistance. But there were still German formations south of the Seine whose orders were to remain. Three of these, 331st, 344th and 17th Luftwaffe, had escaped encirclement in the pocket and had the mission of defending the 'Paris–Orleans gap' between the Loire and the Seine. Far too weak to form line against the spearheads of Patton's army, they would shortly be brushed aside by his armoured divisions and fall to pieces. By August 21st the American armoured divisions were reaching out towards Melun, on the Seine south of Paris, and at Mantes, north of the city, an infantry division had already established a bridgehead on the far bank. Paris was thus encircled around half its circumference and must fall as soon as its garrison – which had orders to hold the city as a bridgehead – was overcome. The garrison was not strong. It consisted of a 'security' division, the 325th, and twenty batteries of 88 mm anti-aircraft guns, with seventeen-year-old crews, which could at a pinch be deployed in an anti-tank role; Colonel Meise, on the staff of the German commander of the city, had pointed out that they were superfluous in their orthodox function because 'the Allies are never going to bomb Paris'.

But nor were they going to fight for it. Hitler's and their strategies at this moment were completely mismatched. While he, with hopelessly misplaced optimism, saw Paris as a bridgehead across the Seine, through which his Normandy army might make a quick retreat to his new defence line along the Somme and Marne rivers, Montgomery and Eisenhower saw it as a sponge which would profitlessly absorb good troops in the capture and afterwards enormous quantities of food and fuel needed for the advance to the German frontier. Neither Allied general used the term 'useless mouths'; but the harsh logic of that old concept of siege warfare underlay Supreme Headquarters' outline plan for the next phase of operations: 'If taken early, Paris will become a serious limitation to our ability to maintain forces in operation'; the feeding of its inhabitants would 'entail a civil affairs commitment equal to maintaining eight divisions in operation' – or about a fifth of the force at Eisenhower's disposal (due to assume direct control of the land battle on September 1st, major strategic decisions were now increasingly falling to him). The immobilization of eight divisions would interrupt one or other of the two most promising operations currently on hand: the essential effort to cut off as much as possible of the fugitive Fifth Panzer and Seventh Armies, by sweeping along the south bank of the Seine from Mantes-Gassicourt to the estuary; and the subordinate but dramatic opportunity to thrust Patton's Third Army eastward from its bridgehead at Melun and Troyes towards Lorraine and the Siegfried Line. Montgomery in his directive to the Allied armies written on August 20th therefore warned that it was not General Eisenhower's intention to take Paris 'until it is a sound military proposition to do so'.

## Insurrection

The Allied generals had discounted the intentions of the Resistance. Like Warsaw Paris sheltered a secret army with the will, and some of the means, to bend the strategy of the forces of occupation and those of the conquerors standing beyond its outskirts. Its actions would now determine when, and how, the battle for Paris would be fought.

The Paris Resistance was far smaller than the force with which Bor-Komorowski had begun the insurrection in Warsaw. And, unlike the Home Army, it was many organizations rather than one. Effective opposition to the German occupation had been slow to develop in France and then grew from many budding points. Until the German invasion of Russia in June 1941 the Communist Party, by its nature the most apt for clandestine activity, had matched the occupiers' policy of 'correctness'. And, until November 1942, the population of the unoccupied zone, south of the Loire, had dutifully accepted the authority of Marshal Pétain's government in Vichy. The only declared opponents of the armistice of 1940 operated in the north of France, drawing their inspiration from the pre-war political parties of the left and from contact with de Gaulle's organization in London. His ambition naturally was to unite all forms of resistance under the banner of Free (later Fighting) France, but it was not until May 1943, by which time the Communist Party had put itself in the forefront of opposition to German occupation, that he succeeded in persuading all groups, of whatever party or affiliation, Catholic, military or trade union, and wherever located, to accept the legitimacy of a National Council of Resistance.

Even then the CNR remained a confederacy, and one without much force at its disposal. The French countryside offers little terrain suitable for guerrilla activity; and the extremely efficient and overlapping network of governmental power – police, gendarmerie, *Renseignements généraux*, *Surveillance du territoire*, as well as the agencies of préfecture, canton and commune – all of which were at the disposal of officialdom, German or Pétainist, made subversion a risky business for the individual. It was not until the rigorous imposition of forced labour decrees in mid-1942 that young Frenchmen, presented with the stark choice of resistance or deportation to Germany, began to choose the former in any number. And even so their choice did little to harm the German war effort. Arms were few and localities willing to run the risk of reprisals attendant on sheltering an active maquis band fewer still. And so it was literally to the *maquis* – the brush-covered slopes of the Massif central or the bare upland plateaux of Savoie far from centres of population and industry – that the larger bands of the resistance had to take, where they enjoyed relative immunity from German anti-partisan columns at the humiliating price of keeping themselves to themselves. When they erred, retribution was swift and terrible. In March 1944 the maquis on the plateau de Glières in Haute Savoie, which had been launching raids against German lines of communication in the area, was destroyed in a single brutal operation; and as late as July 1944 the Germans found the force to visit the same fate on another highland maquis at Vercors in the Dauphiné.

Significantly each was commanded by officers of the regular army, who had gone underground after the German occupation of the *Zone libre* in November 1942. To their maquis they had been able to bring not only their military skills but also access to stocks of arms hidden from the authorities in 1940–41. It was these weapons, as much as those parachuted to them by the British Special Operations Executive, which had allowed them to carry battle to the enemy. The Paris Resistance, at the beginning of August 1944, enjoyed no such resources. Colonel Rol, head of the communist networks in the city, estimated the number of arms available at only 400, about a quarter of the armament at the disposal of Bor-Komorowski on the same date.

That arms were so scarce was due in part to the pattern of the campaign of 1940, which had been fought far from the capital and so left no tidewrack of weapons to be hidden by patriots, in part by the co-operation of the French authorities with the German disarmament commission (lovingly created by Hitler to match that which Versailles had inflicted on Germany in 1919). But there was another cause of want: Special Operations Executive and the Gaullist organization in London, fearful of feeding the power of the communists, whose strength lay in the cities, had taken care to see that the preponderance of parachute drops fell in the open country: between February and May 1944, 76,000 Sten guns and 28,000 pistols were parachuted into France, but only 118 and 14 respectively were consigned to Paris.

De Gaulle carried his mistrust of the communists – founded less on hostility to their ideology than on his vision of a France liberated from party politics – beyond denying them arms. His extraordinary success thus far in sustaining a unique and independent role for himself among the Allied leaders had lain in his skill in manipulating all the organizations of external and internal resistance – those he had founded himself, those the Allies had foisted on him, those spontaneously created – to his advantage. His technique was either to pack them with his own nominees – his recipe for dealing with Giraud and the Committee of National Liberation at Algiers in 1943 – or to cap a paramount organization which had escaped from his control with another of his own. By the beginning of 1944 he had judged that the CNR had fallen too heavily under the influence of its communist element, the *Franc-Tireurs et Partisans* (FTP). His solution, which served another of his purposes (that of seeking constantly to exaggerate the size of the armed forces at the disposal of Fighting France), was to create in February 1944 a general staff for what he denominated the French Forces of the Interior (FFI). These, comprising the Gaullist *Armée Secrète* and the military resistance movement, *Organisation de Resistance de l'Armée*, which had come into being after the German occupation of the *Zone libre*, as well as the FTP, were put directly under the command of General Koenig, hero of the Free French epic at Bir Hakim and de Gaulle's chief of staff. Shortly afterwards Eisenhower was persuaded to recognize him as a co-equal of the other national commanders – British, Canadian and American – under Supreme Headquarters Allied Expeditionary Force.

He at once began to issue orders to all resistance units inside France. But de Gaulle was already aware that the communists had, where strong enough, taken charge of local FFI structures and, where not, were tending to operate independently. With an eye to the political future, therefore – and, like the FTP, he saw resistance largely as a means to future political power – he decided to reserve the essential functions of Koenig's general staff, supply, signals and finance, to yet another organization. This, the Military Delegations, belonged directly to his Provisional Government in London, of which it effectively formed the defence ministry. And because it held the purse – from which arms and money were parachuted into France – it determined which maquis should have the means to fight and which not.

He was particularly concerned that the Paris maquis should not fight. Not only did he wish to spare the city itself from destruction (Warsaw, where he had served as a military adviser in 1920, was much on his mind). He was also determined that the capital should be liberated from without rather than within, where the communists formed the strongest element in the resistance and might use a local victory to frustrate at the last moment his four-year pilgrimage to the seat of government. On August 16th, therefore, he despatched the head of the Military Delegations, Jacques Chaban-Delmas, who had been recalled to London for consultations, with specific instructions to the Paris FFI to await the entry of Allied forces and under no circumstances to unleash a 'premature rising' against the rump of the German garrison.

They were instructions which the Paris FFI received with very bad grace. Its chief, Rol, was a communist and as anxious as any comrade to monopolize for the party and the FTP the glory and the fruits of an early liberation. His second-in-command was a regular officer, Colonel de Marguerittes, alias Lizé, whose political views were those of an orthodox soldier but who, stout warrior that he was, chafed at inactivity when the enemy's weakness invited attack. Both, moreover, were acutely conscious that elsewhere in France the FFI was in open conflict with the remnants of the German army — passages of arms later to be characterised as the National Insurrection — and were shamed at the thought that the forces in the capital should alone be seen to fail to strike. On the afternoon of August 17th, therefore, Lizé and his chief of staff drew up orders for the occupation the following day of all public utilities and municipal and government offices in what the Germans called 'Greater Paris'.

There were a bewildering number. Besides the *mairies* of the twenty *arrondissements* into which Paris is divided, the office of the Prefect of the Department of the Seine in the Hôtel de Ville was obviously a key point, as was the Préfecture de Police, on the Ile de la Cité. The residences of the President of the Republic (Palais de l'Elysée) and Prime Minister (Hôtel Matignon), the Chamber of Deputies (Palais Bourbon) and the Senate building (Palais du Luxembourg) all had important symbolic significance. So naturally did the ministries and also, though they were too strongly guarded for the resistance to attempt a direct assault on any, the various German headquarters, chief of which was the office of the Commander of Greater Paris, the Hôtel Meurice in the rue de Rivoli.

Some of these buildings were empty or occupied only by caretakers. Others were still in the possession of legitimate office-holders, appointed either by the municipality or the government in Vichy.

Whatever their state, however, there were too many of them, it soon became clear, for the communists to occupy all, particularly as FTP strength lay principally in the eastern arrondissements, XVIII, XIX and XX, at the opposite end of the city from the official quarter. Rol's orders, though issued, could not therefore be carried out and August 18th passed without the general uprising he and Lizé desired. Yet they sensed a growing demand for action in the population of Paris itself. The railwaymen had been on strike since August 12th, and the police, whom the Germans were trying to disarm, since August 15th. They determined to put de Gaulle's representatives to the test on the following day. The forum chosen was the National Resistance Council, which met at 11 a.m. to hear their demand for a proclamation of general insurrection. The communists were represented on it by the Paris Liberation Committee, which saw itself as the future municipal council, de Gaulle by his Delegate General (Chaban-Delmas's political opposite number) Parodi. Parodi resisted the communist case vigorously. He pointed out that the Allies intended to bypass Paris and that a rising might leave it a field of ruins – as Hitler was to order the city commander to make it three days later. But, while he argued, he took account of the danger that obedience to de Gaulle's orders might bring: that he would be left an impotent spectator of a battle which the local resistance, communist and non-communist alike, would unleash anyhow, with irretrievable damage to the Gaullist cause resulting either from victory or defeat. Eventually, therefore, he decided to add de Gaulle's authority to the call to arms.

But while the politicians argued, the people – or, to be precise, the police – had acted. Policemen, it is a cliché, are survivors of all political change. And the Paris police had indeed remained stolidly on duty throughout the occupation and co-operated with the German authorities when necessary. But co-operation had rankled with many of them and by August 1944 the resistance was strong in their ranks, where, as elsewhere, it took a politically tripartite form. All three police resistance groups had, however, agreed on August 18th to co-operate in direct action and on the following morning a group of 3,000 entered the Préfecture de Police and hoisted the tricolour – not flown in Paris since 1940 – over the roof. Rol, who happened to be passing at that moment on his way to a clandestine meeting, was as surprised as anyone else in the city to see it, and more surprised to be turned away when he demanded admission. When he got back dressed in the uniform he had worn as a Republican soldier in the Spanish Civil War, it was to find de Gaulle's nominee as Prefect of Police, Charles Luizet, installed and in charge of the defence.

Rebuffed, Rol bicycled off to his headquarters in the basement of the Paris sewage administration in Montparnasse. Thence he could put himself in touch with the many groups which would obey his orders and, during the morning of August 19th, began to do so. By early afternoon most of the places he and Lizé had earmarked for occupation two days before were in the hands of the FFI, traffic had stopped in the streets, citizens were sheltering indoors and the intermittent rattle of small-arms fire could be heard all over the inner city. The fighting, except at the Préfecture de Police and the *mairie* at Neuilly, where the Germans brought up some old tanks, was not intense. But, like drizzle in summer, it had clearly set in and had begun to yield a steady drip of casualties. About 125 French people were to be killed during the day, most of them *résistants*. They, in their turn, were to kill about 50 Germans.

# Truce

The outbreak of fighting had taken the commander of Greater Paris, Generalleutnant Dietrich von Choltitz, unawares. Appointed to the post only two weeks before, he had been chosen by Hitler because of his reputation for unvarying obedience and his great experience in defensive operations; he had just come from commanding a corps in the Cotentin. It is alleged that, at the interview at Rastenburg when he received his orders, Hitler instructed him to leave Paris utterly destroyed, 'nothing must be left standing, no church, no artistic monument'. The words, if spoken, were not written down and Choltitz arrived in Paris apparently without special instructions. But his orders were certainly to defend the city vigorously, and on August 11th, after four days in office, he had been given the prerogatives of a fortress commander. For centuries, all over Europe, the meaning of that status in time of siege had been well understood: absolute authority over all within the siege lines, civilian as well as military, and legal power to appropriate or demolish private and public property for their defence.

He had initially assumed, however, that he was to defend the city at its perimeter, along a notional line drawn by his predecessor around the southern and western suburbs. And although he had taken certain precautions for the demolition of the Paris bridges, should that become necessary, he had not envisaged having to fight within the city itself and certainly not against the inhabitants. Nor did he wish to do so. Prussian though he was in appearance, in an Erich von Stroheim style, cropped above the ears, thick of body and short in the leg, he was neither brutal nor philistine. His personal code was that of the honourable soldier and, as a former page of the queen of Saxony, he had no difficulty in appreciating the aesthetic significance of the city on which the Wittenburgs had modelled Dresden. But, like Hitler's other recently appointed fortress commanders, he had reasons beyond those of automatic military obedience for fulfilling his orders to keep Paris German. He had left his wife and children in Germany, and knew that their welfare depended upon his fidelity.

With skirmishing spreading throughout the official quarter, military vehicles ambushed and ablaze in the streets and the crowds of shirt-sleeved young *résistants* swelling as fast as they could improvise FFI armlets, he was obliged to sustain his side of the fight. And, though all too conscious of the civic disaster which would flow from the interruption of public services in a city of three million, a stream of inquiries from Model, at St Germain-en-Laye, and Jodl, at Rastenburg, forced him to press forward with preparations to dynamite the electrical power plants, telephone exchanges and railway stations, as well as the forty-five bridges of the city and a dozen of its most famous buildings – Les Invalides, Palais du Luxembourg, Palais Bourbon, Quai d'Orsay, Ministère de la Marine – which housed occupation staffs.

The prospect of a sustained insurrection horrified others who were not party to the fight. One was Otto Abetz, German ambassador to the Vichy government, whose wraiths still inhabited the capital (on August 13th Laval had actually returned for a moment with the notion of reconvening the Third Republic's Chamber of Deputies and extracting from it the powers which would have allowed him to greet the Allies as a legitimate head of government; but not even the Gestapo was prepared to countenance that charade). Another was the Swedish consul-general, Raoul Nordling. As his fellow-countrymen Bernadotte and Wallenberg were to do on the other side of Europe a little later, he now prepared to act in the best traditions of neutral diplomacy. He had already seen Choltitz in an attempt to halt deportations of French political prisoners to

Germany. On the morning of August 20th he telephoned with an offer to arrange a truce with the other side. Choltitz gave his agreement in principle. Thanks to the intervention of Abetz, who had transmitted a calculated complaint to Ribbentrop about the army's 'brutality' to the Parisians, he felt his standing at Rastenburg was sound for the moment. And, for his own part, he reasoned that a truce might foment the antagonisms he knew existed within the politically divided resistance, setting them against each other instead of against his men. During the afternoon, therefore, on his assurance that members of the FFI would be treated as legitimate combatants and would not be attacked in their positions as long as the Germans were undisturbed in theirs, firing from the FFI strongholds spluttered to a halt. And, by a bizarre coincidence, Choltitz was actually able that evening to confirm the terms of the truce directly with Parodi, who had been arrested by chance while on his way from the meeting of the National Resistance Council which had accepted Nordling's mediation.

The meeting, however, had lacked a quorum. The communists, busy with manifestos and infernal machines, had been represented by only a single member, who had been outvoted. Rol's reaction, when he heard of the truce, was immediately to denounce it and during the next day, Monday, August 21st, sporadic fighting broke out again. Colonel Lizé joined Rol in rejecting the truce and late that afternoon actually issued a call for the building of barricades – some were already in existence, the outcome most likely to alarm de Gaulle, who was acutely conscious of the danger of a second Commune, about the safe inheritance of his patrimony. The National Resistance Council was therefore reconvened in the evening, with full communist representation, and the decision taken to abrogate the truce officially at the end of the next twenty-four hours.

During Tuesday, August 22nd, however, the tide of the fighting started to run the insurgents' way. Choltitz's troops in the heart of the city had always been few. Their freedom of movement was now much restricted by the barricades and they were not being reinforced. Colonel Rol accordingly made a remarkable move. Believing that the gains made – largely by communist groups – would present de Gaulle and the Allies when they entered with the *fait accompli* of a city under FTP control, he approached Parodi, the Gaullist delegate-general, with the offer to abide by his decision to end or prolong the truce. Parodi, who had spent the day achieving his own purpose, the installation in the abandoned ministries of their future secretaries-general, weighed the military risk against the political attraction of a submission by the FTP to his authority and chose the latter.

Both men were calculating as if the insurrection had already achieved its object, but Choltitz, reduced though his power had been by the spread of the barricades and the rising toll of German casualties, was not yet to be counted out of the struggle for the city. During August 22nd he received yet another order for its defence from Hitler, by far the strongest so far. 'In history the loss of Paris always meant the loss of France. Therefore the Führer repeats his order to hold the defence zone in the advance of the city ... Within the city every sign of incipient revolt must be countered by the sharpest means ... [including] the execution of ringleaders ... The Seine bridges will be prepared for demolition. Paris must not fall into the hands of the enemy except as a field of ruins.' Shortly after its reception, he asked the Swede Nordling to see him again. He began by complaining at the breakdown of the truce and at the inability of the leaders with whom he had been in touch to control their followers. Soon, he emphasized, they would drive him into carrying out the demolitions which all civilized men would wish to avoid. Nordling explained, as he had done before, that the insurgents were a coalition, in which left and right sought to steal a march on each other and could be brought to heel only by a superior force. To Nordling's astonishment, Choltitz conceded that he accepted that analysis and was now prepared to allow Nordling to pass through his lines, make contact with the Allies and arrange for their prompt arrival in the capital to overawe its dissidents.

# De Gaulle

Choltitz was later to offer a variety of reasons for his decision. The best was that he had despaired of reinforcement (Hitler had airily promised him two skeleton panzer divisions from Denmark), of suppressing the revolt, even of carrying out at that late stage any systematic demolitions, and was anxious only to make honourable surrender to regular troops. The reservation which he made, but carefully kept to himself, was that his conception of an honourable surrender required a stout show of resistance before he raised the white flag. His brief meeting with Nordling thus upset many expectations: Parodi's, that he could repossess Paris for de Gaulle by negotiation; Rol's, that he could legitimize communist claims on power by winning Paris in battle; and Eisenhower's, that he could avoid a battle for Paris altogether. But the capture of Paris by Allied troops would upset the Gaullists most of all, for their leader had long set his heart on taking Paris himself. His vision of what was 'right', of a solution 'worthy of France', demanded it; but so too did the ambiguity of his position.

Now that de Gaulle has passed into history, it is difficult to recall that there was a time when his co-equals in the Allied leadership of the Second World War denied his claims to parity. The 'Free French epic' has been subsumed within the story of a career which seemed destined towards triumph, as inevitably during its unwinding as in retrospect. But as late as August 1944 even the Allied leaders with whom he was most frequently and closely in touch were not yet prepared to recognize him as legitimate head of a legitimate French government-in-exile. He had been, certainly, a minister of the last government of the Third Republic. He was, certainly, a general – very junior and of the lowest rank – in the French army. He had been, certainly, the most senior French officer to reject the armistice of June 1940 from the outset. But he had not been able to demonstrate that the powers of the Republic were inherent in his person or that they had migrated with him from France to England. Nor had he yet been able to show that the popular will had transferred spiritual sovereignty from wherever it currently resided – perhaps still in Pétain's *Etat Français* – to his Provisional Government. It did not of course help his case that he overstated his claims, overplayed his hand, dealt in tantrums, sulks, insults, postures, silences, Olympian detachment, political self-righteousness, moral holier-than-thouery and, when it suited his book, double-dealing and backstairs intrigue characteristic of the Third Republic at its most underhand. All that might have been overlooked (though so too, without it, might have been his claims) had there not been genuine doubts about the legality of his organization and his personal acceptability to the French population. As late as March 1944 Marshal Pétain had made a state visit from Vichy to Paris and been ecstatically received. Currently, not only in Paris, but throughout the provinces of France there were thousands – soon to be hundreds of thousands – of active *résistants* not only of the left but also of the right and centre on whom the label *gaulliste* did not fit.

'Général, nous voilà', was not a cry which the crowd of liberated Paris could be guaranteed to chorus.

Hence Parodi's preoccupation with installing the Gaullist nominees in the buildings of the ministries, almost before they had been vacated by the Germans or the Vichyists. Hence the urgency with which de Gaulle had despatched his *commissaires-généraux* to occupy the prefectoral offices of each *départment* as it was liberated. Hence above all his search for some means to forestall American or British troops in the formal military entry to the capital. The initial Allied intention to bypass Paris had suited his plans, for there was a Free French formation in Normandy, the 2nd Armoured Division, which Eisenhower had long promised should eventually have the honour of entering Paris. The rising had awakened his old anxieties of being cheated of his prize. The news of Choltitz's *démarche* to the Allies – transmitted via Parodi's radio station – raised them to fever pitch. He had written to Eisenhower on August 21st to 'threaten politely' that if the Supreme Commander would not release the division, he would take the responsibility of ordering it to Paris himself. And when his emissary, Juin, brought him the news that Eisenhower was not to be moved, he endorsed an independent decision by Leclerc, the commander of the 2nd Armoured, to start its reconnaissance elements towards the capital without American approval.

His frustration at his inability to determine events was heightened by his lack of a fixed base of operations. He had, until August 20th, made but one brief visit to France, and that a day trip to address the population of Bayeux, where he was so little expected that the first official representatives he met in the town, two policemen wheeling bicycles, failed altogether to recognize him and had to inquire his name. In the interim he had returned to Algiers, seat of the National Committee which only his co-exiles, the Czechs, Poles, Norwegians, Yugoslavs and Belgians, among the Allies would accept as the Provisional Government, and had thence flown to Washington. He went at the invitation of Roosevelt, implicitly to reconcile their personal antagonism and official differences – the President had always taken the General's 'egoism' in bad part, besides choosing to regard the Gaullists merely as one of several groups with claims to share in the postwar government – and although the meeting was a partial success, he had come back to Algiers without the United States' *de jure* recognition. He was now nevertheless determined to establish himself in France, but, since he needed Allied permission to visit the country, had been forced into the humiliating pretence of expressing a wish to inspect the liberated areas in order to extract it. It was therefore merely *en mission* that he had eventually arrived at Cherbourg on August 20th and he had peripateted via Rennes and Laval before arriving, on August 22nd, at the first place where he might establish an official presence, the country seat of French presidents at Rambouillet. While *en route* he still had no assurance that he could proceed from there to Paris, that Leclerc's recon-naissance column would not have been called back by the Americans, that the Allies would not have preceded it, that the FTP would not have won the battle for the city or that Choltitz would not have reduced it to the 'field of ruins' which the Führer wanted.

But now a stroke of misinformation suddenly directed events, and in his favour. A number of missions, besides Nordling's, had made their way through the German lines around Paris on August 22nd. One, led by the chief of staff of the FFI in Paris, Roger Gallois, had succeeded in reaching Patton's headquarters, where Gallois had managed to convince Bradley's chief intelligence officer that the truce was still in force (which it was not), that it was due to expire the following day (it had already broken down), that Choltitz would then probably crush the insurrection (unlikely) but that he would withdraw at the approach of regular troops (not his intention). 'To avoid bloodshed, it was essential that Allied soldiers enter the city promptly at noon, August 23rd.' These misrepresentations swiftly reached Eisenhower, who had already been shaken in his decision to bypass Paris by de Gaulle's threat to take Leclerc's division under direct command. Eisenhower was rare among Allied leaders in holding de Gaulle in high regard. He had, at Algiers in 1943, given the assurance to de Gaulle in person that a French force would liberate Paris, and had arranged that Leclerc's division should be transferred from North Africa to England before the invasion for that purpose. He had been impressed by the combativeness of the FFI units which had sprung to life at the approach of the Allied armies and was grateful for the part they had played in mopping up the remnants of German resistance. He also detected how strongly devoted many of them were to de Gaulle and how ready they were to accept him as the national leader. The FFI's appeal, via Gallois, gave him a neat excuse to repay the FFI for its help and further the cause of a man he admired. Because it was made on military, not political grounds, and by an integral element of his command, which the FFI theoretically was, he might represent a change of mind to Washington and London as a purely operational decision. Change his mind he now did accordingly, so that, late in the afternoon of August 22nd, Leclerc could hasten from a suddenly convened meeting with Bradley to shout to his operations officer, 'Gribius ... mouvement immédiat sur Paris!' For him it was the culmination of a four-year pilgrimage from humiliation to glory.

# La Division Leclerc

At the heart of de Gaulle's anomalous position among the exiled leaders lay the fact – to be camouflaged but never successfully hidden – that so few Frenchmen had been willing to declare at the outset for Free France. It did not really matter that he was not a head of state or government: the exiled cabinets of Belgium, Norway and Denmark were accorded full recognition as allies even though their kings remained within the occupied homeland. It did not matter that he brought with him not a scrap of territory, national or colonial, where his authority ran: Poland and Czechoslovakia were both totally occupied and indeed dismembered, yet Sikorski and Beneš were recognized as sovereign national leaders. It did not even matter that Pétain was the undoubted constitutional successor of President Lebrun: given that he had abolished the Third Republic by fiat, Britain – and later the United States – had good grounds for denouncing the legitimacy of the *Etat Français* had they so chosen. But numbers – of ships, of soldiers and, distressing though it was to admit it, of hearts – were with the Marshal and, unless and until de Gaulle could begin to match them, Allied interests lay in keeping a back door to Vichy open.

Such numbers he could not match. The great majority of French servicemen marooned in England after the armistice of June opted to go home, and were allowed to do so; at the end of 1940 only 7,000 soldiers and sailors had donned the Cross of Lorraine and of those the largest contingent was a demi-brigade of the Foreign Legion, by definition not French in nationality. And even fewer Frenchmen, however strong their anti-German feeling, had shown themselves ready to take the yet more extreme step of quitting France to join de Gaulle in England. Some corners of the empire – the New Hebrides, the French Congo, Equatorial Africa – were declared to be Free

French by local hot-heads. The military attachés in several Latin American capitals declared for him, as did a number of senior colonial officials who guessed that old enemies in Pétain's new regime would now settle scores. But the trickle of committed Gaullists – the term was not yet current – who found their way across the Pyrenees to his side in London after June 18th, 1940 was pitifully thin, and composed for the most part of the young and unknown. He looked in vain for companions of his own quality. Until the arrival of Leclerc.

Leclerc – properly the Vicomte Jacques-Philippe de Hautecloque; the pseudonym was assumed to protect his wife and six children from reprisals – belonged firmly within the society of which de Gaulle's family was an appendage, the conservative, Catholic aristocracy of the north. English readers would recognize the Haute-cloques in the d'Archevilles of Mottram's *Spanish Farm*. It exactly denoted the social distance between them that Leclerc's father, a regular officer and a landowner, had sent Philippe to the Jesuit school in Paris of which de Gaulle senior was headmaster. But Leclerc was much more than a son of the château, a Georges d'Archeville with a contempt for the Germans and an urge to shine in the cavalry. Cavalryman he was but he had also passed first into the *Ecole de Guerre* and stood on the threshold of a brilliant career when disaster overtook the French army in 1940. He might still have enjoyed preferment in the Armistice Army, that rump of a hundred thousand soldiers which Hitler, with woundingly calculated tit-for-tat, allowed Pétain to keep in being in the *Zone libre*; brainboxes and *particules* were to flourish there, all quick with explanations that real patriotism lay towards Vichy and easy sneers at the brigadier *de fausse particule* who claimed to embody France in London. He had not even thought of it. Recognizing defeat when he saw it, he had obtained his divisional commander's permission to leave the battle-field, had twice escaped from German hands on his way out of France and had arrived in London only a week after the armistice to demand a fighting command. The paucity of de Gaulle's troops denied him one. But the general had another task for which he needed a capable subordinate. Anti-Vichy declarations in French West and Central Africa promised him a foothold there, and in August he sent Leclerc to Nigeria with orders to consolidate the military situation. While his own expedition to Dakar in September failed, Leclerc was able to capture Gabon and thence to transfer to

Fort Lamy in the colony of Chad, where the garrison had come over to de Gaulle.

It was not large nor particularly French. The bulk of the soldiers were black, Senegalese of the Régiment de Tirailleurs de Tchad, their officers a Kiplingesque bunch – d'Ornano, Dio, Massu – who had chosen to make their lives, and so sink their careers, far from the *métropole*. But the Senegalese were legendary warriors and d'Ornano's subalterns a swashbuckling crew. With them behind him, and even though a thousand miles of the Sahara lay between his base and the nearest hostile position, Leclerc found means to carry the war to the enemy. In February 1941, at the end of a gruelling trek across the wastes, he fell on the Italian garrison in the oasis of Kufra in southern Libya and seized it for Free France. Under the tricolour he had hoisted over the fort, he led the officers who had accompanied him in an oath 'not to abandon the fight until the flag of France shall fly again over Metz and Strasburg'. The significance of the formula was a double one: his promotion (1922–4) at St Cyr had chosen the denomination 'Metz et Strasbourg' to celebrate the return to France of the two provinces of which those cities were the capitals; it had been a condition of the armistice of 1940 that they should again be incorporated in the Reich. Leclerc was dedicating himself not only to victory over Germany but to the repudiation of Vichy and all its craven compromises.

In 1942 he made another raid into enemy territory and captured several places in the Libyan province of Fezzan, accompanied this time by patrols of the British Long Range Desert Group, which had established contact with him across the wilderness. And at the end of the year he abandoned his base in Chad for good and took the whole of his command up into Tunisia to join the Anglo-American armies which had rendezvoused there after the twin victories of Alamein and Algiers. A consolidation of Free French forces could now take place, of Leclerc's column with the brigade which Koenig had commanded with such tenacity at the glorious defeat of Bir Hakim the previous year. But Koenig's force was as heterogeneous as his own: some Foreign Legionaries, a regiment of Moroccan Spahis, some remnants of Dentz's Army of the Levant, which had 'rallied' after the tragic little fratricidal war in Syria and the Lebanon in 1941. And it was not much stronger. If two divisions were to be formed on their cadres, and such was de Gaulle's wish, they would have to incorporate recruits from the only source of French manpower, available, the Army of Africa. For the Koenig division, destined to fight in the Mediterranean, that entailed no difficulty, for it could be filled out with regiments of Algerian and Moroccan mountaineers, whose former employment by Vichy could be forgiven because they were mercenaries. But the Leclerc division, chosen in March 1943 for transfer to the gathering invasion army in England, would have to be composed as far as possible of native Frenchmen if it were properly to represent the nation at the liberation. And those of the Army of Africa – officers foremost, but men also – were soldiers to whom *le Serment de Koufra* had been thrown down not as a challenge but as a reproach.

It is easy now to pour scorn on the soldiers who chose to serve Vichy in the Armistice Army, easier still those who continued at duty with the Army of Africa. Unlike those in the *métropole*, they were beyond the reach of the Germans, and outside the effective authority of Vichy. But, even if they had their families with them, they had other reasons for preferring Pétain to de Gaulle. Legality and the legend of Verdun apart, both of which the Marshal embodied, Vichy represented much that was to be valued by the officers of a defeated France. It kept alive a part of the historic French army against the day when the whole might be reconstituted. It promised an end to the corrupt and defeatist spirit of the Third Republic which traditionalists in the officer corps invoked as the 'real' explanation of the débâcle of 1940. Vichy honoured institutions, above all the church, and fostered others, like the nationalist youth movements, *Chantiers de Jeunesse*, *Équipes sociales* and *Compagnons de France*, through which a healthier spirit of discipline, service and the outdoor life could be inculcatted in the next generation. The movements' fondness for knickerbocker trousers and Celtic impedimenta invests photographs of their jamborees, to modern eyes, with strong overtones of *Tintin* and *Asterix*, but senior officers of the period thought them worth hefty patronage. Above all, however, Vichy was a guarantee of French sovereignty in the empire. In the Far East, by agreement with the Japanese, it saved Indo-China from the fate undergone by Malaya, Burma, the Philippines and the Dutch East Indies. Along the Mediterranean shore, it preserved the French presence in Tunisia, Morocco and Algeria. Those were not stations where, in the piping days of peace, the grandees of the metropolitan army had chosen to serve. But the diminishment of French power at home disproportionately enhanced the importance, real and symbolic, of French Africa. And, by cleverly playing on the strategic danger which its fall – to a British drive from Egypt, to a Free French advance from the equatorial colonies – would level at German interests in southern Europe and the Atlantic, Vichy diplomacy had actually been able to exclude most of the Army of Africa from the disarmament provisions of the Armistice. Its officers, when they confronted the minority who had chosen the other path in 1940, had grounds for arguing therefore that they too had trodden the road of patriotism, and had swallowed their pride to do so.

Leclerc, who had seen his column as 'a sort of shining spearhead', was as ready as any of his Jacobins to throw these casuistries back in the teeth of those who uttered them. Pétain, for him, was the 'hook on which men hang their cowardice'. But his idealism was realistic. The Americans had promised him the equipment for a full armoured division, the strongest force which Free France had yet fielded. To man it he would enlist any Frenchmen who would do duty. From the Army of Africa, therefore, he took two regiments of artillery. From the Dakar garrison, which had now 'rallied', he took a tank regiment, the 12th Chasseurs d'Afrique, which had smuggled thither a handful of armoured vehicles from under the noses of the German disarmament commission in 1941. The North African garrison yielded the manpower for another, the 12th Cuirassiers. The navy, the most pro-Vichy of all the services, provided a battalion of Fusiliers-Marins to form the anti-tank regiment; his admonition to its officers was particularly stringent: 'You have been doing nothing for three years but now you have your chance. You have to regain the right to be respected.' The reconnaissance regiment, the 1st Spahis Marocains, was Gaullist. It had escaped from Syria in 1940 to join the British in the Eritrean campaign. The infantry, Gaullist from the start, had reluctantly to be remade. The Senegalese would not do as liberators and so, against their will and their officers' – had they not been good enough to march in the front rank of Nivelle's 'victory' offensive of 1917? – were sent home, to be replaced by Frenchmen. The Régiment de marche du Tchad would return to France as a white regiment. Christian Arabs from the Lebanon, who had 'rallied' after the defeat of the Army of the Levant in 1941, provided the engineers. The third tank regiment, the 501st Chars de Combat, was built on a nucleus of original enthusiasts who had declared for de Gaulle in London in 1940.

From these disparate elements – *marsouins, bigorres, Cuir, Chass d'Af* – representing not only the two opposed camps of Pétainism and Gaullism, but the three unmingling streams of which the old army was composed, *métropolitain, colonial, Africain*, Leclerc set out to make in the next twelve months a single fighting organization. An important binding agent was the complement of officers who had escaped to Africa from the Armistice Army, out of the disgust with Vichy, before the Allied landings of 1942; they might properly claim a foot in both camps. The brotherhood of St Cyr melted hearts also; difficult to hold at arm's length a *copain de promotion*, even harder a *bazar* one had crowned with his *casoar* at the *baptême* of *Marne et Verdun* or *Amitié Franco-Britannique*. And was that carefully chosen title not in itself a reminder of past hopes which deserved to be revived? But the most powerful agent in healing the division was the personality of Leclerc himself. Brave with the total indifference to danger of the real cavalier, proud without conceit, impassioned without bigotry, selfless, relentless, he stamped ruthlessly on all expressions of mutual disregard – 'cowards and shirkers' from one side, 'rebels and adventurers' from the other – and drove all to work. Men had to be picked and trained, the tricks of new equipment learnt, the complex tactics of a formation of all arms endlessly rehearsed. First in Morocco, then in England, the 2nd Division blindée (armoured division) – soon the 'Deuxième DB' to all who belonged to it – practised to make itself a match for the Germans who had tossed aside the *divisions cuirassées* of 1940 with such humiliating ease. By the eve of D-Day it was judged battleworthy by Supreme Headquarters and on August 1st crossed to France to come under Patton's command.

## Liberation

In two weeks of combat at Alençon and Argentan, on the southern flank of the Falaise pocket, the division had proved itself a skilful and flexible instrument of war. It had made much of the going in the drive to close the neck of the pocket from the south and, but for Bradley's change of mind, might have been the formation which met the Poles and Canadians at Chambois. Switched eastward before the junction, it was on the evening of August 22nd, when Leclerc returned to his headquarters with his electrifying news, laagered in open country south of Argentan. It had been settling down for another quiet night, the seventh since its relief from the battle for Alençon. Word of the new mission threw all into activity. Head-quarters tents suddenly showed light through the canvas as orders were typed and commands telephoned. The division was to move in three columns, commanded by Dio (one of the Chad originals), Langlade and Billotte. Each was to be formed of a half-track infantry battalion of the Régiment de marche du Tchad, a squadron of Spahis in reconnaissance, a squadron of the Fusiliers-Marins tank destroyers, an artillery regiment, and one of the tank regiments: the Cuirassiers with Dio, Chasseurs with Langlade, Chars de Combat with Billotte. All night the crews humped ammunition and hauled jerricans of fuel, ran up motors, raced their last few doubtful runners through workshops. Next morning, at first light, a throbbing, blue-fumed mass of 3,000 vehicles, 12,000 men aboard, stood on the line of departure.

Many had never seen Paris. Some, *pieds noirs* of Algiers and Oran or children of emigrants to the Americas and the South Seas, had landed in France for the first time three weeks before. But their tanks and scout cars were blazoned, in the French style, with splendid affirmations of homecoming. The Cuirassiers had adopted the names of the towns first liberated in the invasion battle, Caen, Evreux, Lisieux, Cherbourg, Rennes, Lorient; the Chasseurs those of old royal provinces, Béarn and Guyenne, or Imperial Marshals, Lannes and Murat. The Chars de Combat preferred battles, those of Napoleon's will o' the wisp campaign before Paris in 1814 – Romilly, Montmirail, Champaubert – or the grim episodes of the Meuse and Vosges of the previous war – Douaumont, Mort-Homme, Laffaux, Vieil-Armand. The Fusiliers-Marins alone chose to recall origins rather than destination. Their tank destroyers bore the names of the winds which carry sailors to safe harbour or drive the illfound and unwary to run for shelter, Bourrasque, Cyclone, Ouragan, Orage, Tempête, Astral, Simoun, Sirocco. Both sorts would blow over Paris in the coming days.

The division was still 120 miles short of the city, and the whole of August 23rd was spent in a breakneck drive down narrow depart-mental roads towards the outskirts, via Sées, Mortagne, La Loup and Maintenon. Leclerc travelled at the point and reached Ram-bouillet in mid-afternoon. There he found General de Gaulle already installed in the presidential residence, killing anguished time with English cigarettes and a volume of Molière extracted from the library (his sense of protocol forbade him to make any other use of the head of state's perquisites). A tactical conference ensued. Leclerc explained that Bradley had started forward an American infantry division, the 4th, on his right, which was to assist in the capture. The plan was that it should make its approach from the east, the French from the west. Leclerc judged however that his allotted route, via St Cyr and Versailles, was the more heavily defended and he therefore proposed shifting his weight towards the Americans to beat them to the finish. De Gaulle, with the enigmatic remark that Leclerc was a lucky man to liberate Paris, appeared to approve. 'Go quickly', he said, 'we cannot have another Commune.'

Leclerc now issued precise objectives to his three column commanders. Langlade was to cross the Seine at the Pont de Sèvres, enter the city at the Porte de St Cloud and aim for the Arc de Triomphe. Dio was to cross the line of the outer boulevards at the Porte d'Orléans and take possession of the Ecole Militaire–Invalides–Eiffel Tower. Billotte was to enter by the Porte d'Italie on the same axis and aim for the Panthéon and the Ile de la Cité. Each represented an area of symbolic importance, of known German resistance and of possible demolition.

Leclerc's objections were well selected but not his lines of advance. Langlade, taking the ceremonial route past Versailles and St Cyr (ruined but days before by a Flying Fortress raid) found resistance spirited but patchy. It centred on small groups of tanks and mobile anti-tank guns which defended villages and crossroads until outflanked and then withdrew. By early afternoon the subgroup Massu had pushed almost to Route nationale 186 at Jouy-en-Josas. Twenty years later, a little farther down the road at Petit Clamart, de Gaulle would survive the most serious of the attempts made on his life by the intransigents of the OAS. Massu, whose victory in the Battle of Algiers was to give that conspiracy its *raison d'être*, now won his first experience of street fighting in the back gardens of this shabby little suburb. For four hours his dismounted half-track crews stalked anti-tank guns and motorised 20 mm cannon through hedges and orchards. Three Shermans were lost in tank-to-tank fights; a wet and overcast afternoon denied all recourse to air support. Eventually at a cost of a dozen dead, some of whom had made the long journey from Fort Lamy itself, Jouy-en-Josas was taken and the Spahis, pressing their Stuart tanks to the crest of the high ground beyond, saw the valley of the Seine below and signalled to Langlade in triumph that the Arc de Triomphe was only three hours away.

Langlade, however, could only enter the city in company with Dio and Billotte. And they in mid-afternoon of August 24th had a real battle on their hands. Two small tributaries of the Seine, the Yvette and the Bièvre, lay across their path and could be crossed only at the existing bridges, which were here dominated by the buildings of the Paris *banlieue*. That over the Yvette at Longjumeau was bounced by twin companies of the Chars de Combat and the Tchad infantry and a subsidiary island of resistance at Massy was overcome by Dio's 12th Cuirassiers. But on the Bièvre, Billotte found himself confronted by a well-prepared triangle of strongpoints commanding Route nationale 20, the broad southern highway into the city which had become his main axis of advance. To his left lay the little industrial suburb of Antony, to his front the village of Croix de Berny, to his right the fortress of Fresnes prison. Throughout the afternoon, Billotte's leading elements fought to drive the German anti-tank gunners from the crossroads at Croix de Berny and by 7 p.m. had it in their hands. But Fresnes, from which fire swept the Paris road, still held out. It was garrisoned by the German military defaulters who had the day before been confined in its cells, supported by several anti-tank guns; an 88 mm was ensconced in the sepulchral gateway of the prison itself. At a range of three hundred yards along the sweep of the avenue de la République, a duel opened between the anti-tank gunners and three French tanks. One was manned by a native of Fresnes who had crossed the *Zone libre* and Spain to join de Gaulle, another by an escaped prisoner of the Gestapo who had been held in the prison.

The Germans' first shot set the leading Sherman ablaze; its commander died in sight of the church where he had been married. The second tank destroyed the 88 mm with its return of fire. The third, driven by the former internee, crashed through the gateway, tossing the wreck of the gun aside, and took possession of the central courtyard. But the battle had taken an hour and had cost four more Shermans, caught in enfilade from guns sited at other points around the prison perimeter. Billotte reckoned that he must regroup; some of his tank commanders were signalling a lack of fuel and ammunition; he had only two hours of daylight left on this overcast evening. Reluctantly, because he could feel the hot impatience of de Gaulle on his neck and sense the growing crisis within the city, Leclerc decided to halt for the night beyond Fresnes and open his final assault next morning.

During the evening, however, he came under increasing pressure from Gerow, the American corps commander to whom he was subordinate, to maintain progress, or surrender the right of first entry to the accompanying Americans. Gerow and Bradley were exchanging on the radio sarcastic remarks about Frenchmen 'dancing to Paris' — there had, in the intervals of the fighting, been impromptu celebrations in the little towns along the way — and of 'advancing on a one-tank front' to avoid the fighting which would damage French homes. The gibes were unfair. The German anti-tank guns were more numerous than the Americans, advancing on a weakly defended sector, realized. But the threat alarmed Leclerc and, as he had essayed three days before, he now determined to slip a reconnaissance column into Paris as a token of intention. Summoning a captain of the Tchad infantry, Raymond Dronne, he ordered him to take a platoon of infantry and a troop of three tanks of the Chars de Combat and by any means find a route into the city.

Slipping along byways in the gathering dusk and then, as the city closed round his column, down side streets and back turnings, Dronne found the Porte de Gentilly unguarded, crossed the Place d'Italie through crowds who half-recognized that the silhouettes of his vehicles were unfamiliar, ran the gauntlet of a burst of fire from an isolated German picket in the Gare d'Austerlitz, crossed the Seine by the Pont d'Austerlitz and drove up the right bank along the Quai des Célestins. At 9.30 p.m. his three tanks, Montmirail, Champaubert and Romilly, drew to a halt outside the Hôtel de Ville. He was within a few hundred yards of von Choltitz's headquarters at the other end of the rue de Rivoli.

The news of his arrival brought the bells of Paris to life and disturbed the sombre little dinner party the general was giving for his immediate staff in the Meurice. He listened for a moment and then withdrew to telephone Army Group B at St Germain-en-Laye. Twenty-four hours earlier he had called Speidel, the chief of staff, to assure him with heavy irony that he had received Hitler's order to leave Paris a 'field of ruins', had placed three tons of dynamite in the crypt of Notre Dame and was preparing to block the Seine by felling the Eiffel Tower across it. Now, when Speidel appeared on the line, Choltitz raised the receiver to capture for him the noise of rejoicing from the steeples. He asked if there were any further orders. The two men – one a July 20th conspirator who had thus far covered his tracks, the other one of the Führer's disenchanted – understood each other perfectly. Speidel said he had nothing to say. Choltitz asked him to see to the welfare of his wife and family and bade him farewell.

The bells, word of mouth and signals from the vanguard of the Deuxième DB along the civilian telephone network kept Paris on tenterhooks throughout the night. But the crowds which thronged the southern faubourgs and the long avenues reaching to the heart of the city had no certainty yet of the identify of the troops coming to their liberation. They had heard that there were French soldiers in the city. But they were expecting an American army. The morning was misty, with the promise of a hot August sun which the last four days had withheld, and the mist muffled the sound of tank tracks and engines from the approaching columns. Occasionally the rattle of a burst of firing carried northward. Then suddenly, a little after 7 a.m. the vehicles were seen. The crowds were thin beyond the outer boulevards. Inside the line of the old fortifications, beyond the Porte d'Orléans and Porte d'Italie, along the sweep of the avenue du Maine and the rue St Jacques, they were ranked twelve and twenty deep on the pavements, straining for a glimpse of the first arrivals. The khaki tanks and half-tracks they had heard of appeared, fronts painted with the white star of the Allied armies. But the heads in the turrets were wearing caps they had seen before – red *calots* of Spahis, blue of the Cuirassiers, the fez of the Chasseurs d'Afrique, the unmistakable pom-poms of the Fusiliers-Marins. Their liberators were French.

'Within a quarter of an hour, we were caught up in the atmosphere of a full-blooded Fourteenth of July', recorded Captain de la Horie of the Chasseurs d'Afrique. Food and drink was passed, pressed, hurled into the vehicles of the division, which time and again were brought to a halt as the crowds burst across the roads, retreating to leave the youngest and prettiest cast by the tide on their armoured decks. An unbroken roar of cheers and greetings – 'Vive la France, vive la division Leclerc' (suddenly its name was known in every corner of Paris) – carried the columns forward, rising to such a pitch that the tank crews, many of them Parisians frantic to see parents, wives, sweethearts again after years of parting, often without the passage of news from either side, grew hoarse with the effort of shouting messages and scribbled names and telephone numbers on scraps of paper, passing them into the throng in the hope that the recipients would find time from their rejoicing to dial news of the prodigal.

Thus a crop of tiny, poignant tragedies. For as the columns neared the centre, they began to hit the ring of strongpoints in the ministries and public monuments still occupied by German soldiers with orders to engage the enemy. And at least three of the liberators who had sent messages ahead, Lieutenant Bureau to his father, Sergeant Laigle to his fiancée, Private Ferracci to his sister, were killed by fire from these last-ditch warriors before they could make their rendezvous. Fighting was particularly fierce around Dio's objectives at the Ecole Militaire and Invalides, where trees and open space gave the defenders cover and good fields of fire. The foreign office building on the Quai d'Orsay was set ablaze in the exchange of fire and a Sherman knocked out during five hours of fighting which cost the German garrison fifty dead. There was heavy fighting too on Langlade's axis. His men began the morning by clearing the huge Renault factory of Germans, then swung through the Porte St Cloud into the Paris of the *haute bourgeoisie* following the rue Michel-Ange, avenue Mozart and rue de la Pompe to the foot of the avenue Victor Hugo. The Arc de Triomphe stood before them. Massu was determined to be first to pay tribute to the tomb of the Unknown Warrior beneath its vault, and launched his jeep up the long incline. His armour followed. At the moment that he bowed his head before the eternal flame, a 75 mm shell from a German tank parked in the Place de la Concorde at the far end of the Champs Elysées whistled through the arch itself, disturbing the folds of an enormous tricolour which the *sapeurs-pompiers* of Paris were suspending from the keystone. By instantaneous recall of a figure remembered from a school day lesson on the geography of Paris the gunner of one of his escorting tanks set 1,800 metres on to his sight and destroyed the German with his first return of shot. Then Massu gathered his followers up and started on a triumphal *tour d'honneur* to follow its trajectory down the long vista. He was also bound towards the Meurice.

Choltitz had passed the morning in his office, occasionally leaving the hotel to speak to soldiers manning positions along the rue de Rivoli and in the Tuileries Gardens opposite; but until well after noon the defenders of this battlefield de luxe were not disturbed. At about 11.30 a.m. however, Choltitz found himself in direct touch with the enemy via the offices of the Swedish consul-general. One of his officers was visiting the consulate when Captain de la Horie arrived with an ultimatum from Leclerc calling on the Germans to end resistance at once, 'in order to avoid the useless shedding of any more blood'. The document was shortly in Choltitz's hands and almost as soon back again with Nordling, together with an explanation that a German officer's honour forbade him to surrender without a fight. At about 2 p.m. therefore, bearing operational orders which read like a sightseer's guide – 'advance through the Tuileries Gardens as far as the Pont de la Concorde', 'approach the Hôtel Meurice via the Opéra and rue St Honoré', 'enter the Hôtel Meurice by way of the rue de Rivoli' – three platoon/troop groups of the Tchad and Chars de Combat set out from the Hôtel de Ville to make the demonstration the general required.

He, however, had prudently not informed his outposts that a quick surrender was his intention and realistic combat quickly broke out along the line of the arcades which shelter some of the most expensive shops in the world. Three Germans were killed at the foot of the statue of Jeanne d'Arc while sprinting to change position in the Place des Pyramides. A Tchad infantryman was killed under the walls of the Louvre. Three Shermans were set on fire in the Place de la Concorde by grenades thrown from upper windows into their open turret hatches, and there was a brisk battle for possession of Gabriel's serene palaces which close its north side, the Ministère de la Marine and the Hôtel Crillon. But bound by bound, from one pillar of the arcades to the next, the Tchad infantrymen drew nearer to the front door of the Meurice and at about 2.30 p.m. the first Frenchman burst in. On his heels raced Lieutenant Henri Karcher, who, plunging through the smoke released by a phosphorus grenade, took the stairs at a run and pressed some surrendering Germans to show him to Choltitz's office. Entering and saluting, he asked the general if he spoke German. 'Yes, probably better than you', was the answer. Karcher, overcoming his excitement, introduced himself as an officer of 'the army of General de Gaulle' and invited the commander of *Gross-Paris* to make his surrender.

The formalities were quickly completed. A jeep took Choltitz to the Préfecture de Police, where Leclerc was starting a delayed lunch in the banqueting chamber. In the billiard room next door the two men conferred over terms of capitulation and then put their signatures to a typewritten document. It arranged for an immediate ceasefire, surrender of all German personnel and equipment, identification of all prepared demolitions and the despatch of German officers to all outlying strongpoints to take to their garrisons the message of capitulation. The last provision was essential because, while the conference proceeded, heavy fighting still raged in and around the Palais du Luxembourg, which was not finally brought to a halt until 7 p.m. As the two generals appended their signatures, there was a disturbance at the entrance. Colonel Rol, had appeared, Ledru-Rollin like, to set his seal of approval on the surrender. Leclerc had carefully taken it in his own name and that of the Provisional Government of the French Republic, thus breaching the instructions of Supreme Headquarters that it alone was entitled to negotiate terms with the enemy. Rol, whom the Division Leclerc had not bothered to collect from his headquarters (as it had Chaban-Delmas from his at the Place Denfert-Rochereau) insisted on a co-signature and, tiring Leclerc with his arguments, prevailed. Pressed further, Leclerc actually altered the document to make it a surrender to the 'Commander of the FFI in the Ile de France'.

Literary attempts to capture the victory for one party or another were vain. For all the bravura of the resistance, and nearly a thousand members of the FFI had been killed in the six days of insurrection, Paris recognized its liberators in the Division Leclerc. Home of legitimacy as much as of revolution, it hungered in 1944 not for the Commune but for the reassurance of French uniforms, French words of command, French generals. On August 26th it got three. Leclerc and Koenig marched together in the front rank of the great crowd of *résistants*, internal and external, which descended throughout the hot afternoon from the Arc de Triomphe to Notre Dame for a solemn Te Deum of gratitude for deliverance. A little ahead of them both walked de Gaulle, already teaching the crowds those stiff sacerdotal gestures which would become the hallmark of the strangest personal politics of postwar Europe. A king uncrowned, he chose for his apotheosis the same simple khaki service dress worn by his subordinates. The roll call of their victories – Bir Hakim, Fezzan, Kufra – inspired by his sublime resolve had restored its dignity.

# EPILOGUE

## *From the Atlantic Wall to the Iron Curtain*

AS THE DIVISION LECLERC celebrated with the Parisians the triumphant repossession of their unravaged city, the rest of the Allied armies were hurrying the remnants of Army Group B across the Seine. They were few enough. Of the 50 infantry and 12 panzer divisions which Supreme Headquarters West had had under its command during the Battle of Normandy, only 24 infantry divisions and 11 panzer divisions preserved any semblance of organization. The panzer divisions were down to 10 tanks each. The infantry divisions were at one-quarter strength. Best preserved were the formations which had belonged to Army Group G, south of the Loire. Surprised in their positions on the Riviera by the Allied force committed to the 'Second D-Day', August 15th, the majority had been able to escape up the valley of the Rhône, ahead of the pursuing Americans and French of the Sixth Army Group. But they were too few to bring any real reinforcement to their comrades who had fought the Battle of Normandy, too few indeed to do anything more than head for the safety of the Siegfried Line. Hitler had hoped that another line he had designated on his situation map, that of the Somme and Marne, would provide a refuge for the Normandy survivors, along which they might stand while the Reich was ransacked for reserves of men and equipment. But meanwhile he had forbidden the construction of any fortifications on that position, lest the news of the work dishearten the soldiers holding Normandy. Now that he needed the line, Model warned him that its defence would require thirty fresh infantry divisions, which he had not got. And as a result the Allies brushed past it in the night of September 3rd, the armoured car crews which led the chase failing altogether to notice that they had crossed an obstacle of any significance. A day later, September 4th, these spearheads entered Brussels, at the end of a pell-mell advance of 110 miles in two days, a feat unequalled in war, and to a reception almost without parallel. For three days and nights Brussels celebrated without restraint, and two weeks later the reverberations of the welcome still rumbled on.

Brussels's liberation confirmed beyond cavil the result of the Battle of Normandy. It now ranked to stand beside the three other great disasters which had overtaken the German army in the war thus far, Stalingrad, Tunisia, and the recent battle in White Russia, which was simply known as the Destruction of Army Group Centre. How did it compare?

Stalingrad still struck most chill into German hearts; none at home would forget the three days during which the state radio had played nothing but the solemnest of solemn martial music, the 'Eroica' and Bruckner's Seventh Symphony, endlessly repeated. Hitler himself could not forget it, complaining in the spring of 1944 to an army doctor that his nights were filled with 'staff maps in the dark and my brain goes grinding on and ... I can sketch exactly where every division was at Stalingrad. Hour after hour it goes on ...' But terrible though Stalingrad had been in human terms, it had eventually cost Germany only twenty divisions, of which only two were armoured; about one-tenth of the number in Russia and one-fifteenth of the army's whole strength. Enough remained to mount at Kursk during the following summer the largest armoured offensive undertaken by the German army in the whole war. And while the defeat lost Germany much ground – the army was not to see the Volga again – it still left her forward line 500 miles inside Russia and strongly established at many points. The Tunisian capitulation had, in contrast, eliminated the German presence in a whole theatre of operations and ended Hitler's hopes of sustaining the war outside Europe. It had also destroyed Italy's empire and accelerated that country's withdrawal from the Axis. But, though 125,000 German soldiers had fallen prisoner to the Allies at Tunis, the number of divisions lost had been quite small, only eight. Thus in scale the disaster was not much larger than that suffered by the British in Malaya and Burma in the spring of 1942, with which in strategic significance it stands comparison.

The Destruction of Army Group Centre was altogether different. The result of an offensive opened by the Russians on June 22nd, 1944, timed deliberately to coincide with the third anniversary of Barbarossa, it had been launched by 140 Soviet rifle and tank divisions against the German Fourth and Ninth Armies. Attacking

on a front of 350 miles, they had in three weeks driven forward 250
miles, from the Dnieper to the Niemen, to re-cross the Polish border
of 1939 and halt within fifty miles of East Prussia itself. And in the
process 300,000 German soldiers were killed or taken prisoner and
28 divisions written off the German order of battle, dissolved as if
they had never existed. For several weeks an enormous gap had
yawned in the line covering the eastern approaches to Germany and
it had been only the headlong pace of the Russian advance,
over-reaching the capacity of their supply columns to keep step with
the vanguard, which had spared Hitler the wholesale collapse of his
north-eastern front.

The Destruction of Army Group Centre, little known as a battle
though it is in the West, must therefore count among the greatest
defeats ever inflicted in warfare. And yet, if strict comparisons are
made between its results and those of Normandy, it may yet appear
that the Western Allies' victory was the greater. The Allies committed far fewer divisions to Normandy than did the Russians against
Army Group Centre, only thirty-four in all; even after making
allowance for the smaller size of Russian divisions and the larger
number of Western 'corps' and 'army' troops in the divisional slice,
the ratio between effort expended and result achieved stands very
much in their favour. The number of enemy divisions destroyed also
counts to the Western Allies' balance. Such calculations are complicated. In the middle of September, when the German high command in the West began to put its books in order, it was able to show
that almost every division which had fought west of the Seine was
still represented in some form on the new line which had been
established in Holland and along the West Wall. But in most cases
only by fragments. The twelve armoured divisions, which should
have fielded 1,800 tanks, could show only 120; 2,200 had been
destroyed in the Normandy battle. Of the 48 infantry divisions
under Rundstedt's command on June 6th, only 21 still stood in the
order of battle in mid-September. Three had been evacuated from
the West altogether. Nine were being reconstructed in the Replacement Army. Seven were besieged in French ports. Eight had been
dissolved as beyond repair. And of the twenty-one in nominal
existence, eight were classified as remnants. Twenty-seven infantry
divisions had therefore been ground to dust by the British and
Americans, and eleven of the twelve panzer divisions reduced to
bits and pieces. Five hundred thousand German soldiers had dis-

appeared in the process; a quarter of a million of them were dead.

But there was more to the Allies' victory than that. A whole 'OKW theatre' had been obliterated in a single campaign. 'Supreme Commander West' remained one of the major appointments in the OKW chain of command, together with Italy and Scandinavia. But while in the first week of June its boundaries had stretched from the Riviera and the Pyrenees to Finistère and the Belgian coast, they enclosed only ten weeks later little more territory than that marked by the western frontier of the homeland itself. And the loss of France and Belgium was much more than symbolic in its importance. France had been the golden goose of German Occupation policy. *Mein Kampf* and the experience of 1918, when the kaiser's armies had occupied the whole of White Russia and the Ukraine, had conditioned Germans to expect that in a future war their wheatbowl would lie in the east. But France had consistently contributed as much food to German tables as the whole of the occupied east during 1941–4, as well as 500,000 of the 2,700,000 horses requisitioned to move the Wehrmacht's tactical transport and artillery. On top of that her industry and natural resources had also been ruthlessly exploited for German benefit, and her state revenues systematically taxed to pay not only for the cost to Germany of occupying the country but of many other German military expenses incurred beyond her borders. Three-quarters of French iron ore, half her bauxite and 15 per cent of her coal production was compulsorily exported to Germany, a traffic to which 85 per cent of rail movements in France was dedicated in 1944. The total value of goods and services extracted in the last full year of occupation, 1943, equalled a quarter of Germany's whole national product in the last full year of June 1938.

And the effect of the loss of France was not merely negative. Though a million French prisoners-of-war had been held in Germany since 1940, and half a million French workers had been recruited, voluntarily or compulsorily, into Germany's domestic labour force, there still remained a large pool of men of military age within the country. By 1944 some were already living a life of active or passive resistance outside settled society and would freely offer their services to the Provisional Government as soon as it had established itself. To their number would shortly be added the contingents which the Provisional Government began to conscript for the national army. The result was quick to appear. In July 1944 there had been only a single French division on the national territory. By mid-August, with the arrival on the Riviera of the Anvil force, there were to be five. By the beginning of 1945 there would be seven, almost all by then wholly French in composition, as a result of the replacement of the Algerian and Moroccan regiments in their ranks by units of the maquis. While the German army was shrinking in size, therefore, and finding the recruitment of fit, native men to replace casualties increasingly difficult, the French army was growing, and adding appreciable numbers to the swelling weight of Allied soldiers now pressing against Germany's western defences.

Late in time though the Second Front had come, its results therefore ranked as the greatest military disaster Hitler had yet suffered in the field. And it entailed further military setbacks of the most critical nature. The loss of the French Atlantic ports was virtually to bring to an end his ability to prosecute a U-boat war against Allied shipping. Any hope of reviving it lay in the development of new submarines, still under test in the Baltic, and the need to safeguard their testing grounds would require him in October to accept the otherwise pointless confinement of Army Group North in the Kurland peninsula, where it was to remain until the end of the war. At the same time the loss of the French and Belgian coasts deprived the Luftwaffe of its outer chain of early warning radar and, as the end of the fighting in France also released Bomber Command and the US Eighth Air Force from the ground support role they had played during Goodwood and Cobra, the cities of Germany were now to be exposed to renewed attack, against which the Luftwaffe's fighter squadrons could make a less effective showing than ever before.

So thick and fast were troubles to accumulate for Hitler in the autumn of 1944, however, that neither the Allied victory in Normandy nor the strategic disadvantages which flowed from it were to stand out for long from the rollcall of disaster. On the heels of the destruction of Army Group Centre, the Red Army, now numbering 500 divisions, with 15,000 tanks, was to launch a succession of offensives into the bleeding eastern flank of the Reich. In mid-July it had broken through the German defences south of the Pripet marshes, and by early August the spearheads of that thrust had made contact with those which had destroyed Army Group Centre. Together they stood on the Vistula just east of Warsaw. At the same moment, the Ukranian Fronts of the Red Army advanced towards Bulgaria and into Romania, both of which speedily made peace with the invaders, by prior arrangement. The loss of Romania was particularly damaging because its oil wells at Ploieşti were by then Germany's main source of natural oil. And, as had become monotonously repetitious, another sixteen German divisions disappeared along with them into the Russian maw, the bulk belonging to the Sixth Army which Hitler had recreated to keep alive the memory of its predecessor destroyed at Stalingrad.

And yet at the turn of the year, Hitler's Germany was no nearer imminent collapse than it had been in the summer. By frantic measures of rearmament and recruitment, a new strategic reserve had been assembled, which endowed Hitler once again with the power to counter-attack and so, locally at least, impose an initiative. The locality in which he chose to do so was in the Ardennes on the western front. And though the closure of this offensive, after an initial but illusory success, coincided with the opening of a new and deeply menacing Russian attack through Poland towards Berlin, the Red Army did not carry through its stroke to the capital itself. During February a strange lull fell over all the battlefronts and persisted until the beginning of April. It was incomplete in places, particularly in East Prussia, where the Russians ground inexorably towards the Baltic, and in Hungary, scene of a final and remarkable German counter-attack towards the oilfields near Lake Balaton. But, in general, winter imposed a solstice on the fighting.

Not only winter. Logistics, the enemy of bad and over-successful generalship alike, had laid its hand on the encircling Allied armies. The means of their advance on all fronts, east and west, was identical, the six-wheel GMC truck. The Americans supplied the Russians with 375,000 of this model during the war, mostly before 1945. They themselves had nearly 20,000 in transport companies in France, as well as thousands of others in the echelons of combat units. And, since the fighting everywhere destroyed the railway systems over which it passed, the truck had become literally the vehicle of military manoeuvre. But, like the ship of the desert, it was both consumer and supplier. As the distance between the point from which it picked up supplies and that where it delivered them increased, so too in direct proportion did the inroads it made on its most essential load, fuel. At the end of 1944 the fuel depots for both the Russian and Anglo-American armies were several hundred miles behind their fighting lines; in the west on the Normandy beaches and western Channel ports, in the east beyond the Vistula. And until those depots could be moved forward, by the re-opening of railways and ports and the laying of pipelines, the armies which depended upon them were haltered where they stood by invisible but almost inflexible bonds.

The Germans, in contrast, though also by a familiar strategic law, had actually eased their logistic problems by retreating. The relief was to be short-lived, for in the first quarter of 1945 the Anglo-American strategic bomber force could direct the weight of its attack against the railway system east and west of the Rhine, with disastrous effects on the movement of coal and so very swiftly on the production of steel and its manufactured products. But for a short while an interlude of deceptive stability descended on the battle-fronts, in the west from mid-January to mid-February, in the east from mid-February to mid-April. Hitler's optimism revived. To visitors to the Chancellery, where he had established his head-quarters again, he spoke as in the past of wonder weapons and of the inevitable and imminent falling-out of Russia and the United States. With his staff he discussed coming operations in the east which would knock the Russian armies off balance and release the tank forces necessary to defend the Rhine – which the Allies had not yet crossed. He had become possessed by the philosophy of the eleventh hour, of the night being darkest before the dawn, and sustained his spirits with the belief that, like Frederick the Great in the worst moment of the Seven Years War, he had only to keep his nerve for all eventually to turn in his favour.

The trust in a miracle was illusory. But retrospectively the six months between the end of the Battles of Normandy and Army Group Centre and the appearance on the Rhine and the Oder of the armies which had won them certainly had something miraculous for Germany about them. The Allies' failure to capitalize on their great victories could not be laid at the door of logistic difficulties alone. It had also to do with the continuing ability of German industry to produce, despite every sort of damage to railways, factories and fuel sources which the Allied bombers could inflict, and to the extra-ordinary resilience of the German army.

The army's fighting power was legendary. Alone among those of the First World War, it had retained its morale and cohesion almost to the very end, and in the process brought about the disintegration of the Russian army, inflicted something close to breakdown on the French and Italian armies, and visited a severe moral crisis on the

British army. In 1945 it was to demonstrate an even greater and more remarkable resolution. In East Prussia, in Silesia, on the Vistula and at Lake Balaton, it was to lose men in hundreds of thousands, many killed by weapons of mass destruction it could no longer match or forced to throw their lives away resisting tank attacks with short-range, hand-held missiles. And yet it would continue to fight until denied room for its battlefield. How the Germans resisted the advance of the Red Army as they did remains a mystery. Fear of falling prisoner to a pitiless enemy played its part; so too did the resolve to spare German women and children from the terror of a Russian occupation. The long columns of refugees which set off beside the fighting formations whenever they were forced to give ground were a chilling reminder to the soldiers that they, and only they, now stood between the enemy and the disintegration of the nation.

But external stimuli were not the whole explanation. The fighting spirit of the German army derived ultimately from its own character. Unlike the American army, or even the British, which for all its parade of territorial titles was quite lax about matching them with the regional origins of its soldiers, the German army had always taken the greatest care to see that its units were formed of men from the same province or city, that replacements for casualties also came from the same places and that returned wounded went back to the units with which they started. Thus, even though the army diminished rapidly in size during the first months of 1945, its essential nature was not changed. As Silesians, Franconians, Bavarians, Brandenburgers were driven inexorably inwards on the heartland, their determination to resist was heightened by the increasing proximity of their own home bases. Only their tenacity, they knew, could stem the great *Volkswanderung* which the campaign on the eastern frontiers had set in motion. Like the warriors of the Teutonic tribes of old, they were resolved if necessary to die where they stood, should that be necessary to protect the uprooted population from the eastern invader.

There is a limit, of course, to what human will and courage can achieve. And in April that limit was reached by the Germans. Their Army Groups B, G, Centre, South, once separated by 2,000 miles of conquered Europe, were now pressed back to back along the meridian of the homeland. Knowledge that the demarcation line between the Western and Russian zones of occupation ran along the

Elbe stimulated a final effort of resistance on the river, even after Hitler's suicide on April 30th, so that refugees from the east might find a way into future western territory before a ceasefire was imposed. But Hitler's successor, Dönitz, recognized that the arrangement of a ceasefire was his first and only real duty of state. It came into force everywhere on May 8th. By then the Allied armies had been in touch across the remnants of the German front for nearly two weeks; troops of the American V Corps had met Russians of the first Ukrainian Front at Torgau on the Elbe on April 25th.

The ten months which separated Germany's two fatal defeats – the destruction of Army Group B in Normandy and Army Group Centre in White Russia – and her eventual collapse have been taken in retrospect to imply a fundamental fault in Allied strategy. Two mistakes in particular are identified: Eisenhower's preference for a 'broad front' advance to the German border in September and Stalin's abandonment of the drive along the Baltic in February. A 'narrow front' advance, it is held, would have got an Allied force across the Rhine before winter, and so isolated the industrial centre of the Ruhr. Persistence on the Baltic route would have brought the Russians to Berlin at the beginning of March instead of the end of April.

There is no doubt some weight in both these contentions. It does seem as if the leaders chose to be guided in these decisions by political rather than strictly strategic considerations. Eisenhower's rejection of the narrow thrust seems to have been dictated by his desire to keep both the American and British halves of his army in action simultaneously rather than risk disappointing one of the Allied peoples – it would in this case have been the Americans – by consigning its national army to inactivity. Stalin, for his part, was anxious to see that the Balkans were safely secured as a buffer zone for Russia's postwar security and was prepared to resist the pull even of Berlin in order to do so.

Yet there is no certainty that different – in the critics' view better – strategies would have significantly shortened the war. The rate of advance of the two converging armies after their great victories of July imposed strains on their systems of supply and transportation which would have been heightened unbearably by the effort to sustain it. Moreover, both offensives, in Normandy and White Russia, had derived much of their effect from being fought where they were. Both battlefields were at the far edge of the German operational area. Both could be, and were, isolated from adjoining theatres by the systematic cutting of the railway systems which led into them. Both were relatively unfortified – for, as we have seen, the Atlantic Wall was but the thinnest of crusts, which was easily cracked on the first day of the amphibious assault. The defences which gave the British and Americans such difficulty later were improvised in the course of the fighting.

Given that Hitler could find new formations to replace those lost in White Russia and Normandy, therefore, a second great effort, nothing less than a battle for the frontiers of Germany itself, may be seen to have been a necessity before the Eastern and Western allies could finally overcome the power of the Wehrmacht and take possession of its homeland. And those formations were found. Twenty-five scaled-down 'People's Grenadier' divisions, ten panzer brigades, three parachute divisions from the Luftwaffe were created in the west in the autumn and, after the majority had been lost or disabled in the Ardennes offensive, numbers were made up by drafting Todt Organization workmen, police and the staff and demonstration units of training schools to the front. Himmler's SS, whose order of battle had always been inflated by units of largely symbolic value, redoubled its efforts to produce formations to which the title of division could be given. And in the last resort the civil population, organized as the *Volkssturm* under party control and equipped with captured enemy weapons, could be thrown into the battle for the defence of the eastern cities. At Breslau in Silesia, 35,000 soldiers and 15,000 *Volkssturm* held out though encircled from mid-February until a week after the end of the war, when only 20,000 remained alive and unwounded.

Another people, under another leader, might have been shocked into capitulation by the great defeats of the summer of 1944. The Germans under Hitler displayed a resistance to catastrophe at the front, round-the-clock bombing at home, and the fearful psychological and material hurt entailed by both, which flew in the face of reason and of every Allied expectation. Or did it? The occupation zones agreed by the Eastern and Western allies in 1944 and modified at Yalta in February 1945 to allow room for a French share, were divided between them by a line following the Elbe and Werra rivers. The final fighting line coincided with this Inner German Border, as it would come to be called in later years, with a remarkable degree of accuracy. Only in Saxony did the American advance spill over into what would after the surrender become Russian jurisdiction.

Allowance must be made for Dönitz's foreknowledge of the zonal agreement. It was that which stiffened the resolve of the German soldiers on the Elbe to hold the river until the Allied spearheads should reach it. For, as long as they did so, the refugee population of the east would have time to cross from future Russian into future Western territory. But the neat approximation of the military and diplomatic maps was not brought about by the last-minute desperation of the Wehrmacht. The document which revealed the Allies' post-war plans for Germany does not seem to have come into German possession until early April. And by then the German armies, east and west, were already almost back to back.

Rather it was as if the Allies had accepted what lay in Hitler's mind, which, as so often in his touch with that of the German people, also represented their inner will: that every inch of German soil would have to be fought over before they would be brought to accept defeat. Hence even as late as March 28th, with the Rhine already crossed and the Ruhr about to be encircled, Eisenhower could still write to Montgomery as if a great battle lay ahead. 'My plan is simple, it aims at dividing and destroying the enemy forces and joining hands with the Russian army. My purpose is to destroy the enemy forces and his power to resist.' Hence, as if by symbiosis, the extraordinary spasm of final combat which convulsed Germany in late March and during April. Ten thousand German prisoners were captured by the British and Americans every day in March and the figure rose to 30,000 a day during April. But those Germans still at liberty battled on, fighting and dying at every river line between the Rhine and the Elbe, counter-attacking when they could and compelling the enemy to turn into rubble every other provincial town they approached. Ibbenbüren, Verden, Lingen in the British area, defended here by a division of sailors, there by an NCO school, held out for days at a time, to be taken only after tactical air power had thrown down the houses on to their defenders' heads. In the American Zone south of the Ruhr, the Germans in the Harz mountains resisted for ten days in mid-April and at Crailsheim and Heilbronn in Württemberg counter-attacked strongly enough to cut off an American armoured division, reduce it to dependence on aerial resupply and eventually force it to break out and withdraw. And in Berlin, where Hitler had promised that the Russians would suffer their greatest defeat, the garrison came near to exacting from them a price for their victory as heavy as that of Stalingrad. In the twelve days of fighting which the reduction of the city required, it is estimated that 200,000 Russian soldiers became casualties.

The armies which breasted to a halt against the line of armistice in the first week of May had, therefore, been stretched to the point of exhaustion. The American army, still growing in numbers from divisions shipped directly from the training camps at home, had best been able to absorb the punishment of the last months. But the British was already shrinking in size, as existing units were dissolved to make good losses in others. The Canadians had used up their pool of volunteers for overseas duty. The French, though not short of men, had neither the money nor means to equip them. The Russians, with 500 divisions in the field, appeared at the peak of their strength; but their formations were bulked out with the old, the very young and the unfit, conscripted as a desperate measure to replace the seven million servicemen who had been killed since 1941.

Even amid the devastation and despair to which a year of fighting and three years of bombing had reduced the land they were now to occupy, the armies were therefore content to enjoy the peace they had won. The prospect of transfer to the Pacific and another ordeal by fire was soon dissipated. Though eighty Russian divisions were railed eastward across the Soviet Union in mid-summer for the autumn offensive into Manchuria, no British or American division which had fought in north-west Europe was engaged against the Japanese. The vast majority of Allied servicemen were demobilized directly from Germany to their homes. And the demobilization was rapid. Between August 1945 and June 1946 the United States Army was reduced from 8 million to 1·5 million men, the British army by June 1947 from 3 million to 400,000. The Russian army, 12 million strong at the end of the war, numbered 3 million by the end of 1947. The Polish army-in-exile had disappeared altogether; but 55,000 of the 228,000 Poles abroad in 1945 chose to return home to live under communist government. Only the French, with wars still to fight in a vain effort to retain its pre-war empire, chose to expand rather than reduce its army. Leaving three divisions of the Army of the Rhine and Danube to occupy its zone in Baden and Württemberg, it shipped all its regular soldiers eastwards for the start of the long campaign in Indo-China. Its neighbour, the British Army of the Rhine, counted only two divisions after 1946, the American for a while only one, the 1st Infantry. Even the Group of Soviet Forces Germany, giant among the Allied armies of occupation, had its strength fixed at a mere twenty divisions. For the first year of occupation the conquering armies were outnumbered by their captives, the 8 million former members of the Wehrmacht who, in long columns, marched out from their makeshift detention camps each day to pick over the rubble of their homeland.

In Normandy, where the first great breach in the defences of Hitler's fortress had been won, the rubble was being cleared from the towns and villages over which the armies had battled. Two hundred thousand buildings in the province had been destroyed. Some places had been devastated as severely as those in the Zone of the Armies in 1914–18. In the village of Vesly, over which Patton's army had rumbled in August, 655 out of 700 inhabitants had lost their homes, at Saintenay 151 out of 245 houses had been destroyed. Lisieux, Coutances, St Lô, Falaise, Argentan, were in ruins. Caen was a mountain of broken stones; 9,000 of its 15,000 buildings had been bombed or shelled flat. And it was not as if Normandy were the only zone of devastation in France, which had actually suffered greater damage during the Second than the First World War. Nine hundred thousand buildings had been damaged or ruined in 1914–18, twice that number in 1939–44. And while the French economy had boomed in the first conflict, it had been systematically robbed under German occupation.

The tragi-comedy of French politics in the postwar years promised badly for the work of reconstruction. But while the parties bargained and squabbled in the capital, the formidable machine of French bureaucracy harnessed American aid and native energy to a labour of unsung but spectacular achievement. The devastation of the First World War was not made good until 1928. By 1951 most of ruined Normandy had been rebuilt. Le Havre by 1950 was once again a functioning port with a magnificent transatlantic terminal. By 1954 Caen was reborn, the capstone to its rebirth the reconstruction of the spire of the church of St Pierre toppled in the great air raid of July 7th, 1944. The Mount of William the Conqueror's Castle, cleared of the jumble of buildings which had disguised its outline for centuries, rose above broad tree-lined boulevards in a new town plan which brought urbanists from around the world to admire its distinction and humanity.

There was another work of reparation to be done; the gathering in of the bodies of the soldiers who had died in Normandy's fields and orchards. Buried where they had fallen in the ten weeks of fighting, or thrown together in the mass graves into which the victims of the Falaise pocket were heaped, in the years after the departure of the armies they were disinterred and brought together into more fitting places. The bodies of the 9,000 American dead not repatriated were buried together under a forest of white cruciform headstones at St Laurent above Omaha Beach. At Orglandes 10,000 German soldiers were interred in collective graves, marked by monumental granite reproductions of the Iron Cross. The British, with their genius for the funereal and' with the experience of a previous labour of memorialization behind them, worked by a different and more intimate method. Northern France and Flanders was already covered by a patchwork of the small, gardened cemeteries of the Imperial War Graves Commission into which had been gathered the million casualties of the First World War. Its landscape architects, obedient to the rules laid down by Lutyens and Kipling thirty years before, now began to reproduce in Normandy the Stones of Remembrance, Crosses of Sacrifice, pergolas, mown walks, rose beds and flowering shrubs among which it had become traditional that the dead of British battlefields should lie.

At both Ranville and Bayeux, close to the centres of fierce fighting on the Orne and Odon, space had to be made for 2,000 graves. At other spots, Douvres-la-Délivrande, Combes-en-Plaine, Fontenay-le-Pesnel, the cemeteries could be smaller, small enough to be hidden among the regrown hedgerows from all but the most determined visitor. But, as the native flowers of the English countryside took root and blossomed more colourfully from one summer to the next beside the headstones, visitors in growing numbers began to make the cross-Channel journey to seek them out. Many came for reasons of bereavement or out of comradeship with lost friends; others came in organized parties, reunions of veterans who had been that way in the invasion months. In time the visits acquired formality. Towns in Britain from which the troops had left to embark for the liberation entered into formal association with the French towns to which they had brought it, and delegations of mayors and councillors began to acquire an annual acquaintance with wreath-layings, *vins d'honneur* and substantial municipal cuisine. Regiments, too, incorporated the Normandy pilgrimage into their round of ceremony, finding the funds to raise memorials to their exploits on the sea fronts of the small watering places where they had landed, and to despatch bandsmen and colour-parties to do them honour at the appropriate anniversary. During the 1960s the sight of red poppies in white-gloved hands and the sound of the Last Post bugled across sand dune and esplanade became a familiar ingredient of Normandy tourism, something for which campers would gather and which caravanners would halt to contemplate for a small moment of sentimentality and half-comprehension.

Other soldiers also came to make the return, serious students of the great amphibious, airborne and armoured operations which were their profession's most recent extended exercise of its business easily available for analysis. In the immediate postwar years analysis took second place to something like self-congratulation, since the memory of the risk run in committing the liberation armies to the unknown dangers of the Channel and the Atlantic Wall still bulked largest in the visitors' minds. Later, attention would focus on the issue of leadership, particularly at small-unit level, as veterans explained to officers unblooded by any postwar experience what a battle was like: at what distance the enemy was encountered; what was seen, heard, smelt; what soldiers said to each other, to their sergeants, to their platoon commanders; how their sense of self-preservation might be overcome to carry them forward to positions which had to be taken. At the Merville battery, around Pegasus Bridge, under the sea wall at Ouistreham, in the deep-banked lanes by Gavrus, on the skyline of the long cornfields over which the Goodwood tanks had galloped to disaster, there, too, at stated intervals of the year, clumps of pondering sightseers, unmistakably military in tweed jackets and flat caps, became a familiar feature of the Norman summer, disregarded by tractor-drivers and apple-pickers getting in the harvest the countryside had been brought to yield again.

Imperceptibly, these visitations took on a more serious cast as the years of peace attenuated into an anxious present. The formations which had made the great journey from Normandy to the boundary of the Russian zone of occupation in Germany had remained throughout the postwar period exactly where they had come to rest in 1945, replacing their soldiers as tours of duty ended but preserving apparently unchangeably their titles and their stations. The British 2nd Division in Westphalia and the American 1st Division in Bavaria had become over time fixed elements of the local landscape. But so, too, in the east had the formations which Katukov, Bogdanov, Chuikov and Kuznetsov had commanded in the Battle of Berlin, the First and Second Guards Tank Armies, the Eighth Guards and the Third Shock Armies. Demobilization, re-organization and the solidification of the power of the satellite regimes permitted in the early postwar years a gradual withdrawal of Soviet forces from the states of eastern Europe. But the strength of the Group of Soviet Forces Germany remained constant at about twenty divisions from one decade to the next, their status gradually shifting from that of an army of occupation to that of an advance guard of national power as relations between East and West moved from alliance to hostility.

It is difficult to fix the moment at which the frontier between the eastern and western military zones of Germany became known as the Central Front. Its use would have been quite inappropriate in the 1950s, when the western states, though already organized into the North Atlantic Treaty Organization, wholly lacked the force on the ground to match that of the Russians beyond the Elbe. By the 1970s, when thirty years of ideological confrontation had brought into being in Germany an inter-Allied army of formidable size, it had passed into common staff use. And staff thinking about how the Central Front might be defended had moved during the same period from unstated admission of inability to detailed doctrinal formula. The policy of the 1950s, a fighting retreat to the Rhine, had given way in the 1960s to a declared intention to use tactical nuclear weapons against a Russian incursion. The dangers of an escalation to general nuclear war, and natural objection to the devastation of their territory by the Germans, who had come to provide NATO with its most powerful land contingent, led finally to a doctrine of 'forward defence' by conventional forces.

'Forward defence' implied that the mass of Soviet armour, should it ever, and in whatever unforeseeable circumstances, spill over the Inner German Border on to the territory of the Federal Republic, must be resisted where it was encountered, defeated and repulsed. But the disparity in strength between it and the forces NATO could deploy in opposition raised chronic doubt over their capacity to do so. The Group of Soviet Forces fielded ten tank and ten motorized divisions. American, British and German divisions were equal in number. But in numbers of men, tanks and close-support aircraft deployed, the Western Alliance was at a disadvantage of between two and three to one. Moreover, while British and American reinforce-ments for their divisions in the field were at the wrong end of vulnerable sea communications, Russia's reinforcements were land-based and close to hand: eleven divisions in eastern Europe, sixty divisions in European Russia and fifty divisions of non-Russian Warsaw Pact troops, Czechs, Hungarians, Poles, East Germans, immediately behind the Central Front.

If NATO were to believe in its capacity to hold the Inner German Border, it had therefore to find a plausible doctrine of defence, and if possible one based on concrete historical example; not only a set of rules but rules validated by experience in the not too distant past. Where to turn? Neither in Vietnam nor Korea had armoured forces clashed in strength. Britain's campaigns against Rommel in the Western Desert had been fought in conditions topographically too dissimilar from those of central Europe to be a useful source of comparisons; and the same went, despite the modernity of the equipment deployed, for the Arab-Israeli wars. The Russians' success in resisting and repelling the German panzer wedges on the steppe in 1943 offered, by a strange reversal, heartening evidence that blitzkrieg was not invincible; but their method relied on the transformation of the terrain into defended belts of entrenchment and minefield scores of miles deep, something quite inapplicable to the thriving, heavily farmed countryside of Germany.

Where then to turn? Where else had tank met among standing corn, orchard, crops and hedgerow? Where had an armoured army on the defensive given as good as it had got, held a line and won time for reinforcements to arrive? In this aftermath of Normandy there would have been few Allied soldiers prepared to concede that that was Army Group B's achievement. Allied attention remained fixed on the achievement that Overlord had been, on the successful gamble of the Channel crossing and the triumph represented by the winning of the foothold under the guns of the Atlantic Wall.

But time dissolves the emotions of triumph. And the battle had never generated any of that deep-rooted animus between the combatants which forbids sober analysis of its character for generations afterwards. Recriminations by the Canadians against the 12th SS Division apart, the invaders conceded that, by the curious morality of battlefields, the Germans had fought the good fight. Proof, if it were wanted, of their attitude could be found in the Normandy cemeteries where, intermingled with the graves of the British dead, in a fashion unthinkable to those who had fixed the character of the memorialization after 1918, stood the headstones of Silesians and

Saxons who had died on the wrong side of the line at Caen and Bayeux.

And so, in the politically and militarily transformed world of the oil crisis and the inter-continental missile, Normandy became news again: not newspaper news; but news to the editors of the professional military journals whose business is to speculate about the nature of future warfare, and to the authors of those works of 'future history' whose attempt to give it, literally, reality was one of the great publishing successes of the decade. The similarity between the landscapes of Normandy and the Central Front was noted and measured. The battlefield was re-walked, by military tourists whose motives were now exploratory instead of nostalgic. Lines of sight, pockets of dead ground, routes of approach, angles of defilade were plotted and calculated. The war diaries of units long dissolved were disinterred from the archives. Veterans pensioned off years before found that their war stories had a new audience. It was the shape, rhythm and tempo of the fighting in those June and July days nearly forty years before which today's experts sought to recreate, hoping therefrom to draw the elements of a tactical system by which the descendants of the warriors who had fought in Normandy could defend with confidence the distant ceasefire line the victory there had won.

Perhaps there is point to their work. Certainly no European can or should contemplate with complacency the concentration of military power which continues to occupy the centre of his continent so long after the formal closure of the events which called it there. And no western European can rest easy at the disproportion which exists between the force which defends his half of the continent from that which threatens it from the other. But one wonders if the search for reassurance in the example of the German defence of Normandy is not a taking counsel of fears, an indulgence in that 'worst case' theory with which the tough-minded in the world of strategic analysis choose to alarm and provoke their more optimistic fellows? For real hindsight allows us after forty years to see the great Second Front debate, and the battle in which its conclusion resulted, entirely differently from those who argued for and against the running of the risk.

That risk, it was conceded by both British and Americans, was the defeat of the invasion force in its amphibious phase, that is, either offshore or while half-ashore. Might it be got safely to dry land and, as Montgomery put it, a good lodgement area pegged out, both Allies agreed that their superiority in airpower, mobility and material would give it the edge in the battle of the breakout. To that the Americans looked forward with a greater confidence than the British, marked by the memories of the First World War, could muster; but it was not an ordeal from which either shrank. In the event their estimation of the difficulties of the battle ashore were both exceeded and under-fulfilled. Under-fulfilled because, when the German line broke, it did so irreparably; there was no chance for Army Group B to fall back from one river line to another across the breadth of northern France, since it had given its all in the defence of the lodgement area. Exceeded because the Allies had not expected that it would fight so fiercely, successfully and long at the very point where they chose to land.

Had the pessimists in the Allied camp foreseen and been able to persuade the makers of policy that the battle behind the beaches would have lasted as long as it did, it is possible that the invasion would have been further postponed; even that the Second Front protagonists might have lost their case and seen the power of the Western Alliance dedicated to an enlargement of the campaign in Italy and the Balkans. But that would have been to make the gravest of strategic mistakes. For where the Allies felt themselves to be at their most vulnerable in their Second Front strategy was precisely where their greatest strength lay; in their reliance on the sea for the movement of their forces.

The sheer technical difficulty of transferring land forces from ship to shore, emphasized by the disaster of Dieppe, and reinforced by memories of Gallipoli, was the medium of obfuscation. But, as the success of the Sicily and Salerno landings demonstrated, that difficulty had been overcome a year before D-Day by solutions set in hand a year before that: the construction of specialized landing-craft, the creation of major airborne units, the refinement of direct fire support from naval guns and fighter aircraft and the utilization of air power to isolate the landing zone from the rest of the enemy's defended area. Given those innovations, everything in an amphibious strategy then favoured the Allies. For, granted roughly equivalent strength between attacker and defender, what makes an offensive work is surprise. Hitler had twice achieved stupendous surprise over his opponents, but only because of their stubborn self-delusion: in 1940 through the French and British conviction that he must attack over the Belgian plain, in 1941 through Stalin's refusal to believe that he would attack at all. Until the autumn of 1943 there persisted an element of self-delusion in his refusal to elevate the threat from the west to the same plane as the struggle in the east. Thereafter he could blind himself neither to the certainty that the Allies intended to invade nor to the probability that when they did so they would arrive undetected and without warning.

Had the Allies been able to take the measure of his anxiety, they might then with confidence have comprehended the enormous advantages they enjoyed. The Channel, instead of appearing an obstacle, a zone of uncertain weather and hidden obstructions and an enormous field of direct fire for the defenders' weapons, would then have been seen for what it was; an impermeable barrier to German intelligence and the smoothest of broad highways to the weak places in the Atlantic Wall. Indeed, given the Luftwaffe's inability to overfly British airspace from the spring of 1944 onwards and the complete penetration of the Abwehr's network of spies within the United Kingdom, every place on the Atlantic Wall was a weak one. 'He who defends everything', as Hitler's spiritual mentor, Frederick the Great, had warned, 'defends nothing.' And Army Group B, for want of any but the crudest topographical indication as to where the Allies might make their descent, was on June 6th, 1944 defending everything. The result might have been foreseen: the instantaneous concentration of eight first-class divisions against three weak divisions and the almost immediate reinforcement of the attackers by another four divisions. On the first day, therefore, the Allies were to achieve a superiority of four to one on the ground, which the intervention of a single panzer division could do almost nothing to redress.

Gone are such chances from the battlefield, present or future. Wellington's 'other side of the hill' has been conjured out of existence, by the invention of intelligence-gathering devices of which neither he nor even Hitler could have dreamt. No power today could prepare in secret a great seaborne invasion. Its gathering would be spied out from the beginning by satellite reconnaissance. Even less can any power hope to muster undetected a concentration of force in central Europe for an attack across an international boundary in the manner of 1914 or 1940. The sea provides the means, if not today the opportunity, for tanks, troops and guns to leap a hundred miles of space in a single night. Not so communication by land. An army bent on the offensive must monopolize roads and railways for days beforehand, and its political masters find convincing explanations if governments in the target area are not to take their own precautions. Happily the governments of Europe are now agreed that any significant disturbance of the fixed pattern of military deployment is a legitimate occasion for international concern, to be announced before it takes place and monitored while in progress. Perhaps it is stiil proper, none the less, for the peoples who live in the shadow of the armies which line the border between east and west to frighten themselves with the thought of what might happen should they move against each other. It is certainly proper for their commanders to plan how they might defend the ground on which they are stationed should crisis call them to do so. But if they look to Normandy to tell them how to fight the battle, they will see but the lesser part of what the story of the Second Front has to tell. The greater part is that of how easily in the end the Allies won the surprise they scarcely dared grasp at, and how utterly vanished are the circumstances which gave it to them. Dare we guess that D-Day was the last of Europe's great invasions?

# APPENDIX

## British, American and German Divisions in Normandy
### June 6th–August 25th, 1944
#### (with dates of arrival)

## 21st (British) Army Group
### Second (British) Army

| | |
|---|---|
| Guards Armoured Division | June 28th |
| 7th Armoured Division | June 8th |
| 11th Armoured Division | June 13th |
| 79th Armoured Division (specialized armour) | D-Day |
| 6th Airborne Division | D-Day |
| 15th (Scottish) Division | June 14th |
| 43rd (Wessex) Division | June 24th |
| 49th (West Riding) Division | D-Day |
| 50th (Northumbrian) Division | D-Day |
| 51st (Highland) Division | D-Day |
| 53rd (Welsh) Division | June 27th |
| 59th (Staffordshire) Division | June 27th |

### First Canadian Army

| | |
|---|---|
| 4th Canadian Armoured Division | July 31st |
| 1st Polish Armoured Division | July 31st |
| 2nd Canadian Division | July 7th |
| 3rd Canadian Division | D-Day |

## 12th US Army Group
### First and Third US Armies

| | |
|---|---|
| 2nd Armoured Division | July 2nd |
| 3rd Armoured Division | July 9th |

| | |
|---|---|
| 4th Armoured Division | July 28th |
| 5th Armoured Division | August 2nd |
| 6th Armoured Division | July 28th |
| 7th Armoured Division | August 14th |
| 2nd French Armoured Division | August 1st |
| 82nd Airborne Division | D-Day |
| 101st Airborne Division | D-Day |
| 1st Infantry Division | D-Day |
| 2nd Infantry Division | June 8th |
| 4th Infantry Division | D-Day |
| 5th Infantry Division | July 16th |
| 8th Infantry Division | July 8th |
| 9th Infantry Division | June 14th |
| 28th Infantry Division | July 27th |
| 29th Infantry Division | June 7th |
| 30th Infantry Division | June 15th |
| 35th Infantry Division | July 11th |
| 79th Infantry Division | June 19th |
| 80th Infantry Division | August 8th |
| 83rd Infantry Division | June 27th |
| 90th Infantry Division | June 10th |

# Army Groups B and G (German)
(original divisional locations on Map 1, p. xviii)

## Seventh Army

| | |
|---|---|
| 77th Infantry Division | 352nd Infantry Division |
| 91st Infantry Division | 353rd Infantry Division |
| 243rd Infantry Division | 709th Infantry Division |
| 265th Infantry Division | 716th Infantry Division |
| 266th Infantry Division | 2nd Parachute Division |
| 275th Infantry Division | 3rd Parachute Division |
| 343rd Infantry Division | 5th Parachute Division |

## Fifteenth Army

| | |
|---|---|
| 48th Infantry Division | mid-August |
| 84th Infantry Division | by July 30th |

| | |
|---|---|
| 85th Infantry Division | August 5th |
| 326th Infantry Division | by July 30th |
| 331st Infantry Division | by July 30th |
| 344th Infantry Division | mid-August |
| 346th Infantry Division | by June 29th |
| 711th Infantry Division | by June 29th |
| 17th Luftwaffe Field Division | mid-August |

## Nineteenth Army

| | |
|---|---|
| 271st Infantry Division | July 24th |
| 272nd Infantry Division | July 24th |
| 277th Infantry Division | June 29th |
| 338th Infantry Division | mid-August |

## First Army

| | |
|---|---|
| 276th Infantry Division | June 29th |
| 708th Infantry Division | by July 30th |

## From outside France and Belgium

| | |
|---|---|
| 89th Infantry Division (Norway) | early-August |
| 363rd Infantry Division (Denmark) | by July 30th |
| 16th Luftwaffe Field Division (Netherlands) | mid-June |

## Armoured Divisions

| | |
|---|---|
| 1st SS Panzer Division | late June |
| 2nd Panzer Division | in Normandy |
| 2nd SS Panzer Division | late June |
| 9th Panzer Division | early August |
| 9th SS Panzer Division ⎱ from Russia | June 25th |
| 10th SS Panzer Division ⎰ | |
| 12th SS Panzer Division | In Normandy |
| 17th SS Panzergrenadier Division | June 12th |
| 21st Panzer Division | In Normandy |
| 116th Panzer Division | July 20th |
| Panzer Lehr Division | June 8th |

# Order of Battle of the Divisions Treated Extensively in the Text

## US 82nd Airborne Division

505th Parachute Infantry Regiment
507th Parachute Infantry Regiment
508th Parachute Infantry Regiment
325th Glider Infantry Regiment
376th Parachute Field Artillery Regiment
319th Glider Field Artillery Regiment
307th Airborne Engineer Battalion

## US 101st Airborne Division

501st Parachute Infantry Regiment
502nd Parachute Infantry Regiment
506th Parachute Infantry Regiment
327th Glider Infantry Regiment
377th Parachute Field Artillery Regiment
321st Glider Field Artillery Regiment
907th Glider Field Artillery Regiment
326th Airborne Engineer Battalion

## 3rd Canadian Division

The Royal Winnipeg Rifles
The Regina Rifle Regiment
1st Battalion Canadian Scottish Regiment
The Queen's Own Rifles of Canada
Le Régiment de la Chaudière
The North Shore (New Brunswick) Regiment
The Highland Light Infantry of Canada
The Stormont, Dundas and Glengarry Highlanders
The North Nova Scotia Highlanders
17th Duke of York's Canadian Hussars (reconnaissance regiment)
12th, 13th, and 14th Regiments, Royal Canadian Artillery
3rd Anti-Tank Regiment, Royal Canadian Artillery
The Cameron Highlanders of Ottawa (machine-gun regiment)

# 15th (Scottish) Division

8th Battalion The Royal Scots
6th Battalion The Royal Scots Fusiliers
6th Battalion The King's Own Scottish Borderers
9th Battalion The Cameronians
2nd Battalion The Glasgow Highlanders
7th Battalion The Seaforth Highlanders
10th Battalion The Highland Light Infantry
2nd Battalion The Gordon Highlanders
2nd Battalion The Argyll and Sutherland Highlanders
15th Reconnaissance Regiment, Royal Armoured Corps
131st, 181st and 190th Field Regiments, Royal Artillery
97th Anti-Tank Regiment, Royal Artillery
1st Battalion The Middlesex Regiment (machine-gun regiment)

# 11th Armoured Division

23rd Hussars
2nd Fife and Forfar Yeomanry
3rd Royal Tank Regiment
8th Battalion The Rifle Brigade (motor infantry)
3rd Battalion The Monmouthshire Regiment
4th Battalion The King's Shropshire Light Infantry
1st Battalion The Herefordshire Regiment
2nd Northamptonshire Yeomanry (reconnaissance)
13th Regiment, Royal Horse Artillery
151st Field Regiment, Royal Artillery
75th Anti-Tank Regiment, Royal Artillery

# 21st Panzer Division

Panzer Regiment 22
Panzergrenadier Regiment 125
Panzergrenadier Regiment 192
Panzer Artillerie Regiment 155
Panzer Aufklärung Abteilung 21 (reconnaissance)
Panzer Jäger Abteilung 200 (anti-tank)
Panzer Pionier Bataillon 220 (engineers)

# 1st Polish Armoured Division

1st Polish Armoured Regiment
2nd Polish Armoured Regiment
24th Lancers
10th Dragoons (motor infantry)
Podolian Light Infantry
8th Light Infantry
9th Light Infantry
10th Mounted Rifle Regiment (reconnaissance)
1st and 2nd Field Artillery Regiments
1st Anti-Tank Regiment

# 2nd French Armoured Division
# (2e Division blindée)

501e Régiment de Chars de Combat
12e Régiment de Chasseurs d'Afrique
12e Régiment de Cuirassiers
Régiment de marche du Tchad (motor infantry)
1er Régiment de marche des Spahis marocains (reconnaissance)
Régiment blindé de Fusiliers-Marins (anti-tank)
3e Régiment d'Artillerie coloniale
64e Régiment d'Artillerie
40e Régiment d'Artillerie nord-africain
13e Bataillon du Génie (engineers)

# REFERENCES

Full bibliographical details are given in the
Select Bibliography; when not quoted here.

## 1 Journey to the Second Front

1  Stilwell, *Papers*, p. 5.
2  Ibid., p. 16.
3  Ibid., p. 15.
4  Leighton and Coakley, *Global Logistics*, pp. 134–5.
5  Chandler, *Eisenhower Papers*, p. 75.
6  Ibid., p. 179.
7  Pogue, *Marshall*, vol. II, p. 346.
8  Irving, *The Trail of the Fox*, p. 316.

## 2 All-American Screaming Eagles

1  Koskimaki, *D-Day*, p. 19.
2  Ibid., p. 35.
3  Marshall, *Night Drop*, p. 247.
4  Ridgway, *Soldier*, p. 2.
5  Burgett, *Currahee*, pp. 74–5.
6  Koskimaki, *D-Day*, p. 34.
7  Ibid., p. 59.
8  Ridgway, *Soldier*, p. 3.
9  Ibid., p. 4.
10  Koskimaki, *D-Day*, p. 76.
11  Burgett, *Currahee*, pp. 84–5.
12  Koskimaki, *D-Day*, p. 251.
13  Ibid., p. 360.
14  Burgett, *Currahee*, p. 86.
15  Koskimaki, *D-Day*, p. 256.
16  Ibid., p. 279.
17  Marshall, *Night Drop*, p. 261.

18  Ibid., p. 26.
19  Ibid., p. 37.
20  Ibid., p. 218.
21  Ibid., p. 222.

## 3 Canada: to the South Shore

1  C.P. Stacey, *Six Years of War* (Queen's Printer, Ottawa, 1955), p. 339.
2  Goronwy Rees, *A Bundle of Sensations* (Chatto & Windus, 1960), p. 168.

## 4 Scottish Corridor

1  Quoted in Chester Wilmot, *The Struggle for Europe* (Collins, 1951), p. 329.
2  Woollacombe, *Lion Rampant*, p. 53.
3  McElwee, *Argyll & Sutherland Highlanders*, p. 28.

## 5 Yeomen of England

1  Orde, *Household Cavalry at War*, p. 68.
2  David Holbrook, *Flesh Wounds* (Methuen, 1966), p. 131.
3  Orde, *Household Cavalry at War*, p. 68.
4  McKee, *Caen*, p. 259.
5  Liddell Hart, *The Tanks*, p. 365.
6  D.J.L. Fitzgerald, *History of the Irish Guards in the Second World War* (Gale & Polden, 1949), p. 381.
7  McKee, *Caen*, pp. 269–70.
8  Ibid., pp. 270–71.
9  Sellar, *Fife & Forfar Yeomanry*, p. 168.
10  *Story of the 23rd Hussars*, p. 76.

## 6 The Honour of the German Army

1  Irving, *Hitler's War*, p. 663.
2  Ibid.
3  Henry Benrath, *Ball auf Schloss Kobolnow* (Deutsche Verlags-Anstalt, 1932), p. 142.
4  Quoted in Belfield and Essame, *Battle for Normandy*, p. 183.
5  Quoted in Ellis, *Victory in the West*, vol. 1, p. 385.

## 7 'A Polish Battlefield'

1 Warlimont, *Inside Hitler's Headquarters*, p. 451.
2 Zawodny, *Nothing but Honour*, p. 163.
3 *Destiny Can Wait*, p. 221.
4 Florentin, *Battle of the Falaise Gap*, p. 260.
5 Lucas and Barker, *The Killing Ground*, p. 135.
6 Hilary St George Saunders, *Royal Air Force, 1939–45*, vol. III (HMSO, 1954), p. 138.
7 Florentin, *Battle of the Falaise Gap*, p. 221.
8 Ibid., p. 223.
9 Ibid., p. 261.
10 Lucas and Barker, *The Killing Ground*, p. 145.
11 Florentin, *Battle of the Falaise Gap*, p. 276.
12 Ibid., p. 278.

# SELECT BIBLIOGRAPHY

ROBERT ARON, *De Gaulle before Paris* (Putnam, 1962).

—— , *De Gaulle Triumphant* (Putnam, 1964).

EMMANUEL D'ASTIER, *De la Chute à la libération de Paris* (Gallimard, 1965).

J.R.P. BAGGALEY, *The 6th (Border) Battalion the King's Own Scottish Borderers, 1939–45* (Berwick-on-Tweed, 1964).

JACQUES BARDOUX, *La Délivrance de Paris* (Arthaud, 1945).

W.T. BARNARD, *The Queen's Own Rifles of Canada* (Ontario Publishing Co. Ltd, n.d.).

A. BARON, *From the City, from the Plough* (Cape, 1948).

MARCEL BAUDOT, *Libération de la Normandie* (Hachette, 1974).

E. BELFIELD and A. ESSAME, *The Battle for Normandy* (Batsford, 1965).

RALPH BENNETT, *Ultra in the West* (Hutchinson, 1979).

WILL R. BIRD, *North Shore (New Brunswick) Regiment* (Brunswick Press, 1963).

—— , *No Retreating Footsteps: The Story of the North Nova Scotia Highlanders* (n.p., n.d.).

MARTIN BLUMENSON, *Breakout and Pursuit* (Office of the Chief of Military History, Washington, 1961).

—— , *The Duel for France* (Houghton Mifflin, 1963).

G. BLUMENTRITT, *Von Rundstedt* (Odhams, 1952).

W. BOSS, *The Stormont, Dundas and Glengarry Highlanders* (Runge Press, Ottawa, 1952).

PIERRE BOURDAN, *Carnets de retour avec la 2e D.B. en France* (Trémois, 1945).

PATRICE BOUSSEL, *D-Day Beaches Pocket Guide* (Macdonald, 1965).

O. BRADLEY, *A Soldier's Story* (Eyre & Spottiswoode, 1952).

A.E.C. BREDIN, *Three Assault Landings* (Gale & Polden, 1946).

ARTHUR BRYANT, *The Turn of the Tide* (Collins, 1957).

—— , *Triumph in the West* (Collins, 1959).

A. BULTERECK, *Sans Peur: History of the 5th Seaforth Highlanders, 1942–5* (Mackay, 1946).

H.C. BUTCHER, *My Three Years with Eisenhower* (Heinemann, 1946).

DONALD BURGETT, *Currahee* (Hutchinson, 1967).

J.R.M. BUTLER and M.A. GWYER, *Grand Strategy*, vol. III (HMSO, 1964).

A.D. CHANDLER (ed.), *The Papers of Dwight David Eisenhower*, vol. I (Johns Hopkins Press, 1970).

RAY S. CLINE, *Washington Command Post* (Office of the Chief of Military History, Washington, 1951).

W.S. COLE, *America First: The Battle against Intervention* (University of Wisconsin Press, 1953).

LARRY COLLINS and DOMINIQUE LA PIERRE, *Is Paris Burning?* (Simon & Schuster, 1965).

HENRY L. COVINGTON, *A Fighting Heart: An Unofficial History of the 82nd Airborne Division* (Davis, 1949).

W.F. CRAVEN and J.L. CATE, *The Army Air Forces in World War II*, vol. III (University of Chicago Press, 1951).

F.A.E. CREW, *Army Medical Services, Campaigns*, vol. IV (HMSO, 1962).

NAPIER CROOKENDEN, *Drop Zone Normandy* (Ian Allen, 1976).

*Currahee: Scrapbook of the 506th Parachute Infantry Regiment* (Germany, 1945).

ADRIEN DANSETTE, *Leclerc* (Flammarion, 1952).

K.S. DAVIS, *Soldier of Democracy* (Doubleday, 1945).

W. FORREST DAWSON, *Saga of the All American* (Davis, 1949).

RÉMY DESQUESNES, *Le Mur de l'Atlantique en Normandie* (n.p., n.d.).

*Destiny Can Wait: The Polish Air Force in the Second World War* (Heinemann, 1950).

JOHN EHRMAN, *Grand Strategy*, vol. V (HMSO, 1956).

DWIGHT D. EISENHOWER, *Crusade in Europe* (Heinemann, 1948).

L.F. ELLIS, *Welsh Guards at War* (Gale & Polden, 1946).

—— , *Victory in the West*, vols I and II (HMSO, 1962, 1968).

VINCENT J. ESPOSITO, *The West Point Atlas of American Wars*, vol. II (Praeger, 1959).

BERNARD FERGUSON, *The Watery Maze* (Holt, 1961).

*1st & 2nd Northamptonshire Yeomanry, 1939–46* (Brunswick, 1946).

D.J.L. FITZGERALD, *History of the Irish Guards in the Second World War* (Gale & Polden, 1949).

E. FLORENTIN, *The Battle of the Falaise Gap* (Elek, 1965).

CATHERINE GAVIN, *Liberated France* (Cape, 1955).

A. GOSSET, *Caen pendant la bataille* (Ozanne, 1946).

JAN TOMASZ GROS, *Polish Society under German Occupation, 1939–44* (Princeton University Press, 1979).

F. DE GUINGAND, *Operation Victory* (Hodder & Stoughton, 1960).

GORDON A. HARRISON, *Cross Channel Attack* (Office of the Chief of Military History, Washington, 1951).

WERNER HAUPT, *Rückzug im Westen* (Motorbuch Verlag, 1978).

*Historical Record of the Queen's Own Cameron Highlanders* (Blackwood, 1952).

MICHAEL HOWARD, *The Mediterranean Strategy in World War II* (Weidenfeld & Nicolson, 1968).

—— , *Grand Strategy*, vol. IV (HMSO, 1972).

J.J. HOWE, *The 3rd Bn the Monmouthshire Regiment* (Pontypool, 1954).

*I Dywizja Pancerna W Walce* (Editions de la Colombe, Brussels, 1947).

DAVID IRVING, *Hitler's War* (Hodder & Stoughton, 1977).

—— , *The Trail of the Fox* (Weidenfeld & Nicolson, 1978).

J. JAMAR, *With the Tanks of the 1st Polish Armoured Division* (Hengelo, 1946).

GLOVER S. JOHNS, *The Clay Pigeons of St Lô* (Harrisburg, 1958).

S. KORBONSKI, *Fighting Warsaw* (Allen & Unwin, 1956).

GEORGE E. KOSKIMAKI, *D-Day with the Screaming Eagles* (Vantage Press, 1970).

FRANZ KUROWSKI, *Die Panzer Lehr Division* (Podzan Verlag, 1964).

PAUL DE LANGLADE, *En suivant Leclerc* (Fil d'Ariane, n.d.).

ABBÉ LAUNAY, *Dans la tourmente de la guerre* (Vilaire, 1946).

R.M. LEIGHTON and R.W. COAKLEY, *Global Logistics & Strategy, 1940–43, 1943–5* (Office of the Chief of Military History, Washington, 1955, 1968).

B.H. LIDDELL HART, *The Tanks*, vol. II (Cassell, 1959).

W.G. LORD, *History of the 508th Parachute Infantry* (Infantry Journal Press, 1948).

J. LUCAS and J. BARKER, *The Killing Ground* (Batsford, 1978).

WILLIAM McELWEE, *History of Argyll & Sutherland Highlanders, 2nd Battalion, European Campaign, 1944–5* (Nelson, 1949).

ALEXANDER McKee, *Caen, Anvil of Victory* (Souvenir Press, 1964).

S.L.A. MARSHALL, *Night Drop* (Macmillan, 1962).

H.G. MARTIN, *The History of the 15th Scottish Division, 1939–45* (Blackwood, 1948).

HENRY MAULE, *Out of the Sand* (Odhams, 1966).

GUY MERLE, *A l'assaut avec la 2e DB* (Imprimeries Malesherbe, 1949).

WILFRED MILES, *The Life of a Regiment*, vol. v, *The Gordon Highlanders, 1919–45* (Aberdeen University Press, 1961).

ALAN S. MILWARD, *War, Economy & Society, 1939–45* (Allen Lane, 1976).

A. and P. MONZEIN and Y. CHAPRON, *A la charnière (Caen 1944)* (Flammarion, 1947).

JACQUES MORDAL, *La Bataille de France, 1944–5* (Arthaud, 1964).

L.B. OATTS, *Proud Heritage: The Story of the Highland Light Infantry*, vol. IV (Nelson, 1963).

RODEN ORDE, *The Household Cavalry at War* (Gale & Polden, 1953).

FORREST C. POGUE, *George C. Marshall*, vols II, III (Viking Press, 1965, 1973).

*Queen's Own Rifles of Canada* (n.p., n.d.).

G.L.Y. RADCLIFFE, *History of the 2nd Battalion, King's Shropshire Light Infantry in N.W. Europe, 1944–5* (Blackwell, 1947).

LEONARD RAPPORT and ARTHUR NORTHWOOD, *Rendezvous with Destiny: A History of the 101st Airborne Division* (Infantry Journal Press, 1948).

ALEXANDRE RENAUD, *Sainte Mère-Eglise* (Odile Pathé, 1964).

LT-COL. REPITON-PRENEUF, *La 2e D.B.* (Editions Arts et Métiers, 1952).

MATTHEW B. RIDGWAY, *Soldier* (Harper, 1956).

TERENCE ROBERTSON, *Dieppe* (Hutchinson, 1963).

ERWIN ROMMEL, *The Rommel Papers*, ed. B. H. Liddell Hart (Collins, 1953).

A. ROSS and M. GAUVIN, *Le Geste du Régiment de la Chaudière* (Van Veem, Rotterdam, n.d.).

G.E.M. RUFFEE, *The History of the 14th Field Regiment, Royal Canadian Artillery* (Wereldbibliothek, Amsterdam, 1945).

FRIEDRICH RUGE, *Rommel in Normandy* (Macdonald, 1979).

CORNELIUS RYAN, *The Longest Day* (Simon & Schuster, 1959).

R.J.B. SELLAR, *The Fife & Forfar Yeomanry, 1919–56* (Blackwood, 1960).

*A Short History of the 7th Armoured Division* (n.p., n.d.).

MILTON SHULMAN, *Defeat in the West* (Secker & Warburg, 1948).

*The 6th Battalion, Royal Scots Fusiliers* (Ayr, 1962).

HANS SPEIDEL, *We Defended Normandy* (Michael Jenkins, 1951).

C.P. STACEY, *Canada's Battle in Normandy* (King's Printer, Ottawa, 1946).

——, *The Victory Campaign* (Queen's Printer, Ottawa, 1960).

JOSEPH W. STILWELL, *The Stilwell Papers* (Sloane, 1948).

*The Story of the 23rd Hussars, 1940–46* (Germany, 1946).

J.M. SYM, *Seaforth Highlanders* (Gale & Polden, 1962).

*Taurus Pursuant! A Short History of the 7th Armoured Division* (n.p., n.d.).

WILLIS THORNTON, *The Liberation of Paris* (Hart Davis, 1963).

BARBARA TUCHMAN, *Stilwell and the American Experience in China* (Macmillan NY, 1970).

US DEPARTMENT OF THE ARMY, *Utah Beach to Cherbourg* (US Government Printing Office, 1948).

G.L. VERNEY, *The Guards Armoured Division* (Hutchinson, 1955).

W. WARLIMONT, *Inside Hitler's Headquarters* (Weidenfeld & Nicolson, 1962).

MARK S. WATSON, *Chief of Staff, Pre-war Plans & Preparations* (Office of the Chief of Military History, Washington, 1950).

CHARLES WEBSTER and NOBLE FRANKLAND, *The Strategic Air Offensive against Germany, 1939–45*, vol. III (HMSO, 1961).

ALBERT C. WEDEMEYER, *Wedemeyer Reports!* (Holt, 1958).

F.W. WINTERBOTHAM, *The Ultra Secret* (Weidenfeld & Nicolson, 1962).

ROBERT WOOLLACOMBE, *Lion Rampant* (Leo Cooper, 1970).

W. ZAGORSKY, *Seventy Days* (Frederick Muller, 1957).

J.K. ZAWODNY, *Nothing but Honour* (Macmillan, 1978).

# Index

# Index of Formations and Units